Finance and Competitiveness in Developing Countries

As recent events in Southeast Asia have demonstrated, the fragility of a country's financial sector can have severe macro-economic consequences, affecting its ability to manufacture, import and export. Using a combination of case studies and theoretical papers, the contributors address this vital issue by examining the interaction between trade and financial development.

Using detailed trade and firm-level financial data, it is demonstrated that while links between finance and competitiveness are strong, they are not uniform across sectors and countries.

The book examines the link between finance and competitiveness at the macro and sectoral levels in seven different countries: Argentina, Brazil, India, Indonesia, The Philippines, South Africa and Tunisia, and also investigates key international issues, such as:

- the evidence of the impact of exchange rate variability on trade.
- patterns in bank lending.
- trade openness and development.

Finance and Competitiveness in Developing Countries will prove essential reading for those with a professional or academic interest in economic development, trade and competitiveness.

José María Fanelli has a Ph.D. in Economics, specializing in macroeconomics and monetary economics. He is currently Senior Professor of Macroeconomics and former Director of the Economics Department at the University of Buenos Aires. Since 1984 he has been senior researcher at CEDES (the Center for the Study of State and Society) and Conicet (the National Research Council) in Buenos Aires.

Rohinton Medhora received his Ph.D. in Economics at the University of Toronto, where he was also a faculty member in economics. He has published principally in the areas of monetary integration and central banking. At Canada's International Development Research Centre, he has led programs on adjustment policies and poverty, and trade. He is currently responsible for the Centre's social and economic policy programming.

Routledge Studies in Development Economics

Finance and Competitiveness in Developing Countries

Edited by José María Fanelli and Rohinton Medhora

London and New York

First published 2002
by Routledge
11 New Fetter Lane, London EC4P 4EE

Simultaneously published in the USA and Canada
by Routledge
29 West 35th Street, New York, NY 10001

Routledge is an imprint of the Taylor & Francis Group

© 2002 Editorial material and selection, José María Fanelli and
Rohinton Medhora, individual chapters, the respective contributors

Typeset in Times New Roman by
Newgen Imaging Systems (P) Ltd.
Printed and bound in Great Britain by
St Edmundsbury Press, Bury St Edmunds, Suffolk

British Library Cataloguing in Publication Data
A catalogue record for this book is available
from the British Library

Library of Congress Cataloguing in Publication Data

Finance and competitiveness in developing countries/edited by
José María Fanelli and Rohinton Medhora
    p. cm.
   Includes bibliographical references and index.
   1. Finance—Developing countries. 2. Competition—Developing
countries. 3. Developing countries—Commerce.
   4. Finance—Developing countries—Case studies.
   5. Competition—Developing countries—Case studies. 6. Developing
countries—Commerce—Case studies. I. Fanelli, José María, 1959–
II. Medhora Rohinton

HG195 .F527 2001
332'09172'4—dc21   2001019762

ISBN 0-415-24088-3

Contents

Figures

Tables

Contributors

Mejda Bahlous is Associate Professor of Finance at the *Institut des Hautes Etudes Commerciales*, University of Tunis. She obtained her Doctorate in Management Sciences in 1991 from the University of Rennes I, France.

Mohamed Bechri is Professor of Economics at the University of Sousse, Tunisia. He holds a Ph.D. in Economics from the University of Southern California and a *Doctorat de Troisième Cycle* in economics from the University of Paris I, Panthéon-Sarbonne.

Trevor Bell is Professor Emeritus of Economics and Economic History of Rhodes University, South Africa. He holds a Masters degree from Vanderbilt University, USA, and a Ph.D. from Rhodes. His research interests are in South African trade and industrialization, on which he has published extensively.

Rashad Cassim is the Executive Director of the Trade and Industrial Policy Secretariat (TIPS) in Johannesburg, South Africa. He holds a Ph.D. in Economics from the University of Cape Town. His research interests are in trade policy, regional integration and the economics of regulation.

Marouane El Abbassi is Assistant Professor of Economics at the *Institut des Hautes Etudes Commerciales*, University of Tunis. He holds a *Doctorat de Troisième Cycle* in economics from the University of Paris I, Panthéon-Sarbonne.

Riadh El Ferktaji is Assistant Professor of Economics at the *Institut des Hautes Etudes Commerciales*, University of Tunis. He obtained his Doctorate in economics in 1994 from the University of Paris I, Panthéon-Sarbonne.

José María Fanelli has a Ph.D. in Economics, specializing in macroeconomics and monetary economics. He is currently Senior Professor of Macroeconomics and former Director of the Economics Department at the University of Buenos Aires. Since 1984 he has been senior researcher at CEDES (the Center for the Study of State and Society) and Conicet (the National Research Council) in Buenos Aires.

Greg Farrell was Research Officer, Institute for Social and Economic Research, University of Durban-Westville, Durban, until October 1998; he is now an economist in the Research Department of the South African Research Bank, Pretoria.

A. Ganesh-Kumar is Assistant Professor at the Indira Gandhi Institute of Development Research, Mumbai, India. Research interests are in agricultural economics, international trade and applied general equilibrium modelling. Previous publications include 'Agricultural Trade Liberalization: Growth, Welfare and Large Country Effects' (with Kirit S, Parikh, N. S. S. Narayana and Major Panda), *Agricultural Economics* 17(1), 1997.

Paolo Guerrieri is Professor of Economics at the University of Rome, *La Sapienza* and the College of Europe, Bruges, and Director of the International Economic Unit of the Institute for Foreign Affairs of Rome. He is the author of several books and articles on international trade policy, technological change, international political economy, and European integration issues.

Saúl Keifman, majored at the University of Buenos Aires and obtained his Ph.D. in Economics at the University of California-Berkeley. He is currently Professor of Economics and Director of the Master Program in Economics at the University of Buenos Aires and Associate Researcher at CEDES.

Ari Kuncoro is currently Research Associate at the Institute of Economic and Social Research, Faculty of Economics, University of Indonesia. He obtained his Ph.D. in Economics from Brown University, Rhode Island. He is a participant in the Global Development Network sponsored by the World Bank and East Asian Development Network, and the Pacific Economic Council Structure Meeting, a research-oriented body supported by the Asian Pacific Economic Council.

Rohinton Medhora received his Ph.D. in Economics at the University of Toronto, where he was also a faculty member in economics. He has published principally in the areas of monetary integration and central banking. At Canada's International Development Research Centre, he has led programs on adjustment policies and poverty, and trade. He is currently responsible for the Centre's social and economic policy programming.

Mustapha K. Nabli is Regional Chief Economist within the World Bank's Middle East and North Africa Region. He was previously Minister of Planning and Economic Development in the government of Tunisia and Chairman of the Tunis Stock Exchange. He holds a Ph.D. in economics from the University of California at Los Angeles and was Professor of Economics at the University of Tunis and other universities in Europe, Canada and the United States.

Jaime Ros is Professor of Economics and Fellow of the Helen Kellogg Institute for International Studies at the University of Notre Dame. His main research interests include development theory and the macroeconomics of developing countries.

Rodney Schmidt is Program Advisor to the International Development Research Centre and Coordinator of the Vietnam Economic and Environmental Management (VEEM) program, based in Hanoi. Prior to joining IDRC, Dr. Schmidt worked as an economist with the Canadian Department of Finance and the Belize Ministry of Economic Development. He obtained his Ph.D. in economics from the University of Toronto where he also worked as a lecturer. Dr. Schmidt has written several papers on money and finance.

Kunal Sen is Lecturer in Economics at the School of Development Studies, University of East Anglia, UK. Research interests are in macroeconomics and international trade. Previous publications include *The Process of Financial Liberalization in India* published by Oxford University Press and *Economic Restructuring in East Asia and India* published by Macmillan.

Béchir Talbi is Professor of economics at the University of Sousse, Tunisia. He holds a *Doctorat de Troisième Cycle* in economics from the University of Paris X, Nanterre, France.

Maria Cristina T. Terra is Professor of Economics at the Graduate School of Economics, Getulio Vargas Foundation, Rio de Janeiro, and Associate Editor of *The Brazilian Review of Economics*.

Rajendra R. Vaidya is Associate Professor at the Indira Gandhi Institute of Development Research, Mumbai, India. Research interests are in macroeconomics, finance and industrial economics. Previous publications include *The process of Financial Liberalization in India* published by Oxford University Press.

Josef T. Yap is Senior Research Fellow at the Philippine Institute for Development Studies (PIDS). His areas of interest are in macroeconomic policy and econometrics. Dr Yap was recently a consultant at the Regional Economic Monitoring Unit of the Asian Development Bank. He is co-author of the book *The Philippine Economy: East Asia's Stray Cat? Structure, Finance, and Adjustment* (London: Macmillan Press Ltd, 1996).

Acknowledgements

This volume is genuinely a group effort and would not have been possible without the cooperation of a number of persons and organizations.

At IDRC, thanks are due to Rashad Cassim, Marie-Claude Martin, Caroline Pestieau and Andres Rius for their input, encouragement and participation from the very beginning. Lynne Richer at IDRC and Delia Carval at CEDES handled with patience and efficiency the administrative aspects of this project.

The first methodological meeting of the project was hosted by Centro de Estudios de Estado y Sociedad (CEDES) in Buenos Aires, Argentina, in April 1997. We thank in particular Mario Damill and Roberto Frenkel for their participation in this meeting, and CEDES for its management of the logistics. The mid-term meeting of this project was hosted by the Philippine Institute for Development Studies (PIDS), Manila, Philippines, in April 1998. The seminar disseminating the final results of this project was hosted by the Trade and Industrial Policy Secretariat, located at the Johannesburg office of Canada's International Development Research Centre. We thank PIDS and TIPS for their hospitality and organization of an excellent program during our stay with them.

Finally, thanks are due to Nilima Gulrajani at IDRC and Nicole Krull at Routledge for their yeoman work in bringing twelve chapters written by twenty-one economists from all over the world into a coherent and readable whole.

José María Fanelli and
Rohinton Medhora

1 Finance and competitiveness

Framework and synthesis

José María Fanelli and Rohinton Medhora

The issues of international competitiveness and integration in the global economy play a central role in the discussion on development and there is no indication that their importance will decline in the near future. At the analytical level, and often at the policy level as well, competitiveness is seen largely in real or trade terms, at the expense of the key roles that financial factors, and institutional and other micro-level features play in determining how successful a country's trade and competitiveness position is. Trade theories are for the most part silent on financial issues while policy makers cannot afford the luxury of seeing the two as separate or, worse, unconnected. Likewise, once financial issues are brought into the picture it is not possible to ignore the role of the macroeconomic factors and their interaction with the microeconomic structure of the economy.

The main goal of the research project whose results are presented in this book is, precisely, to contribute to filling the theoretical and empirical gap which exists in the development literature regarding the linkages of trade, finance and macroeconomic factors. The project comprised eight country studies (Argentina, Brazil, Uruguay, Indonesia, India, the Philippines, Tunisia and South Africa) which were elaborated according to the same framework and four thematic papers that analyzed the relationship between competitiveness, finance and trade at a more abstract level. In this chapter we present a framework for our analysis and an overview of the key results of the studies. This chapter has two sections. In the first section we discuss why 'achieving competitiveness' is an important policy goal in the developing world and why it is closely associated with the process of catching up. Then, we discuss four stylized facts characterizing developing countries that explain why it is necessary to analyze the relationship between trade, finance and macroeconomic issues. In the second section, we elaborate on our view of the micro/macro and trade/finance linkages. We conclude with the three most important questions that have been targeted in the project.

1. Competitiveness and the developing world

The challenges of economic policy

There are three facts that are crucial to understanding the ongoing debate on development strategies and on economic policy in developing countries. The first is that growth is the most important economic policy goal to these countries. It is true that it would be hard to find someone involved in economic policy-making or politics who would deny or ignore that development is a complex process that entails much more than mere increasing per capita GDP, and, consequently, that the results of a specific economic program should be assessed on the basis of an ample set of indicators including variables related to, say, income distribution and the environment. In practice, however, it is growth that is privileged as *the* measure of economic attainment. One important reason for privileging growth as an indicator of development is that there is a firm consensus among politicians, public opinion, advisors from multilateral agencies and policy makers that it is much easier to undertake the difficult and often painful economic and social changes required to ensure development in a context of sustained growth. Two necessary conditions for sustainable growth are the steady increase of overall productivity and macroeconomic stability. Hence, the preeminence given to growth naturally implies that policies for productivity enhancement and for preserving macroeconomic equilibrium take priority on the economic policy agenda.

The second fact is closely associated with the previous one. If growth is the measure of attainment, how do we know whether a given rate of growth is high or low? In other words, what is an acceptable rate of growth? For a developing country, 'development' means, in the first place, approaching the per capita GDP of industrialized countries and, hence, developmental success means reducing the income gap between the country under consideration and the wealthier ones. In this way, achieving a rate of growth in overall productivity which is higher than the average rate observed in the developed world becomes a key target for economic policy. Under these circumstances, Krugman's (1996) reasoning that the increase in national productivity is what matters to the improvement of the standard of living independently of what is happening with the productivity of the rest of the world may be correct at first sight, but is politically vacuous. The common consensus is that a sound development policy should set the country on a growth path which would help it to catch up with the industrialized economies. To be sure, the primary reason for using the industrialized countries' income as a benchmark is neither the search for national prestige nor the belief that international economic competition across countries resembles competition across firms, but, rather, the need to fix a standard to assess how well a country is doing. It seems only natural to set such a standard at the highest level of welfare observed at a specific moment.

The third fact is that, at present, integration in the global economy is conceived of as central to fueling productivity and fostering growth (Sachs and Warner 1997). One important reason that accounts for the perception of the international economy as a window of opportunity is the increasing interaction in recent decades between domestic economies and the world economy. The most important indicators of this 'globalization' process are the growing share of international trade in world output and an extraordinary rise in capital mobility, including foreign direct investment.[1] In such a context, it is believed that developing countries could enlarge the size of their export markets and use the proceeds coming from higher exports to foster productivity gains via the acquisition of investment goods abroad and improvements in the quality and variety of imported intermediate inputs used in production. The international capital market is also viewed as a potential source of productivity enhancement. Specifically, it is assumed that a greater supply of foreign direct investment means both greater availability of savings and technology, while accessing international capital markets implies accessing not only more foreign savings but also better alternatives for the diversification of national risks. The most important piece of evidence flagged in the literature favoring these ideas is the experience of the Asian Tigers. Many studies have concluded that countries that have expanded most successfully in the postwar period heavily relied on external trade – or at least on an export-oriented strategy – as a source of dynamism for the domestic economy. An additional piece of evidence is that many countries which did not privilege external trade in their development strategy have faced enormous problems not only to sustain growth but also to maintain a reasonable level of macroeconomic stability. Latin American countries usually serve as a paradigm of the problems that the lack of 'outward orientation' can create. It was suggested that the domestic-market-oriented development strategy these countries followed in the postwar period led to the misallocation of investment and recurrent balance-of-payments crises, which were specially marked in the 1980s during the 'debt crisis'.

The lessons drawn from the analysis of concrete development experiences and the theoretical contributions of the 'liberalization' approach to development theory crystallized in the so-called Washington Consensus in the mid-1980s (Williamson 1990). The Washington Consensus was extremely effective at criticizing the inefficiencies of the older development paradigm based on import substitution and state intervention and at establishing new guidelines for the design of policies oriented to liberalizing repressed markets and reducing the size and functions of the state. A good number of developing countries put into practice the policy recommendations of the Consensus. In spite of its success as a framework for designing market-oriented structural reforms and for eliminating many of the inefficiencies of the old development model, the results of the reforms in terms of growth, productivity and macroeconomic stability, nonetheless, were mixed. In general, after a decade of deep reforms, we do not see a spectacular improvement in growth and catching up, not to mention social equity. Under these circumstances, it is not surprising that the Consensus is, at present, under scrutiny (Rodrik 1999).

The three aspects of economic policy that we highlighted – preeminence of growth indicators, the aim of catching up and outward orientation – suggest that an analytical approach which can tackle the policy issues developing countries are now facing should be able to integrate the interactions between the determinants of productivity growth, macroeconomic stability and integration in the global economy in a single analytical framework. The Washington Consensus attempted to make such an integration in the 1980s and it was one of its main virtues. In fact, one could argue that a good part of the popularity of the Consensus was due to its ability to present a guide for policy design in a wide range of areas within a consistent framework. At present, nonetheless, the approach shows difficulties in accounting for a set of highly relevant developments. Given the objectives of our research, there are two features of those developments that we would like to highlight. The first is that many countries that opened their capital markets and undertook trade liberalization did not grow as fast as had been expected. These are, for example, the cases of Turkey, Mexico, the Philippines and Brazil. Argentina, on the other hand, grew much faster than in the 1980s after deepening trade liberalization and privatization, but was severely affected by the Tequila effect and the Asian crisis. The reforms were unable to radically eliminate the tendency to generate 'excessive' current account deficits that had been a structural characteristic of the Argentine economy during the import substitution period. The experience of these countries suggests that high productivity and competitiveness are not automatically achieved as a result of market deregulation, financial and trade liberalization, and integration in the international capital markets. The second is that, somewhat unexpectedly, some of the most successful outward-oriented countries, like Korea and other 'new' tigers like Indonesia, experienced deep macroeconomic disequilibria which matched some of the characteristics of Latin American instability, such as currency attacks, financial fragility and deep falls in the activity level. These facts made it evident that imperfections exist in the functioning of international capital markets which can jeopardize even the most successful countries and that, under such circumstances, outward orientation *per se* is not enough to protect a given country from exposure to capital flows volatility. Likewise, the crises show that macroeconomic instability, financial fragility and the capital structure of the firms are closely associated.

In most cases, the economies facing problems of current account sustainability devalued their currencies in the 1990s. The diagnosis to support devaluation is that the external imbalance is basically a macroeconomic problem: a 'wrong' exchange rate erodes the competitiveness of the economy and prevents the country from competing successfully in international markets. From the static point of view this policy is correct since, if an equilibrium exists, there is always an exchange rate which leaves the balance of payments in equilibrium and permits the country to fully exploit its comparative advantage. When dynamic factors are taken into account however, the experience of developing countries shows that to ensure competitiveness countries need much more than just getting the real exchange rate right. The experience of Latin American countries in the 1980s is particularly relevant in this regard. The systematic use of devaluation as a means of improving competitiveness accelerated inflation and damaged financial intermediation, thereby increasing volatility in both prices and quantities. In this way, the upward correction of the real exchange rate was achieved only at the cost of a sharp worsening of the macroeconomic setting. The effects of increased volatility and the deterioration of financial conditions on investment were devastating. There was a generalized fall in the investment/GDP ratio in the entire region. This, in turn, resulted in the stagnation of productivity and the widening of the productivity gap between Latin America and other more successful developing countries such as the Asian NICs. The ultimate consequence of the attempt to get the real exchange 'right' in a context of high uncertainty and severe financial constraints was the opposite of the effect that was sought for: competitiveness was severely hindered by the lagging evolution of productivity.

To be sure, our reference to the Latin American experience during the debt crisis is not meant to imply that the real exchange rate is irrelevant for a country's competitiveness. The lesson that we do draw, instead, is that competitiveness is a complex issue which has price and non-price dimensions and that embraces micro- and macro-elements which interact with each other. At the micro-level, it is normal for a growing economy to experience rising and falling competitiveness in different industries, since productivity growth is not a uniform process across sectors. If the country is losing competitiveness in many industries simultaneously however, the loss of competitiveness can be caused either by a misalignment of domestic costs or by low average productivity growth *vis-à-vis* the rest of the world. If the problem is the misalignment of relative prices, devaluation may be the cure. But if the problem is lagging productivity, we should not take it for granted a priori that devaluation will be sufficient to enhance competitiveness. When we take into account the micro-dimension of the problem, it is clear that if a country specializes in the least dynamic industries (with flat learning curves, low returns to scale, small scope for innovation) it will enjoy little productivity growth and will lose competitiveness. If this is the case, it is plausible to think that devaluation is not the best response from a long-run perspective. The real problem lies in the specialization pattern and the lagging path of productivity. This makes it clear that trade specialization patterns, productivity growth and current account sustainability are not independent phenomena. In fact, the trade specialization pattern might be a source of macroeconomic instability *per se*. For example, a country which depends on the surplus generated by a narrow set of products with high price volatility to close the external gap can be more unstable than another with a more diversified surplus structure. Additionally, it must be taken into account that micro/macro-interactions are also relevant for the non-price dimensions of competitiveness. A highly unstable environment can hinder the evolution of productivity via its effect on non-price determinants of competitiveness, such as the level of financial deepening. For example, trade liberalization may eliminate an anti-export bias in the economy. In the new scenario one would expect that firms will be restructured to take advantage of the trade opportunities offered. It is very doubtful, however, that firms will in fact get the funds needed for restructuring in a context of credit rationing.

We think that the traditional approach has difficulties with the issue of competitiveness because it tends to ignore the kind of micro/macro-interactions that we are stressing here. In this regard, one particularly inadequate characteristic of the traditional approach is the excessive use of dichotomies as a methodological recourse to simplify the analysis. There are marked dichotomies between micro- and macro-problems, between the real and the financial side, and between open and closed economies. It is undeniable that these dichotomies are powerful simplifying devices, but it is also true that such dichotomies are often maintained even under circumstances in which real/financial and micro/macro-interactions are extremely relevant for a specific economic phenomenon as in the case of the turbulences in 'emerging' economies. In these economies, it is pretty obvious that the problems of macroeconomic sustainability, capital flows and trade specialization are closely interrelated.

Dichotomies play a particularly relevant role in the case of trade theory. There is a long tradition in the field of international economics of sharply separating trade and the 'micro'-question of optimum resource allocation from monetary and macroeconomic issues. For example, the typical international economics textbook is divided into two parts. The first analyzes the real economy with a 'micro'-perspective, omitting the existence of money, financial intermediation and current account disequilibria. The second part studies open economy macroeconomics. In this part the trade specialization pattern plays no role and output is highly aggregated. Some of the agents' financial decisions (domestic vs foreign bonds) come to the forefront and macroeconomic problems like the correct level of the real exchange rate, aggregate domestic absorption, portfolio decisions and balance-of-payments equilibrium take center stage. It is not clear what the relationship between the first and the second part is or how the results of each part are modified by the results obtained in the other.[2] As a consequence of this dichotomy, in the literature on trade, the problem of achieving a sustainable macroeconomic equilibrium is conceived of as being largely independent of the question of competitiveness. Trade imbalances can always be corrected through fiscal, monetary or exchange rate policies because competitiveness problems (i.e. recurrent current account crises) have their roots in inadequate macroeconomic policies rather than in weak productive structures.

The dichotomy between the real and the financial side also plays a significant role in trade theory. It is implicitly assumed that the firms seeking to exploit a competitive advantage can always finance their productive projects and thereby 'real' decisions are isolated from financial ones. In fact, it is implicitly assumed that the latter are irrelevant, as it would be the case under perfect capital markets. In such a world, there is no chance that a firm which is potentially competitive at the international level will be forced to forego trade opportunities either because of liquidity constraints created by credit rationing or because interest rates are abnormally high as a consequence of an excessively volatile macroeconomic setting.

Another important weakness of the standard approach to the competitiveness problem is that it is not clear enough what the sources of a sustained increase in productivity are. This is apparent in the Washington Consensus' policy recommendations. It is generally explicitly assumed that market deregulation and outward orientation (i.e. 'undistorted' integration in the world economy) should be sufficient conditions to ensure an upward trend in productivity. The recent experience of many developing countries suggests, nonetheless, that market deregulation alone is not enough to take full advantage of the creativity of the private sector and to enhance productivity growth. Although it is true that many countries enjoyed important static efficiency gains after the liberalization and opening of the economy, the growth path of productivity and competitiveness has been far from satisfactory from the point of view of catching up and macro-stability.

In this regard, a central weakness of the traditional theory is that it downplays the role of market failures. The assumption that product and factor markets will function well after liberalization may be unwarranted in the case of developing countries, where imperfections are pervasive in the markets for knowledge, human capital, infrastructure services and finance. These markets have a determinant influence on the evolution of productivity.

This criticism of the traditional approach, however, is not meant to imply that we should start from scratch to better understand the interactions of productivity, stability and openness. In the first place, in spite of its flaws, the Washington Consensus has clarified a variety of issues, particularly those related to static economic efficiency and macroeconomic stability originating in monetary and fiscal imbalances. Second, there is a series of more heterodox contributions, both analytical and empirical, which have shed light on key aspects of developing economies. On the analytical side, there were new advances in trade, finance and growth theory which take explicitly into account the existence of market failures and, therefore, are specially useful for the analysis of developing economies which have incomplete market structures. Likewise, researchers working in the technological and industrial organization area have studied the determinants of competitiveness and productivity in developing countries and have showed the limits of the neoclassical approach for analyzing the dynamics of technical change, trade and competitiveness in the developing world.[3] This new intellectual environment has led many researchers to challenge the orthodox interpretation of the Asian NIEs' experience. They demonstrated that many highly relevant facts do not fit into and cannot be accounted for within the liberalization paradigm.[4] From our point of view, these contributions are promising steps towards the construction of a post-Washington Consensus approach. This new approach to development problems will surely integrate many of these recent contributions as its building blocks.

Four stylized facts

In addition to the analytical advances in the study of economies with missing and imperfect markets, any attempt to improve our understanding of the problems of competitiveness and the challenges of economic policy should take into account some specific features that characterize the structure of developing countries. There are four of these features that we would like to highlight because of their relevance for the present investigation.

(a) *Developing countries tend to be more unstable than developed countries from the macroeconomic point of view.* There is a large amount of empirical evidence that documents this fact (IDB 1995). The central point that we would like to emphasize is that a higher degree of volatility in the stochastic processes generating key macroeconomic prices represents a deadweight cost for the economy as a whole which can severely hinder productivity (Fanelli and Frenkel 1995; Ramey and Ramey 1995). The basic reason is that volatility affects the investment rate. Greater volatility means greater risk and, consequently, higher discount rates.

Under these circumstances, the minimum rate of return required for a project to be considered profitable is higher and the rate of investment, *ceteris paribus*, lower. In this way, macroeconomic instability has sizeable economic costs which affect the sources of productivity enhancement at the micro-level, to the extent that investment is correlated with learning, the adoption of new technologies and the acquisition of skills. These micro/macro-linkages could play an important role in explaining the existence of some vicious circles which are very frequently observed in the developing world: the obstacles to developing dynamic comparative advantages force the country to depend on a few export items to finance imports and to close the external gap; this makes the country highly vulnerable to terms of trade shocks and the evolution of key macroeconomic variables becomes more volatile; the volatility of the macro-environment, in turn, hinders the country's capacity to develop new comparative advantages to the extent that a weak investment rate creates an anti-innovation bias. This kind of vicious circle may be relevant in explaining the experience of countries showing chronic balance-of-payments problems and difficulties in strengthening their competitiveness.

(b) *The external constraint is a key source of aggregate instability. This is closely associated with the existing imperfections in international capital markets and the lack of trade diversification.* There are two factors that play a central role in explaining the relevance of the external constraint as a source of macro-instability. The first is the lack of export diversification. When the prices and/or the quantities sold of a good or service which account for a high share of exports fluctuate, large swings in the availability of foreign exchange are likely to result if exports are not diversified. Under circumstances of greater volatility in the supply of foreign exchange, it is reasonable to assume the hypothesis that there will be a higher volatility in key macroeconomic prices (particularly the real exchange rate) and quantities. We consider that the roots of this problem lie in the lack of competitiveness to the extent that the country is unable to diversify sufficiently its exports via the acquisition of comparative advantages in new sectors or specific products.

The second factor has to do with the imperfections in international capital markets. In the context of perfect foreign capital markets, the lack of export diversification should be less of a problem because it would be possible to diversify the risks implicit in the fluctuations of one country's export proceeds by resorting to capital markets. The market would make it possible to combine the financial instruments of countries whose export proceeds are negatively correlated in a well-diversified portfolio. Likewise, countries suffering temporal terms of trade shocks could tap international credit markets in order to stabilize the level of domestic absorption every year around its long-run national income. They would run, say, deficits in bad years and surpluses in good ones. Fluctuations in the terms of trade and, hence, in the availability of foreign exchange would not be an obstacle to exploit investment opportunities and to develop dynamic comparative advantages. Regrettably, international capital markets have proven to be unable to diversify national risks efficiently and to finance temporary current account deficits (Obstfeld and Rogoff 1996; Obstfeld 1998). The existence of a credit constraint means there will be a kind of accelerator mechanism working at the aggregate level. In this way, the imperfections of capital markets on the financial side of the economy become a problem on the real side. When financial constraints exist, a country needs to enhance its competitiveness to avoid a risky dependence on the availability of credit in foreign markets. This association, between the external balance of the economy and macroeconomic instability, is aggravated in the present context of openness and free capital mobility because it seems that herding behavior and other irrational phenomena in international capital markets could be an independent source of volatility for a country whose financial needs are too high or somewhat inelastic in the short run.

(c) *The economic structure comprises sectors characterized by different productivity levels and growth potential.* The economic structure of a country is a complex system that includes physical and human resources, markets, organizations and institutions. It is a well-known stylized fact of the development process that the economic structure experiences systematic changes as skills, technologies and capital accumulate. Chenery and Syrquin (1986), for example, studied a broad set of countries and showed that as economies become industrially mature, manufactured exports tend to move from simpler to more complex activities, use more advanced products and processes within activities, and increase local contents in physical inputs, services and technologies. In a situation of growth and structural change, productivity growth at the aggregate level can be decomposed into a shift in the production structure towards activities with higher levels of productivity and into the growth of productivity in all existing activities (Llal 1995). In such a context, it is very unrealistic to assume that firms in countries showing different stages of development use identical production functions to produce homogeneous products. It seems more plausible to adopt the hypothesis that there will be some technological differences between firms in the same sector in different countries because learning curves and the evolution of technological capabilities in general depend on the previous path of development as well as on the overall economic environment (infrastructure, financial deepening, the quality of government). Under this assumption, comparative advantages are determined not only by the natural endowment but also by dynamic factors associated with technological capabilities and the whole economic environment. A country will not show any tendency to catch up with developed countries if it specializes in low-productivity sectors with low growth potential.

We have seen that the convergence with the productivity level of developed countries is a privileged policy goal. A country, however, cannot freely choose which sectors to specialize in precisely because, in the long run, the path of specialization is determined by factors such as the previous evolution of technological capabilities and accumulation of physical and human capital. When the rate of growth of aggregate productivity (which determines the competitive strength) is very low in a given country, a phenomenon that is often observed is that the country recurrently runs into balance-of-payments problems. Normally it occurs because there is a pressure to maintain the standard of living when a negative shock hits the economy. In this situation, the authorities face a policy dilemma.

To break the inertia behind the lagging path of productivity and induce a 'jump' in competitiveness in order to secure current account sustainability, it is necessary to invest in physical and human capital and technologies. In the short run, however, higher levels of investment could worsen the current account. It is precisely because of this sort of policy dilemma that it is interesting to investigate in detail the micro/macro-linkages between the determinants of the evolution of aggregate and sectoral productivity at the micro-level and competitiveness and current account sustainability at the macro-level.

(d) *Factor markets show severe failures and such failures are much more important than those observed in developed countries. This has an impact on competitiveness and growth.* It is a very well-known fact that there may be significant failures in the factor markets where developing country agents operate. In our research, however, we concentrate on financial markets. It is common to observe the following phenomena in the developing country financial structure: a high degree of segmentation in financial markets which acts against innovative and smaller enterprises; a marked scarcity of long-term credit for the financing of private investment; very low total capitalization of the stock exchange market as compared to the size of the economy; severe difficulties to diversify non-systematic risk because the range of activities quoted in the stock market is very narrow; an elevated degree of financial fragility in the system which – via systemic risk premia – results in excessively high interest rates (Fanelli and Medhora 1998).

When these imperfections exist in the credit markets, firms are not uniformly affected (Fazzari *et al.* 1988; Hubbard 1998). Smaller firms with less net worth or firms producing in more risky sectors or with less marketable assets to be used as collateral will be more affected (Harris *et al.* 1994). In a context of tighter overall financial conditions, these firms will face a disproportionate widening in the external finance premium or will be rationed out of credit markets. This means that when the interest rate rises as a consequence of an increase in volatility induced by a worsening in the macroeconomic situation, the financial conditions will worsen in a disproportionate way for some enterprises. If these enterprises are also those with the most profitable and innovative projects, macroeconomic instability will be extremely costly for productivity growth.

2. Competitiveness: Price and non-price dimensions

From our previous reasoning, it follows that to face the challenges of economic policy and understand the determinants of sustainable growth in a small economy that is open to international flows of goods and finance, we should be able to model the links between productivity growth, macroeconomic stability and financing of the firm. There are a growing number of researchers who are using the problems posed by competitiveness as the pivot of their analysis of these questions. Competitiveness is defined as 'an economy's ability to grow and to raise the general living standards of its population in a reasonably open trading environment without being constrained by balance of payments difficulties' (Haque 1995).

Although some academic economists are reluctant to apply the concept of competitiveness because they consider it to be redundant, we believe that even if it is not strictly necessary as a 'primitive' concept in economic theory, it is still very useful. For one thing, it summarizes in a single concept the problems of growth, openness and productivity which, as we argued before, are at the heart of policymakers' concerns.[5]

A country's competitiveness has two components: price competitiveness and non-price competitiveness. Price competitiveness measures a country's ability to increase its share in world markets by selling at a lower price than its competitors. If price competitiveness were all that mattered, a country's market share would rise (fall) as its real exchange rate or unit labor cost fell (rose) *vis-à-vis* the rest of the world. The limitations of price-competitiveness indicators, however, came to the forefront when Kaldor (1978) found that the industrialized countries which gained market share (West Germany and Japan) were also the ones that experienced a rise in unit labor costs *vis-à-vis* their competitors. Kaldor's 'paradox' suggests that factors other than price, such as product differentiation, technological innovation and capacity to deliver, must also be taken into account (Fagerberg 1988).[6]

The inclusion of non-price factors into the picture naturally calls for an approach more akin to the Schumpeterian view of development. Specifically, this requires recognizing the key role of technology and innovation, of financial constraints and of systemic elements in determining the evolution of competitiveness. In Schumpeterian models of growth in an open economy, the rate of technical progress and the pattern of international trade are jointly and endogenously determined and dynamic comparative advantages become a critical factor (Aghion and Howitt 1997). Finance matters because financial institutions contribute to fostering productivity and hence absolute advantage. Financial intermediaries can spur technological innovation by identifying and funding those entrepreneurs with the best chances of successfully implementing innovative products and production processes. In this way, the development of financial institutions and markets is a critical and inextricable part of the growth process (Levine 1997). Systemic factors need to be integrated into the analysis because technological development significantly depends on the existence of a suitable environment for learning, imitation and innovation. The most relevant systemic factors that are usually highlighted in the literature are the quality of the physical and institutional infrastructure, financial deepening, and the characteristics of the national system of innovation.

The literature stressing the role of non-price and systemic factors, however, has two weak points. The first is that there is no systematic research on the effects of macroeconomic disequilibrium on competitiveness. There are two facts that make this point important: (i) It is undeniable that the macroeconomic regime is a relevant component of the systemic environment in which the firm operates. (ii) As we have stressed, macroeconomic instability is much more significant in the specific case of developing countries. These two facts imply that it is very important to identify what are the channels through which macroeconomic disequilibria affect the microstructure. The second weak point is that the literature analyzing the links between growth and financial deepening has relied excessively on cross-country evidence. As a consequence, too many unanswered questions remain about the concrete features of the causal links between financial constraints, growth and the creation of comparative advantages. We believe that much more empirical research should be done. We need econometric analyses and case studies about both specific countries and industries. A deeper understanding of the micro/macro and real/financial interactions at the country, firm and sectoral levels would greatly contribute to our understanding of the determinants of competitiveness. The main objective of the project whose results we present in this book is, precisely, to contribute to filling this gap in the development literature.

Micro/macro-linkages

One important reason explaining the scarcity of studies analyzing micro/macro-linkages is that, until recently, economic theory made a sharp distinction between the economy's growth trend and cycles. Traditionally, business cycle theorists have analyzed de-trended data and considered the trend as exogenous to the cycle, and growth theorists have focused on characterizing a long-run growth path. One important weakness of this approach is that it cannot account for the existence of stochastic trends (Aghion and Howitt 1997). The view that, under certain circumstances, macroeconomic disequilibrium can have permanent effects on the microeconomic structure implies that temporary shocks are embedded into long-run paths and hence is a view consistent with the approach of some endogenous growth models. It is interesting to notice, in this regard, that although there is consensus on the fact that in developing countries (particularly in Latin America) excessive macroeconomic instability and sluggish growth have not been independent phenomena, there have been no attempts until recently to analyze the effects of volatility on the growth trend. It must be stressed, nonetheless, that temporary shocks can either hamper or benefit growth. We have already given an example in which volatility acts as an obstacle to growth. But we can also easily think of situations in which a temporary boom can have permanent positive effects. Suppose that there is a surge in capital inflows that reduce the interest rate and, as a consequence, credit-constrained firms experience a long period of excess liquidity. It is possible for the higher investment rate that will result from a softer liquidity constraint to have permanent favorable effects on productivity, if learning and skill accumulation are complementary to physical capital accumulation. Mechanisms of this kind have been present in the experience of countries like Argentina and Peru in the 1990s.

When trends are assumed to be stochastic, not only the temporary shocks that hit the economy but also the characteristics of the short-run macroeconomic adjustment path may have long-lasting effects. This fact is a primary source of concern for policy makers. The policy dilemmas associated with the choice between alternative exchange rate regimes is a good example. Policy makers care about the exchange rate regime because the adjustment paths under alternative exchange rate regimes are different. If the effects of the adjustment path on the long-run equilibrium are non-neutral, the adoption of a particular exchange rate regime matters for the evolution of competitiveness. Let us take the example of the recent crises in Asia and Latin America. The balance-of-payments disequilibria typically arose in the context of (approximately) fixed exchange rate regimes. Under such circumstances, there were two basic policy reactions. The most usual option was the devaluation of the currency and the change of the exchange rate regime. Other economies (notably Argentina and Hong Kong), on the contrary, did not resort to devaluation and privileged the maintenance of the regime over the need to correct the exchange rate parity to preserve competitiveness. Devaluation proved to be very effective to correct external imbalances in the short run. Why, then, have there been countries which did not devalue? The case of Argentina is very interesting in this regard. The diagnosis behind the decision to maintain convertibility was that changing the regime would be too costly. The most important costs were considered to be the higher volatility of key relative prices, inflation acceleration and, particularly, the increase in the fragility of the financial system. These costs could more than offset the benefits of correcting the misalignment of the exchange rate in the short run. Independently of whether or not the Argentine authorities were right in their assessment of the costs and benefits of a regime change, the Argentine case clearly shows that relative prices are not the only channel through which macroeconomic factors influence microeconomic decisions and competitiveness.

One important conclusion that our analysis of micro/macro-interactions suggests is that competitiveness means more than just getting the relative prices (and, particularly, the exchange rate) right. The presence of fragmented or missing markets and weak institutions in developing countries determines that externalities, spillover effects, financial constraints and strategic interactions between economic actors are pervasive. Under these circumstances, when, say, a negative macroeconomic shock occurs, the market forces (i.e. relative price changes driven by excess demand) which should automatically restore equilibrium are too weak. As a consequence, there will be a tendency for the disequilibrium to set in motion destabilizing forces such as deep recessions accompanied by high and persistent inflation and/or unemployment. We think that this is an important reason why it is frequently observed that macro-disequilibria in developing countries are deeper and more unstable than the disequilibria observed in economies with a more complete market structure.

When we adopt a more comprehensive view of the determinants of competitiveness, many other elements enter the picture. In the first place, a static equilibrium can be 'bad' from the point of view of both the level of welfare of the population and the incentives for productivity growth and the development of dynamic comparative advantages. It is undeniable that an upward correction in the real exchange rate can be, under certain circumstances, a strong incentive for the production of tradable goods and it is also true that getting the exchange rate right may be of great help in reducing macroeconomic volatility. We should not reduce the issue of the overall economy's competitiveness, however, to the profitability of the tradable sector. For one thing, in the long run human capital accumulation, the development of indigenous technological capabilities, and the quality of the physical, financial and institutional structures critically depend on the efficiency of the non-tradable sector. In the second place, as we have seen, the way in which the correction in the exchange rate is achieved is of no minor importance, since the path of relative prices will likely affect the long-run equilibrium. In sum, in an open economy there is no guarantee that the equilibrium which will result from getting the exchange rate 'right' will not be a sort of 'bottom of the well' equilibrium characterized by sluggish productivity growth and/or high macroeconomic volatility. Obviously, if we assume away market imperfections and dynamic considerations, relative prices can only be distorted if the government interferes in the functioning of markets. Under such circumstances, if the government does not intervene, and we still observe low productivity growth, we should accept that the 'bottom of the well' equilibrium is the best situation for the country under consideration. Such a dismal conclusion, though, is not warranted. Given the characteristics of developing economies, assuming away market imperfections and the role of the factors associated with resource accumulation, finance, and technologies may be an erroneous starting point.

Trade and finance

The traditional theory of international trade emphasizes efficient resource allocation and endowment as the main explanation for a country's specialization pattern. The pattern of specialization and trade does not depend on absolute but rather relative costs of production, which under certain conditions are determined by relative factor endowments. In this setting, the firm is not much more than a production function and does not have to bother with financial questions to carry out its production projects. If the project is good, it is undertaken. It can always be financed in a perfect market setting. Under these circumstances, there is no room for such financial phenomena as credit rationing or financial fragility to influence the firm's decisions regarding production, and hence competitiveness. The 'new' trade theory has clarified the role of economies of scale, externalities, learning by doing, technical progress, product differentiation, and oligopolistic and monopolistic market. The firm is much more complex in this new framework which incorporates some insights from industrial organization theory. But especial consideration of financial issues is yet to be made. There is no systematic treatment of how financial decisions affect competitiveness either at a global or firm level. Indeed, when we depart from traditional trade theory, financial issues become more relevant in determining competitiveness. Compare, for instance, the constant-returns-to-scale static comparative advantage case with the 'learning by doing' dynamic comparative advantage perspective. Finance is unlikely to make a difference in the former as firms of any size and experience will produce always at the same unit cost. However, in the latter case, as experience becomes a crucial determinant of unit costs, new entrants will initially produce at a loss that has to be financed somehow. If capital markets are reluctant to finance these initial losses, firms that have the potential to become competitive will never have a chance, unless government intervenes to correct this market failure.[7]

If we assume that it is possible to explain the competitive performance of a firm without making any explicit reference to financial issues, we are implicitly assuming that Modigliani–Miller's theorem and Tobins' and Fisher's separation theorems hold. The company's funding decisions are irrelevant to the choice of projects. The present value of each project is independent of the way in which it is financed. This assumption is too strong in the context of most developing countries because, as we noticed, there are highly significant failures in factor and capital markets.

If the idealized conditions that define a perfect capital market do not hold, and finance matters, then it will be easy to find two firms with the same potential levels of competitiveness but very different foreign trade performances. One might be able to finance projects very easily while the other might not because of extremely high interest rates or credit rationing. Often in developing countries, suppliers of raw materials and intermediate goods provide credit to their buyers, especially small- and medium-sized ones which do not have access to credit from financial institutions (Petersen and Rajan 1996). This phenomenon has implications for the development of strong and competitive trading firms as well as for the financial intermediation process in a country. Of course, this is a direct consequence of the existence of market segmentation.

Finance also matters for the allocation of resources for another reason. Financial institutions are supposed to screen for the best projects and monitor their development. Consequently, if key segments of the capital markets are missing it implies that there will be less screening and monitoring and, hence, a worse allocation of resources. A company that has no bank monitoring may incur an inefficient allocation of real resources and have a suboptimal risk management. In a modern capitalist economy, the financial institutions have the important task of collaborating in 'picking the winner' in a decentralized way.

Following the lines of thinking of Schumpeter, McKinnon and Shaw and the more recent literature on finance and endogenous growth, Rajan and Zingales (1998) state that capital markets make a contribution to growth by reallocating capital to the highest value use while limiting risks of loss through moral hazard, adverse selection or transaction costs. This implies that the lack of financial development should disproportionately affect those firms that are heavily dependent on external finance. From this hypothesis two testable facts follow: (i) Industries which are more dependent on external financing grow faster in more financially developed countries. (ii) Given that new firms depend more on external finance, financial development favors growth by disproportionately improving the prospects of young firms. The Rajan and Zingales (1998) paper uses the external dependency ratio of firms in different sectors to test these two hypotheses using a panel of developed and developing countries. Their main conclusion is that 'financial development has a substantial supportive influence on the rate of economic growth and this works, at least partly, by reducing the cost of external finance to financially dependent firms' (p. 584). On the basis of the evidence found, Rajan and Zingales advance two conjectures which deserve more research. The first is that 'the existence of a well-developed (capital) market in a certain country represents a source of comparative advantage for that country in industries that are more dependent on external finance'. The second is that 'the costs imposed by a lack of financial development will favor incumbent firms over new entrants. Therefore, the level of financial development can also be a factor in determining the size and composition of an industry as well as its concentration' (p. 584). These conjectures are in line with the two main hypotheses of our project: finance matters and, specifically, finance matters to comparative advantage. In fact, combining Rajan and Zingales' assumptions about external dependency ratios with the analyses of trade specialization pattern and firms' capital structure, we have found additional support for the hypothesis that the level of financial deepening has an impact on competitiveness and trade patterns.

To be sure, the studies presented in this volume portray a picture of finance 'mattering' crucially in determining competitiveness. The link operates through various channels. At the micro and sectoral level, there is almost universal evidence for credit constraints operating to determine the range and nature of trade specialization. The link between credit dependence and 'winning' and 'losing' firms and sectors is remarkably tight, and best illustrated in the cases of Argentina and Brazil. Indonesia and South Africa are illustrations of how the credit constraint has maintained specialization in traditional products. Indeed, an important lesson from the country case studies is how the exploitation of dynamic comparative advantage and genuine infant industry arguments in developing countries depends on the availability of credit, a point highlighted in the Philippines case study.

But not just any credit, as Schmidt argues in his paper, and a point also made in the India and Tunisia case studies. Depending on the regulatory framework and political imperatives within which they operate, banks in particular can lend too much or too little. It is clear from the India, Indonesia and Tunisia studies that the existence of a market failure in the financial sector need not automatically result in an improvement with government intervention. It is here that caution is called for in generalizing and presenting a 'set' of policy recommendations that may then be followed in cookie cutter fashion.

The story and policy lessons emerging from the micro-level are further complicated by the role that finance plays at the macro-level. The Asian crisis brought to the lexicon of economics a word borrowed from the epidemiology literature – contagion. To be sure, high and highly volatile levels of short-term capital played havoc in the frontline countries of any crisis. But with contagion, Argentina and Brazil were compelled to reassess their monetary and exchange rate arrangements as a result of events in East Asia a few months earlier. In addition to short-term volatility, financial flows can have more persistent effects which often go beyond conventional Dutch disease explanations. There is, in all of this, a question of what constitutes the equilibrium exchange rate. But the South Africa study and chapters by Ros and Medhora suggest that this is not just a technical issue. There are important consequences to having an imbalance in the trade and real sectors on the one hand, and the financial sector on the other.

It is at this point that Guerrieri's call for a more nuanced assessment of the link between trade openness and economic development becomes a powerful one. Still, the purpose of this set of studies is not to suggest that no answers exist to complicated situations. Rather, it is to suggest that answers do exist, but they have to be actively sought out, and not inferred from a preferred approach, much less derived from consensus. In large part, deep and well-run financial markets are indispensable to a successful strategy to link competitiveness in trade with economic growth and, ultimately, development. The benefits of having such markets and the costs of not having them are clear. Developing such markets often involves the active intervention of the state, to a point. Finding the balance between market creation and market liberalization is the ultimate challenge that faces all countries.

In sum, we believe that the concept of competitiveness represents a challenge to economic analysis because the level of competitiveness a country shows results from complex interactions of microeconomic, macroeconomic and financial factors and the analytical tools of the traditional approach are not especially useful for analyzing such interactions. Indeed, one important motivation for undertaking the country studies that we present here was, precisely, to investigate whether or not micro/macro and real/financial interactions are as relevant for competitiveness, the trade pattern and current account sustainability as the stylized facts that we have listed above seem to suggest. To be more specific, the hypotheses of our research work have been:

1   Both the degree of macroeconomic stability and the quality of financial markets are relevant in determining the evolution of competitiveness via their influence on non-price factors.
2   The sectoral mix of specialization at the 'micro'-level contributes to determining macroeconomic stability via its influence on the sustainability of the current account. The hypothesis of an imperfect access to international capital markets is crucial for this hypothesis.
3   Financial factors matter at the micro-level via their influence on the firms' capital structure and investment behavior, and they matter for competitiveness to the extent that there may be an anti-innovation or anti-trade bias in the allocation of financial resources.

The studies that follow elaborate on these points and, we trust, highlight their veracity while remaining true to the important distinctions and nuances that always exist across countries and development experiences and, indeed, change over time within countries.

Notes

1 On globalization, see Rodrik (1998).
2 For a paradigmatic example, see Krugman and Obstfeld (1991).
3 See for example Haque (1995) and Guerrieri (1994).
4 See World Bank (1993) and the references there.
5 The authors who propose leaving aside the concept of competitiveness should develop an alternative and more efficient view that can consistently integrate the problems implicit in this concept. Krugman, for example, after uncovering some mistakes which

originated in an incorrect interpretation of competitiveness, calls for a counter–counter revolution which would supersede the Washington Consensus (Krugman 1992). But such a revolution is still wanting.

6 The inclusion of proxies of technological activity (R&D investments, patents granted) and productive capacity (capital stock growth, investment rates) in regressions explaining market shares or trade flows yielded the 'right' signs for the estimated coefficients of price-competitiveness indicators (Fagerberg 1988; Amendola *et al.* 1993; Agénor 1997). The analytical underpinnings of non-price competitiveness determinants are to be found in the new theories of trade and growth as explained, for instance, by Helpman and Krugman (1985) and Grossman and Helpman (1991); see also Ocampo (1991) and Dosi (1991). Other contributions stem from endogenous growth theory. For a comprehensive and consistent presentation of this issue, see Aghion and Howitt (1997) and Fagerberg (1994).

7 We owe this example to Saul Keifman.

References

Agénor, P. (1997) 'Competitiveness and External Trade Performance of the French Manufacturing Industry', *Weltwirtschaftliches Archiv* 133(1): 103–33.

Aghion, P. and Howitt, P. W. (1997) *Endogenous Growth Theory*. Cambridge, MA: MIT Press.

Amendola, G., Dosi, G. and Papagni, E. (1993) 'The Dynamics of International Competitiveness', *Weltwirtschaftliches Archiv* 129(3): 451–71.

Chenery, R. and Syrquin, M. (1986) *Industrialization and Growth*. Oxford: Oxford University Press.

Dosi, G. (1991) 'Una reconsideración de las condiciones y los modelos del desarrollo. Una perspectiva "evolucionista" de la innovación, el comercio y el crecimiento', *Pensamiento Iberoamericano* 20: 167–91.

Fagerberg, J. (1988) 'International Competitiveness', *The Economic Journal* 98: 355–74.

Fagerberg, J. (1994) 'Technology and International Differences in Growth Rates', *Journal of Economic Literature* XXXII: 1147–75.

Fanelli, J. M. and Frenkel, R. (1995) 'Micro–Macro Interaction in Economic Development', *Unctad Review*. New York: United Nations.

Fanelli, J. M. and Medhora, R. (eds) (1998) *Financial Reform in Developing Countries*. London: Macmillan.

Fazzari, S., Hubbard, G. and Petersen, B. (1988) 'Financing Constraints and Corporate Investment', *Brookings Papers on Economic Activity*, No. 1.

Grossman, G. M. and Helpman, E. (1991) *Innovation and Growth in the Global Economy*. Cambridge, MA: MIT Press.

Guerrieri, P. (1994) 'International Competitiveness, Trade Integration and Technological Interdependence', in OECD, *The New Paradigm of Systemic Competitiveness: Toward More Integrated Policies in Latin America*. Paris: OECD Development Centre.

Haque, I. (1995) *Trade, Technology, and International Competitiveness*. Washington, DC: World Bank.

Harris, J. R., Schiantarelli, F. and Siregar, M. G. (1994) 'The Effect of Financial Liberalization on the Capital Structure and Investment Decisions of Indonesian Manufacturing Establishments', *The World Bank Economic Review* 8(1): 17–47.

Helpman, E. and Krugman, P. (1985) *Market Structure and Foreign Trade*. Cambridge, MA: MIT Press.

Hubbard, R. G. (1998) 'Capital-Market Imperfections and Investment', *Journal of Economic Literature* XXXVI: 193–225.

Inter-American Development Bank (IDB) (1995) *Economic and Social Progress in Latin America, 1995*. Washington, DC: Inter-American Development Bank.

Kaldor, N. (1978) 'The Effect of Devaluation on Trade in Manufactures', in *Further Essays on Applied Economics*. London: Duckworth.

Krugman, P. R. (1992) 'Toward a Counter–Counter-Revolution in Development Economics', Mimeo, Harvard University.

Krugman, P. R. (1996) *Pop Internationalism*. Cambridge, MA: MIT Press.

Krugman, P. R. and Obstfeld, M. (1991) *International Economics. Theory and Policy*. Boston: Harper Collins.

Levine, R. (1997) 'Financial Development and Economic Growth: Views and Agenda', *Journal of Economic Literature* XXXV: 688–726.

Llal, A. (1995) 'The Creation of Comparative Advantage: The Role of Industrial Policy', in I. Haque (ed.) *Trade, Technology, and International Competitiveness*. Washington, DC: World Bank.

Obstfeld, M. (1998) 'The Global Capital Market: Benefactor or Menace?', *Journal of Economic Perspectives* 12(4): 9–30.

Obstfeld, M. and Rogoff, K. (1996) *Foundations of International Macroeconomics*. Cambridge, MA: MIT Press.

Ocampo, J. A. (1991) 'Las nuevas teorías del comercio internacional y los países en vías de desarrollo', *Pensamiento Iberoamericano* 20: 193–214.

Petersen, M. A. and Rajan, R. G. (1996) 'Trade Credit: Theories and Evidence', *National Bureau of Economic Research Working Paper*, No. 5602.

Rajan, R. G. and Zingales, L. (1998) 'Financial Dependence and Growth', *American Economic Review* 88(3): 559–86.

Ramey, G. and Ramey, V. (1995) 'Cross-Country Evidence on the Link between Volatility and Growth', *American Economic Review* 85(5): 1138–51.

Rodrik, D. (1998) 'Symposium on Globalization in Perspective: An Introduction', *Journal of Economic Perspectives* 12(4): 3–8.

Rodrik, D. (1999) 'Governing the Global Economy: Does One Architectural Style Fit All?', Mimeo, John F. Kennedy School of Government.

Sachs, J. and Warner, A. (1997) 'Fundamental Sources of Long-Run Growth', *Recent Empirical Growth Research* (Area Papers and Proceedings) 87(2): 184–8.

Temple, J. (1999) 'The New Growth Evidence', *Journal of Economic Literature* XXXVII: 112–56.

Williamson, J. (1990) 'What Washington Means by Policy Reform', in J. Williamson (ed.), *Latin American Adjustment: How Much Has Happened?* Washington, DC: Institute for International Economics.

World Bank (1993) *The East Asian Miracle, Economic Growth and Public Policy*. Washington, DC: Oxford University Press.

2 Finance and changing trade patterns in developing countries
The Argentine case[1]

José María Fanelli and Saúl Keifman

1. Introduction

Structural reforms, the creation of a customs union with Mercosur, and the renewal of capital inflows into Latin America profoundly changed the structure of incentives Argentine firms faced in the 1990s. One important consequence was a higher degree of heterogeneity in the performance of firms and sectors. The non-tradable sector was a privileged recipient of foreign funds as a result of the privatization process and the deregulation of foreign investment. Producers of tradable goods faced greater competition as well as new opportunities from Mercosur markets as well as the availability of inputs and investment goods at international prices. The changing environment affected profitability across and within industries in complex ways and obliged firms to restructure. Some firms adopted offensive strategies to restructure, taking advantage of new market opportunities, implementing organizational improvements and upgrading capital equipment. Other firms, however, followed purely defensive restructuring strategies, their principal objective being to ensure survival in a far more challenging environment. This chapter explores how the changes in the macroeconomic setting and the interactions between developments in trade and finance created winners and losers in Argentina's recent past.

We will examine two different periods of the Argentine experience: the 1983–90 period when economic policies were dominated by the adjustment of the economy to the financial constraints imposed by the international debt crisis, and the period which followed the launching of Convertibility in 1991, when structural reforms and liberalization were implemented. We will place more emphasis on the latter, the richest in transformation, but also the least understood. The second section analyzes the stylized facts related to the evolution of trade and specialization patterns. The third part studies the characteristics of firms' financial structure and portfolio decisions in the context of imperfect capital markets such as those existing in Argentina. The fourth section builds on the stylized facts presented in the previous two sections and advances some hypotheses on micro–macro and trade–finance interactions. In what follows in this introduction, we briefly review the most important features of the overall evolution of the Argentine economy in the period under analysis in order to set the context of our research.

Productivity, competitiveness and growth in postwar Argentina reveal clearly differentiated periods. Until the mid-1970s, the country followed a strategy of import substitution industrialization. Although the economy grew during this period, the average growth rate was much lower than that observed in Latin American countries like Brazil or Mexico that were following the same strategy. In particular, the rate of productivity increase in Argentina was low and the country systematically lost competitiveness. This discouraging evolution in competitiveness, in turn, resulted in recurrent balance-of-payments crises and stop-and-go cycles determined by the availability of foreign exchange. In 1975, the country suffered a huge macroeconomic crisis that set the economy on the brink of hyperinflation. This crisis made it clear that the import substitution strategy had been exhausted as a means of increasing productivity and competitiveness.

From the macroeconomic collapse of the mid-1970s to 1990, Argentina made several fruitless attempts to reform its economy. Two features that were prevalent until 1990 are highly relevant to the topic of this book: the recurrent balance-of-payments crises which resulted in major macroeconomic instability, and the strong drop in the demand for domestic financial assets which gave rise to an unprecedented tightening in the rationing of credit toward productive firms, even for larger ones. It is not surprising that investment activity collapsed during this period and that productivity stagnated. Under such circumstances, the need to close the current account deficit required a sharp trade-off between living standards and competitiveness since the only way to gain competitiveness in the short run was to reduce domestic costs via huge devaluations. The maxi-devaluations of the 1980s, however, affected not only human welfare and competitiveness but also macroeconomic stability. Consequently, the economy underwent two hyperinflationary episodes by the end of the period.

In the 1990s the situation changed radically. In the first place, structural reforms were deepened. The process to open the trade and capital accounts, as well as the liberalization of the financial system, was completed, and state-owned firms were privatized. In the second place, price stability was achieved via the implementation of a currency board scheme which pegged the Argentine peso to the US dollar (the so-called Convertibility Plan). Third, the greater availability of foreign finance and the fall in international interest rates relaxed the external financial constraint significantly, thus eliminating one of the causes of macroeconomic disequilibria during the debt crisis. This is perhaps the most important fact that distinguishes the 1980s from the 1990s. In the 1990s it was possible to finance the higher trade and current account deficits resulting from the structural reform and stabilization processes. One significant factor generating the current account deficit was the recovery in the private demand for capital goods. Another important factor was that the private agents also increased their demand for consumption goods. In this way, the recovery in investment was not accompanied by savings, leading to a widening in the private deficit.

These macro-developments have had very important consequences at the micro-level. While the increased macro-stability reduced uncertainty in decision making, the greater availability of credit dramatically softened the credit rationing that firms were facing. Both factors heavily contributed to reversing the stagnant path of productivity, particularly in the manufacturing industry. Exports have shown a greater dynamism during the 1990s as compared to the 1980s, in spite of the real appreciation of the peso, while the overall economy has been growing at around 6 per cent per annum. This might indicate that the loosening up of financial constraints made a difference, probably, via investment and productivity. Table 2.1 shows the evolution of some key macroeconomic variables.

In the 1980s there was a systematic fall in the domestic demand for financial instruments because of the extreme uncertainty. In the 1990s, the upsurge in capital inflows, together with the recovery in the demand for domestically issued financial assets in a context of increasing stability, led to an increase in financial deepening. This can be seen in Figure 2.1, which shows the evolution of M4 and total credit. This not only softened the tight credit rationing of the 1980s, but also opened up opportunities for firms to innovate in the form of financing capital projects. Despite these remarkable changes, however, the new situation of the 1990s presents an important weakness. The macroeconomic equilibrium is highly dependent on the stability of capital inflows, and the recent Mexican and Asian crises have made it clear that international flows into 'emerging' countries are

Table 2.1 Evolution of selected macroeconomic variables

Period average	Real GDP growth (%)	GDP deflator change (%)	Investment/ GDP (%)	Current account (billion USD)	Real exchange rate (1990 = 100)	Openness (X + M)/ GDP (%)
1983–90	−0.2	911.6	17.1	−1.4	103.6	15.7
1991–7	6.2	23.1	21.0	−5.7	78.4	27.6

Source: Elaborated on the basis of Ministry of Economy data.

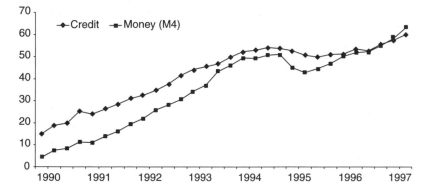

Figure 2.1 Evolution of money and credit (millions of pesos).
Source: Elaborated on the basis of Central Bank data.

far from stable. The figure also records the sharp reversal experienced by the financial deepening process in 1995 as a result of the Tequila effect. It took over one year for the economy to recover from the consequences of the instability triggered by the crisis. In fact, a more severe crisis was avoided only because of measures taken by both the Central Bank as lender of last resort, and by the IMF in providing external support.

2. Trade specialization and competitiveness: The stylized facts

This section is devoted to establishing the 'trade facts', that is, the evolution and structure of trade flows in the recent past, the evolution of productivity and domestic costs and their relationships with the current account.

After a poor performance in 1983–90, trade flows increased dramatically in 1991–6. However, as imports grew much faster than exports, the trade balance turned negative. An important factor behind the growth in exports was the launching of Mercosur (Southern Cone Common Market) in 1994. Import growth, in turn, was driven by GDP growth, a real currency appreciation and trade liberalization.

Regarding the pattern of inter-industry specialization, food items remained the main source of foreign exchange in the 1980s and the 1990s. This dependence on primary sectors was reinforced in the 1990s as fuels became a surplus sector while most manufactures increased their negative contribution to the trade balance. The rise in capital goods imports (machinery and transport equipment) was an important factor behind this development.

A more detailed examination of trade flows, however, shows that intra-industry trade experienced a significant and continuous increase throughout the 1980s and the 1990s. That is to say, all sectors exported and imported more, including deficit sectors (manufacturing) which managed to increase their exports, especially in the 1990s.

Real unit labor costs declined in the 1980s and rose in the 1990s, mainly as a result of the ups and downs of dollar wages. Labor productivity grew dramatically in the 1990s (after a slip in the 1980s) thanks to higher capacity utilization, technological change and the resumption of investment activity.

Overall evolution of trade flows

The performance of trade flows between 1983 and 1990, the years of financial restraint, was rather disappointing (see Figure 2.2). Imports remained stagnant, hardly surprising given the lack of GDP growth. Exports, in turn, grew at 6.7 per cent per annum, well below the 10.1 per cent annual growth rate recorded by world exports. Additionally, exports behaved countercyclically[2] and were also strongly influenced by commodity prices. The annual average of the trade balance was 3.9 billion USD in 1983–90. In other words, the goal of generating trade surpluses to serve the foreign debt was accomplished at a high social cost.

From 1991, trade flows increased dramatically. Imports took the lead, growing at a 34 per cent yearly rate, mainly fueled by lower tariffs, real currency

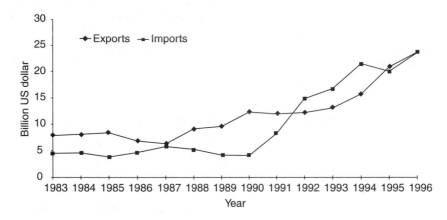

Figure 2.2 Trade flows, 1983–96.

Source: Elaborated on the basis of Ministry of Economy data.

appreciation and output growth. This brought about a trade deficit from 1992, but exports soon caught up, closing the gap in 1995 and 1996. Between 1990 and 1996, the annual rate of export growth was 11.6 per cent, which favorably compared to the annual growth rate in world exports which was 7.6 per cent. Most of Argentina's export growth took place in 1994–6, at a 22 per cent yearly rate. Something remarkable about the export surge initiated in 1994 is that it seems to have broken the aforementioned countercyclical pattern, occurring not only during the Tequila's recessionary year (1995) but also in expansionary years, such as 1994 and 1996. Trade balances in this period averaged a 1.2 billion USD annual deficit, though this figure masks a yearly 4 billion USD deficit in 1992–4 and a near balance situation in 1995–6.

As a result of the growth in trade flows, Argentina has recently become a much more open economy. Total real trade flows as a percentage of real GDP[3] have increased from an average of 16 per cent in 1983–90 to an average of 28 per cent in 1991–6.[4]

Changes in the pattern of inter-industry trade specialization

Table 2.2 provides information on the sectoral contributions to the trade balance[5] according to aggregate Standard International Trade Classification (SITC) commodity groupings. This indicator is adjusted by the overall trade balance. When the economy began to adjust to the debt crisis (1983–4), only food items made a positive contribution to the trade balance. By the end of the first period (1988–90) two more groups, Agricultural raw materials and Other manufactures, added positive contributions to the trade balance, while the remaining ones (Fuels, Ores and metals, Chemical products, Machinery and transport equipment) reduced their deficit shares.

Table 2.2 Contributions to the trade balance

	1983–4	*1985–7*	*1988–90*	*1991–3*	*1994–6*
Food items	647.50	556.07	448.35	521.50	456.43
Agricultural raw materials	−20.40	−7.87	2.21	3.20	16.73
Fuels	−58.06	−67.59	−40.02	45.07	75.66
Ores and metals	−42.95	−38.69	−41.62	−17.63	−10.83
Chemical products	−173.69	−157.69	−155.79	−100.59	−103.41
Other manufactures	−97.26	−12.89	18.86	−90.89	−73.60
Machinery and transport equipment	−255.23	−271.35	−231.05	−359.71	−361.32
Unallocated	0.09	0.01	−0.93	−0.95	0.35
Cereals	301.39	175.97	91.32	110.93	97.99
Crude and manufactured fertilizers	−7.47	−7.28	−7.08	−4.42	−11.60
Crude petroleum	0.00	3.78	4.06	24.72	77.44
Medical and pharmaceutical products	−18.09	−20.48	−16.54	−14.80	−16.40
Textile fibers, yarn and clothing	5.56	23.71	31.07	14.90	8.96
Metals and metal manufactures	−66.45	−16.96	7.82	−5.72	−11.31
Machinery	−206.89	−234.99	−201.73	−268.42	−279.84
Transport equipment	−48.34	−36.36	−29.32	−91.28	−81.49

Source: Elaborated on the basis of Ministry of Economy data.

Table 2.3 Aggregate indices of intra-industry trade (based on SITC three-digit groupings)

Indices	*1983–4*	*1985–7*	*1988–90*	*1991–3*	*1994–6*
Grubel and Lloyd	0.159	0.205	0.250	0.273	0.320
Aquino	0.151	0.196	0.253	0.276	0.326

Source: Elaborated on the basis of Ministry of Economy data.

Changes in the intra-industry pattern of trade

Indices of contributions to the trade balance are good indicators of the pattern of inter-industry specialization. When trade is driven by comparative advantage, that is all there is to know. Trade is also driven by economies of scale, however, which affects the volume of intra-industry trade. Therefore, the evolution of indices of intra-industry trade gives important information on the structure of the economy since they measure the exploitation of economies of scale and the degree of technological sophistication of an economy.

Table 2.3 shows the evolution of intra-industry trade as measured by the indices proposed by Grubel and Lloyd,[6] and Aquino,[7] based on SITC three-digit groupings. They both show a dramatic increase in the significance of intra-industry trade, which more than doubles between 1983–4 and 1994–6.

The evolution of manufacturing trade flows, output, productivity and domestic costs

To better understand this story, we now focus on the evolution of the manufacturing sector that underwent serious structural change. The ratio of the trade balance in manufacturing to gross output rises from a surplus position in 1986 (1.7 per cent), peaks in 1990 as a result of a deep recession and hyperinflation (8.5 per cent), and then falls dramatically reaching a 5.4 per cent deficit in 1996 for the overall manufacturing (Table 2.4). This might suggest that manufacturing is one of the big losers of the opening-up process and that Argentina is being dein-dustrialized. Furthermore, this ratio falls in most manufacturing branches. This ratio, however, conceals the fact that both imports and exports increased faster than total production (of course, the former more quickly than the latter). The rise in the imports to gross output ratio from 3.4 per cent in 1990 to 20 per cent in 1996 is hardly surprising given the mix of currency appreciation and drastic tariff reductions. It is more remarkable that export ratios also improved from 12 per cent in 1990 to 15 per cent in 1996. We have already mentioned that export growth in the mid-1990s seems to have broken the old countercyclical pattern. We now see that manufacturing is part of this change in behavior. Naturally, this parallel increase in both imports and exports is closely related to the important rise in intra-industry trade mentioned above.

Table 2.4 Manufacturing: trade-balance-, exports- and imports-to-output ratios (%)

	1986	1987	1988	1989	1990	1991	1992	1993	1994	1995	1996
$(X-M)/Q$	1.7	0.7	3.0	5.8	8.5	2.7	−3.9	−5.2	−8.1	−3.1	−5.4
X/Q	5.1	4.7	6.6	9.4	12.0	10.1	8.9	9.8	10.6	14.7	14.9
M/Q	3.4	4.0	3.6	3.6	3.5	7.4	12.8	15.0	18.8	17.8	20.3

Source: Elaborated on the basis of Ministry of Economy data.

$(X-M)/Q$: trade-balance-to-output ratio; X/Q: exports-to-output ratio; M/Q: imports-to-output ratio.

Table 2.5 Manufacturing: indices of output, labor productivity and unit labor costs

	1986	1987	1988	1989	1990	1991	1992	1993	1994	1995	1996
Q	128.6	130.2	121.2	110.6	100	109.9	121.1	127.3	135.2	125.8	132.4
Q/L	108.2	111.4	100.8	102	100	110.7	119.9	127.2	133.7	138.2	146.6
WL/QE	76.7	70.2	81.2	45.3	100	112.3	133.2	136.6	137.7	136.9	136.0
WL/QEP_x	93.5	78.6	78.8	44.8	100	107.9	122.7	126.4	124.6	114.6	112.3
WL/QEP_m	92.9	80.0	83.5	48.0	100	107.6	126.4	133.9	132.4	124.5	120.9

Source: Elaborated on the basis of Ministry of Economy data.

Q: output index; Q/L: labor productivity index; WL/QE: US dollar unit labor cost index; WL/QEP_x: US dollar unit labor cost index deflated by export prices; WL/QEP_m: US dollar unit labor cost index deflated by import prices.

Table 2.6 Export growth and investment

Variable	Coefficient	t-statistic
Independent	6.18	2.34
Constant	1.35	5.47

Adj. $R^2 = 0.09$; observations included $= 65$.

In order to measure the importance of trade developments in the 1990s, it should be noted that they took place in a context of a swift growth in manufacturing output (see Table 2.5). The driving force behind the expansion in manufacturing output was productivity growth since employment actually declined. Indeed, the record of labor productivity growth in manufacturing between 1990 and 1996 was remarkable. Total manufacturing labor productivity increased by 46.6 per cent, or a 6.6 per cent annual rate of growth between 1990 and 1996. According to Katz (1997), these developments made it possible to reduce the productivity gap between Argentina and the United States from 45 to 33 per cent during the same period.[8] We are also certain that part of the measured growth in productivity is due to cyclical rather than structural factors as manufacturing output reached a trough in 1990. This is an important point to keep in mind when trying to ascertain and gauge its sources, something we do not attempt to do in this paper.

Despite higher labor productivity, real unit labor costs[9] increased for the manufacturing sector and most of its branches as the increment in productivity only partially compensated for the growth in dollar wages caused by the currency appreciation that took place from 1991.

We suspect that there is a connection between the jump in productivity and the recovery of investment spending which increasingly satisfied its demand via capital goods imports. If it is true that investment has affected productivity significantly in the recent past, then it has also influenced competitiveness through its impact on unit labor costs. In this regard, learning how investment is financed becomes crucial to understanding the linkage between trade flows and finance. In a context of credit rationing, access to credit might become the binding constraint on investment decisions thereby hampering productivity change and the growth of trade flows. We found some preliminary evidence on the linkage between investment levels and export growth based on a regression run with data from sixty-five manufacturing branches in 1994–7, as shown in Table 2.6. The dependent variable is the growth rate of the export-to-output ratio between 1994 and 1997, and the independent variable is the average investment-to-value-added ratio in 1994–6. We are aware of the limitations of this piece of evidence but this is as far as we can go given the available data.

3. Competitiveness, finance and macroeconomic stability

The objective of this section is to assess the extent to which finance matters in explaining the degree of success or failure of firms and industries in Argentina. The question is relevant because changes on the financial side of the economy were as marked as those that occurred on the real side in the last two decades. Furthermore, since Argentina's capital markets are far from perfect, it seems plausible to assume that finance does matter in explaining not only the results of the restructuring process launched in the 1990s, but also the kinds of strategies specific firms chose.[10] In what follows, we will try to shed some light on this issue based on available empirical evidence, using data from the financial system and the sample of firms listed on the Buenos Aires Stock Exchange.

We begin with some evidence on how the amount of credit generated by the formal system influences the activity level of manufacturing in order to set the context for the analysis that follows on the financial decisions of firms in manufactures.[11] Our hypothesis is that, in a context of pervasive imperfections in financial markets (rationing), the availability of real credit in the banking system (crtot) has a strong influence on the activity level of manufacturing (gdp) in the short run, while there is a long-run relationship between the stock of real credit and the activity level of manufactures (eqns (2.1)–(2.3)).

$$\log gdp_t = \delta_1 + \delta_2 \log crtot_t + s_t, \tag{2.1}$$

$$\Delta \log gdp_t = \delta_3 (\log gdp_{t-1} - \delta_1 - \delta_2 \log crtot_{t-1}) + \delta_4 \Delta \log gdp_{t-1}$$
$$+ \delta_5 \Delta \log crtot_{t-1} + \delta_6 + z_{1t}, \tag{2.2}$$

$$\Delta \log crtot_t = \delta_7 (\log gdp_{t-1} - \delta_1 - \delta_2 \log crtot_{t-1}) + \delta_8 \Delta \log gdp_{t-1}$$
$$+ \delta_9 \Delta \log crtot_{t-1} + \delta_{10} + z_{2t}. \tag{2.3}$$

Table 2.7 details the results obtained using this error correction model (ECM).

The coefficient of credit in the long-run equation (δ_2) is positive and significant at the 5 per cent level and so it seems that these two variables are co-integrated. As coefficients δ_3 and δ_5 are also significant while coefficients δ_7 and δ_8 are not, it seems that credit Granger-causes manufacturing GDP. In sum,

Table 2.7 Credit and manufacturing activity level

Coefficient	Estimated value	t-statistic
δ_1	0.87	—
δ_2	0.29	21.4
δ_3	−1.43	−4.7
δ_4	0.53	−2.5
δ_5	−0.27	−3.0
δ_6	0.01	1.0
δ_7	0.75	1.3
δ_8	−0.15	−0.4
δ_9	−0.40	−2.4
δ_{10}	0.04	1.7

Adj. $R^2 = 0.48$; observations included $= 32$; sample period: 1989:3/1997:2.

the evidence is consistent with the hypothesis of a relevant influence of credit on manufacturing output.

Competitiveness and asset accumulation: Winners and losers

In this part of the study, we focus on the micro-level and try to investigate whether, and in which way, financial factors were relevant in determining success or failure in an environment with higher external competition. To this end, we use the empirical evidence provided by the balance-sheet data of the sample of firms listed on the Buenos Aires Stock Exchange. We work with different aggregates of firms. First, we differentiate between firms which produce non-tradable goods and services (mostly newly privatized public utilities) and firms in the manufacturing industry which, in the new open-economy environment, belong to the tradable sector. Given our goals we concentrate on the tradable sector and use non-tradables as a benchmark. Second, we work with disaggregates within the tradable sector so as to identify interactions between real and financial factors at the sectoral level, and elaborate hypotheses on the financial variables determining the success or failure of firms. Third, in order to isolate the features associated with market imperfections we use other criteria to divide up the sample by, for example, the size of the firm.

In spite of the important recovery in manufacturing output achieved in the 1990s, the value of total assets of the industrial firms in our sample was only 20 per cent greater in the first half of 1997 than in 1986.[12] This fact, however, conceals marked differences in the firms' dynamic paths in each manufacturing branch. In order to capture such differences, we have classified the manufacturing firms in the sample according to the branches they belong to, and then split them into two groups: 'winners' and 'losers'.[13] A branch is defined as a winner if a representative firm's assets have grown by more than the average and as a loser if they have not. Figure 2.3 shows the evolution of the assets of winner and loser firms.

The contrast between the evolution of assets of the firms in the winner and loser sectors is striking. While the real value of the assets of the winners more than doubled, the aggregate assets of the losers were much lower in 1997 than in 1986. While winners increased the size of their assets, investment in the latter sectors became negative. Figure 2.3 clearly shows that there was a break in the dynamic path of the variables under study at the beginning of the 1990s, followed by the amplification of the differences in the economic behavior of losers and winners. The important questions from the point of view of our study are, on the one hand, whether financial factors matter in explaining these facts and, on the other, whether there are relevant linkages between finance and changes in international competitiveness. In answer to the second question, the stylized facts of the overall evolution of competitiveness in the branches in which loser and winner firms produce are highly relevant. These are summarized in Tables 2.8 and 2.9.

From the tables, it seems that both winner and loser firms faced important changes in factors affecting competitiveness. First, all cases showed a marked increase in the imports-to-output ratio (except tobacco). This can be interpreted as evidence that these firms were experiencing far tougher competition from abroad.

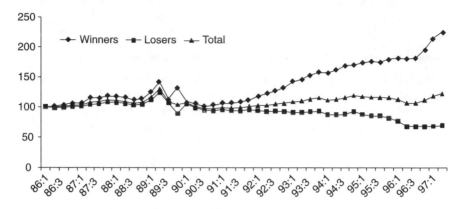

Figure 2.3 Evolution of total assets (1986:1 = 100).

Source: Elaborated on the basis of Sistema de Information Bursatil data.

Table 2.8 Evolution of key real variables of loser sectors (1991/6; %)

Sector	Output growth	Labor productivity growth	Labor costs growth	Exports/ output		Imports/ output		Trade balance/ output	
				1991	1996	1991	1996	1991	1996
Textiles	−7.6	23.1	22.9	4.1	7.6	5.9	14.7	−1.8	−7.1
Paper-cell.	30.3	30.3	35.8	4.0	9.8	9.4	24.7	−5.4	−14.9
Metals	27.7	63.2	−6.2	20.1	17.1	9.6	13.2	10.5	3.9
Chemicals	29.8	30.2	24.2	9.1	10.4	19.1	24.8	−10.0	−14.7

Source: Elaborated on the basis of INDEC data.

Table 2.9 Evolution of key real variables of winner sectors (1991/6; %)

Sector	Output growth	Labor productivity growth	Labor costs growth	Exports/ output		Imports/ output		Trade balance/ output	
				1991	1996	1991	1996	1991	1996
Food	23.9	23.8	36.4	26.0	32.0	1.5	2.9	24.5	29.1
Wood	−4.3	15.3	−11.6	1.8	7.9	7.1	11.0	−6.1	−3.9
Petroleum	1.3	203.0	−34.8	6.9	8.1	1.3	3.5	−1.2	−2.2
Electrical machinery	40.1	71.6	−16.1	3.2	5.0	37.0	58.2	−1.8	−21.2
Tobacco	14.1	89.0	−41.5	1.1	0.6	0.1	0.1	1.0	0.5
Non-metallic	2.7	28.5	29.6	4.0	4.3	4.0	11.0	0.0	−6.7
Transport equipment	85.6	75.8	−32.9	7.2	11.2	15.4	37.4	−4.0	−22.0

Source: Elaborated on the basis of INDEC data.

Second, all branches responded to the challenge by increasing productivity and most managed to increase output levels. Another positive feature is that the exports-to-output ratio also increased (except tobacco). Nonetheless, sectoral trade deficits widened (except food).

One important difference in the performance between loser and winner branches is that the former experienced increased labor costs while the latter managed to reduce them (with a few exceptions: metals among losers and food and non-metallic products among winners). The fact that labor productivity grew much faster in most winner branches probably explains that outcome. All this means, *ceteris paribus*, that winner firms were better positioned during the restructuring process. If we assume that the increase in total assets is a reasonable proxy for investment, it is clear that one specific and highly relevant difference between winners and losers is that the former were able to invest and adopt a more offensive strategy while the latter reduced their assets and increased their productivity implementing a defensive restructuring of the firm. Why were winners able to adopt a more offensive strategy based on increases in investment? In order to assess the role of market imperfections, we first examine the determinants of investment in assets and, second, study the differential patterns in which loser and winner firms fulfill their financial requirements.

One hypothesis we would like to investigate is whether the chosen strategy was either defensive or offensive because of firms' ability to access the necessary funds to finance their restructuring. We utilized panel data for the 1986–97 period to analyze the determinants of changes in firms' assets and to check for the presence of market imperfections. On theoretical grounds, the first candidate in the search for determinants of a firm's investment decision (Δasset) is its rate of profit (profit). In a context of perfect capital markets the firm should invest in all projects that are profitable under existing market conditions. When imperfections in financial markets are present, however, cash flow and the ability to access credit markets also matter.[14] We utilized the operational income of the firm (income) and leverage (leverage, measured as the total-debt to asset ratio) as proxies for cash flow and the ability to obtain funds from credit markets, respectively, and estimated the model represented in eqn (2.4).

$$\Delta \text{ asset}_{it} = \alpha_{1i} + \alpha_2 \text{profit}_{it} + \alpha_3 \text{income}_{it} + \alpha_4 \text{leverage}_{it} + u_{it}. \quad (2.4)$$

Using the fixed-effects approach we found that the three exogenous variables were significant at the 5 per cent level, as shown in Table 2.10. The empirical evidence,

Table 2.10 The determinants of asset accumulation

Variable	Coefficient	t-statistic
profit	18.70	4.24
income	0.43	2.23
leverage	3.30	3.00

Adj. $R^2 = 0.51$; $F = 65.1$; D–W $= 2.06$; total panel observations: 140.

then, does not reject the hypothesis that there exist imperfections in capital markets that constrain asset accumulation. Given this evidence, the question that naturally arises is whether there are any systematic differences in the way in which aggregate agents finance their stocks. In the next part, we focus on the evolution of stocks (particularly on the liabilities side of the firms' balance sheets) and examine whether these reveal some clues that help answer this question.

Imperfect capital markets and patterns of finance

Firms' decisions about the proportion of debt and net worth on the balance sheet are much more complex when market failures exist. In a world where the supply of credit at the ongoing interest rate is not infinitely elastic and the cost of the funds raised from distinct sources can differ significantly, the managers in charge of the capital budgeting process face additional restrictions. In such a context, the decision over the mix of owned and borrowed capital is crucial. It is not only essential to maximize the present value of a firm's assets but also to minimize the probability of unexpected increases in financial fragility which could result in financial distress and even bankruptcy. Figure 2.4 shows the evolution of total assets, liabilities and net worth of the aggregate of firms in the industrial sector. Between 1986 and 1996, total assets of aggregated manufacturing firms grew. Between 1986 and 1990 large swings in the value of real debts and a sharp drop during the hyperinflationary period (1989–90) made it harder for firms to satisfy their financial requirements.

In the 1990s, financial deepening and capital inflows increased credit supply allowing firms to increase their leverage after a long period of tight rationing. This picture, however, conceals important differences between winners and losers. Figure 2.5 shows the evolution of the most important items that define the balance sheet of winners: net worth, assets and liabilities.

As can be seen, the substantial growth in the value of assets is accompanied by a still higher increment in the stock of total liabilities. As a consequence, there is a systematic elevation in the leverage ratio. In fact, the augmentation in the stock of debt held by winners in the 1990s is impressive, between 1990:4 and 1997:2 it grew by 229 per cent. The evolution of the stock of debt, however, exhibits a greater variance than net worth and assets. Furthermore, the fact that the higher level of uncertainty caused by the Tequila crisis in the 1995 to mid-1996 period induces a sharp but temporary reversal in the upward trend of the leverage ratio, and a fall in the real value of the outstanding stock of debt, suggests that the winners' ability to access credit markets did not suffice to isolate them from macroshocks. Figure 2.6 showing the performance of the losers' balance-sheet items is very different from that of the winners.

There are two salient features in the evolution of financial variables in the case of losers. The first is that the three variables under study exhibit a clear downward trend. It seems that it has been very difficult for losers either to generate funds internally or raise them in capital markets. Under such circumstances, they were even unable to maintain the size of their firms. The second feature is that the

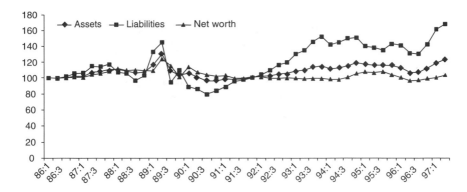

Figure 2.4 Pattern of finance, manufacturing (1986:1 = 100).
Source: Elaborated on the basis of Sistema de Informacion Bursatil data.

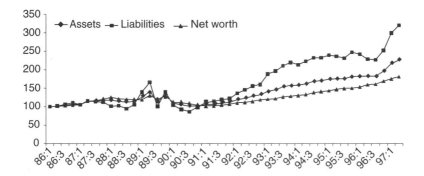

Figure 2.5 Pattern of finance of winners (1986:1 = 100).
Source: Elaborated on the basis of Sistema de Informacion Bursatil data.

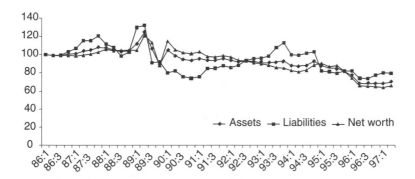

Figure 2.6 Pattern of finance of losers (1986:1 = 100).
Source: Elaborated on the basis of Sistema de Informacion Bursatil data.

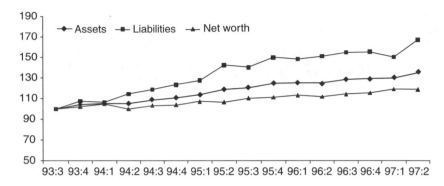

Figure 2.7 Pattern of finance of the non-tradable sector.

Source: Elaborated on the basis of Sistema de Informacion Bursatil data.

effects of macroeconomic shocks on the balance sheet of losers differ from the case of winners. Loser firms were able to increase their leverage in the context of the greater macroeconomic stability in the 1991–4 period much like winners. Unlike winners, however, losers never recovered from the fall in the stock of debt and leverage ratio caused by the Tequila crisis, forcing them to undertake a defensive restructuring of their balance sheets. This hypothesis is consistent with Minsky's view on the changes in financial fragility throughout the business cycle and with Bernanke's approach regarding the effects of credit crunches on the external premium that firms pay for external finance.[15] In both cases, market imperfections play a crucial role in determining the change in the level of fragility of (financially) heterogeneous agents.

The balance sheets of non-tradable producers are shown in Figure 2.7. The aggregate of non-tradable firms in the sample is a good standard to check for market segmentation because it is basically composed of firms that are, on average, larger in size and produce in sectors where the variance of cash flow is much lower. A priori, these firms should suffer from the effects of market imperfections less than manufacturing firms.

The pattern in the relationship between assets, liabilities and net worth reproduces the one corresponding to winners in the 1990s. There is a fact, nonetheless, that sharply differentiates this group from both the winners and losers: the effects of the Tequila crisis are hardly discernible in the graph. It is clear that these larger firms with a low standard deviation in cash flow have much more stable access to financial markets and are, thus, better equipped to resist macroeconomic shocks.

Market segmentation and foreign credit

We have seen that larger firms show lower financial volatility and seem to access long-term finance more easily. On the other hand, it can be argued that the accumulation of abundant liquidity can be a good strategy to avoid a liquidity crunch and maintain creditworthiness for managers facing excessive instability in the long-run segment of capital markets. *Ceteris paribus* the size of the firm, a strong liquidity position can increase the firm's access to long-run finance. Based on this reasoning, we investigate whether the ability to obtain long-run finance (leverlp) is explained by the size of the firm measured by the value of total assets (assets) and the real value of liquidity (liquidity). We used quarterly observations from the panel of manufacturing firms to estimate eqn (2.5).[16] Table 2.11 presents the results obtained using the fixed-effect approach.

$$\text{leverlp}_{it} = \gamma_{1i} + \gamma_2 \log \text{assets}_{it} + \gamma_3 \log \text{liquidity}_{it} + h_{it}. \qquad (2.5)$$

All variables are significant at the 5 per cent level. This means that the hypotheses that there exists a segmented market for long-run credit on the one hand, and that managers use liquidity to signal a strong financial position as a means to soften the rationing of long-term funds on the other are both plausible.

Additional evidence on the issues under consideration can be obtained by looking at the evolution of different types of debt instruments and their distribution across the aggregates of firms. In the 1990s, the greater availability of long-term finance permitted enterprises to augment the proportion of long-term assets in the portfolio without jeopardizing the soundness of their financial positions. At the macroeconomic level this took the form of a strong recovery in the investment/GDP ratio. At the microeconomic level, though, the distribution of the increase in long-term credit among firms was far from even. Figure 2.8 shows

Table 2.11 The determinants of the long-run debt ratio

Variable	Coefficient	t-statistic
log assets	0.11	3.6
log liquidity	0.03	2.1

Adj. $R^2 = 0.814$; $F = 1,288$; total panel observations $= 585$.

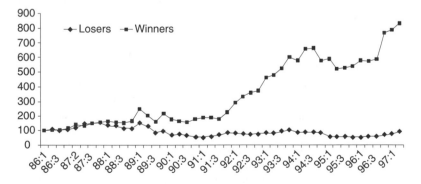

Figure 2.8 Evolution of long-run liabilities (1986:1 = 100).

Source: Elaborated on the basis of Sistema de Informacion Bursatil data.

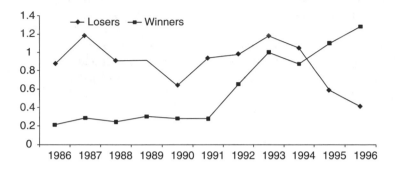

Figure 2.9 Evolution of net-denominated debt (millions of USD).

Source: Elaborated on the basis of Sistema de Informacion Bursatil data.

the evolution of real long-term liabilities of losers and winners within the manufacturing industry.

While the real value of long-run liabilities in the case of winners shows a pronounced upward trend reaching a 1997 value which is eight times its 1986 level, that of the losers fluctuates around a mean of zero growth. Hence, the low (and even negative in some firms) investment demand of losers may be correlated with difficulties in obtaining long-term finance.

One important characteristic of financial underdevelopment is the inability to generate long-run debt instruments. Argentina is no exception to this rule and, consequently, international capital markets are a crucial alternative source of long-term finance. Likewise, in the particular case of Argentina, the growth of the dollarized segment contributed to the prolongation of debt contracts. The consequence of all this is that there tends to be a positive correlation between the proportion of long-run finance and the proportion of dollar-denominated debt held in the portfolio. Figure 2.9 shows the evolution of the dollar-denominated stock of debt in our sample of manufacturing firms.

The upward trend in the dollar-denominated debt of the winners is very strong while the opposite is true in the case of losers. At the beginning of the 1990s, the upsurge in capital inflows increased the availability of finance for the entire manufacturing industry. However, after the Tequila crisis, while winners could recover creditworthiness in international markets, losers could not. Why were losers unable to recoup credibility? A reasonable hypothesis is that the losers were less able to adapt to the post-Tequila scenario and, consequently, lost creditworthiness. The tight rationing triggered by the Tequila effect in financial markets may have become an insurmountable obstacle for some firms to adapt to the new export-oriented scenario without implementing a defensive strategy. The question is why they tried to increase efficiency by means of a defensive strategy.[17] We cannot give a definitive answer to these questions because more research (and particularly more data) is necessary, but we think that we have enough evidence to show that the interactions between finance and competitiveness merit more attention.

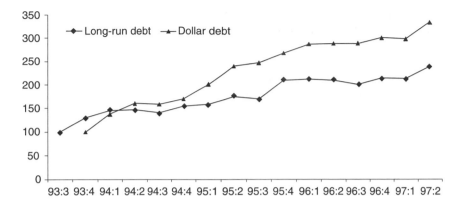

Figure 2.10 Evolution of debt items in the non-tradable sector (1993:3 = 100).

Source: Elaborated on the basis of Sistema de Informacion Bursatil data.

The data on the evolution of non-tradable firms is consistent with the previous approach regarding the influence of segmentation and rationing on the productive strategies of the firms.

As Figure 2.10 shows, corporations in the non-tradable sector have privileged access to international markets and to long-run funds. The supply of foreign finance, on the other hand, seems to be much more stable than in the case of the other aggregates under analysis. The Mexican crisis, for instance, had much softer consequences on the ability of these firms to tap international capital markets to fulfill their financial needs.

Patterns of specialization and finance

Following Schumpeter, McKinnon and Shaw and the more recent literature on finance and endogenous growth, Rajan and Zingales (1998) state that capital markets make a contribution to growth by reallocating capital to the highest value use without substantial risk of loss through moral hazard, adverse selection or transaction costs. This implies that the lack of financial development should disproportionately hinder firms who are typically dependent on external finance. From this hypothesis two testable facts follow: (i) Industries which are more dependent on external financing grow faster in more financially developed countries. (ii) Given that new firms depend more on external finance, financial development favors growth by disproportionately improving the prospects of young firms.

One problem in testing these hypotheses is that the true optimal capital structure of firms cannot be observed in financially underdeveloped countries. Rajan and Zingales make two assumptions in order to overcome this problem and identify the 'technological' demand for external financing that a firm operating in a specific industry would choose in a perfect capital market. The first is that capital markets in the United States, especially for the large firms listed on the stock exchange, are relatively frictionless and, therefore, it is reasonable to assume that the observed ratio of external finance reflects the technological demand for external financing of the industry. Second, such a technological demand carries over to the same industries in other countries. On the basis of these assumptions, they identify the industry's technological demand for external finance using US data. The variable used is the external dependency ratio or EDR (capital expenditures minus cash flow from operations divided by capital expenditures), shown for nineteen ISIC sectors in the fourth column of Table 2.12.

The Rajan and Zingales paper utilizes these EDRs to test the two aforementioned hypotheses using a panel of developed and developing countries. Their main conclusion is that 'financial development has a substantial supportive influence on the rate of economic growth and this works, at least partly, by reducing the cost of external finance to financially dependent firms' (p. 584).

On the basis of the evidence found, Rajan and Zingales advance two conjectures that deserve more explanation. The first is that 'the existence of a well-developed (capital) market in a certain country represents a source of comparative advantage for that country in industries that are more dependent on external finance' (p. 584). The second is that 'the costs imposed by a lack of financial development will favor incumbent firms over new entrants. Therefore, the level of financial development can also be a factor in determining the size composition of an industry as well as its concentration' (p. 584). These conjectures are in line with the two main hypotheses of our project: finance matters and, specifically, finance matters to comparative advantage. In fact, combining Rajan and Zingales' assumptions about EDRs with our previous analysis on the trade

Table 2.12 Trade specialization and external dependence ratio

Rank	ISIC sector	CTB	EDR (%)
1	Food products and beverages	42.5	14.0
2	Leather, fur products and footwear	5.8	−11.0
3	Petroleum refineries	4.0	18.5
4	Basic metal products	2.1	9.0
5	Tobacco	0.1	−45.0
6	Wearing apparel	0.0	3.0
7	Furniture	−0.1	24.0
8	Printing and publishing	−0.2	20.0
9	Non-metallic mineral products	−0.3	19.0
10	Wood and cork products	−0.4	28.0
11	Textiles	−0.9	40.0
12	Metal products	−1.5	24.0
13	Paper	−1.8	18.0
14	Rubber and plastic products	−2.0	68.5
15	Professional and scientific equipment	−2.6	96.0
16	Transport equipment	−8.0	31.0
17	Industrial chemicals and other chemicals	−9.5	19.0
18	Electrical machinery	−11.8	77.0
19	Non-electrical machinery	−15.4	45.0

Source: Elaborated on the basis of Table 2.2 and table I in Rajan and Zingales (1998: 566–7).

specialization pattern and firms' capital structure, we can find additional support for the hypothesis that the level of financial deepening has a bearing on competitiveness and trade patterns.

In order to test the hypothesis about the relationship between finance and comparative advantage in Argentina, we ranked the ISIC sectors according to sectoral contributions to the trade balance (CTB), an indicator of comparative advantage that is included in the third column of Table 2.12. If finance matters for comparative advantage, there should be a negative association between the order of the sectors ranked by CTB and their order ranked by the EDR. In a financially underdeveloped country like Argentina, one would expect that sectors which have a greater probability to develop their potential comparative advantage would be those with a lower dependency ratio. We computed the Spearman rank correlation coefficient between the external dependence ratios and the contributions to the trade balance and found a very strong association between the two rankings: 0.98.

A second piece of evidence regarding the role of finance in trade has to do with the general hypothesis that those economies with weak capital markets develop a bias against new firms and innovators. In this sense, the lack of access to external finance acts as a barrier to entry. If this is true, firms which show stronger competitive advantage and, hence, are successful in export markets should tend to be older (traditional firms with established reputations and/or access to international capital markets) and larger in size. Likewise, there should be an important degree of concentration with few firms exporting a high share of total exports. In order to evaluate whether these hypotheses are relevant in the case of Argentina, we used the ranking of the top 1,000 exporter firms. The sample explains around 90 per cent of total exports. On the basis of such data it is possible to construct concentration indices and analyze the characteristics of the most successful exporter firms.

Table 2.13 clearly shows that there is a strong concentration in export markets. The top five firms account for 20 per cent of exports while fifty out of 1,000 firms explain 63.2 per cent of total exports. Likewise, the characteristics of the firms which appear at the top are telling: the overwhelming majority are either large

Table 2.13 Indices of concentration of exports

Position in the ranking	Accumulated value of exports (million USD)	Share of total exports (%)
Top five	4,977	20.0
Top ten	7,535	30.3
Top twenty	11,004	44.4
Top fifty	15,686	63.2
Top 100	18,202	73.4
Top 500	23,509	94.8
Bottom 100	45	0.02
Bottom 500	1,285	5.2

Source: Elaborated on the basis of Revista Mercado 1998 data.

traditional exporter firms (many of them belonging to 'grupos' – national hold-ings) or multinational corporations.[18] As we have seen in the previous section, the larger firms have better access to both international and domestic capital markets. Hence, it is plausible to assume that finance is much less of a binding constraint for decision making in the case of these firms. On the other hand, it is clear that firms operating in either non-traditional industrial sectors and/or innovative firms are not present. These facts are consistent with the predictions that follow from our approach: the level of a country's financial deepening should be considered a very important non-price determinant of competitiveness.

From macro to micro: Credit fluctuations and financial volatility

In highly unstable countries like Argentina in the 1980s, the most important sources of instability are usually inflation and macroeconomic disequilibria. Fanelli and González Rozada (1998) show that volatility has not been constant in Argentina and has sharply declined under the Convertibility Plan. Here, we check whether volatility is relevant to firms' financial decisions at the micro-level and explore differences in winners and losers and the tradable and non-tradable sec-tors' financial behavior. In a capital market where segmentation and market fail-ures are pervasive it seems reasonable to expect a priori that financial volatility differs if capital structure and access to capital markets differ among firms.

We have shown that more fragile firms face wider variation in their access to credit markets when shocks occur. Under such circumstances, we should observe a greater volatility in the evolution of the stock of debt in the case of losers. However, if macro-volatility has a bearing on the microstructure, we should also observe a reduction in overall volatility under Convertibility to the extent that the standard deviation of expectations will be lower. We will present some evidence of these facts below.

In Table 2.14 we have estimated the trend of the debt series and taken the unexplained portion of the total variance of the dependent variable $(1 - R^2)$ as a proxy for the level of volatility built into the time series.

Since the unexplained portion of the variance of the liabilities series is signif-icantly lower in the case of winners, these results are consistent with the hypoth-esis that the financial position of losers is more volatile than that of winners. The table also presents the volatility of income. The objective is to show that there is practically no difference in the amount of volatility in the income of winners and losers. In other words, the higher volatility in the evolution of the stock of debt cannot be attributed to a higher volatility in the flow of income.[19] Imperfections in capital markets do matter when explaining the facts under study.

Table 2.15 can be used to check for differences in financial volatility in trad-able and non-tradable sectors. The methodology is the same as before. The table shows that all volatility indicators classify the group of firms in a way which is coherent with our previous arguments: the losers are first in the volatility ranking and the services sector is last. This occurs independently of the item on the bal-ance sheet. The volatility of liabilities is higher than the volatility of assets in the

Table 2.14 Volatility measures for liabilities and income:
manufacturing industry (1986:2–1997:2)

Dependent variable	Trend coefficient	Volatility $(1-R^2)$ (%)
log liabilities winners	2.5	19.8
log liabilities losers	−0.6	69.6
log income winners	0.6	93.2
log income losers	−0.3	93.8

Table 2.15 Volatility measures of balance-sheet items in services and
manufacturing (1993:3–1997:2)

Group of firms	Liabilities volatility	Income volatility	Assets volatility	Net worth volatility
Services	6.9	47.6	2.6	6.3
Winners	23.9	70.8	9.3	11.3
Losers	47.0	95.8	33.4	43.8

three groups. This means that the short-run fluctuations in the stock of debt around its long-run trend are more frequent and greater in size than the same kinds of changes in the case of assets held by agents. This can be interpreted as evidence that when a disequilibrium occurs in agents' portfolios, the velocity of asset adjustment toward equilibrium values is lower than the velocity with which liabilities adjust. This is why firms are vulnerable to sudden and unexpected changes in credit conditions when a shock of a certain magnitude occurs. Debtor firms are 'tied' to assets more than creditors are 'tied' to the debt instruments that firms issue. This implies that, *ceteris paribus*, the more unstable and volatile the conditions are to access credit markets, the greater is the preference of the firm for flexible assets. Under conditions of increasing uncertainty, the managers will develop a strong preference for flexibility. The data suggest that this reasoning is not misleading. If we rank the firms by the volatility of their assets using Table 2.15, losers rank first, followed by winners while non-tradable firms come last. This coincides with the previous findings regarding the ability of different groups to access capital markets in a context of segmentation, and also suggests that tradable sectors suffer from a competitive disadvantage *vis-à-vis* the non-tradable sector from the financial point of view.

4. Conclusions: Trade specialization and micro–macro and trade–finance interactions

After a long period of high inflation, economic stagnation and recurrent balance-of-payments crises, Argentina has achieved macro-stabilization in the 1990s. In addition, structural reforms such as trade liberalization and privatization of state-owned enterprises were implemented. In turn, these developments were accompanied by the rebound of economic growth and investment, a rapid rise in trade flows, the resumption of capital inflows, an important increase in the level of financial deepening, as well as a real currency appreciation and higher current account deficits. The doubling of exports and the boom of imports, particularly manufactures, was the flip side of a process that created both winners and losers.

In spite of higher trade flows and greater intra-industry trade, the inter-industry pattern of specialization has not been upgraded and the country's balance of payments still remains vulnerable to foreign shocks, as proven by the Tequila effect, the Southeast Asian crisis and Brazil's devaluation of the 'real'. We believe that both micro–macro-interactions and finance mattered in all these cases.

An important question that we tried to answer is whether finance has played any role in the winner/loser game. We found evidence that supports the existence of important imperfections in Argentine capital markets that constrain asset accumulation, as cash flow and leverage ratios are significant determinants of asset changes, besides profits. In this regard, the fact that loser firms, that is to say, firms that contracted, seemed to have been less successful in increasing productivity suggests that financial market imperfections have forced these firms to pursue defensive restructuring strategies.

Furthermore, we found that asset size and liquidity also affect access to long-run finance, and verified that loser firms have had very little access to long-term funding and foreign sources of credit.

We collected evidence for the hypothesis that finance also plays an important role in determining the pattern of trade specialization. More specifically, we found an almost perfect (0.98) negative correlation between the pattern of inter-industry trade of Argentina and the EDRs computed by Rajan and Zingales (1998), which suggests that the lack of financial development is distorting the pattern of trade against sectors that are more dependent on external finance.

Finally, we examined the effects of financial volatility stemming from macro-instability on winners and losers. While the difference in income volatility between winners and losers is minor, the volatility of liabilities has been much higher for loser firms. In addition, the fact that firms in the non-tradable sector suffered from much lower levels of volatility in all categories of balance-sheet items than manufacturing firms (whether winner or loser) shows how financial market imperfections hinder firms in the tradable sector.

We conclude that the main lesson from the Argentine case study is that non-price determinants of competitiveness such as the level of financial development and macroeconomic stability are highly relevant to the degree of success of trade liberalization and financial opening.

Notes

1 We are grateful to Martín González Rozada for his superb econometric advice and Sebastian Katz for his helpful research assistance.
2 All jumps match recessionary years: 1985, 1988, 1989 and 1990.
3 See Table 2.1, last column.

4 Measuring the same variables in nominal terms yields no increase because of the fall in the relative price of tradables *vis-à-vis* non-tradables, caused by the currency real appreciation.

5 The contribution of sector (or industry) i to the trade balance (CTB$_i$)is defined as

$$CTB_i = [(X_i - M_i) - (X - M) * (X_i + M_i)/(X + M)]/[(X + M)/2],$$

where X_i and M_i are exports and imports of good i, respectively, and X and M are total exports and imports. Summation of CTB$_i$ over i equals 0. See Guerrieri (1994).

6 The Grubel and Lloyd index of intra-industry trade for country j and industry i is defined by

$$B_{ij} = (X_{ij} + M_{ij} - |X_{ij} - M_{ij}|)/(X_{ij} + M_{ij}).$$

The Grubel and Lloyd indices of intra-industry trade can be aggregated according to the following:

$$B = \left[\sum_i (X_{ij} + M_{ij}) - \sum_i |X_{ij} - M_{ij}| / \sum_i (X_{ij} + M_{ij}) \right].$$

7 Grubel and Lloyd indices have been criticized for being sensitive to the overall trade imbalance. Aquino suggested another index of intra-industry trade which corrects for aggregate trade imbalances in the following way:

$$Q_{ij} = \left[(X_{ij}/X_j + M_{ij}/M_j) - |X_{ij}/X_j - M_{ij}/M_j| / (X_{ij}/X_j + M_{ij}/M_j) \right].$$

The aggregate Aquino index of intra-industry trade for country j is, in turn,

$$Q_j = \left[\sum_i (X_{ij}/X_j + M_{ij}/M_j) - \sum_i |X_{ij}/X_j - M_{ij}/M_j| / \sum_i (X_{ij}/X_j + M_{ij}/M_j) \right].$$

8 These figures merit a word of caution. Official statistics on recent expansion in manufacturing value added and, therefore, productivity, might be somewhat overestimated as they do not adjust for the fall in the ratio of value added to gross output that took place in the 1990s, most likely, as a result of the opening up of the economy. Until better estimates are available, we can only conjecture on the order of magnitude of the bias. Our guess is that actual productivity growth has been, nevertheless, outstanding in the 1990s.

9 Unit labor costs (ULC) are computed according to the following definition:

$$ULC = W/[(Q/L) * P],$$

where W is the hourly wage rate, Q/L is output per hour worked, and P is either one of three prices: export price, import price or the peso/US dollar exchange rate.

10 Levine (1997) discusses this issue in the context of endogenous growth theory.

11 For an overall assessment of Argentina's financial deepening process with an emphasis on the role of credit factors in the business cycle, see Fanelli *et al.* (1998).

12 The activity level in 1986–7 represents a peak in industrial production for the 1980s during the debt crisis.

13 The branches represented are food, fuels and petroleum, metals, textiles, transport equipment, electric machinery, tobacco, chemicals, non-metallic products, paper and cellulose, wood products and others.

14 See on this issue, Fazzari *et al.* (1988) and Harris *et al.* (1994).

15 See Minsky (1977) and Bernanke *et al.* (1993).

16 The variable leverlp is defined as the long-run debt/total assets ratio, h_{it} is the error term. We corrected for the presence of first-order autocorrelation.
17 Unfortunately, firms that did not survive the Tequila effect are not included in our sample and are, therefore, outside of this discussion.
18 The top twenty exporting firms are YPF, Cargill, Ford, Aceitera Gral Deheza, Grupo Fiat, Volkswagen, Vicentin, Nidera, Louis Dreyfus, Aerolineas Argentinas, Molinos Río de la Plata, Siderca, La Plata Cereal, Oleaginosas Moreno, Continental, Prod. Sudamericanos, Perez Companc, Guipeba, Toepler and Renault.
19 We will see below, though, that income volatility was higher for the losers in the 1990s.

References

Bernanke, B., Gertler, M. and Gilchrist, S. (1993) 'The Financial Accelerator and the Flight to Quality', *National Bureau of Economic Research Working Paper*, No. 4789.

Fanelli, J. M. and Frenkel, R. (1995) 'Micro–Macro Interaction in Economic Development', *UNCTAD Review*: 129–55.

Fanelli, J. M. and González Rozada, M. (1998) 'Convertibilidad, Volatilidad y Estabilidad Macroeconómica en Argentina', Mimeo.

Fanelli, J. M., Rozenwurcel, G. and Simpson, L. (1998) 'Argentina', in J. Fanelli and R. Medhora (eds), *Financial Reform in Developing Countries*. London: Macmillan.

Fazzari, S., Hubbard, G. and Petersen, B. (1988) 'Financing Constraints and Corporate Investment', *Brookings Papers on Economic Activity* 1: 141–95.

Guerrieri, P. (1994) 'International Competitiveness, Trade Integration and Technological Interdependence', in *The New Paradigm of Systemic Competitiveness: Toward More Integrated Policies in Latin America*. Paris: OECD Development Centre.

Harris, J. R., Schiantarelli, F. and Siregar, M. G. (1994) 'The Effect of Financial Liberalization on the Capital Structure and Investment Decisions of Indonesian Manufacturing Establishments', *The World Bank Economic Review* 8(1): 17–47.

Katz, J. (1997) 'The Dynamics of Technological Learning during the ISI Period and Recent Structural Changes in the Industrial Sector of Argentina, Brazil and Mexico', Mimeo.

Levine, R. (1997) 'Financial Development and Economic Growth: Views and Agenda', *Journal of Economic Literature* XXXV: 688–726.

Minsky, H. P. (1977) 'A Theory of Systemic Fragility', in E. I. Altman and A. W. Sametz (eds), *Financial Crises*. New York: Wiley.

Rajan, R. and Zingales, L. (1998) 'Financial Dependence and Growth', *American Economic Review* 88(3): 559–86.

3 Finance and changing trade patterns in Brazil[1]

Maria Cristina T. Terra

1. Introduction

Balance-of-payments crises have been recurrent throughout Brazilian history. The depth and length of these crises depend basically on the country's vulnerability to external shocks and its capability to generate the necessary trade surplus after an adverse external shock. These, in turn, depend on trade diversification and competitiveness. With more diversified exports and imports, the country becomes less vulnerable to specific sector shocks. Increased competitiveness, furthermore, should facilitate trade balance reversals. This chapter focuses on one possible determinant of competitiveness, which is the existence of credit constraints. In a world with no missing markets, no informational asymmetries and no transaction costs, credit supply and demand should be equalized by an appropriate interest rate level, with no need for a financial sector. A vast literature, both theoretical and empirical, studies the effects on the economy when these conditions do not hold. In the real world, information asymmetries and transaction costs for acquiring information create the need for a financial system. The role of the financial sector is then, in summary, to allocate savings to the best investment projects, to monitor managers and to diversify risk (see Levine (1997) for a discussion on the roles of the financial system). In such an environment, financial system imperfections create credit restrictions, which in turn may affect firms' investment decisions. Hence, financial sector underdevelopment may be harmful for growth.

Moreover, it is plausible to presume that firms in different sectors have different financial needs. Rajan and Zingales (1998) compute the external financing pattern for different industries in the United States, and they arrive at large disparities among them. If that is the case, the effect of credit restrictions should not be equal among industries. In this chapter, I try to identify whether Brazilian firms are credit constrained, and the relation between industries' financial needs and their competitiveness.

The period from 1974 to 1997 is studied, comprising four different situations with respect to macroeconomic environment, trade policy and balance-of-payments conditions. They are briefly described below.

Period 1

From 1974 to 1982 the country was suffering from the adverse trade balance effects of the two oil shocks. Despite implementation of import restrictions and export promotion policies, a large current account deficit mounted up over the period. The economy was nevertheless growing rapidly (7 per cent per year on average), thanks to large capital inflows.

Period 2

From 1982 to 1990 the economy experienced the effects touched off by the Mexican moratorium declared in 1982. Even stronger trade barriers were imposed, and capital flows were very timid. The current account suffered a drastic reduction, from a 6 per cent deficit in 1982 to zero balance in 1984. The economy faced major macroeconomic instability, with two-digit monthly inflation rates in the late 1980s, and several unsuccessful price stabilization programs were attempted.

Period 3

From 1990 to 1994 the macro-instability scenario did not change, but drastic trade liberalization was carried out. There was an upsurge of capital inflows to Brazil, following the Latin American trend.

Period 4

From 1994 to 1997 macro-stability finally was achieved, together with even stronger capital inflows. Increasing current account deficits gave rise to concerns about sustainability.

This chapter is divided into six sections. Section 2 describes the economic environment over the time period studied, emphasizing the four distinct periods outlined above. Section 3 analyzes trade pattern evolution in Brazil over time. Section 4 studies the extent to which Brazilian firms have been credit constrained. Section 5 synthesizes the results from Sections 3 and 4, analyzing possible influences of finance on the evolution of trade specialization. Section 6 concludes.

2. Economic environment

Trade policy

Brazil has a long history of external trade intervention. After the Second World War, it engaged in an import substitution strategy that lasted for decades, following the trend in most Latin American countries. Import substitution meant a gradual process of industrialization based on domestic market protection and subsidies for investments in specific industrial sectors. From the mid-1960s to 1973, the country carried out slow import liberalization, combined with export promotion policies, which included frequent exchange-rate devaluations, subsidized credit and tax and tariff exemptions for export activities. This combination of policies resulted in an important shift in the composition of exports, favoring industrial goods to the detriment of traditional coffee exports. Coffee as a share of total exports was around 40 per cent in 1964, dropping to only 20 per cent in 1973. The degree of diversification of imports did not achieve that of exports. Although some import substitution occurred in the intermediate and capital goods sectors, there was no substantial expansion of domestic oil production. Imports continued to be concentrated on oil and intermediate and capital goods. These are known as the 'miracle' years in Brazil. Gross national product grew at an astonishing average yearly rate of 11.1 per cent, and annual industrial growth averaged 13.1 per cent over the period.[2]

Period 1

Oil prices quadrupled at the end of 1973, and they would increase again in 1979. Since oil was an important part of Brazilian imports (20 per cent in 1974), there was a severe impact on the trade balance, which changed from a modest surplus to a 4.7 billion USD deficit in 1974. The current account deficit deteriorated substantially, increasing from 1.7 billion USD in 1973 to 7.1 billion USD in 1974. The government chose not to depreciate the real exchange rate. Non-essential imports were discouraged, and the country borrowed internationally to level its balance of payments and ensure the country's fast growth path. A dynamic export promotion policy was then implemented to compensate for the anti-export bias created by the import restraints.[3] Average growth from 1974 to 1982 was indeed high – 6.6 per cent average GDP growth for the period (Table 3.1).[4]

Period 2

A new shock hit the economy in 1980 – the increase in international interest rates. From 1975 to 1979, the LIBOR averaged 7.8 per cent, and world inflation 8.9 per cent.[5] Thus, over the period real interest rates were negative on average. From 1980 to 1984, however, the LIBOR averaged 13.0 per cent and world inflation only 1.2 per cent. As most of Brazilian external debt was at floating interest rates, debt service increased substantially. The 1982 Mexican moratorium induced a capital flow reversal from Latin America. The increasing current account deficits could no longer be financed by capital inflows, so that a large trade surplus would have to be generated to provide foreign reserves to pay the debt service, and thereby equilibrate the current accounts (Table 3.1). A rapid trade surplus was achieved by further import repression and active export promotion policies.[6] An industrial policy was also conducted, granting fiscal incentives and subsidized credit from the state development bank to selected firms.

Although a restrictive trade policy had been in place in Brazil for decades, its justification changed over time, in three distinct phases. First, from the First World War to the early 1970s it was part of an active import substitution program. Then,

Table 3.1 Selected macroeconomic data

	Inflation (%)	GDP growth (%)	Current account (% GDP)	Exports (% GDP)	Imports (% GDP)	Oil[a] (% imports)	Coffee (% exports)	Terms of trade	International reserves[b] (million USD)	Real exchange rate[c]
1974–82	63.6	6.6	−4.7	7.3	8.4	33.6	13.0	125.2	7011.9	91.2
1983–90	699.0	3.2	−0.7	10.3	5.8	30.9	7.4	103.2	8,756.3	175.4
1991–4	1,261.4	−0.2	0.2	8.6	5.7	11.6	3.7	112.5	26,044.3	155.4
1995–7	11.9	4.2	−3.3	6.4	7.2	2.9	4.3	115.2	56,521.7	123.7
1990	1,794.8	3.2	−0.8	7.0	4.6	21.1	3.5	114.8	9,973	130.3
1991	478.1	−4.6	−0.4	8.2	5.4	16.0	4.4	117.6	9,406	151.2
1992	1,149.1	0.3	1.6	9.6	5.5	14.9	2.7	109.3	23,754	163.4
1993	2,489.1	−0.8	−0.1	9.0	5.9	8.5	2.8	109.1	32,211	160.2
1994	929.3	4.2	−0.3	7.8	5.9	7.1	5.1	114.0	38,806	146.6
1995	22.0	5.7	−2.5	6.5	6.9	5.2	4.2	115.3	51,840	126.4
1996	9.3	4.2	−3.2	6.4	7.1	5.2	3.6	115.0	60,110	121.4
1997[d]	4.3	2.7	−4.0	6.4	7.6	0.7	5.2		57,615	123.3

Sources: Boletim do Banco Central do Brasil, FUNCEX, International Financial Statistics (IMF).

Notes

a Oil and natural gas.
b International liquidity.
c e (WPI/CPI): nominal exchange rate, multiplied by US wholesale price index, divided by Brazilian consumer price index.
d Current account, export and import data up to July.

from the early 1970s to the early 1980s, the intent was to improve the deteriorating trade balance due to the oil shocks. Finally, from the early 1980s to 1990, it served as a drastic measure to deal with the debt crisis. Trade policy during the first phase was designed as an incentive to selected sectors, whereas in the other two phases, and especially in the third, trade policies in the form of both tariff and non-tariff barriers were created due to the macroeconomic instability.[7]

The effect of these policies on relative prices distorted microeconomic incentives. By the end of the 1980s, a maze of incentives and disincentives was in place. It is important to emphasize the harm of such a distorted and arbitrary system. It was prone to stimulate rent-seeking activities, drawing resources to the unproductive activity of seeking special treatment. It also displaced entrepreneurial effort from productive activities to seeking the best path through the maze of policy incentives.

Periods 3 and 4

A much-needed trade liberalization process was initiated by a new government in 1990. The BEFIEX program was immediately terminated (no new contracts were to be signed). Trade liberalization was to be carried out in three steps:

1   the abolition of all 'special regimes' for imports;
2   the abolition of all quantitative restrictions and their replacement by tariffs; and
3   the lowering of tariffs, according to a preannounced schedule to be over four years. By the end of the liberalization process in 1995, all tariffs would be in the range 0 per cent to 40 per cent, averaging 20 per cent.

Trade liberalization was carried out as planned. Import levels did not increase during the 1990–3 period, despite the lowering of tariffs and elimination of quantitative import restrictions. Two factors contributed to this: the real exchange-rate devaluation during 1990–1 (between January 1990 and December 1992 the real devaluation amounted to 36 per cent), and the low economic activity during the period (the average GDP growth rate was negative 2 per cent).

Brazil, as other Latin American countries, experienced a capital inflow upsurge in the 1990s. There was a substantial capital inflow increase after the implementation of the Real Plan, a successful price stabilization program introduced in July 1994. Real exchange-rate appreciation resulted, producing a mounting current account deficit, now led by a steep increase in imports. The reliance on capital inflows was severely questioned after the Mexican crisis in December 1994. This led to a partial reversal in trade liberalization. Some quantitative restrictions were temporarily reintroduced, and tariffs were increased for those products most responsible for increased imports.

Real exchange rate, trade flows and the current account

Figure 3.1 shows the evolution of the real exchange rate and its volatility,[8] and Figure 3.2 shows the current account, imports and exports as a percentage of GDP from 1974 to 1996. The charts are divided into the four subperiods described above.

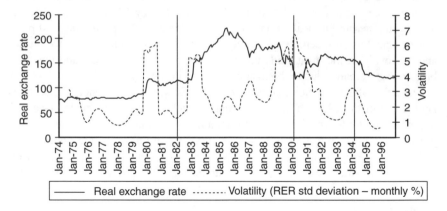

Figure 3.1 Real exchange rate: level and volatility.

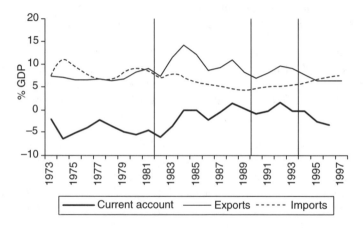

Figure 3.2 Current account.

Period 1

During the first period, the real exchange rate (RER) appreciated more than in the other periods. The crawling-peg exchange-rate regime maintained low RER volatility, except for the maxi-devaluation episode in 1979. Imports, which had increased substantially after the oil price increase, decreased steadily until 1979 due to a restrictive trade policy. The second oil price increase caused the trade balance to deteriorate, leading to the currency maxi-devaluation in 1979. Figure 3.2 shows the jump in export share after the devaluation (it increased from an average of 6.8 per cent of GDP during 1973–9 to 8.5 per cent in 1980). The current account was negative throughout the period, reaching negative 6 per cent of GDP in 1982, despite the trade balance surplus in that year. The current account deficit was caused by the high debt service cost, due to the increase in international interest rates. The country nevertheless experienced high GDP growth rates over the period (Table 3.1).

Period 2

There was a sharp RER devaluation during the debt crisis, accompanied by higher volatility. The RER volatility increased over the period, reaching its peak in 1990. The period was characterized by deep macroeconomic instability. As shown in Table 3.1, inflation reached extremely high rates. Several heterodox price stabilization attempts managed to reduce inflation from two-digit monthly figures to zero in a very short period of time, only for it to take off again after failure of the plans. Not even the crawling-peg regime pursued was capable of preventing high RER volatility.

The more devalued RER was accompanied by a substantial trade balance improvement, led mainly by increasing exports, as shown in Figure 3.2. The current account moved from negative 6 per cent of GDP in 1982 to a near-zero balance over the whole period. The investment rate decreased during the period. The sharp balance-of-payments adjustment was accompanied by bitter recession: GDP decreased 4.2 per cent and 2.9 per cent in 1982 and 1984, respectively. High growth rates were experienced from 1985 to 1987, but they decreased again towards the end of the decade.

Period 3

The third period started with very high RER volatility, during a short period of RER appreciation. The RER depreciated again, but to a lower level compared with the second period, while RER volatility decreased substantially. The current account maintained its near-zero balance, while imports started an upward trend, following the 1990s trade liberalization. GDP growth rates were near zero or negative over the period.

Period 4

The nominal exchange rate was allowed to float during the first months after the Real Plan's implementation in June 1994, causing a RER volatility increase. The capital inflow during the period caused the exchange rate to rise, leading to higher imports. The current account moved from a zero balance at the beginning of the period to a 3.2 per cent deficit in 1996. Annual growth rates were between 4 and 6 per cent during 1994–6, but in 1997 growth declined to 2.7 per cent.

Labor productivity and unit labor cost evolution

Labor productivity was stationary between the mid-1980s and 1990.[9] As shown in Figure 3.3, it then increased continuously between 1990 and 1996 at an average annual rate of approximately 7 per cent. Over the whole period it increased

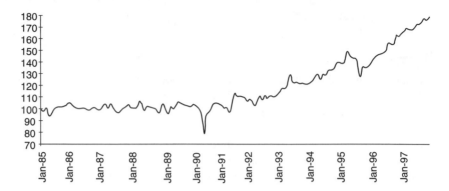

Figure 3.3 Labor productivity in industry (seasonally adjusted data – Jan-85: 100).

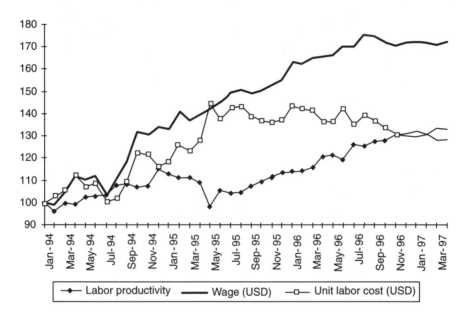

Figure 3.4 Labor productivity, wage and unit labor cost in industry (seasonally adjusted data – Jan-94: 100).

by more than 50 per cent. To a large extent, this productivity increase reflects the impact of greater international competition encountered by domestic producers.

Labor productivity is a basic factor in explaining competitiveness. Hence, one would expect that the significant productivity increase in Brazil has been translated into greater competitiveness. At least since 1994, however, this has not been the case, since wages for most of the period have grown faster than labor productivity.

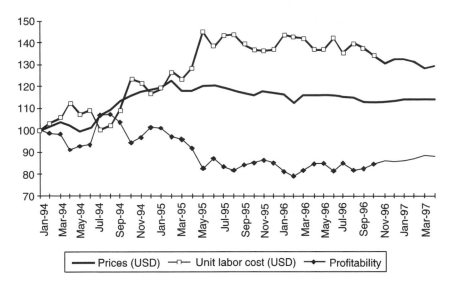

Figure 3.5 Unit labor cost, prices in USD and profitability (seasonally adjusted data – Jan-94: 100).

Figure 3.4 shows labor productivity evolution, wages in US dollars and the unit labor cost (ULC is the ratio of wages in dollars to productivity) for the industrial sector as a whole. The ULC provides an indication of labor costs measured in the relevant foreign currency per unit of output. Wages in dollars grew continuously, totaling a 70 per cent increase between 1994 and 1997. Labor productivity, in turn, increased by 32 per cent. ULC increased by 40 per cent until mid-1996 and has been falling somewhat since then. The ULC increase in the initial period resulted from the fact that wages grew faster than productivity, and vice versa in the later period.

Hence, for the period as a whole, to the extent that the ULC is a good measure of competitiveness, the latter has not increased since 1994. Based on this criterion, overall competitiveness fell until mid-1996 and it has recovered slightly since then.

The price of tradable goods in dollars and 'profitability' as measured by firms' profit margin may be more refined measures of competitiveness. Figure 3.5 shows the evolution of the industrial goods producer price index (PPI), and the ratio between PPI and ULC as a measure of aggregate profit margin. PPI increased around 20 per cent between January 1994 and mid-1995 and then decreased approximately 10 per cent. Profitability fell 20 per cent and then recovered. Both the lower price index in dollars and the profitability increase in the more recent period resulted from the ULC reduction.

Summarizing the main findings in this section, three aspects may be highlighted. First, external shocks, such as the oil price hikes and external debt crisis, had crucial roles in determining both the macroeconomic environment and trade policy choices. Second, trade liberalization had a positive effect on productivity during the 1990s. Third, the macroeconomic environment played a decisive role in ULC evolution, and hence competitiveness.

3. Trade pattern evolution

This section analyzes the pattern of trade since 1974, using several indexes that characterize trade patterns.

Contribution to trade balance

The first index used to characterize trade patterns in Brazil is the contribution to trade balance (CTB) index. Table 3.2 presents the performance of this index from 1974 to 1997, in a ten-sector aggregation.[10] The index of contribution of industry *i* to trade balance was calculated using eqn (3.1):

$$\text{CTB}_i = \frac{2}{(X + M)}\left[(X_i - M_i) - \frac{(X_i + M_i)(X - M)}{(X + M)}\right], \tag{3.1}$$

where X_i and M_i are exports and imports of industry *i*, respectively, and X and M are total Brazilian exports and imports, respectively.

The first term of the index represents net exports (by sector), whereas the second represents 'neutral' net exports, that is, net exports (by sector) that would be observed if the share of each product in overall net exports were equal to its contribution to total trade. Thus, the index value equals zero for a given period when the ratio of the net sector exports to overall net exports is equal to the sector's contribution to total trade. Its value will be positive or negative depending on whether net exports are larger or smaller relative to the 'neutral' value. Note that if a country is running a trade deficit, a product may show a positive sign even if its imports are larger than its exports. The opposite is true for a trade surplus.

Figures 3.6a and b show the index evolution for each of the ten industries. Note that the industries in Figure 3.6a have a much stronger contribution to trade balance than those of Figure 3.6b: the scale in Figure 3.6a ranges from −0.6 to +0.6, whereas in Figure 3.6b it ranges from only −0.1 to +0.1. Lines have been drawn on the years corresponding to the periodicity used above.

There were important changes in the composition of imports and exports over the period. The food and beverages sector presented the largest CTB decrease in absolute terms over the period. Its CTB fell from 0.50 in 1974 to 0.22 in 1997, representing a 54 per cent decrease. This shows the increasing importance of other industries in Brazilian exports over the period. The strongest change occurred between the first and the second periods (the oil shock and debt crisis periods), when the food and beverages CTB decreased from an average of 0.43 to 0.22. After the Real Stabilization Plan, it increased slightly. Food and beverages remains the sector with highest CTB.

Energy material, on the other hand, exhibited the largest swing in CTB. Over the first period (oil crisis), energy material CTB decreased from −0.26 in 1974

Table 3.2 Contribution to trade balance (ten-sector aggregation)

	Food products and beverages	Textiles, apparel and footwear	Transport equipment	Metal products	Chemical products	Wood, paper and products	Construction material	Machinery	Energy material	Other industries
1974–82	0.4288	0.0702	0.0229	0.0371	−0.0740	0.0175	−0.0011	−0.1244	−0.3660	−0.0110
1983–90	0.2223	0.0601	0.0312	0.1366	−0.0793	0.0266	0.0012	−0.0903	−0.2953	−0.0133
1991–4	0.1532	0.0467	0.0158	0.1805	−0.0945	0.0437	0.0019	−0.1337	−0.1918	−0.0217
1995–7	0.1980	0.0271	−0.0199	0.1540	−0.0774	0.0478	0.0004	−0.1776	−0.1282	−0.0243
1990	0.1750	0.0515	0.0428	0.1856	−0.0947	0.0320	0.0003	−0.1417	−0.2322	−0.0186
1991	0.1327	0.0537	0.0330	0.2135	−0.0986	0.0326	0.0009	−0.1286	−0.2191	−0.0201
1992	0.1485	0.0562	0.0360	0.1749	−0.0903	0.0406	0.0010	−0.1273	−0.2161	−0.0235
1993	0.1513	0.0429	0.0133	0.1736	−0.0910	0.0481	0.0034	−0.1273	−0.1924	−0.0219
1994	0.1803	0.0340	−0.0191	0.1599	−0.0982	0.0534	0.0021	−0.1515	−0.1395	−0.0214
1995	0.1807	0.0263	−0.0433	0.1640	−0.0773	0.0602	0.0018	−0.1649	−0.1225	−0.0249
1996	0.1940	0.0303	−0.0120	0.1646	−0.0740	0.0428	0.0001	−0.1747	−0.1386	−0.0324
1997	0.2193	0.0248	−0.0045	0.1336	−0.0809	0.0403	−0.0007	−0.1932	−0.1233	−0.0154

Sources: IBGE and FUNCEX.

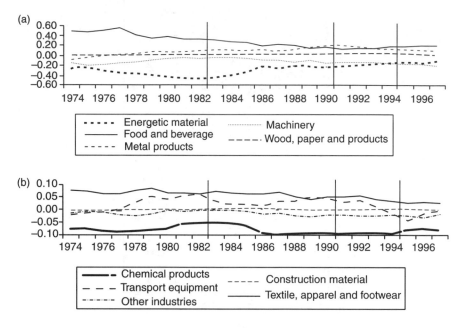

Figure 3.6 Contribution to trade balance. Industries in (a) make a stronger contribution
compared to those in (b).

to −0.46 in 1983. From 1983, on the other hand, it increased to −0.12 in 1997.
This movement reflects the decreasing importance of oil in Brazilian imports. In
1974 this sector had the lowest CTB, and in 1997 it had given up its last position
to machinery (which was second to last in 1974).

In percentage terms, the sectors that underwent the largest changes in CTB
were wood, paper and products, and metal products, increasing 285 per cent and
291 per cent, respectively.

Transport equipment CTB decreased steeply over the last period. Its value
increased during the first period, from −0.0191 in 1974 to +0.0593 in 1982.
During the second period its value averaged 0.0312, thereupon falling from 1992
to its lowest value of −0.433 in 1995.

Both exports and imports became more diversified over the period. The index
variance across sectors ranged from 0.038 to 0.052 in the 1970s and early 1980s.
It started decreasing steadily in 1983, and its value has been around 0.013 in the
past few years.[11] This means that the index has become more uniformly distrib-
uted across sectors over time. Hence, exports and imports have become less
concentrated in specific sectors.

Revealed comparative advantage

The other index used to assess each sector's role in inter-industry trade is
Balassa's index of revealed comparative advantage (RCA). This index measures

the relative importance of a sector in a country's total exports with respect to the relative importance of that sector in world total exports. It is given by eqn (3.2):

$$RCA_{ij} = \frac{(X_{ij}/X_j)}{(X_{iW}/X_W)},$$

(3.2)

where X_{ij} is country j's exports by industry i, X_j is country j's total exports, X_{iW} is world exports by industry i, and X_W is total world exports.

The evolution of RCA indexes is shown in Table 3.3. The index has been calculated for the period from 1986 to 1997, for ten aggregated sectors. The largest movement occurred in the wood, paper and products sector. Its RCA increased 85 per cent over the period (from 1.16 to 2.15). The CTB of that industry increased 42 per cent over the same period, indicating that its increased importance in Brazilian exports surpassed the increase of the sector's importance in world exports. Other significant changes are a 22 per cent decrease in the RCA for textiles, apparel and footwear, also following its decrease in CTB, and a 22 per cent and 29 per cent increase in transport equipment and construction material, despite those sectors' decrease in CTB.

The sectors presenting the highest RCA in 1997 are food and beverages (3.15), metal products (2.82), and wood, paper and products (2.15). The lowest ones are machinery (0.31) and chemical products (0.43).

Intra-industry trade

The Grubel and Lloyd intra-industry trade measure, presented in Table 3.4, is calculated with eqn (3.3):

$$B_i = \frac{(X_i + M_i) - |X_i - M_i|}{(X_i + M_i)},$$

(3.3)

where its aggregate values, shown in the last column of Table 3.4, are calculated with eqn (3.4):

$$B = \frac{\sum(X + M) - \sum|X - M|}{\sum(X + M)}.$$

(3.4)

The aggregate index shows a steady increase over time. As for the index's evolution for the different industries, it increases for most of them. The most spectacular increase was in the textiles, apparel and footwear industry. The Grubel and Lloyd index started at 29 per cent in 1974, decreased until reaching its lowest level of 12 per cent in 1981, and then increased until reaching 82 per cent in 1995. For metal products, on the other hand, the index decreased substantially.[12] As the performance of the index indicates, the advent of Mercosur had a positive effect on intra-industry trade levels.

Table 3.3 Revealed comparative advantage – Balassa's index (ten-sector aggregation)

	Food products and beverages	Textiles, apparel and footwear	Transport equipment	Metal products	Chemical products	Wood, paper and products	Construction material	Machinery	Energy material	Other industries
1986	3.1364	1.1520	0.7125	2.4402	0.4022	1.1629	0.6125	0.3245	0.5530	0.2955
1987	3.1567	1.1759	0.9625	2.3162	0.3107	1.0862	0.5708	0.3070	0.6740	0.3179
1988	2.9034	1.0938	0.8728	2.7100	0.2979	1.2804	0.5841	0.2993	0.8320	0.2173
1989	2.7652	1.0613	0.9287	2.8408	0.3457	1.1800	0.6370	0.3268	0.6682	0.2672
1990	2.9444	1.0293	0.8708	3.1946	0.3788	1.3065	0.5866	0.3103	0.5170	0.3176
1991	2.5808	1.0515	0.8072	3.5885	0.3857	1.3874	0.6111	0.3198	0.4882	0.3471
1992	2.6849	1.0564	0.9717	3.4264	0.3357	1.5768	0.6735	0.3314	0.5301	0.3291
1993	2.8163	1.1443	0.9949	3.4320	0.4525	0.8081	0.8957	0.3526	0.6067	0.2902
1994	3.1015	0.9062	0.9535	2.9531	0.3896	1.8603	0.7600	0.3186	0.6384	0.3221
1995	3.1510	0.8935	0.8725	2.8121	0.4389	2.1495	0.7896	0.3123	0.6017	0.3382

Table 3.4 Grubel and Lloyd intra-industry index (ten-sector aggregation)

	Food products and beverages	Textiles, apparel and footwear	Transport equipment	Metal products	Chemical products	Wood, paper and products	Construction material	Machinery	Energy material	Other industries	Aggregate
1974–82	0.3246	0.1861	0.7243	0.7583	0.3304	0.7272	0.7983	0.4835	0.1408	0.7427	0.3979
1983–90	0.2802	0.2426	0.5522	0.2889	0.6499	0.3438	0.6177	0.8725	0.5049	0.8904	0.4547
1991–4	0.4139	0.4578	0.7170	0.2704	0.5842	0.3265	0.6929	0.7544	0.4381	0.9340	0.5128
1995–7	0.5141	0.7746	0.8747	0.4238	0.5318	0.5545	0.9487	0.5149	0.3624	0.7341	0.5657
1990	0.3699	0.3811	0.5646	0.2933	0.5601	0.4016	0.7762	0.7057	0.4298	0.9710	0.4731
1991	0.4593	0.3992	0.6223	0.2639	0.5545	0.4121	0.7380	0.7440	0.3977	0.9581	0.4912
1992	0.3557	0.3206	0.5731	0.2502	0.6464	0.2762	0.6701	0.8176	0.4277	0.9837	0.4791
1993	0.3998	0.5137	0.7352	0.2620	0.6156	0.2975	0.6177	0.7853	0.4375	0.9164	0.5213
1994	0.4410	0.5977	0.9374	0.3054	0.5205	0.3203	0.7458	0.6709	0.4896	0.8776	0.5597
1995	0.5707	0.8184	0.7929	0.4304	0.4931	0.5238	0.9418	0.5122	0.3750	0.6969	0.5640
1996	0.5694	0.8017	0.8884	0.4227	0.5142	0.6204	0.9430	0.4770	0.3118	0.6165	0.5601
1997	0.4021	0.7038	0.9428	0.4183	0.5879	0.5194	0.9612	0.5555	0.4005	0.8888	0.5731

4. Liquidity constraints, finance pattern and corporate investment

This section studies Brazilian companies' financing decisions, and the extent to which they have been financially constrained. The empirical investigation uses balance sheet data for firms that are required by law to publish them. The data was collected by IBRE (Instituto Brasileiro de Economia, Getúlio Vargas Foundation) from the *Gazeta Mercantil* and *Diário Oficial*, from 1986 to 1997, with the number of firms each year ranging from 2,091 to 4,198. From the original sample, I selected those firms which had data published for all years considered[13] – from 1986 to 1997 – a total of 550 firms. Non-industrial firms were excluded, as well as those with missing data. The sample used is composed of 468 firms, broken down by sector as in Table 3.5.

The data has two breaks over time, one in 1990 and the other in 1994, due to changes in balance sheet reporting criteria after the implementation of inflation stabilization plans (the Collor Plan in 1990 and the Real Plan in 1994). All the analyses are carried out taking into account those two breaks in the time series.

The time frame for which we have firms' level data is shorter, including only three of the four periods described earlier. The analysis in this section will therefore divide the period from 1986 to 1997 into three subperiods: the

Table 3.5 Sample firms broken down by sector

Sector	Number of firms	Average value of assets[a] (1994–7)
Apparel and footwear	16	151,226,212
Beverages	15	599,900,102
Chemical products	71	814,435,409
Drugs	11	137,409,771
Electric equipment	28	338,754,575
Food products	70	170,390,346
Furniture	4	35,992,189
Leather	3	19,429,112
Machinery	38	176,597,031
Metal products	60	606,166,766
Non-metal products	30	371,050,142
Other industries	9	92,482,669
Paper and products	19	857,736,540
Perfumery and soap	3	24,547,019
Plastic products	8	74,543,359
Printing and publishing	11	97,283,390
Rubber products	1	17,969,577
Textiles	40	121,148,883
Tobacco	1	409,941,742
Transport equipment	23	256,891,434
Wood products	7	252,427,396

Note
a In 1996 constant Reals.

macro-instability and balance-of-payments crisis period (1986–90), the macro-instability and trade liberalization period (1990–4), and the macro-stability and capital inflow period (1994–7).

Pattern of finance

The analysis starts with a description of the firms' patterns of finance. The set of firms is divided into subcategories, trying to identify possible differences in finance patterns across different groupings, or across different time periods. Two leverage measures are calculated: the ratio between liabilities and assets, and the ratio between debts[14] and assets. Figure 3.7 presents both measures' evolution for the whole sample of firm averages, and Table 3.6 presents the averages across periods. Over the first period, liabilities and debts were stable in relation to total asset ratios, averaging 35 per cent and 11 per cent, respectively. There was a slight increase in both measures during the second period. Firms were clearly becoming more leveraged over the last period, 1994–7, when liabilities averaged 47 per cent and debts 16 per cent of total assets.

First, the sample of firms is divided into subgroups based on an a priori hypothesis with respect to firms' credit accessibility. It is reasonable to assume

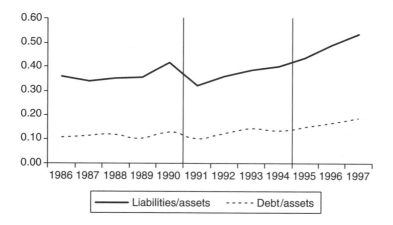

Figure 3.7 Industrial firms.

Table 3.6 Pattern of finance

	Debts/assets			Liabilities/assets		
	Mean	*Median*	*Standard deviation*	*Mean*	*Median*	*Standard deviation*
1986–9	0.11	0.08	0.12	0.35	0.32	0.17
1990–3	0.13	0.09	0.13	0.37	0.35	0.18
1994–7	0.16	0.13	0.18	0.47	0.41	0.41
1986–7	0.14	0.11	0.12	0.40	0.36	0.21

that larger firms would have more access to credit markets than smaller ones. As Gertler and Gilchrist argue:

> [W]hile size *per se* may not be a direct determinant [of capital market access], it is strongly correlated with the primitive factors that do matter. The informational frictions that add to the costs of external finance apply mainly to younger firms, firms with a high degree of idiosyncratic risk, and firms that are not well collateralized. [T]hese are, on average, smaller firms.
>
> (1994: 313)

The finance pattern evolution for those two groups of firms is indeed interesting, as shown in Figures 3.8a and b. Although leverage measured as liabilities as a share of total assets does not differ between the two groups of firms, the debts to assets ratio is quite different between them. Large firms have a higher debts to assets ratio throughout the whole time frame compared to small firms.

There are two possible explanations for the higher indebtedness of large firms compared to that of small firms. Low debt for small firms may be either the result of pure financial decisions or an indication of the credit restrictions they face. If the first alternative is true, some firms simply chose to use fewer external loans, and those are coincidentally the small ones. If the latter is true, a group of firms was credit restricted, and therefore it was not possible for them to be more leveraged. The empirical exercise performed in the next subsection tries to identify which explanation is more consistent with the data.

Rajan and Zingales (1998) construct a measure of external dependence for different industries, using data on external finance for US industries. They assume

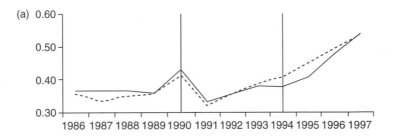

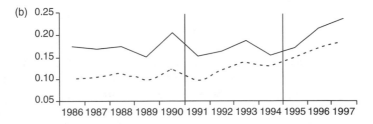

Figure 3.8 Liabilities/assets (a) and debts/asssets (b) ratios for large (——) and small (----) firms.

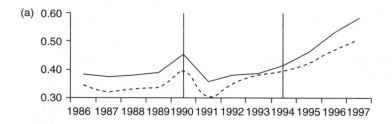

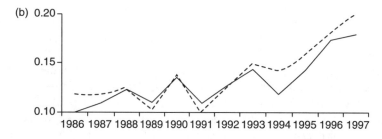

Figure 3.9 Liabilities/assets (a) and debts/assets (b) ratios for more (——) and less (----) financially dependent firms.

that there is a technological reason for some industries to depend more on external finance than others. They argue that

> ... to the extent that the initial project scale, the gestation period, the cash harvest period, and the requirement for continuing investment differ substantially between industries, this is indeed plausible. Furthermore, we assume that these technological differences persist across countries, so that we can use an industry's dependence on external funds as identified in the United States as a measure of its dependence in other countries.
>
> (Rajan and Zingales 1998: 563)

By using the measure constructed in that paper, firms also have been divided according to their external dependence: firms in the sectors exhibiting more external dependence have been separated from those firms in sectors presenting less finance dependence.[15] It is interesting to note that in Brazil, as Figure 3.9a shows, more financially dependent firms are on average more leveraged than less financially dependent firms, looking at the ratio of liabilities to assets.[16] That is, firms more in need of external finance according to the external dependence measure exhibit greater use of external finance. With respect to the debts to assets ratio, there is no pattern for the difference between these two groups: in some periods firms in less dependent sectors have a higher debts to assets ratio, compared to more dependent ones, whereas in other periods they have a lower measure (Figure 3.9b).

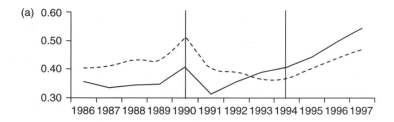

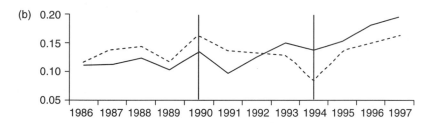

Figure 3.10 Liabilities/assets (a) and debt/assets (b) ratios for domestic (——) and multinational (----) firms.

Finally, the sample of firms is divided between multinational and domestic firms. The motivation for this division is that multinational firms may have more access to international credit markets, and therefore be less credit constrained. In both leverage measures, Figures 3.10a and b show higher leverage for multinational firms until 1993, and higher leverage for domestic firms since then.

Credit constraints

There is ample literature that seeks empirical evidence of credit constraints by looking at the firm's investment decision. Fazzari *et al.* (1988) were the first of several to estimate models of investment demand, including cash flow, as an independent variable. The reasoning is that if firms are not credit constrained, their cash-flow variations should not affect investment decisions, after investment opportunities are controlled for. Equation (3.5) is the general form for the investment equations they estimate:

$$(I/K)_{it} = f(X) + g(CF/K)_{it} = u_{it}, \tag{3.5}$$

where I_{it} and K_{it} represent investment and capital stock of firm i at time t, X represents a vector of variables affecting firms' investment decisions, according to theoretical considerations, and u_{it} is an error term. In some specifications, the Q investment model is estimated by using Tobin's q as the vector X, and including the cash-flow variable in the equation. In other specifications, the accelerator model of investment is used, and the X vector is replaced by contemporaneous and lagged sales to capital ratios.

Using a different method, Whited (1992) estimates Euler equations for an optimizing investment model under two different assumptions: when firms are credit constrained, and when they are not. Gertler and Gilchrist (1994), on the other hand, study whether small and large firms respond differently to monetary policy. They find that smaller firms have a much stronger response to monetary tightening than larger firms, indicating they are more credit constrained. All these studies use data for US firms.

The accelerator model specification from Fazzari *et al.* (1988) will be reproduced for Brazilian data to identify the existence (or not) of credit constraints.[17] The empirical exercises performed here are based on the sales accelerator investment demand model, where investment is explained by current and past sales. Cash flow is included as an explanatory variable for investment, as shown in eqn (3.6):

$$(I/K)_{it} = \beta_i + \beta_0(S/K)_{it} + \beta_1(S/K)_{i,t-1} + \beta_2(S/K)_{i,t-2} + \alpha(\text{CF}/K)_{it} + u_{it}, \quad (3.6)$$

where S_{it} represents the sales of firm i at time t. Cash flow should not be a significant explanatory variable for investment, except when firms are credit constrained. That is, the parameter α should not be significant for firms that are not creditconstrained, and it should be positive and significant for credit-constrained firms.

Table 3.7 presents the initial results. All regressions include firm-specific effects and two dummies: one for 1990 and another for 1994 to account for the breaks in the data.[18] First, the investment accelerator model is estimated without including cash flow as an explanatory variable. The best specification for our data is the one including two lags of the sales variable. As column 1 of Table 3.7 shows, variations in the sales variables explain 52 per cent of investment changes. When cash flow is included in the regression, independent variables explain 81 per cent of investment variations, and cash flow has a positive and significant coefficient (with t-statistics of 10.1). According to our conjecture, this is an indication that firms were credit constrained over the time period studied.

One should note, however, that the period under study encompasses two distinct situations with respect to capital inflows. From 1986 to 1994 there was very little external capital inflow into Brazil, and from 1994 to 1997 current account deficits increased substantially, reaching 4 per cent in 1997, as shown in Table 3.1. It is possible that the higher capital inflow increased the credit supply, therefore lessening firms' credit constraints. A slope dummy for cash flow for the period 1994–7 has been included in the regression. This variable equals cash flow and capital ratio for the years 1994–7, and is zero for the rest of the period. If firms were less credit constrained over 1994–7, this slope dummy should not be positive. That is not the case though. The slope dummy coefficient is positive, with a t-statistic of 1.93. Thus, there is no evidence that firms became less credit constrained with the external capital inflow.

The next step is to investigate possible differences in credit constraints across groups of firms. First, as argued in the previous subsection, it is reasonable to expect that small firms are more credit constrained than large ones. The sample is then split according to firms' size, and the regression results are presented in columns 4–7.[19] Cash-flow coefficients are also positive and significant for both

Table 3.7 Regression results (dependent variable: investment)

Independent variable and summary statistics	Whole sample			Large firms		Small firms	
	1	2	3	4	5	6	7
$(CF/K)_{it}$		1.339 (10.111)	0.882 (3.708)	1.985 (4.793)	1.860 (7.220)	1.313 (8.405)	0.852 (3.662)
CF/K slope dummy 1994–7			0.553 (1.933)		0.138 (0.407)		0.604 (2.005)
$(S/K)_{it}$	−0.284 (−3.975)	−0.127 (−5.462)	−0.118 (−5.115)	0.233 (1.299)	0.239 (1.267)	−0.137 (−6.695)	−0.134 (−6.764)
$(S/K)_{i,t-1}$	0.284 (3.467)	0.101 (3.397)	0.084 (3.106)	−0.319 (−1.632)	−0.328 (−1.553)	0.112 (3.926)	0.100 (3.755)
$(S/K)_{i,t-2}$	−0.034 (−0.034)	−0.001 (−0.069)	0.004 (0.341)	0.034 (0.882)	0.038 (0.902)	−0.004 (−0.309)	−0.001 (−0.121)
R^2	0.515	0.807	0.816	0.863	0.863	0.792	0.805
Number of firms	468	468	468	75	75	393	393
Number of observations	4,680	4,680	4,680	750	750	3,930	3,930

Notes: The dependent variable is investment–capital ratio. The CF/K slope dummy is a variable that has value equal to CF/K for the years 1994–7, and zero in all other years. All regressions have been estimated using firms' fixed effects and dummies for the years 1990 and 1994, but the coefficients are not reported. The t-statistics in parentheses are based on White heteroskedasticity-consistent standard errors.

groups of firms (columns 4 and 6). Hence, there is no evidence that larger firms are less credit constrained than smaller firms.[20]

Second, international credit markets may be more accessible for multinational firms, compared to domestic ones. Columns 1–4 in Table 3.8 present the results for the regressions estimated for multinational and domestic firms separately. Again, all cash-flow coefficients are positive and significant, indicating credit constraints for both groups. There is an important difference in the cash-flow slope dummy in the period 1994–7 for the two groups, though for domestic firms this coefficient is positive and significant, and for multinationals it is negative, with a *t*-statistic of − 1.238. This can be interpreted as an indication that multinational firms were less credit constrained over the period 1994–7, when there was a large capital inflow. Hence, the capital inflow seems to have lessened only multinational firms' credit constraint.[21]

The sample has also been divided according to external dependence, using Rajan and Zingales' (1998) measure, and the estimated regressions are presented in Table 3.8, columns 5–8. The cash-flow coefficients are significant in all regressions, but the coefficient is higher for less dependent firms. One interpretation is that less dependent firms would use less external finance; therefore their investment would be more cash flow sensitive. The cash-flow slope dummy is positive, but not significant for both subsamples.

The results so far indicate credit restrictions across the whole sample of firms, and also across subgroups formed by larger and smaller, more and less externally dependent, multinational and domestic firms. The only instance of credit-constraint reduction was among multinational firms, from 1994 to 1997.[22]

Further results

Kaplan and Zingales (1997) argue that investment-cash-flow sensitivities do not provide a useful measure of finance constraints, introducing controversy regarding the validity of this methodology. An alternative empirical exercise is then performed, without the use of cash flows. It was motivated by Rajan and Zingales (1998).

Rajan and Zingales (1998) investigate the effect of financial sector development on industrial growth. Their main hypothesis is that 'industries that are more dependent on external financing will have relatively higher growth rates in countries that have more developed financial markets' (p. 562). They use industry-level data for several countries to estimate an equation where industry growth is explained by the interaction between an industry's external dependence and the country's financial development, controlling for country indicators, industry indicators, and that industry's share in the country's economy. That is, they have an equation that tries to capture possible variables that explain differences in industry growth rates in different countries, and they include a new variable in the equation, namely external dependence times financial development. Their conjecture is that if financial development is indeed important for growth, the coefficient of this

Table 3.8 Regression results (dependent variable: investment)

Independent variable and summary statistics	Multinational		Domestic firms		More dependent		Less dependent	
	1	2	3	4	5	6	7	8
$(CF/K)_{it}$	1.098 (5.939)	1.367 (6.738)	1.437 (8.036)	0.878 (3.737)	1.022 (6.040)	0.644 (2.883)	1.573 (9.014)	1.304 (7.613)
CF/K slope dummy 1994–7		−0.284 (−1.238)		0.737 (2.278)		0.520 (1.669)		0.302 (1.175)
$(S/K)_{it}$	−0.152 (−1.762)	−0.151 (1.794)	−0.148 (−6.346)	−0.136 (−6.413)	−0.128 (−5.466)	−0.121 (−5.516)	−0.091 (−1.904)	−0.086 (−1.811)
$(S/K)_{i,t-1}$	0.040 (0.591)	0.052 (0.714)	0.115 (3.752)	0.098 (3.516)	0.128 (2.879)	0.108 (2.644)	0.037 (1.087)	0.033 (0.993)
$(S/K)_{i,t-2}$	0.040 (1.130)	0.037 (1.040)	−0.006 (−0.469)	−0.002 (−0.193)	−0.016 (−1.139)	−0.011 (−0.796)	0.031 (2.001)	0.031 (2.155)
R^2	0.918	0.918	0.785	0.802	0.765	0.780	0.844	0.846
Number of firms	46	46	413	413	179	179	289	289
Number of observations	460	460	4,130	4,130	1,790	1,790	2,890	2,890

Notes: The dependent variable is investment–capital ratio. The CF/K slope dummy is a variable that has value equal to CF/K for the years 1994–7, and zero in all other years. All regressions have been estimated using firms' fixed effects and dummies for the years 1990 and 1994, but the coefficients are not reported. The t-statistics in parentheses are based on White heteroskedasticity-consistent standard errors.

Table 3.9 Credit to private sector (% GDP)

	Argentina	Brazil	Philippines	France	Germany	India	Mexico	South Africa	Tunisia	Uruguay	United States
1991	12.5	33.1	17.8	96.6	89.7	25.6	20.2		53.8	28.5	66.7
1992	15.2	54.3	20.6	96.7	90.7	26.6	27.2	62.7	54.0	27.5	63.3
1993	16.5	82.2	26.4	92.0	96.5	25.7	30.4	62.4	53.9	27.0	62.5
1994	18.2	45.5	29.1	86.1	98.8	25.2	36.6	65.5	53.8	25.6	62.7
1995	18.1	30.8	37.5	84.9	99.8	24.3	26.7	67.5	54.5	28.3	65.0
1996	18.1	26.3	49.0	81.8	104.9	25.6	16.4	70.5	49.1	28.8	65.6
1997	19.3	26.0	56.5	80.7	108.2		12.7	73.5	50.2	31.1	67.1

Source: International Financial Statistics, IMF.

Table 3.10 Regression results (dependent variable: investment)

Independent variable and summary statistics	Whole sample 1	Winners 2	Losers 3
Interaction (external dependence × firm size)	308.985	206.645	959.942
	(2.601)	(2.276)	(3.508)
$(S/K)_{it}$	−0.284	−0.325	−0.272
	(−3.996)	(−4.831)	(−3.092)
$(S/K)_{i,t-1}$	0.283	0.277	0.286
	(3.482)	(4.375)	2.608
$(S/K)_{i,t-2}$	−0.035	−0.032	−0.036
	(−1.235)	(−1.515)	(−0.793)
R^2	0.516	0.502	0.533
Number of firms	468	235	233
Number of observations	4,680	2,350	2,330

Notes: All regressions were estimated using firms' fixed effects, but the coefficients are not reported. The *t*-statistics in parentheses are based on White heteroskedasticity-consistent standard errors.

interaction variable should be positive: more dependent industries would tend to grow faster in a more financially developed environment.

I borrow this idea from Rajan and Zingales (1998) in the following way. It seems plausible to take Brazil as a financially constrained economy. As shown in Table 3.9, Brazil has low domestic credit as a proportion of GDP compared to developed countries. In this financially constrained environment, more dependent firms that have access to credit should be relatively better off. Less dependent firms, on the other hand, should not be much affected by credit access. Hence, when explaining cross-firm investment levels, more dependent firms would tend to invest more when they have more access to credit, in a credit-constrained environment.

The empirical implementation is carried out by estimating the investment accelerator model, including the interaction between external dependence and credit access. Firm size is used as a proxy for credit access. If Brazil has a credit constrained economy, and if firm size is a good proxy for credit access, the coefficient for the dependence and firm size interaction term should be positive. Table 3.10 presents the results. The estimated regression for the whole sample of firms is presented in column 1. The coefficient for the interaction term is indeed positive and statistically significant; more dependent and larger firms do invest more.

In this empirical specification, it makes no sense to divide the sample of firms into large and small, or more and less dependent, because the criteria used for such divisions are already contained in the new independent variable used. An alternative grouping of firms is used, based on asset growth. One group, denoted 'winners', is composed of those firms that presented an above-average asset growth rate over the period, and the other group, 'losers', is composed of firms with asset growth rate below average. The interaction term (external dependence times firm size) is positive and significant in both subgroups, as shown in columns 2 and 3. It is interesting to note, though, that the coefficient is more than four times larger for the group of loser firms.[23]

5. Credit constraints and trade patterns

Section 3 describes industrial trade pattern evolution in Brazil, and Section 4 investigates the extent of credit constraint faced by Brazilian firms. In this section, I try to interact these two analyses in order to extract some evidence of the working of credit constraint as one of the sources of comparative advantage.

I divide time into the four subintervals used in previous sections: oil crisis (1974–82), debt crisis (1982–90), trade liberalization (1990–4) and capital inflow (1994–7). Trade barriers increased over the first two periods, and started being removed in the late 1980s. Trade pattern evolution over the first two periods would not necessarily represent the response to comparative advantages, but rather to distorted incentives. During the last two periods, on the other hand, trade distortion diminished substantially, and trade pattern evolution can be taken as an expression of the countries' comparative advantages.

CTB averages are calculated for each subinterval, identifying whether they are significantly different across subintervals, at a 5 per cent significance level. The results are presented in Table 3.11. *Winners* are sectors which significantly increased their CTB from one period to the next; *losers* are those significantly decreasing their CTB; and *stagnant* are the ones that showed no significant change. The most interesting features of the pattern observed in Table 3.11 are the following:

- Machinery is a winner from the first to the second periods only, that is, under trade distortions. It is a loser from the second to the third, and stagnant from the third to fourth.
- Drugs, plastic products and electric equipment follow a similar pattern. They are stagnant from the first to second periods, and losers over the other periods.
- The opposite is true for the sectors wood products, furniture, leather and tobacco. These sectors are losers from the first to the second periods (except tobacco, which was stagnant), and they are winners through the other periods.
- Food products, metal products and rubber products are also interesting cases: the first is a losing sector across all periods, except from third to fourth, and the opposite is true for the other two sectors.
- Textiles is a losing sector in all periods.

It is reasonable to conclude that Brazil shows no comparative advantage in machinery, drugs, electric equipment and textiles, and shows comparative advantage in wood products, furniture, leather and tobacco. Our main question is whether finance was one of the sources of this comparative advantage. Looking at the external dependence measure, it is interesting to note that the four sectors with lack of comparative advantage are among the seven most externally dependent

Table 3.11 Contribution to the trade balance across periods

	1982–90 over 1974–82	1990–4 over 1982–90	1994–7 over 1990–4
Metal products	↑	↑	↓
Rubber products	↑	↑	↓
Paper and products	↑	↑	=
Apparel and footwear	↑	=	↓
Non-metal products	↑	=	=
Machinery	↑	↓	=
Tobacco	=	↑	↑
Beverages	=	=	=
Transport equipment	=	=	↓
Perfumery and soap	=	=	↓
Chemical products	=	↓	=
Other industries	=	↓	=
Drugs	=	↓	↓
Electric equipment	=	↓	↓
Plastic products	=	↓	↓
Furniture	↓	↑	↑
Wood products	↓	↑	↑
Leather	↓	↑	↑
Printing and publishing	↓	=	↓
Food products	↓	↓	↑
Textiles	↓	↓	↓

Notes: ↑: winners; ↓: losers; =: stagnant.

ones. Tobacco and leather, on the other hand, are the two least externally dependent – actually, they have negative measures of external dependence.

For a statistical comparison of the two measures – CTB and external dependence – the correlation between the two is calculated for each year, and the results presented in Table 3.12. Not only is the correlation between CTB and external dependence negative, it also decreases over time. This means that, on average, more externally dependent industries have lower CTB measures, and this negative relation is stronger over time.

The nature of the relation between CTB and external dependence is investigated in panel data regression, where external dependence by sector is used as an explanatory variable of CTB. The results are presented in column 1 in Table 3.13. The coefficient of external dependence is not significantly different from zero, and solely fixed effects explain 78 per cent of cross-sector variation in CTB. The correlation between the two measures, presented in Table 3.12, indicates that the relation between them changes over time. An interaction term between external dependence and time is then used as explanatory variable of CTB. As shown in column 2 in Table 3.13, this interaction term has a negative and significant coefficient. These results do not change when both the interaction term and external dependence are used as explanatory variables (see column 3 in Table 3.13).

Table 3.12 Correlation coefficient between external dependence and CTB

1974	−0.14	1989	−0.29
1975	−0.18	1990	−0.32
1976	−0.20	1991	−0.29
1977	−0.18	1992	−0.31
1978	−0.22	1993	−0.30
1979	−0.24	1994	−0.35
1980	−0.18	1995	−0.35
1981	−0.19	1996	−0.39
1982	−0.22	1997	−0.39
1983	−0.23	*Averages*	
1984	−0.22	1974–82	−0.20
1985	−0.25	1982–6	−0.25
1986	−0.28	1986–90	−0.29
1987	−0.27	1990–4	−0.32
1988	−0.27	1994–7	−0.37

As I argued in the beginning of this section, the pattern of trade evolution between 1974 and 1990 was responding to distorted trade incentives, whereas after trade liberalization in the 1990s it could have become an expression of the country's comparative advantages. In order to capture possible differences of the effect of external dependence over the two periods, I have run a regression including two variables as explanatory variables for CTB: external dependence, and a slope dummy for external dependence for 1990–7. The slope dummy equals external dependence for the years 1990–7, and equals zero in all other periods. As presented in column 4 in Table 3.13, the coefficient for external dependence is again not significantly different from zero, and the slope dummy coefficient is negative and significant. This indicates that external dependence explains cross-sector variations in CTB for the period from 1990 to 1997, but not from 1974 to 1990. When all three variables are included in the regression (column 5 in Table 3.13), the only significant coefficient is the negative coefficient for the slope dummy.

The results indicate that external dependence has a negative effect on cross-sector CTB for the period from 1990 to 1997, and no relation in the previous period studied. That is, sectors less external dependent are the ones with higher CTB during the period under more liberalized trade in Brazil.

6. Conclusion

This chapter has sought to investigate whether credit constraints may have influenced trade pattern evolution in Brazil. The analysis started with a description of economic development over the time period studied – 1974–97. The Brazilian economy suffered several large external shocks over the period, leading, along with other factors, to major macroeconomic disturbances. Macroeconomic volatility was extremely high over the 1980s and early 1990s. Since the implementation of the Real Plan in mid-1994, the country has experienced relative macroeconomic

Table 3.13 Regression results (dependent variable: contribution to trade balance index)

Independent variable and summary statistics	1	2	3	4	5
External dependence	−3.50E−04 (−3.79E−16)		5.41E−04 (5.05E−16)	1.42E−04 (1.03E−16)	−1.50E−03 (−1.02E−15)
Interaction (external dependence X time)		−3.40E−04 (−7.01)	−3.40E−04 (−7.00)		−2.21E−05 (−0.18)
External dependence slope dummy 1990−7				−7.21E−03 (−7.13)	−6.85E−03 (−3.64)
R^2	0.780	0.820	0.82	0.828	0.826

Notes: The dependent variable is contribution to trade balance index. The external dependence slope dummy is a variable that has value equal to external dependence for the years 1990−7, and zero in all other years. All regressions were estimated using sectors' fixed effects, but the coefficients are not reported. All regressions include twenty-one sectors, with observations from 1974 to 1997.

stability. Trade policy was characterized by two main situations: severely restrictive trade policy until the late 1980s, and more liberalized trade in the 1990s.

Trade pattern evolution was described through a series of indexes, and they identified a clear trade diversification in the course of the time period studied. Notably, the sector food and beverages represented a very important export sector at the beginning of the period, and its importance thereupon decreased substantially. An interesting feature of trade pattern evolution is the reversal in some sectors' CTB after trade liberalization in the 1990s. Some sectors, such as machinery, drugs, plastic products and electric equipment, presented increasing (or non-decreasing) trade balance contributions over the restricted trade period, and decreasing contributions after liberalization. The opposite is true for some other sectors, such as wood products, furniture, leather and tobacco.

Credit constraints were investigated using a firm's balance sheet data. The empirical exercise tried to answer two questions: whether firms are credit constrained, and whether credit constraints differ among different groups of firms. Following an influential trend in the empirical literature in this area, an investment accelerator model was estimated, including cash flow as an explanatory variable. If firms are not credit constrained, the cash-flow coefficient should not be significant, once investment determinants are controlled for. Estimated results indicated that Brazilian firms are indeed credit constrained. The only instance in which credit constraints seemed softer was among multinational firms, during the period 1994–7.

After describing trade pattern evolution, and establishing that Brazilian firms are credit constrained, the concluding question is: is there a link between credit constraint and trade pattern? The link is investigated by comparing the contribution to trade balance index to sectoral external dependence. External dependence is a measure constructed by Rajan and Zingales (1998) that indicates the amount of external finance an industry would use in an environment with no credit restrictions. Contributions to trade balance and external dependence are negatively correlated, that is, in any given year, sectors with higher CTB are the ones with lower external dependence on average. It is interesting to note that the negative correlation becomes stronger over time, especially after trade liberalization, when trade started to reveal the economy's comparative advantages with less artificial distortions. This is an indication that sectors less in need of external financing would be relatively better off in Brazil, which we identified as a credit-restricted economy. Thus, credit restrictions may be a source of comparative advantage.

Notes

1 I am grateful for helpful comments and suggestions from José Fanelli, Saul Keifman, Naércio Menezes and seminar participants at the IDRC workshop on Finance and Changing Patterns in Developing Countries, FEA – Universidade de São Paulo, and the PRONEX seminar held at Getulio Vargas Foundation. I am especially grateful to Edward Amadeo, with whom this project started, for many insightful conversations, and the elaboration of the section on labor productivity and unit labor cost evolution. I thank Patrícia Gonçalves, from IBRE, Getulio Vargas Foundation, for kindly furnishing

data on Brazilian firms' balance sheets, Carla Bernardes and particularly Cristiana Vidigal for superb research assistance. Financial support from IDRC is gratefully acknowledged. I also thank CNPq for a research fellowship.

2 For an overview of the period from 1964 to 1973, see Bonomo and Terra (1999).

3 BEFIEX (Comissão para a Concessão de Benefícios Fiscais a Programas Especiais de Exportação) coordinated export incentives. Long-term (usually ten-year) contracts were signed between BEFIEX and the exporting firm, in which the firm would commit to a certain amount of exports over the period, and in exchange it would have reduced import duties and taxes. The program was effective – during the 1975 to 1990 period exports grew over 7 per cent a year on average, accompanied by impressive diversification.

4 For further details, see Simonsen (1988).

5 World inflation is measured here as the rate of increase in world export prices in US dollars.

6 Among other measures, the government created the 'Law of Similar National Products', determining that a product could not be imported if there existed a similar good being produced domestically.

7 See Bonelli *et al.* (1993).

8 Real exchange-rate volatility is measured as the monthly real exchange-rate standard deviation for a twelve month period. The measure is centered, i.e. the measure for June corresponds to the standard deviation from January to December. The real exchange rate was measured as $RER = e.(WPI)/CPI$, where e is the nominal exchange rate published by the Brazilian Central Bank, WPI is the US wholesale price index and CPI is the Brazilian consumer price index (INPC series from IBGE).

9 In this section, the time period analyzed is shorter due to lack of data.

10 FUNCEX provided by monthly sector data for imports and exports.

11 Looking at the CTB index for a twenty-three-industry aggregation, its variance ranged from 0.0061 to 0.0115 in the 1970s and early 1980s, going down to around 0.002 for the past few years.

12 The Aquino intra-industry trade index has also been calculated, and the results are similar to the ones reported here for the Grubel and Lloyd index.

13 This procedure may bias the sample of firms used, but I argue that the bias should not favor the result I am investigating. We are trying to identify whether firms are credit constrained. It is plausible to believe that firms which survived throughout the period studied should not be the more credit-constrained ones. Hence, if this (possibly) biased sample presents credit constraints, the unbiased sample should also be credit constrained.

14 The measure for debt is the long- and short-term loans on the firm's balance sheet. Liabilities include all other accounts under liabilities, such as dividends and taxes to be paid.

15 Firms which are less dependent on external finance are those in the following sectors: furniture, chemical products, wood products, transport equipment, textiles, machinery, perfumery and soap, electric equipment, plastic products, drugs, and other industries.

16 Note that Rajan and Zingales' external dependence measure refers to all sorts of external financing, not only loans.

17 It is very difficult to replicate Whited (1992) for Brazilian data, due to a lack of data on some crucial variables. For the same reason, it is also not possible to replicate the Q model of investment used in Fazzari *et al.* (1988).

18 All regressions were also estimated in first differences, and the results were qualitatively similar to the ones reported here.

19 Instead of splitting the sample into subgroups, another specification is also used, which will be denoted here as 'slope dummy specification'. In this specification, slope dummies are included in the regression with the whole sample of firms, which was equal to cash flow for the alternative groupings of firms, and zero otherwise. These slope dummies should capture differences in the cash-flow coefficient for the different groups of firms. The same qualitative results were obtained.

20 As a further result, in the slope dummy specification, the slope dummy for large firms is not significantly different from zero. Therefore, the null hypothesis that the cash-flow coefficient is equal for the two groups of firms cannot be rejected.

21 In both other specifications – slope dummies and first differences – the slope dummy coefficient for 1994–7 is negative *and* significant for the group of multinational firms.

22 All regressions were also run including only one and three lags for sales, and the results were unchanged.

23 All cash-flow regressions were also estimated for the groups of winner and loser firms separately, but no difference between them was identified in those regressions.

References

Bonelli, R., Fritsch, W. and Franco, G. H. B. (1993) 'Macroeconomic Instability and Trade Instability in Brazil: Lessons from the 1980s and 1990s', in A. Canitrot and S. Junco (eds), *Macroeconomic Conditions and Trade Liberalization*. Washington, DC: Inter-American Development Bank.

Bonomo, M. and Terra, C. (1999) 'The Political Economy of Exchange Rate Policy in Brazil: 1964–1997', *Inter-American Development Bank Working Paper Series*, R-367.

Fazzari, S. M., Hubbard, R. G. and Petersen, B. C. (1988) 'Financing Constraints and Corporate Investment', *Brookings Papers on Economic Activity* 1: 141–206.

Gertler, M. and Gilchrist, G. (1994) 'Monetary Policy, Business Cycle, and the Behavior of Small Manufacturing Firms', *Quarterly Journal of Economics* 109(2): 309–40.

Kaplan, S. and Zingales, L. (1997) 'Do Investment Cash Flow Sensitivities Provide Useful Measures of Financing Constraints?', *Quarterly Journal of Economics* 88(3): 169–215.

Levine, R. (1997) 'Financial Development and Economic Growth: Views and Agenda', *Journal of Economic Literature* 25: 688–726.

Rajan, R. G. and Zingales, L. (1998) 'Financial Dependence and Growth', *The American Economic Review* 88(3): 559–86.

Simonsen, M. H. (1988) 'Brazil', in R. Dornbusch and F. Helmes (eds), *The Open Economy: Tools for Policymakers in Developing Countries*. New York: Oxford University Press.

Whited, T. M. (1992) 'Debt, Liquidity Constraints, and Corporate Investment: Evidence from Panel Data', *The Journal of Finance* XLVII(4): 1425–57.

4 International competitiveness, trade and finance

India[1]

A. Ganesh-Kumar, Kunal Sen and Rajendra R. Vaidya

1. Introduction

In 1990–1, the Indian economy underwent a severe balance-of-payments crisis. By the summer of 1991, India's foreign exchange reserves covered less than two weeks of imports. The immediate cause of the crisis was the increase in world oil prices and the drop in the remittances of migrant workers from the Gulf following the annexation of Kuwait in September 1990. There was a realisation among Indian policy-makers, however, that 'the roots of the crisis were more structural in nature and lay in the import-substituting industrialisation (ISI) strategy followed by successive Indian governments since independence' (Agrawal *et al.* 1995: 161). While the ISI regime had enabled India to develop a large and diversified manufacturing sector, the net result of the protectionist policies was 'the growth of a high-cost, capital-intensive domestic industry that was by and large incapable of withstanding international competition' (p. 175). Not only did these policies severely inhibit India's export performance, they also served to limit the possibility of growth based on domestic demand.[2] In spite of four decades of import-substitution policies, production in the Indian manufacturing sector remained greatly import intensive. As a consequence, with India's trade regime providing little incentive to export, growth based on domestic demand would lead to balance-of-payments problems sooner or later.[3]

In June 1991, the new government that assumed office (led by P. V. Narasimha Rao) embarked on an economic reform programme along with several macro-stabilisation measures. One of the major long-term objectives of the reforms was to increase India's international competitiveness, both in relation to its past and to the fast-growing economies of East Asia. While the 1991 reforms could be seen as a continuation of the deregulation measures that were initiated in the mid-1980s by the Rajiv Gandhi government, they were far more comprehensive in scope and radical in substance. The macroeconomic stabilisation programme initiated in 1991 yielded immediate benefits, with foreign exchange reserves recovering from just over 1 billion USD at the time of the crisis to over 6.4 billion USD at the end of 1992–3. The inflation rate, which had peaked at 17 per cent in 1991, came down steadily to 7 per cent in 1992–3. Real output growth, which had dipped to 1.2 per cent in 1991–2, recovered to 4 per cent in 1992–3. It is far from clear, however, whether the long-term goal of the 1991 reforms with regard to international competitiveness has been achieved.

International competitiveness refers to the ability of a country to expand its share in world markets. The standard view on competitiveness is that it is essentially determined by factor endowments and comparative advantage. Thus, to exploit comparative advantage, it is necessary to minimize various distortions in the economy and 'to get the prices right'. In recent years, two more views have emerged: One argues that technological differences across firms, industries and countries are an important determinant of competitiveness. The other view locates competitiveness in the firm's investment decisions and hence in its ability to obtain investible funds. Both these views stress the importance of non-price factors and provide an important role for the government to build technological capabilities and to ensure a financial environment that is able to identify and allocate resources to the best investment projects.

In this study, we examine the international competitiveness of India's manufacturing sector. We take the view that competitiveness is a multifaceted issue and that no single theory (and the associated measures) adequately captures its complexity. We thus use several measures of competitiveness to examine the relative importance of various factors that influence it. Section 2 deals with competitiveness at the aggregate and sectoral level. Here we assess the relative importance of the real exchange rate and trade specialisation patterns in explaining India's trade flows. We also examine the link between labour costs and competitiveness. Further, we explore the technological intensity of India's exports. In Section 3, we analyse one important determinant of competitiveness, i.e. the financial environment. Specifically, we ask the question: to what extent has the Indian financial sector provided an enabling environment for successful export performance by manufacturing firms in the post-1991 period? We attempt to answer this question in two steps. First, we examine firms' sources and uses of funds to discern whether there is any systematic relationship between export performance and financing patterns. Next, we estimate investment functions for a sample of firms in the Indian manufacturing sector to see whether finance constraints are less severe for the exporters as compared to firms whose sales are primarily to the domestic market.

We begin with a more explicit consideration of trade, industrial and financial sector policies in India and the periodisation of the policy regime that we have used in our study.

Policy regimes and periodization

The Indian policy regime can be categorised into three distinct phases. The first phase was the era of planning from 1951 to 1984 when the state had strict control over resource allocation. The second period was a period of partial deregulation from 1985 to 1991 when the state retained a major role in resource allocation even as private agents were given greater freedom in investment decisions. Finally, in the post-1991 period, resource allocation was primarily market driven.[4]

In what follows, we provide a brief overview of the economic policies followed in each period.[5]

1951–84

During this period, India had a highly restrictive trade and industrial policy regime. Nearly all imports were subject to discretionary import licensing or were 'canalised' by government monopoly trading organisations. The only exceptions were commodities listed in the Open General License (OGL) category. Capital goods were divided into a restricted category and the OGL category. While import licenses were required for restricted capital goods, those in the OGL could be imported without a license subject to several conditions. Intermediate goods were also classified into the banned, restricted and limited permissible categories plus an OGL category. As these names suggest, the first three lists were in order of import licensing stringency. The import of consumer goods was, however, banned. Like imports, exports were also subject to an elaborate licensing regime. To counteract the anti-export bias of the trade regime however, there were a large number of export incentives for manufactured goods.

The principal instrument of industrial policy was an elaborate industrial licensing framework under the Industries Development and Regulation Act of 1951. The Act stipulated that no new units (above a certain size) could be set up nor substantial expansion be made to existing units without a license from the government. The Monopolies and Restrictive Trade Practices Act (MRTP) became effective in 1970 to ensure against concentration of economic power and check restrictive trade practices. Foreign investment in India was regulated by the Foreign Exchange Regulation Act (FERA) of 1974.

With respect to financial sector policy, there was a period of increasing financial repression from the early 1970s. In 1969, fourteen of the largest commercial banks were nationalised followed by six more in 1980. Moreover, commercial banks were increasingly pressured to lend to the 'priority sector', comprising agriculture, small-scale industry, retail trade, transport operators, professionals and craftsmen. While the commercial banks essentially provided short-term credit to the manufacturing sector, long-term loans were provided by All India Development Banks like Industrial Development Bank of India and Industrial Credit and Investment Corporation of India. These term-lending institutions depended a lot on the government for resources (usually subsidised heavily), and their allocation of long-term loans to firms was strictly monitored by the government according to plan priorities. Interest rates both of commercial banks and term-lending institutions were controlled by the government. The stock markets too were controlled by the government with respect to pricing, quantum and timing of new issues.

Finally, with respect to exchange rate policy, the rupee was pegged to the pound sterling till 1975 (except for a brief period when the rupee was pegged to the US dollar). In September 1975, the peg was altered to a basket of currencies with undisclosed weights. For much of the period, the peg was 'passive', with the sole intention of keeping the real exchange rate constant.

1985–91

With the advent of the Rajiv Gandhi government in 1985, piecemeal reforms were initiated in trade and industrial policy. Several initiatives were taken to limit the role of licensing, expanding the scope for contribution by large business houses to growth, encouraging modernisation and allowing existing firms in certain industries to achieve minimum economic level of operations. The shift from quantitative import controls to a protective system based on tariffs initiated in the mid-1970s was considerably quickened from 1985 onwards. Also, beginning in the mid-1980s, there was a renewed emphasis by the new administration on export promotion. The number and value of incentives offered to exporters were increased and their administration streamlined. The allotment of REP licenses – tradable import entitlements awarded to exporters on a product-specific basis – became increasingly generous. There was also a steady devaluation of the Indian rupee during this period. Effectively, India operated an 'active' crawling peg from 1986 onwards to produce a sharp real depreciation of the rupee in the period 1986–90.

Post-1991

As noted earlier, the year 1991 marked a watershed in Indian economic policy. As a part of the structural adjustment programme, quotas on the imports of most machinery and equipment and manufactured intermediate goods were removed. REP licenses were abolished and a large part of the import licensing system was replaced by tradable import entitlements linked to export earnings. There was also a significant cut in tariff rates, with the peak tariff rate reduced from 300 per cent to 150 per cent and the peak duty on capital goods cut to 80 per cent. There was, however, little change in trade policy with respect to consumer goods which remained banned. With respect to industrial policy, industrial licensing was abolished altogether except for a select list of environmentally sensitive industries. MRTP was substantially revised so that regulations restricting the growth and merger of large business houses were eliminated. FERA was altered in 1993 so that the earlier policy of restricting foreign investment became one of actively promoting it.

From 1991 to 1993, India moved gradually to full current account convertibility of the exchange rate, first in March 1992, *with the replacement of the tradable import entitlements, with a dual-exchange rate system*, and then in March 1993, moving to a unified 'market-determined' exchange rate system (i.e. a managed float). Nonetheless, strict controls over the capital account, especially capital outflows, remain.

In the financial sector, from the point of view of the financing decisions of firms, the two most important changes were the deregulation of interest rates (both of commercial banks and term-lending institutions) and the freeing of pricing restrictions on new issues of shares through the stock markets.

Our study is mostly confined to the 1985–91 and post-1991 policy regimes. In the next section, we attempt to trace the effects of these policy changes on export competitiveness of the Indian manufacturing sector. Specifically, we look for breaks in the trend in competitiveness across these two periods. In Section 3, where we analyse financial factors at the firm level, we confine ourselves to the post-1991 period for obvious reasons.

2. Productivity and the price determinants of competitiveness

In this section, we assess the relative importance of the real exchange rate and labour productivity (and domestic costs) in explaining India's trade performance in the recent past. We begin with overviews of India's trade performance and the evolution of the current account. We then attempt to determine the importance of the real exchange rate in explaining India's competitiveness in both total and manufacturing exports. Next we examine in detail India's trade specialisation patterns. We compute export shares and indices of revealed comparative advantage to assess competitiveness at a sectoral level. 'Winner' and 'loser' industries are then identified and the links between competitiveness, labour productivity and domestic costs are explored. We end by examining alternate measures of trade specialisation such as intra-industry trade and the technological complexity of exports.

Overview of trade flows

India had a persistent deficit in the trade account during the period 1971–96 (Figure 4.1). The trade deficit as a percentage of GDP was smaller in magnitude in the 1990s as compared to the 1980s. This, in spite of a rapid increase in imports as a ratio of GDP, was due to a strong performance by the export sector. It is clear that due to the sharp increase in both the ratios of exports to GDP and imports to

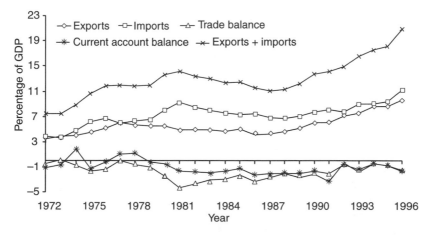

Figure 4.1 India's exports, imports, trade balance, current account balance and openness measure.

GDP since the mid-1980s, the economy has been increasingly 'open' during this period (Figure 4.1).[6] There has also been a steady increase in manufacturing exports as a proportion of India's total exports since the 1980s, from less than 60 per cent in 1979–80 to about 75 per cent in 1995–6. Nonetheless, market shares of India's total and manufacturing exports in world exports have not improved substantially and continue to remain at less than 1 per cent. There does not seem to be any perceptible increase in the annual growth rates of both total and manufacturing exports in the post-1991 period. For the period 1981–90, the average annual growth rates for total and manufacturing exports were 9.4 and 11.8 per cent, respectively, while for the period 1991–6 the average annual growth rates for total and manufacturing exports were 8.9 and 9.9 per cent, respectively. Therefore, the 1991 reforms do not seem to have had any perceptible positive effect on India's export performance.

Evolution of the current account and the real exchange rate

It is evident from Figure 4.1 that it is only in the early 1980s that India had large deficits in the current account. In the 1990s, while India still had a deficit in its current account, the current account deficit to GDP ratio was considerably lower than in the 1980s. We have already observed earlier that India had a rapidly falling deficit in its trade balance from the early 1980s as exports grew rapidly during this period (see Figure 4.1). Moreover, the real effective exchange rate (REER) had been steadily depreciating since the mid-1980s (Figure 4.2). During this period, India followed a policy of steadily devaluing the rupee in combination with other export promotion measures to boost exports. Clearly then, the worsening current account deficit in the 1980s cannot be attributed to a weakly performing export sector.

Figure 4.2 Real effective exchange rate of the rupee (1979 = 100).

Joshi and Little (1994) argue that the increase in the current account deficit to GDP ratio in the 1980s could be linked to an increase in the investment–savings gap. Underlying this was the widening fiscal deficits of the central government, with the public investment–savings gap increasing from 7.1 per cent of GDP in 1982–4 to 8.4 per cent of GDP in 1985–9. With the fiscal retrenchment initiated in 1991, there was a narrowing of the investment–savings gap in the 1990s and a consequent decrease in the current account deficit to GDP ratio. Thus, the large current account deficits of the 1980s could be attributed to a macroeconomic imbalance (related to a widening fiscal deficit) rather than a stagnant export sector or an inappropriate real exchange rate. The structural adjustment programme of 1991 led to some correction in this imbalance and, hence, a more sustainable current account deficit. It should be noted, however, that in contrast to its behaviour in the mid-to-late 1980s, the real exchange rate (RER) has shown a slight appreciation in the very recent past.

We have observed earlier that India followed a discretionary crawling peg in the 1970s and 1980s to maintain an 'appropriate' level of the RER. Yet there were periods, particularly in the early 1980s, when the nominal exchange rate was kept fixed in spite of a high inflation rate prevailing in the domestic economy. It is commonly agreed that sustained RER misalignment may contribute to severe macroeconomic disequilibria and a balance-of-payments crisis. Moreover, there is evidence to suggest that more 'successful' countries owe much of their success to having been able to maintain the RER at its 'appropriate' level (Edwards 1994). To what extent can it be argued that India had 'misaligned' RERs during the period under consideration? Elbadawi (1994) estimates the degree of misalignment in India's real exchange rate for the period 1965–88. The degree of misalignment is defined as the deviation of the actual RER from the equilibrium RER. The latter is itself the level of the RER which allows the economy to simultaneously attain internal equilibrium (i.e. the non-tradable market clears, the budget is balanced and portfolio equilibrium holds) and external equilibrium (the current account is in balance). Elbadawi has developed a model of the equilibrium RER where the equilibrium RER is determined by domestic absorption and government expenditures (both as ratios of GDP), terms of trade and a measure of the degree of 'openness' of the economy. Elbadawi finds that except for 1965 and 1986, which witnessed episodes of overvaluation of 16.3 per cent and 10.6 per cent, respectively, the period is characterised by single-digit RER misalignments, most of which are actually quite small. This, according to the author, supports the view that 'India, while maintaining an elaborate ensemble of economic controls, has nonetheless adopted a rather conservative macroeconomic policy' (Elbadawi 1994: 126).

Aggregate competitiveness

To measure competitiveness at the aggregate level, we use the constant market share (CMS) analysis. According to the CMS method, the proportionate increase in exports over time comprises a number of effects: (a) standard growth effect,

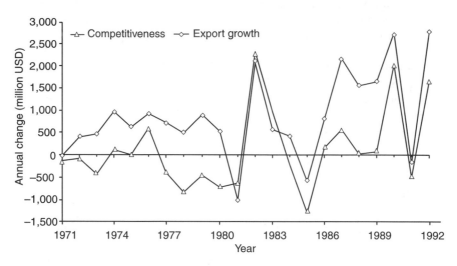

Figure 4.3 India's competitiveness and export growth – all commodities (SITC two-digit level).

(b) commodity composition effect, (c) market distribution effect, and (d) a residual effect which may be termed 'competitiveness'. In other words, the increase in exports can be 'explained' in terms of four factors: the general growth of world exports to the focus destination; the commodity mix of exports and differential growth in import demands; the extent to which the particular market represents growing centres of demand; and finally, a residual term which captures the net gain or loss in the market shares presumably due to changes in the relative price and/or quality of the product, not to mention the marketing effort and skill of the exporters.[7]

The estimates of each of the above-mentioned effects depend on the 'standard' against which the focus country's exports to the focus destination is to be compared. This study has used the world standard, assuming that the commodity composition of world exports bears a reasonably good relationship to that of the focus exporter.

The CMS methodology is used to decompose the annual change in India's total exports, all commodities and manufacturing commodities separately, over the period 1970–92.[8] The data set used is the World Trade Database from Statistics Canada made available through the NBER (Feenstra *et al*. 1997). Based on the trade data from the United Nations Statistical Office, this database provides on a consistent basis the annual bilateral trade values for all countries of the world over 1970–92.[9]

In Figure 4.3, we plot the competitiveness measure for *all* commodities as obtained from the CMS methodology along with the annual growth of total exports. Similarly, in Figure 4.4, we plot the competitiveness measure only for *manufacturing* commodities along with the annual growth of manufacturing exports. In both cases, the change in competitiveness is correlated with export growth. However, there is a closer correlation between the growth rate and the

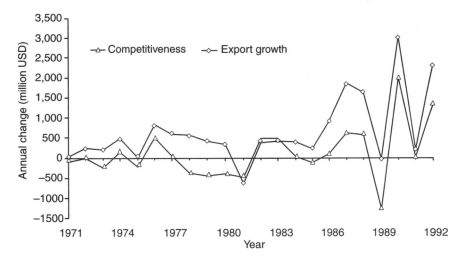

Figure 4.4 India's competitiveness and export growth – manufacturing commodities (SITC two-digit level).

Table 4.1 Decomposition of India's exports (%)

	World trade effects	Commodity effects	Market effects	Competitive effects	Export growth – actual (USD 000)
All commodities					
1971–5	−66.4	28.3	50.7	87.5	2,415,207.2
1976–80	168.7	−14.2	14.8	−69.3	3,583,957.3
1981–5	6.6	12.9	−22.9	103.5	1,473,356.8
1986–90	87.9	7.3	−20.5	25.3	8,965,485.2
1991–2	−140.3	1.7	78.5	160.2	2,598,590.4
Manufacturing					
1971–5	32,964.5	−17,278.3	18,974.5	−34,560.7	933,390.1
1976–80	128.3	−1.5	17.9	−44.6	2,740,358.5
1981–5	52.0	−11.2	6.1	53.0	810,632.4
1986–90	−604.6	−35.0	−277.6	1,017.2	7,394,295.2
1991–2	182.3	−3.3	−111.1	32.1	2,531,672.7

change in competitiveness of manufacturing commodities than there is between the growth rate and the change in competitiveness for all commodities (the correlation in the former case is 0.861 as compared to 0.796 for the latter case). This indicates that competitiveness may play a greater role in determining the export performance of the manufacturing sector than it does for all other sectors.

The CMS methodology decomposes the change in a country's exports into four components – the world trade effect, the commodity composition effect, the market effect and the competitiveness effect. In Table 4.1, we decompose exports into these four components for all commodities and for manufacturing commodities. We find that the relative importance and the direction of change of the four components for all commodities is quite different from the relative importance of these components for manufacturing commodities for most subperiods. For example, in 1971–5 and in 1986–90, the competitiveness effect is large in magnitude (and opposite in direction, for the period 1971–5) for manufacturing exports as compared to all exports. This may indicate that the factors explaining competitiveness for manufacturing exports may be different from those explaining competitiveness for all exports. The periods 1971–5 and 1986–90 are striking in that we find that for manufacturing exports, the competitiveness effect is negative and large in magnitude in the first period and positive and, again, large in magnitude for the second period. What explains these large variations in the aggregate competitiveness of both total exports and total manufacturing exports? We examine this below.

The real exchange rate and aggregate competitiveness

The real exchange rate is often viewed as the most important determinant of the overall competitiveness of an economy. We examine this relationship for aggregate competitiveness measured over all commodities (CMSA) and over manufacturing commodities (CMSM) as estimated earlier using the CMS methodology (Table 4.2). Towards this, we regress CMSA on the change in the real exchange rate (RER) (Model 1a), and on the change in the nominal exchange rate (NER) and the inflation differential between India and the US (INF) (Model 1b). Similarly, we regress CMSM on the change in the real exchange rate (RER) (Model 2a), on the change in the nominal exchange rate (NER) and the inflation differential between India and the US (INF) (Model 2b), on the change in the sector-specific real exchange rate (RERM) (Model 2c), and, finally, on NER and on the sector-specific inflation differential between India and the US (INFM) (Model 2d). A linear functional form was specified and estimated using ordinary least squares (OLS) over the period 1971–92.

For CMSA, the change in RER is positive and significant at the 5 per cent level, albeit with a lag (Model 1a). The current change in RER was found to be insignificant. Decomposing the RER into its components, we find that it is the change in NER with a lag that explains the variations in CMSA (Model 1b). Similarly, for CMSM, the change in RER is positive and significant with a lag (Model 2a), with the decomposition again indicating that it is the change in NER that matters (Model 2b). Further, sector-specific RER does not have as much explanatory power as the economy-wide RER (Models 2c and 2d).

As noted earlier, India has followed an active exchange rate policy to boost exports since the mid-1980s. The evidence above shows that such a policy has indeed been effective. With a shift towards a more market-determined exchange rate since 1991 however, such a policy option may no longer be available.

Table 4.2 Real and nominal exchange rate, inflation differentials and competitiveness

Dependent variable	Explanatory variables						$\bar{R}^2$	D–W
	Constant	$\Delta RER(-1)$	$\Delta RERM(-1)$	$\Delta NER(-1)$	$\Delta INF(-1)$	$\Delta INFM(-1)$		
ΔCMSA (1a)	−58,864.2 (−0.32)	439,952.2 (3.01)*					0.287	1.846
ΔCMSA (1b)	−216,538.0 (−0.99)			7,520,050.0 (3.28)*	−2,184,505.0 (−0.59)		0.309	2.007
ΔCMSM (2a)	−17,959.2 (−0.13)	316,787.7 (2.99)*					0.285	2.797
ΔCMSM (2b)	−97,534.9 (−0.59)			5,047,609.0 (2.92)*	−2,036,369.0 (−0.74)		0.247	3.006
ΔCMSM (2c)	−6,400.6 (−0.04)		476,982.1 (2.36)*				0.185	2.795
ΔCMSM (2d)	−133,039.6 (−0.81)			4,640,995.0 (2.67)*		2,650.5 (0.001)	0.225	3.073

Notes: t-tests are reported in brackets; * indicates significance at the 5 per cent level.
ΔCMSA: change in competitiveness − all commodities; ΔCMSM: change in competitiveness − manufacturing; ΔRER(−1): 1 period lag in change in real exchange rate − all commodities; ΔRERM(−1): 1 period lag in change in real exchange rate − manufacturing; ΔNER(−1): 1 period lag in change in nominal exchange rate; ΔINF(−1): 1 period lag in change in inflation differential between India and USA − all commodities; ΔINFM(−1): 1 period lag in change in inflation differential between India and USA − manufacturing.

Trade specialisation patterns

Data

The database used is obtained from the International Economic Data Bank (IEDB) at the Australian National University and provides trade and industry data at the ISIC four-digit level. The source of the industry data is UNIDO's *Industrial Statistics* databank, which in turn is compiled from the *Annual Survey of Industries* published by the Central Statistical Organisation, India. The export data is obtained from the United Nations *Trade Database* and uses a commodity concordance developed by the United Nations and further refined by the IEDB. The commodity concordance involves a mapping from the SITC classification system used by the *Trade Database* of the United Nations in reporting export data to the ISIC classification system used by the UNIDO in reporting industry data. While all the commodities that are usually included in the SITC definition of manufacturing exports (SITC 5 to 8 less 68) have been reclassified according to their industry of origin at the ISIC four-digit level, the ISIC classification contains some additional commodities not included in the SITC classification. As is well known, one limitation of the SITC classification of manufacturing exports is that it excludes processed food items and tobacco products (which are included in SITC 0 and 1). In contrast, the ISIC (i.e. industry-based) classification of manufacturing includes all such commodities in ISIC 311 (food products), 313 (beverages) and 314 (tobacco products). Furthermore, the ISIC classification of manufacturing also includes non-ferrous metals (ISIC 372), which are usually excluded from the SITC-based classification of manufacturing. Therefore, the coverage of manufacturing exports using the ISIC-based definition (i.e. the definition used in this chapter) may be considered to be more comprehensive than the more commonly used SITC-based definition.

Export shares and indices of revealed comparative advantage

In Table 4.3, we present the top two dozen commodities (at the ISIC four-digit level) in terms of export shares in India's total manufacturing exports over the period 1971–96. It is evident from the table that the shares of ISIC 3211 (spinning, weaving and finishing of textiles) and ISIC 3231 (tanneries and leather finishing) have declined significantly in the period under consideration from a total of around 34 per cent in 1971–5 to less than 14 per cent in 1991–6. On the other hand, the shares of ISIC 3220 (wearing apparel excluding footwear) and ISIC 3901 (jewellery and related articles) have increased in this period from a total of less than 8 per cent in 1971–5 to around 32 per cent in 1991–6. Basic industrial chemicals (excluding fertilisers, ISIC 3511) also seem to be increasingly important in India's manufactured export basket over time. The shares of most other commodities do not show any significant change in trend over the period 1971–96. It is also evident from Table 4.3 that these twenty-four commodities have consistently accounted for more than 85 per cent of the manufacturing

Table 4.3 Export shares of select commodities

ISIC Industry code and name	1971–5	1976–80	1981–5	1986–90	1991–6
3111-SLGHTRG, PREP, PRESERV MEAT	1.2	1.6	1.7	1.0	0.8
3115-MANUF VEG, ANL OILS+FATS	7.3	4.6	3.1	2.6	3.8
3116-GRAIN MILL PRODUCTS	3.1	6.4	7.8	4.6	4.1
3118-SUGAR FACTORIES REFINERS	7.0	3.5	1.3	0.1	0.5
3121-MANUF OF FOOD PRODS NEC	1.1	1.3	1.3	0.9	0.6
3211-SPINNG, WEAVG, FINSHG TEXTS	24.6	14.8	12.3	10.5	11.9
3212-MAN MDUP TXT GDS EX WEARG APP	7.5	3.4	2.7	1.3	0.8
3214-CARPETS	2.0	3.0	4.3	3.9	3.3
3220-MANUF WEARG APP EX FTWR	4.9	10.1	13.7	18.0	19.7
3231-TANNERIES, LTHER FINISHNG	9.2	7.9	5.7	4.4	1.7
3233-MAN PRODS LTER EXC FWR, APP	0.3	0.4	0.9	1.4	1.7
3240-MAN FTWR EX RUBBR, PLASTC	0.9	1.3	2.9	3.7	2.8
3511-BASIC IND CHEMS EXC FERT	1.5	1.7	1.8	3.8	5.3
3522-DRUGS+MEDICINES	0.8	1.3	2.5	2.6	2.6
3523-SOAP, CLNS PRPS, PERF, COSM	0.4	0.7	1.4	1.0	0.7
3530-PETROLEUM REFINERIES	0.8	0.5	4.2	6.9	2.5
3710-IRON+STEEL BAS INDS	4.2	6.5	1.2	1.7	3.8
3720-NON-FER METAL BASIC IND	2.5	2.5	0.4	0.5	0.9
3819-FAB MET PRD EX MACH EQP NEC	1.2	2.1	1.6	1.1	1.5
3824-SPEC IND MACH+ EQP EX 3823	0.9	1.0	1.3	1.4	0.9
3829-MACH, EQUIP EX ELECT NEC	0.9	1.2	1.2	0.9	1.1
3839-ELEC APPAR+ SUPPLIES NEC	0.9	1.0	1.4	1.1	0.5
3843-MOTOR VEHICLES	1.8	2.6	2.6	1.9	2.4
3901-JEWELRY+RELATED ARTICLES	3.0	6.4	9.4	13.1	12.1
Cumulative share of the above 24 commodities	88.0	85.8	86.7	88.4	86.0

Note: Export share of industry i = (export of industry i/India's total manufacturing exports) $*$ 100.

exports during this period. This seems to suggest that India's manufacturing exports have not diversified over the past twenty-five years.

We computed the revealed comparative advantage (RCA)[10] of India's manufacturing exports for each year over the period 1971–96.[11] The RCA computations showed that for a vast majority of industries, India is just not competitive in export markets as indicated by RCAs that are less than 1 over the entire period. In the post-1991 period, India was most competitive in ISIC 3901 (jewellery), followed by ISIC 3214 (carpets). In the case of jewellery, in particular, the increase in RCA has been dramatic, from 2.4 in 1971–5 to 12.8 in 1991–6. Other commodities whose export competitiveness has been increasing over the period 1971–96 are ISIC 3116 (grain mill products), ISIC 3220 (manufacture of wearing apparel excluding footwear), ISIC 3233 (manufacture of leather excluding footwear, apparel) and ISIC 3551 (tire and tube industries). Commodities with declining competitiveness are ISIC 3212 (manufacture of made-up textile goods excluding wearing apparel) and ISIC 3231 (tanneries and leather finishing).

Winner and loser sectors

In order to determine which industries 'gained' and which industries 'lost' in competitiveness, we adopt a non-parametric approach involving essentially a *t*-test (and an associated *F*-test) on the sample mean of RCAs across different subperiods of interest. The theme of the *t*-test is to split the whole time series of RCAs into two subsamples (say, Period I and Period II), compute the means of the series over the subsamples and test for equality or inequality of these two subsample means. At a given level of significance, a significant positive (negative) *t*-statistic would indicate a significant increase (decrease) in the mean level of the RCAs in Period II compared to Period I. An insignificant *t*-statistic would indicate equality of the mean level of the RCAs between the two subperiods, i.e. the RCAs are more or less constant over the full sample. The mathematical expression for the test statistic can be found in Brockett and Levine (1984) and Kanji (1993).

As we have noted in Section 1, the Indian economy has undergone two sets of reforms in the recent past, once in 1985, and the second in 1991. To see whether these two rounds of reforms have had any discernible effect on external competitiveness of the Indian manufacturing sector, we conduct the *t*-test on the sample means of RCAs once between the periods 1970–84 and 1985–91 and a second time between the periods 1985–91 and 1992–6. An industry whose RCA showed a significant increase (decrease) is considered to be a 'winner' ('loser') industry over the relevant period. Industries whose RCA did not show a significant change are considered to be 'stagnant'. We confine the *t*-tests to those industries which had RCAs greater than one for at least one of the subperiods. The results are tabulated in Table 4.4. A summary of these results is reported in Table 4.5.

From these results it is clear that some industries have gained in competitiveness while others have lost following the two rounds of reforms. Furthermore, there have been more winners than losers after the 1991 reforms as compared to the earlier reforms of 1985. Only one industry, namely leather products (excluding

Table 4.4 t-Test on sample means of RCAs

ISIC Industry code and name	Sample mean		t-statistic	Significance level (%)	Sample mean		t-statistic	Significance level (%)
	1970–84	1985–91			1985–91	1992–6		
3115-MANUF VEG, ANL OILS+FATS	3.8139	3.0220	−1.58	12.89	3.0220	4.8482	2.33	4.20
3116-GRAIN MILL PRODUCTS	3.8752	5.9993	3.41	0.34	5.9993	7.6897	1.44	21.04
3118-SUGAR FACTORIES REFINERS	3.3591	0.5569	−4.09	0.08	0.5569	1.8683	2.31	6.01
3121-MANUF OF FOOD PRODS NEC	2.7737	1.8439	−3.44	0.88	1.8439	1.0759	−2.81	2.29
3211-SPINNG, WEAVG, FINSHG TEXTS	5.0223	3.6114	−4.15	0.05	3.6114	4.4774	2.14	5.78
3212-MAN MDUP TXT GDS EX WEARG APP	17.4034	6.5477	−5.24	0.01	6.5477	3.8569	−3.56	0.92
3213-KNITTING MILLS	—	—	—	—	0.8682	1.0096	0.45	66.15
3214-CARPETS	8.3973	12.8104	4.75	0.02	12.8104	12.3311	−0.48	64.17
3215-CORDAGE ROPE, TWINE INDS	—	—	—	—	0.5291	1.7030	6.62	0.01
3220-MANUF WEARG APP EX FTWR	3.1098	4.9518	5.24	0.00	4.9518	5.0752	0.33	75.05
3231-TANNERIES, LTHER FINISHNG	25.5586	13.4599	−2.89	0.91	13.4599	5.0011	−5.09	0.14
3233-MAN PRODS LTER EXC FWR, APP	2.0642	4.9482	2.84	1.01	4.9482	5.9971	2.28	4.58
3240-MAN FTWR EX RUBBR, PLASTC	1.9479	3.9214	8.61	0.00	3.9214	3.1289	−8.39	0.00
3511-BASIC IND CHEMS EXC FERT	—	—	—	—	0.7722	1.2161	3.13	1.21
3521-PAINTS, VARNISH LACQUERS	1.2697	1.4107	0.36	72.37	1.4107	0.1447	−7.22	0.02
3522-DRUGS+MEDICINES	1.3252	2.1755	1.18	25.03	2.1755	1.5513	−1.20	25.65
3523-SOAP, CLNS PRPS, PERF, COSM	1.8687	1.8269	−0.09	92.98	1.8269	0.7205	−3.98	0.26
3530-PETROLEUM REFINERIES	0.2373	1.7062	4.90	0.17	1.7062	0.9406	−2.54	3.88
3551-TIRE+TUBE INDUSTRIES	0.8314	1.1584	1.11	28.11	1.1584	1.7966	2.50	4.66
3692-CEMENT, LIME AND PLASTER	1.1028	0.4034	−2.45	2.47	0.4034	2.0359	2.77	3.96
3699-NON-MET MINL PRODS NEC	1.2433	0.8894	−1.17	25.72	0.8894	2.0929	5.32	0.11
3710-IRON+STEEL BAS INDS	—	—	—	—	0.4119	1.1236	4.07	0.23
3811-CUTLY, HAND TLS, GEN HDWRE	1.3135	1.0637	−2.41	2.81	1.1584	1.7966	2.50	4.66
3813-STRUCTURAL METAL PRODUCTS	1.0962	0.6143	−5.05	0.01	—	—	—	—
3819-FAB MET PRD EX MACH EQP NEC	1.1295	0.8542	−2.63	1.57	0.8542	1.0363	1.15	27.74
3844-MOTOR CYCLES+BICYCLES	2.1411	2.2228	0.16	87.62	2.2228	2.5623	0.72	48.61
3901-JEWELRY+RELATED ARTICLES	5.8760	13.3393	9.55	0.00	13.3393	12.7182	−0.57	57.87
3903-SPORTING+ATHLETIC GOODS	1.9433	1.1650	−3.37	0.29	1.1650	0.9652	−1.54	16.19

Note: t-Tests were done only for those industries for which the average RCA is greater than one in at least one of the subperiods.

Table 4.5 Winner and loser industries

1985–91 over 1970–84	1992–6 over 1985–91		
	Winners	Losers	Stagnant
Winners	Man Prods Lter Exc Fwr, App	Petroleum Refineries Man Footwear Ex Rubber, Plastics	Grain Mill Products Carpets Manuf Wearing App Ex Footwear Jewelry + Related Articles
Losers	Spinning, Weaving, Finishing Texts Cutly, Hand Tls, General Hardware Sugar Factories Refiners Fab Met Prd Ex Mach Eqp Nec	Manuf of Food Prods Nec Man Mdup Txt Gds Ex Wearing App Tanneries, Leather Finishing	Sporting + Athletic Goods
Stagnant	Manuf Veg, Anl Oils + Fats Tire + Tube Industries	Paints, Varnish Lacquers Soap, Clns Prps, Perfumes, Cosm	Drugs + Medicines Motor Cycles + Bicycles

footwear and apparel), has been winning over both rounds of reforms. In contrast, three industries have lost in both rounds of reforms. These are food products (NEC), textile goods (excluding wearing apparel) and product of tanneries and leather finishing. There have been some industries which gained in one round of reforms but lost in another round, such as footwear (excluding rubber and plastics) and sugar factories. One possible explanation for this could be that these industries may have gained/lost (as the case may be) due to inter-industry effects of the reform measures that dominated the direct effects of reforms.

Evolution of labour productivity and unit labour costs

It is well recognised in the literature that a key determinant of external competitiveness is unit labour costs (see Fagerberg 1988). To what extent this hypothesis is relevant in the Indian context is of great significance given that India is perceived to be a labour-surplus economy. There has been a significant increase in labour productivity in the manufacturing sector since the early 1980s, with a levelling off in the 1990s (Figure 4.5). Real wages followed labour productivity for much of the 1970s and 1980s, leading to no perceptible change in unit labour costs during this period. In the late 1980s however, there was a slight decline in unit labour costs in the manufacturing sector, as labour productivity growth overtook growth in real wage per worker. In the early 1990s, with stagnation in labour productivity, unit labour costs began to increase. We observe that the movements in unit labour costs during the 1980s and early 1990s seem to have a fairly strong negative correlation with India's market share in world manufacturing exports.

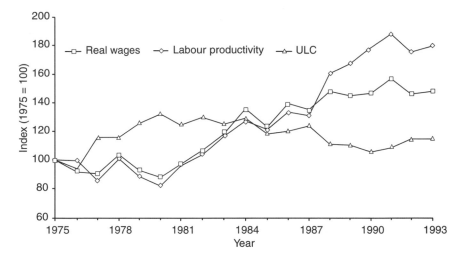

Figure 4.5 Labour productivity, real wages and unit labour costs (ULC).

During the early 1980s, with little change in unit labour costs, there was no significant change in India's market share. With the decline in unit labour costs in the late 1980s, India's market share improved. Finally, in the early 1990s, with a slight increase in unit labour costs, there was a fall in India's market share. There is preliminary evidence, then, that at the aggregate level, the behaviour of unit labour costs may have played an important role in determining India's international competitiveness in the period under consideration.

Data on changes in unit labour costs by industry show that there is no consistent pattern on unit labour cost growth across industries (Table 4.6). In keeping with the trend in unit labour costs at the aggregate level however, a larger proportion of industries witnessed declining unit labour costs in the period 1986–90 as compared to the periods 1982–5 and 1991–2. The correlation coefficients between growth in unit labour costs and the change in RCAs across industries indicate that for the period 1982–5, growth in unit labour costs in a particular industry may be negatively correlated with the change in the international competitiveness of that industry (the correlation coefficient between the two is −0.25). On the other hand, there is little correlation between growth in unit labour costs and the change in RCAs for the other two subperiods. Moreover, when we attempted to relate changes in unit labour costs with the classification of industries into winners and losers, no discernible pattern emerged at the sectoral level on the linkage between domestic costs and export competitiveness (see Table 4.6). It should be noted nonetheless that such an analysis is *incomplete* until we can compare the evolution of unit labour costs at the sectoral level in India with a world norm. Clearly, what is of relevance for export competitiveness of a particular sector is the relative movement of its domestic costs with respect to the

Table 4.6 Percentage change in unit labour costs (ULC), India, 1982–92

ISIC Industry code and name	1982–5	1986–90	1991–2	Winner/loser	
				1985–91 over 1970–84	1992–6 over 1985–91
3111-SLGHTRG, PREP, PRESERV MEAT	0.23	−0.03	−0.23	—	
3112-MANUF OF DAIRY PRODUCTS	0.27	−0.03	0.34		
3113-CANNG, PRES FRUITS VEGS	−0.03	0.15	−0.04		
3114-CAN, PRES, PRS OF FISH, CRUS	0.06	0.04	0.16		
3115-MANUF VEG, ANL OILS+FATS	0.00	0.16	0.37	Stagnant	Winner
3116-GRAIN MILL PRODUCTS	0.08	0.14	0.32	Winner	Stagnant
3117-MANUF OF BAKERY PRODUCTS	0.15	0.07	0.21		—
3118-SUGAR FACTORIES REFINERS	−0.10	0.13	0.15	Loser	Winner
3119-MANUF COCOA, CHOC+SUG CONF	0.01	−0.57	0.34		
3121-MANUF OF FOOD PRODS NEC	−0.07	0.16	0.40	Loser	Loser
3122-MANUF OF PREPD ANL FEEDS	0.12	0.10	0.37		
3131-DISTG, RECTG, BLENG SPIRITS	0.16	0.09	0.28		
3132-WINE INDUSTRIES	0.10	0.25	−0.50		
3133-MALT LIQUORS AND MALT	0.14	0.04	0.44		
3134-SFT DRNKS+CARB WTRS IND	0.12	−0.02	0.08		
3140-TOBACCO MANUFACTURES	−0.01	0.06	0.23		
3211-SPINNNG, WEAVG, FINSHG TEXTS	0.07	0.02	0.27	Loser	Winner
3212-MAN MDUP TXT GDS EX WEARG APP	N/A	0.38[a]	0.22	Loser	Loser
3213-KNITTING MILLS	0.17	0.15	0.20		
3214-CARPETS	N/A	−0.73[a]	−0.21	Winner	Stagnant
3215-CORDAGE ROPE, TWINE INDS	N/A	0.30[a]	−0.05		
3219-MANUF OF TEXTILES, NEC	N/A	−0.07[a]	0.27		
3220-MANUF WEARG APP EX FTWR	0.12	0.08	0.35	Winner	Stagnant
3231-TANNERIES, LTHER FINISHNG	0.12	−0.02	0.28	Loser	Loser

Industry					
3240-MAN FTWR EX RUBBR, PLASTC	0.10	0.11	0.18	Winner	Loser
3311-SAWMLS, PLNG OTH WD MILLS	0.10	0.00	0.28		
3312-MAN WD, CNE CNTS, SML CNWR	−0.08	0.02	0.33		
3319-MAN WOOD CORK PRODS NEC	0.05	0.04	0.35		
3320-MAN FURN, FIXT EX PRIM MTL	0.16	−0.01	0.29		
3411-MAN PULP, PAPER, PAPERBOARD	0.14	−0.02	0.30		
3412-MAN CONTS, BXES PPR, P/BRD	0.17	−0.03	0.47		
3419-MAN ART PULP, PPR, P/BRD NEC	−0.09	0.33	0.19		
3420-PRNTNG, PUBLNG ALLIED IND	0.07	0.07	0.07		
3511-BASIC IND CHEMS EXC FERT	0.20	0.00	0.39		
3512-FERTILISERS PESTICIDES	0.10	0.11	0.04		
3513-SYN RESINS ETC EXC GLASS	0.01	0.12	−0.01		Loser
3521-PAINTS, VARNISH LACQUERS	0.11	0.02	0.22	Stagnant	
3522-DRUGS+MEDICINES	0.07	0.07	0.24	Stagnant	Stagnant
3523-SOAP, CLNS PRPS, PERF, COSM	0.08	0.07	0.10	Stagnant	Loser
3529-CHEMICAL PRODUCTS NEC	0.10	−0.01	0.25		
3530-PETROLEUM REFINERIES	0.09	−0.02	0.20	Winner	Loser
3540-MISC PRODS OF PETR, COAL	0.15	0.14	0.13		
3551-TIRE+TUBE INDUSTRIES	−0.10	0.20	0.13		Winner
3559-MANUF OF RUBBER PRODS NEC	0.05	0.03	0.42	Stagnant	
3560-PLASTICS PRODUCTS NEC	0.05	0.14	0.31		
3610-POTTERY, CHINA, EARTHWARE	0.24	−0.02	0.22		
3620-GLASS+GLASS PRODUCTS	0.00	0.08	0.24		
3691-STRUCTURAL CLAY PRODUCTS	0.20	0.06	0.13		
3692-CEMENT, LIME AND PLASTER	−0.06	0.04	0.45		
3699-NON-MET MINL PRODS NEC	0.09	0.08	0.22		
3710-IRON+STEEL BAS INDS	0.11	−0.01	0.32		
3720-NON-FER METAL BASIC IND	0.10	0.13	0.21		
3811-CUTLY, HAND TLS, GEN HDWRE	0.08	0.04	0.14	Loser	Winner
3812-FURN+FIXT PRIM OF METAL	0.05	0.04	0.71		
3813-STRUCTURAL METAL PRODUCTS	0.09	0.30	0.10		
3819-FAB MET PRD EX MACH EQP NEC	0.09	0.07	0.28	Loser	Winner

Table 4.6 Continued

ISIC Industry code and name	1982–5	1986–90	1991–2	Winner/loser	
				1985–91 over 1970–84	1992–6 over 1985–91
3821-ENGINES+TURBINES	0.07	0.07	0.08		
3822-AGRIC MACHINERY AND EQUIP	0.14	0.04	0.32		
3823-METAL+WOODWORKING EQUIP	0.14	0.03	0.29		
3824-SPEC IND MACH+EQP EX 3823	0.04	0.08	0.20		
3825-OFF, COMPUTG, ACCOUNTG MACH	0.06	0.25	0.16		
3829-MACH, EQUIP EX ELECT NEC	0.12	0.10	0.13		
3831-ELEC IND MACH+APPARATUS	0.11	0.06	0.24		
3832-RADIO, TELE, COMM EQP, APPAR	0.13	0.11	0.08		
3833-ELEC APPLNCS+HOUSEWARES	0.11	–0.09	0.28		
3839-ELEC APPAR+SUPPLIES NEC	0.16	0.02	0.14		
3841-SHIPBUILDING+REPAIRING	0.11	–0.14	0.25		
3842-RAILROAD EQUIPMENT	0.08	0.01	0.33		
3843-MOTOR VEHICLES	0.10	0.17	0.31		
3844-MOTOR CYCLES+BICYCLES	0.14	0.10	0.22	Stagnant	Stagnant
3845-AIRCRAFT	0.02	0.10	0.24		
3849-TRANSPORT EQUIPMENT NEC	0.24	0.25	0.01		
3851-PROF, SCIEN, MSRG, CNTRL EQU	0.05	0.08	0.20		
3852-PROF, SC, MSRG, CONT EQU NEC	0.02	0.26	0.46		

3853-WATCHES+CLOCKS	0.21	0.13	0.36	Stagnant
3901-JEWELRY+RELATED ARTICLES	-0.19	0.53	-0.30	Winner
3902-MUSICAL INSTRUMENTS	-0.39	0.35	0.02	
3903-SPORTING+ATHLETIC GOODS	0.04	0.04	0.20	Loser
3909-MANUF INDUSTRIES NEC	-0.03	0.12	0.21	Stagnant
Correlation with change in RCA	-0.253	0.072	0.006	

Notes
a Some years are not available and the average has been adjusted for missing data.
N/A: data not available.

domestic costs of the destination country and that of other competitors in the same sector.

Alternate measures of trade patterns

Hitherto, our analysis has been based on an implicit assumption that trade specialisation is based on comparative advantage emanating from perfectly competitive domestic and international markets. In reality however, markets, both in India and abroad, would generally be characterised by product differentiation and economies of scale. We look at two measures of competitiveness that incorporate such assumptions.

Measures of intra-industry trade[12]

If a significant proportion of the industrial sector is characterised by imperfect competition, measures of intra-industry trade may indicate the extent of product differentiation and the presence of economies of scale in a particular industry. Furthermore, with trade reforms, one would expect an increase in the share of intra-industry trade in total industry trade as firms specialise in the production of certain products and not in others within an industry group (Helpman and Krugman 1989). As is clear from Figure 4.6, there has been a significant increase in aggregate intra-industry trade in the Indian manufacturing sector since the mid-1980s. Interestingly, one notes a slight downturn in total intra-industry trade in the mid-1990s. Measures of intra-industry trade by industry[13] show that the industries with the highest share of intra-industry trade in total trade (0.8 and above) are ISIC 3215 (cordage, rope and twine industries), 3311 (sawmills, plying mills), 3312 (wooden and cane containers), 3521 (paints, varnishes, lacquers), 3620 (glass and

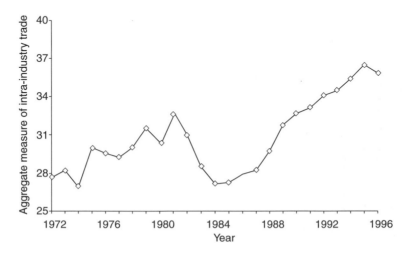

Figure 4.6 Aggregate intra-industry trade.

glass products), 3691 (structural clay products), 3710 (iron and steel basic indus-tries), 3819 (fabricated metal products), 3831 (electrical industrial machinery), 3833 (electrical apparatus and supplies) and 3843 (motor vehicles).[14] It is an open issue, however, to what extent the high volumes of intra-industry trade evident in these industries are due to the existence of scale economies and differentiated products or due to industry classifications that are not comprehensive enough (see Loertscher and Wolter 1980).

Technological complexity of exports

A classification of India's manufactured exports by technological complexity indi-cates that India's manufactured exports are very much at the low end of the 'tech-nology spectrum' (Table 4.7).[15] Labour-intensive and resource-based products are the two dominant categories in India's manufacturing export basket. There has been some increase in the total share of scale-intensive, differentiated and science-based products in India's manufacturing exports from 18.1 per cent in 1980 to 23.2 in 1995. Nonetheless, it is far below that of China (38.4 per cent), Malaysia (79 per cent) and Thailand (53.6 per cent).[16] A closer look at the 'winners' in either of the two subperiods, 1985–91 and 1992–6, shows that these are either labour-intensive, resource-intensive or scale-intensive products.

The comparison with China is particularly revealing. As of 1995, 9.7 per cent and 16.3 per cent of China's manufactured exports were in science-based goods and differentiated products, respectively, as compared to 5 per cent and 4.1 per cent for India. Differentiated products are technology-intensive engineering prod-ucts while science-based products use leading-edge technologies (Lall 1998). Both these types of goods could be classified as 'high technology'. While China and India are both large labour-surplus economies with comparative advantage in labour-intensive manufactures, China is also diversifying into the low-medium technology end of export-oriented activity, with India doing poorly in this area. Clearly, the relatively slow progress in 'climbing up the technology ladder' with respect to exports may act as a constraint on India's long-term export perform-ance and growth potential.

The evidence presented in this section does not allow for an unequivocal inter-pretation of the role of price factors in determining India's external competitiveness.

Table 4.7 Distribution of manufactured exports by technological complexity (%)

Category	1980	1995
Resource based	26.5	31.4
Labour intensive	55.4	45.3
Scale intensive	11.2	13.5
Differentiated	4.1	4.7
Science based	2.8	5.0

Source: Lall (1998).

While at the aggregate level, the real exchange rate and unit labour costs seem to have a definite link with external competitiveness in the Indian context, the picture is far less clear at the sectoral level. This may indicate the importance of firm-level and industry-level non-price factors that may impinge on export performance. We explore in the next section one important determinant of competitiveness at the firm level, namely the availability of external finance. This factor acquires greater significance in the context of the wide-ranging reforms in the Indian financial sector since 1991.

3. Competitiveness and finance

There is widespread agreement in the literature that price competitiveness is a necessary but not a sufficient condition for export success. Among the non-price factors, the ones most commonly identified in Indian policy discussions are technology upgradation, product quality and infrastructural bottlenecks. One non-price factor that has received less attention, however, is the financial environment, i.e. the extent to which the financial sector provides an enabling environment for successful export performance. In the context of this study, an important question that arises is whether there has been any relationship between export performance of firms and financial factors in the Indian context. This question can be framed in two parts. First, is there a systematic relationship between export performance and the financing patterns? Here, we classify firms in certain selected industries into three categories, namely 'domestic firms', 'winning exporters' and 'losing exporters'. For each of these categories, we study the *Sources and Uses of Fund Statements* as well as a few other financial performance indicators to look for differences in their financing patterns and financial performance.

Second, do successful exporters face less information-based capital market imperfections than the not-so-successful exporters? Modern theories of finance which attempt to explain differences in financing patterns across firms emphasise differences in costs associated with different providers of funds. It stresses the lack of substitutability between internal sources (retained profits and depreciation) and external sources (different types of debt and new equity) of funds. This imperfect substitutability arises primarily due to asymmetric information between the suppliers and users of funds and incentive problems between managers and owners of the firm. It has generally been argued that these information asymmetries and incentive problems make external funds more costly than internal funds. In the new equity markets, this manifests as a 'lemons premia' (as pointed out by Myers and Majluf 1984) and in credit markets as credit rationing or loan mis-pricing (as pointed out by Stiglitz and Weiss 1981, and others). Further, this view contends that the cost differential between internal and external funds would vary across firms depending upon the extent of the information asymmetry. Besides, this view also suggests that simple transaction costs might also vary across firms. The implication of a higher cost of external funds is that internal funds would be more important than external funds in financing investments. Clearly, to the extent that a firm is forced to depend on internal sources for investment, its growth is said to be finance constrained.

If exporting firms are finance constrained then this would be a major impediment to sustaining their competitiveness in international markets.

In what follows, we explore this hypothesis by estimating investment functions which explicitly allow for the presence of finance constraints, i.e. models that allow the costs of internal and external sources of finance to be different (see Hubbard (1997) and, in the Indian context, see Athey and Laumas (1994)).

Classification of firms

Classification of firms into the above three categories proceeds as follows: firms are first categorised as 'domestic firms' and 'exporting firms' based on the share of exports in their total sales. If the exports to sales ratio of a firm exceeds 5 per cent over more than half the number of years in the sample period, then the firm is considered to be an 'exporting firm' whereas it is a 'domestic firm' otherwise. The reasoning behind this first level of categorisation is that there exist a large number of firms even in the tradable sector (be they winner or loser industries) who primarily sell only in the domestic market.[17] Issues such as export competitiveness obviously are of little relevance to these 'domestic firms'. 'Exporting firms' are then further classified into 'winning exporters' and 'losing exporters' based on a comparison of the annual growth rates of their exports *vis-à-vis* the annual growth rate of exports for the industry to which they belong. If the growth rate of exports of a firm exceeds the industry export growth rate for more than half the number of years in the sample period, then the firm is classified as a 'winning exporter'; otherwise it is considered a 'losing exporter'. It may be noted here that this way of classifying exporting firms into winners and losers is largely consistent with the procedure adopted earlier for classifying industries.[18]

Furthermore, this procedure allows for the possible existence of winning exporters within a losing industry and vice versa. Consider, for example, a losing industry (the analogy runs similarly for winning industries also), i.e. an Indian industry whose exports are growing but whose RCA is falling over time.[19] The growth rate of exports of some firms in this industry may be higher than the industry average. We consider such a firm to be a winner firm as it has outperformed the industry. This indicates that there could be some firm-specific characteristics (unobserved as yet) that enable such firms to outperform the industry. Similarly, a losing firm is one which has not been able to match the industry performance in terms of export growth, again perhaps due to certain firm-specific characteristics. We feel that it may be important to distinguish these two types of firms.

This analysis is done for firms belonging to five industries. Earlier, we have identified 'winner' and 'loser' industries based on whether their RCAs have been increasing or falling over time, respectively. Three winner industries from that classification, namely ISIC 3220 (manufactured wearing apparels excluding footwear), ISIC 3511 (basic industrial chemicals excluding fertiliser) and ISIC 3901 (jewellery and related articles), and two loser industries, ISIC 3211 (spinning, weaving, finished textiles) and ISIC 3839 (electrical apparatus and supplies NEC), have been selected for this analysis. The average share of these industries in total exports over the period 1991–6 was 19.7 per cent, 5.3 per cent, 12.1 per cent, 11.9 per cent and 0.5 per cent, respectively (see Table 4.3).

The database used is PROWESS provided by CMIE, Mumbai. The PROWESS names for the above industries are readymade garments, industrial chemicals, gems and jewellery, cotton textiles and electrical machinery, respectively. It must be noted that the mapping from ISIC to PROWESS may not be perfect. Only those firms for which data are available for all the years of the sample period are considered for the analysis here. Table 4.8 reports the number of firms in the balanced panel for the three categories for the sample period, 1993–7.

Descriptive statistics on financial variables

The indicators of the financial performance of firms used here are assets, export–sales ratio and profitability ratio (profit before interest, depreciation and taxes to sales). Movements in these indicators over the time period 1993–7 are studied by pooling firms across industries within each category. We present in Table 4.9 the average values of these variables. It may be noted that these summary statistics for the 'exporters' reported in these tables are estimated over winning and losing exporters combined. The following broad conclusions emerge:

1   The average size and the rate of growth in assets are found to be the lowest for domestic firms. Among exporters, winning exporters outperform the losing exporters in both average asset size and growth.
2   The export to sales ratio, which was similar for both winning exporters and losing exporters at the beginning of the period, grew for the former while it fell for the latter.
3   Winners and domestic firms, on an average, have been more profitable than the losers. Moreover, this ratio has been more or less stable over the years for all three groups.
4   We also found that the correlations between assets (i.e. firm size), profitability and the export to sales ratio were all insignificant.[20]

The above patterns must, however, be interpreted with caution as all these three variables show substantial variation across firms within the groups for each year.

Table 4.8 Sample size (sample period: 1993–7)

	Domestic	Winner	Loser	Total
Ready-made garments	0	4	3	7
Cotton textiles (cloth)	13	12	10	35
Electrical machinery	58	19	9	86
Industrial chemicals	44	15	11	70
Gems and jewellery	0	2	4	6
Total	115	52	37	204

Note: The number of exporting firms equals the sum of winners and losers.

Table 4.9 Firm characteristics

Average over firms	Firm type	1993	1994	1995	1996	1997
Assets	Domestic	70.56	93.64	121.54	151.38	183.38
	Winners	100.68	132.79	186.08	235.81	264.39
	Losers	73.78	99.22	131.38	156.97	169.08
	Exporters	89.50	118.84	163.34	203.04	224.77
Export to sales ratio	Domestic	0.01	0.01	0.01	0.01	0.01
	Winners	0.25	0.27	0.29	0.31	0.32
	Losers	0.26	0.28	0.26	0.24	0.23
	Exporters	0.26	0.28	0.28	0.28	0.28
Profitability ratio	Domestic	0.16	0.16	0.17	0.17	0.06
	Winners	0.16	0.17	0.13	0.17	0.15
	Losers	0.15	0.14	0.15	0.15	0.12
	Exporters	0.15	0.16	0.14	0.16	0.14

Source: Firm-level data are from PROWESS, CMIE, Mumbai. The aggregates reported are based on the authors' calculations.

With the exception of profitability, the other two variables have coefficients of variation greater than 1.0.

We now examine the sources and uses of funds to see if there are differences in the financing pattern of firms in these three categories. The sources and uses of funds statements for the domestic firms, and all exporters (winners and losers) are reported in Table 4.10. These statements for winning exporters and losing exporters are reported in Table 4.11. The following broad patterns emerge:

1   In 1993, the average amount of funds raised and used was more or less identical across the three groups. Over time, however, winning exporters on an average have been able to raise more funds from various sources than losing exporters and domestic firms.

2   Across all the three groups and over the entire period, external sources are the most important, accounting for more than 60 per cent of the funds raised.[21] For domestic firms, the importance of internal sources has risen by over 10 percentage points. For winning exporters, the importance of internal sources has fallen over time by around 5 percentage points. For losing exporters, no clear pattern is found in the share of internal sources.

3   Within external sources, funds raised through capital markets have been most significant for the winning exporters.

4   On an average, borrowings have been more important for domestic firms and losing exporters than for winning exporters.

5   The share of gross fixed assets in the uses of funds has risen substantially for the winning exporters. There seems to be no discernible trend for losing exporters and for domestic firms.

The broad conclusions above seem to suggest that exporters as a group are likely to be less financially constrained than domestic firms. Further, it is likely that winning

Table 4.10 Sources and uses of funds – domestic and exporting firms

	Domestic firms					Exporting firms				
	1993	1994	1995	1996	1997	1993	1994	1995	1996	1997
Sources of funds										
Internal sources	23.9	26.1	34.7	39.1	32.0	29.9	25.1	22.7	27.1	33.1
Retained profits	10.2	20.5	22.2	27.1	15.8	14.8	15.2	14.8	16.9	7.7
Depreciation	13.7	5.6	12.6	12.0	16.2	15.1	9.9	7.9	10.2	25.4
External sources	76.1	73.9	65.3	60.9	68.0	70.1	74.9	77.3	72.9	67.0
Capital markets	34.4	40.9	30.4	7.0	14.0	39.0	47.3	41.1	12.7	27.9
Fresh capital (excl. Bonus issue)	5.4	9.4	4.3	2.9	3.1	6.7	7.0	6.2	2.4	1.9
Share premium	6.1	16.9	31.8	8.4	3.2	20.5	33.1	27.9	8.7	10.3
Debentures/bonds	23.1	14.0	−5.8	−4.2	7.2	11.4	5.3	5.1	1.6	15.3
Fixed deposits	−0.2	0.6	0.2	−0.2	0.5	0.4	2.0	1.9	0.0	0.5
Borrowings	29.9	16.7	23.3	32.8	42.7	27.4	11.2	18.5	43.3	20.9
Bank borrowings	9.5	−0.8	17.2	13.1	18.0	15.1	2.4	11.1	31.0	−4.4
Financial institutions	16.7	13.1	5.2	5.2	8.5	10.9	2.4	7.0	8.4	16.5
Loans from corporate bodies	0.5	−0.3	2.6	−0.9	3.4	2.1	−0.3	0.9	−0.2	2.6
Other borrowings	3.2	4.7	−1.6	15.4	12.8	−0.7	6.7	−0.6	4.1	6.3
Current liabilities and provisions	11.8	16.4	11.6	21.2	11.3	3.7	16.4	17.7	16.8	18.1
Sundry creditors	6.0	12.0	6.3	15.3	9.1	8.7	11.8	11.8	12.1	13.7

Uses of funds

Gross fixed assets	62.4	55.0	40.1	56.2	50.7	45.8	38.0	37.9	53.6	74.6
Work in progress	36.4	17.0	−20.0	12.4	16.2	2.0	1.9	10.4	8.9	13.5
Investments	3.8	15.2	8.2	0.0	0.5	4.1	17.5	17.2	1.4	1.6
Current assets	33.8	29.8	51.7	43.9	48.8	50.1	44.6	44.9	45.1	23.8
Inventories	7.4	2.3	14.0	11.2	9.2	18.4	11.6	13.0	13.1	4.4
Debtors	17.7	13.9	23.7	25.8	21.2	23.0	16.2	13.7	20.7	5.7
Cash and bank balances	0.9	1.1	1.0	2.1	6.8	−6.7	2.8	5.9	−1.1	7.2
Total sources/uses of funds	2,137.3	2,779.7	3,343.4	3,810.4	4,053.1	1,710.5	2,875.9	4,300.6	3,892.6	2,337.3
Total sources/uses of funds-average	18.6	24.2	29.1	33.1	35.2	19.2	32.3	48.3	43.7	26.3
Total sources/uses of funds-standard deviation	66.2	96.0	66.8	77.7	110.0	52.2	83.0	100.0	86.0	61.0
Total sources/uses of funds-minimum	−23.6	−5.5	−8.5	−7.7	−29.7	−79.2	−7.0	−6.3	−2.1	−86.4
Total sources/uses of funds-maximum	591.3	745.2	451.1	538.5	844.8	378.4	550.2	611.1	480.9	429.8
No. of companies in panel	115	115	115	115	115	89	89	89	89	89

Source: Firm-level data are from PROWESS, CMIE, Mumbai. The aggregates reported are based on authors' calculations.

Note: Individual items of sources and uses of funds are reported as percentages of the total while the rest are in Rs Crores.

Table 4.11 Sources and uses of funds – winning and losing exporters

Source of funds	Winner exporting firms					Loser exporting firms				
	1993	1994	1995	1996	1997	1993	1994	1995	1996	1997
Internal sources	29.6	27.3	21.5	24.9	23.0	30.3	21.2	25.5	32.8	70.6
Retained profits	15.1	18.6	14.0	15.8	5.8	14.5	9.3	16.7	19.6	14.9
Depreciation	14.6	8.7	7.5	9.1	17.3	15.8	12.0	8.8	13.2	55.7
External sources	70.4	72.7	78.5	75.1	77.0	69.7	78.8	74.5	67.2	29.4
Capital markets	58.0	47.2	45.0	13.6	36.3	12.8	47.5	32.4	10.4	-3.4
Fresh capital (excl. bonus issue)	9.1	6.3	6.5	3.0	2.8	3.3	8.1	5.6	1.1	-1.3
Share premium	31.5	37.3	31.4	8.0	14.8	5.3	25.8	20.0	10.6	-6.7
Debentures/bonds	17.1	2.1	4.4	2.7	17.8	3.5	10.9	6.6	-1.3	5.9
Fixed deposits	0.2	1.5	2.7	0.0	1.0	0.6	2.8	0.2	0.0	-1.3
Borrowings	21.4	7.9	15.1	43.6	29.1	35.8	16.9	26.1	42.6	-9.9
Bank borrowings	13.1	0.3	12.6	29.7	5.2	17.9	6.2	7.9	34.3	-40.5
Financial institutions	8.7	3.1	3.6	12.1	23.8	14.0	1.0	14.8	-0.9	-10.8
Loans from corporate bodies	2.0	-1.3	0.6	-0.1	0.3	2.3	1.4	1.6	-0.4	11.0
Other borrowings	-2.4	5.8	-1.6	2.0	-0.2	1.6	8.3	1.7	9.6	30.4
Current liabilities and provisions	-9.0	17.5	18.4	17.8	11.6	21.2	14.3	16.0	14.2	42.6
Sundry creditors	2.5	11.2	12.1	13.0	5.9	17.2	12.8	11.0	10.0	43.1

Uses of funds

Gross fixed assets	42.3	36.9	40.9	60.3	75.1	50.7	39.8	31.1	36.1	72.7
Work in progress	−6.7	7.6	15.7	10.7	12.5	13.8	−8.0	−1.9	4.3	16.9
Investments	6.1	13.6	9.8	−1.9	4.6	1.3	24.2	34.0	9.8	−9.6
Current assets	51.6	49.5	49.3	41.6	20.3	48.1	36.1	34.9	54.0	36.9
Inventories	19.2	12.5	11.3	14.2	6.0	17.3	10.2	16.8	10.1	−1.5
Debtors	25.2	17.5	15.9	18.5	6.8	20.0	13.9	8.6	26.2	1.4
Cash and bank balances	−13.5	3.5	7.6	−2.1	4.7	2.7	1.7	1.9	1.5	16.2
Total sources/uses of funds	991.3	1,823.4	2,988.8	2,804.9	1,844.5	719.1	1,052.5	1,311.8	1,087.7	492.8
Total sources/uses of funds – average	19.1	35.1	57.5	53.9	35.5	19.4	28.5	35.5	29.4	13.3
Total sources/uses of funds – standard deviation	57.0	81.1	104.1	96.4	72.2	45.6	86.7	93.8	67.5	37.7
Total sources/uses of funds – minimum	−79.2	−0.2	−0.6	−0.1	−81.6	−9.5	−7.0	−6.3	−2.1	−86.4
Total sources/uses of funds – maximum	378.4	550.2	611.1	480.9	429.8	184.9	393.8	534.4	369.1	175.9
No. of companies in panel	52	52	52	52	37	37	37	37	37	37

Source: Firm-level data are from PROWESS, CMIE, Mumbai. The aggregates reported are based on the authors' calculations.

Note: Individual items of sources and uses of funds are reported as percentages of the total while the rest are in Rs crores.

exporters are less financially constrained than losing exporters. In the next section we attempt to estimate investment functions separately for these categories to test the extent of financial constraints that firms in various categories face.

Investment function

Specification[22]

In the empirical literature on firms' investment behaviour, two sets of hypotheses relating to finance constraints are usually tested. First, the presence of a finance constraint is explored using the specification for a panel of firms in eqn (4.1):

$$\left(\frac{I}{K}\right)_{i,t} = a_i + bQ_{i,t} + c\left(\frac{IS}{K}\right)_{i,t} + \varepsilon_{i,t} \tag{4.1}$$

where I is investment, K is capital stock, Q is an estimate of Tobin's q, IS is internal sources of funds, ε is the error term, i is the firm subscript and t is the time subscript. If in the above specification the estimated coefficient c turned out to be positive and significant, it is taken as evidence in favour of the finance constraint hypothesis. Sometimes, besides IS, a variable measuring leverage is also added to the above specification.

The second hypothesis explored in this literature is the so-called 'excess sensitivity hypothesis', which states that the degree of finance constraints varies across firms of different characteristics representing inter-firm differences in information costs. In order to test the excess sensitivity hypothesis, firms are grouped into 'high information cost' and 'low information cost' categories based on some a priori criteria (such as firm size). A higher value for the estimated coefficient c for the 'high information cost' group points to the excess sensitivity of this group to financing constraints.

Empirical work within this framework in the developing country context is sparse. In the few studies available, Tobin's q is replaced by a traditional sales-accelerator model of investment. In this approach, fluctuations in output/sales motivate capital spending. To such a model, cash flow and leverage ratios are added to capture finance constraints. A typical specification is as follows in eqn (4.2) (see Harris *et al.* 1994):

$$\frac{I_{i,t}}{K_{i,t-1}} = \alpha_1 \frac{\Delta S_{i,t}}{K_{i,t-1}} + \alpha_2 \frac{IS_{i,t}}{K_{i,t-1}} + \alpha_3 \frac{D_{i,t}}{K_{i,t-1}} + v_{i,t} \quad \text{where} \quad v_{i,t} = \varepsilon_{i,t} + \lambda_i + \eta_t$$

$$\tag{4.2}$$

I is investment, K is capital stock, S is sales, IS is internal sources of funds, D is debt, v is error term, λ is the time-invariant firm-specific effect, η is a common time effect, ε is the idiosyncratic component of the error term, i is firm subscript and t is time subscript. Positive and significant estimates of α_2 indicate the presence of finance constraints. Tests of the excess sensitivity hypothesis can be done as described earlier. The coefficient α_3 reflects the premium above the safe rate that must be paid as the debt to capital ratio increases and it may vary across groups of firms.

In this study, we intend to estimate an investment function such as eqn (4.2) to test for the presence of finance constraints. Earlier, we had seen that the share of external finance in the total sources of funds is larger for exporters than for domestic firms. Moreover, external funds raised through capital markets as a percentage of total external funds are higher for exporting firms. The relative success of exporters in raising funds through capital markets possibly suggests that these firms might belong to the low information cost category while the domestic firms might belong to the high information cost category. From the perspective of the suppliers of funds, the quality of investment projects is likely to be superior for exporters who have a proven record in international markets – given that international markets are perceived to be highly competitive. The flip side to this is that success (or mere continued presence) in domestic markets, which were largely protected in the pre-1991 regime, is not sufficient assurance that the firm will remain successful in the increasingly competitive environment that is evolving in the domestic product markets since 1991. This suggests that finance constraints are likely to be more severe for domestic firms than for exporters (excess sensitivity hypothesis). In an exactly analogous way, even among exporters, losers are likely to face more severe finance constraints than winners (winners and losers as we defined above). In what follows, we attempt to empirically test the above propositions.

It may be noted here that the criteria we have used to classify firms into high and low information cost categories are, to our knowledge, unlike any used hitherto in the literature. Traditionally, a common criterion used to distinguish firms into high and low information cost has been firm size (usually measured in terms of net fixed assets). We also attempt to evaluate if the above-mentioned excess sensitivity hypothesis (exporters versus domestic firms) holds after controlling for firm size.

Prior to 1991, the Indian Government strictly controlled the creation of new firms and the expansion of existing firms through a rigid licensing regime in accordance with plan priorities. The plans had both industry-specific real capacity targets and a financial plan to ensure the realisation of these targets. Control was exercised on the financial side by public ownership of financial institutions providing long-term loans to the private corporate sector. The government provided subsidised credit to these financial institutions, which were in turn directed to the private corporate sector at a fixed rate of interest implying that these institutions had a limited screening role to perform. Private corporate firms faced severe restrictions on the pricing, quantum and timing of new issues and the government also forced certain industry-specific debt/equity ratio norms on firms, leaving little leeway for firms to choose their capital structure.

In such a scenario, *de facto*, finance did not matter for investment and the traditional finance literature that focuses on informational asymmetries and agency costs faced by suppliers of funds can be argued to be of little relevance for the pre-1991 period. Furthermore, during the period 1991–3, rapid changes were taking place in the financial sector so we chose to exclude these years from our analysis. We, therefore, estimate the investment function for the period 1993–7.

Empirical results

The investment functions are estimated using the pooled data, namely for five years (1993–7) across 204 firms (total 1,020 observations). For the construction of the dependent variable (I/K) and explanatory variables ($\Delta S/K$, IS/K and D/K), we need a measure of the real capital stock. We estimate the beginning of the period capital stock from book value using a method similar to that of Athey and Laumas (1994). The following assumptions are made:

1   All the firm's capital has an identical useful life L_i.
2   The firm's initial end of period capital stock equals the book value of net fixed assets in current rupees.
3   Firms use the straight line method of depreciation and actual depreciation is exponential with depreciation $1/L_i$.
4   All investments are made at the beginning of the year and all depreciation is subtracted at the end of the year.

We estimate the beginning of the period's capital stock by eqn (4.3):

$$K_{i,t} = \left(\frac{P_t}{P_{t-1}}\right)[I_{i,t-1} + K_{i,t-1}]\left[1 - \left(\frac{1}{L_i}\right)\right], \tag{4.3}$$

where P is the wholesale price index of capital goods.

Besides the above three explanatory variables, we also construct various dummy variables to represent firms according to different categories such as domestics, winners, losers, etc. Table 4.12 lists the variable notations used and also their definitions.

Finance constraints – Overall sample

The investment function – eqn (4.2) – for the entire sample (i.e. no distinction is made between domestics, exporters, etc.) is estimated using panel data techniques (a) in levels allowing for both firm and time effects, and (b) in first differences allowing only for time effects. Time effects were found to be insignificant in both cases whereas firm-specific effects were found to be significant in the levels. Table 4.13 reports the GLS estimates for the levels regression and OLS estimates for estimation in first differences. The positive and significant coefficient for IS/K shows that for the entire sample financial constraints are important in explaining investment behaviour.

Table 4.12 Variables and their definition

Notation	Definition
$\Delta S/K$	Change in sales as a ratio of real capital stock
IS/K	Internal sources as a ratio of real capital stock
D/K	Long-term debt as a ratio of real capital stock
EDUMMY	Dummy variable: one for exporting firm, zero otherwise
EIS/K	EDUMMY * IS/K
ED/K	EDUMMY * D/K
WDUMMY	Dummy variable: one for winning exporter firm, zero otherwise
WIS/K	WDUMMY * IS/K
WD/K	WDUMMY * D/K
LDUMMY	Dummy variable; one for losing exporter firm, zero otherwise
LIS/K	LDUMMY * IS/K
LD/K	LDUMMY * D/K
SF	Dummy variable: one for small firms (NFA < Rs 25 crore)
LF	Dummy variable: one for large firms (NFA ⩾ Rs 25 crore)
SFIS/K	SF * IS/K
SFD/K	SF * D/K
SFD	SF * DDUMMY
SFE	SF * EDUMMY
LFE	LF * EDUMMY
SFDIS/K	SFD * IS/K
SFEIS/K	SFE * IS/K
LFEIS/K	LFE * IS/K
SFDD/K	SFD * D/K
SFED/K	SFE * D/K
LFED/K	LFE * D/K
WW	Dummy variable: one for winner firm in winning industry, zero otherwise
LW	Dummy variable: one for loser firm in winning industry, zero otherwise
WL	Dummy variable: one for winner firm in losing industry, zero otherwise
LL	Dummy variable: one for loser firm in losing industry, zero otherwise
WWIS/K	WW * IS/K
LWIS/K	LW * IS/K
WLIS/K	WL * IS/K
LLIS/K	LL * IS/K
WWD/K	WW * D/K
LWD/K	LW * D/K
WLD/K	WL * D/K
LLD/K	LL * D/K

Exporting firms versus domestic firms

To test the excess sensitivity hypothesis between exporting and domestic firms, dummy variables are introduced into the regression for both the intercept and the slope coefficients attached to IS/K and D/K. The dummy variable takes the value one for exporting firms and zero for domestic firms. The estimation is carried out using OLS without allowing for any firm-specific effect or time effect.[23]

The regression results in both levels and in first differences are reported in Table 4.14. It is seen that the slope dummy attached to IS/K is negative and significant in both the levels and first-difference regressions. This suggests that finance the constraint is less binding for the exporting firms than for domestic firms upholding the excess sensitivity hypothesis. We, therefore, re-estimate the investment function separately for the domestic firms and for exporting firms (Table 4.14). These show that the finance constraint is unambiguously binding for domestic firms. For exporting firms the coefficient of IS/K is clearly lower than that for the domestic firms in both the levels and first-difference regressions. There is, however, some ambiguity as to the significance of the coefficient between the levels and first-difference regressions.

Table 4.13 Investment function estimates – all firms

	Levels[a]		First difference[b]	
Constant	0.0843	(2.82)[c]	−0.0113	(−0.85)
$\Delta S/K$	0.0133	(2.90)	0.0100	(2.19)
IS/K	0.5406	(37.85)	0.6417	(40.20)
D/K	0.0973	(3.66)	−0.2106	(−6.33)
D-o-F	813		608	

Notes
a In levels, estimation is using GLS allowing for firm-specific effects.
b In first-differences, estimation is using OLS.
c t-values are reported in parentheses.

Table 4.14 Investment function estimates – exporting firms versus domestic firms

	Levels			First difference		
	All firms	Domestic firms	Exporting firms	All firms	Domestic firms	Exporting firms
Constant	0.0902	0.0898	0.1943	−0.0235	−0.0218	−0.0310
	(8.17)	(7.05)	(17.80)	(−1.49)	(−1.19)	(−2.34)
EDUMMY	0.1029			−0.0065		
	(5.55)			(−0.27)		
$\Delta S/K$	0.0143	0.0361	−0.0002	0.0095	0.0232	0.0016
	(3.18)	(4.39)	(−0.04)	(2.31)	(2.92)	(0.43)
IS/K	0.5169	0.4577	0.0718	0.6686	0.6299	−0.0345
	(36.15)	(19.15)	(3.03)	(45.15)	(25.41)	(−0.78)
EIS/K	−0.4609			−0.7280		
	(−13.8)			(−12.2)		
D/K	0.1723	0.2241	0.0490	−0.2929	−0.2556	0.1024
	(6.65)	(6.68)	(1.13)	(−9.34)	(−6.33)	(1.37)
ED/K	−0.1253			0.3910		
	(−1.94)			(3.60)		
D-o-F	1,013	571	441	605	341	263

Note: Estimation is using OLS. t-values are reported in parentheses.

Small versus large firms

As indicated earlier, firm size has often been used as a criterion to classify firms into high information cost and low information cost categories. From our point of view, it is important to ensure that the excess sensitivity hypothesis between domestic firms and exporters continues to hold after controlling for firm size. Towards this end, we first define a firm to be a small firm if its net fixed assets are less than Rs 25 crore (i.e. Rs 250 million).[24] Dummy variables for small firms and large firms are accordingly defined. Investment functions incorporating size effects are estimated first without distinguishing exporters and domestic firms (Table 4.15) and next by making this distinction (Table 4.16).

From Table 4.15 we find that the slope dummy for small firms attached to IS/K is negative and significant (in both levels and first differences), indicating that finance constraints are less important for small firms than for large firms – a somewhat counter-intuitive result. A similar conclusion was arrived at by Athey and Laumas (1994), who attribute it to the government's policies that favoured small firms.

We now turn to the question of whether the excess sensitivity hypothesis between exporters and domestic firms holds after controlling for size. We concentrate on the slope dummies attached to IS/K which correspond to small domestic firms, small exporting firms and large exporting firms. From the results reported in Table 4.16, we see that these slope dummies are negative and significant (in both levels and in first differences). Moreover, the results suggest that the finance constraint is less severe for (a) small exporters than for small domestic firms, and (b) large exporters than for large domestic firms.[25] Thus, the excess sensitivity of domestic firms to finance constraints over exporting firms holds well across firms of similar size.

Winning and losing exporters

A similar approach as above is adopted to test the excess sensitivity hypothesis between winning exporters and losing exporters. Two sets of dummy variables are used to distinguish the winners and losers *vis-à-vis* the domestic firms. As above, the dummy variables are used in both the intercept and slope terms. Table 4.17

Table 4.15 Investment function estimates – small versus large firms

	Levels		First difference	
Constant	0.1260	(10.16)	−0.0204	(−1.22)
SF	0.0439	(2.55)	−0.0044	(−0.19)
$\Delta S/K$	0.0060	(1.38)	0.0053	(1.35)
IS/K	0.5466	(39.21)	0.6864	(48.48)
SFIS/K	−0.4728	(−17.07)	−0.7383	(−15.15)
D/K	0.1303	(5.21)	−0.3235	(−10.79)
SFD/K	−0.1181	(−1.90)	0.4145	(3.91)
D-o-F	1,013		605	

Note: Estimation is using OLS. *t*-values are reported in parentheses.

Table 4.16 Investment function estimates – exporting firms versus domestic firms and small versus large firms

	Levels		First difference	
Constant	0.1021	(5.98)	−0.0302	(−1.31)
SFD	0.0714	(3.03)	0.0013	(0.04)
SFE	0.0701	(2.77)	0.0062	(0.18)
LFE	0.0690	(2.13)	0.0035	(0.11)
$\Delta S/K$	0.0060	(1.39)	0.0052	(1.32)
IS/K	0.5465	(38.69)	0.6887	(48.18)
SFDIS/K	−0.4286	(−9.23)	−0.6815	(−8.37)
SFEIS/K	−0.4888	(−14.77)	−0.7717	(−12.8)
LFEIS/K	−0.0850	(−0.62)	−0.4311	(−2.60)
D/K	0.1298	(5.10)	−0.3304	(−10.95)
SFDD/K	−0.4606	(−2.73)	−0.0128	(−0.04)
SFED/K	−0.0751	(−1.14)	0.4638	(4.19)
LFED/K	−0.1130	(−0.76)	0.2101	(0.80)
D-o-F	1,007		599	

Note: Estimation is using OLS. *t*-values are reported in parentheses.

Table 4.17 Investment function estimates – winning and losing exporters

	Levels			First difference		
	All firms	Winners	Losers	All firms	Winners	Losers
Constant	0.0902	0.2181	0.1575	−0.0235	−0.414	−0.0170
	(8.19)	(14.94)	(9.67)	(−1.49)	(−2.36)	(−0.86)
WDUMMY	0.1267			−0.0133		
	(5.50)			(−0.46)		
LDUMMY	0.0667			0.0064		
	(2.69)			(0.19)		
$\Delta S/K$	0.0137	−0.0051	−0.0003	0.0095	−0.0203	0.0042
	(3.06)	(−0.54)	(−0.05)	(2.31)	(−1.76)	(1.10)
IS/K	0.5184	0.1087	0.0492	0.00684	0.0812	−0.0557
	(36.27)	(2.88)	(1.60)	(45.05)	(0.74)	(−1.17)
WIS/K	−0.4391			−0.6498		
	(−8.98)			(−4.43)		
LIS/K	−0.4797			−0.7419		
	(−11.0)			(−11.3)		
D/K	0.1710	0.0016	0.1122	−0.2928	0.1104	0.1738
	(6.61)	(0.03)	(1.75)	(−9.30)	(1.41)	(0.58)
WD/K	−0.1727			0.3875		
	(2.06)			(3.46)		
LD/K	−0.0608			0.4629		
	(−0.66)			(1.09)		
D-o-F	1,010	256	181	602	152	107

Note: Estimation is using OLS. *t*-values are reported in parentheses.

reports the estimation results. The slope dummies attached to IS/K for both winners and losers turn out to be negative and significant as expected. Nonetheless, when the investment function is estimated separately for winners and losers, the coefficient of IS/K turns out to be substantially lower for both these types of firms than for the domestic firms (Table 4.14). In fact, in first differences the coefficient is insignificant for both these categories.

These results should, however, be interpreted with caution. While the excess sensitivity of domestic firms versus the exporters is clearly established, the same cannot be said between winners and losers. Possibly this is due to the fact that sample size is rather small for the winners and losers. It may be pointed out here that while the criteria used to categorise firms into domestics and exporters are rather straightforward, the same cannot be said about the criteria used to categorise exporters into winners and losers. This is because we have essentially compared the annual growth rate of a firm's export with a benchmark growth rate of the relevant industry's exports. One may expect that the growth rate in exports is more volatile for individual firms than for the industry as a whole. Considering that we have only five years of data this could lead to misclassification of some firms as either winners or losers, thus affecting our results.

Another possible reason for not obtaining clear results at the level of winner and loser firms could be that we have not controlled for the fact that a winner/loser firm belongs to a winner/loser industry. We attempt to control for this factor below.

Winner/loser–industry/firms

A priori we would expect that the information cost would be the least for winner firms in winner industries, followed by loser firms in winner industries, winner firms in loser industries, loser firms in loser industries, and finally domestic firms in that order. Accordingly, the severity of finance constraints would increase in the above order.

We define dummy variables that distinguish firms into four categories, namely winner firms in winner industries, winner firms in loser industries, loser firms in winner industries and loser firms in loser industries. Distinction of domestic firms by winner/loser industries is not made here since the focus is on the severity of finance constraints within different categories of exporting firms. Table 4.18 reports the results of this dummy variable regression.

These results indicate that:

1   The severity of finance constraints is highest for domestic firms followed by exporting firms in loser industries and is the least for exporting firms in winner industries (compare the coefficients of WWIS/K and LWIS/K on the one hand with those of WLIS/K and LLIS/K on the other).
2   The above expected progression in the severity of finance constraints is found to hold true for exporting firms within loser industries but not for exporting firms within winner industries (compare the coefficients of WWIS/K with LWIS/K and that of WLIS/K with LLIS/K).

Table 4.18 Investment function estimates – winner/loser–industry/firms

	Levels		First difference	
Constant	0.0903	(8.20)	−0.0234	(−1.49)
WW	0.1147	(3.50)	−0.0141	(−0.34)
LW	0.0530	(1.54)	−0.0027	(−0.06)
WL	0.1307	(3.71)	−0.0181	(−0.53)
LL	0.0583	(1.62)	0.0106	(0.25)
$\Delta S/K$	0.0130	(2.88)	0.0107	(2.59)
IS/K	0.5205	(36.30)	0.6652	(44.99)
$WWIS/K$	−0.4411	(−8.35)	−0.6810	(−3.29)
$LWIS/K$	−0.5069	(−10.34)	−0.8731	(−11.26)
$WLIS/K$	−0.4089	(−2.95)	−0.5808	(−2.80)
$LLIS/K$	−0.3125	(−3.11)	−0.4234	(−3.52)
D/K	0.1692	(6.53)	−0.2897	(−9.27)
WWD/K	−0.1073	(−0.94)	0.5439	(3.74)
LWD/K	−0.0566	(0.59)	0.2794	(0.54)
WLD/K	−0.2328	(−1.99)	0.1614	(0.97)
LLD/K	0.0846	(0.24)	0.7865	(1.09)
D-o-F	1004		596	

Note: Estimation is using OLS. *t*-values are reported in parentheses.

Coefficients of $\Delta S/K$ and D/K

The coefficient of the accelerator ($\Delta S/K$) is in most of the cases positive and significant in both levels and first-difference regressions as expected. The exceptions are the regressions in first differences for exporters, winners and losers, and in levels for winners and losers. With respect to the coefficient of the leverage term (D/K), however, no clear pattern emerges either on the sign of the coefficient or its significance. This could perhaps be due to the small size of our sample. We may note here that some other studies have also reported similar results (see Hall 1992; Harris *et al.* 1994).

Examining the financing patterns of firms, we have found that winning exporters have been able to raise more funds from various sources than losing exporters and domestic firms. Furthermore, there is evidence to suggest that while financial constraints are important in explaining investment behaviour for all firms in our sample, they are less binding for exporting firms, particularly those in the winner industries.

4. Stylised facts on micro–macro and trade–finance interactions

Trade specialisation and sustainability of current account

From the policy-maker's perspective, issues such as patterns of trade specialisation and competitiveness are of interest primarily because of their implications for the link between economic growth and current account sustainability. It is well known that the current account balance is influenced both by micro-factors (such as trade specialisation and competitiveness) and macro-factors (mainly the savings–investment gap). In India, in the 1980s and 1990s, macro-factors played a dominant role in determining the current account balance (as has been noted in Section 2). Our findings suggest that with greater amounts of resources flowing into the exporting sectors since the 1991 reforms, poor export performance due to resource constraints is unlikely to be a source of concern for current account sustainability. Other factors, however, such as the lack of adequate infrastructural facilities (roads, ports, power, etc.) may prove to be a generalised constraint on the supply side, which could affect export performance and thus ultimately the trade balance.

Labour costs and trade competitiveness

The non-dynamism of the export sector has long been an issue of policy concern in India. Given India is a labour-surplus country, it has been suggested that trade patterns should follow comparative advantage and that India should specialise in the export of labour-intensive commodities. The 1991 reforms were an attempt to provide an impetus to India's manufacturing exports, especially of the labour-intensive type. There is little evidence, however, of a significant increase in manufacturing exports (labour intensive or otherwise) in the post-1991 period. Moreover, we do not observe any correlation at the sectoral level between unit labour costs and export competitiveness. The lack of importance of price factors in determining competitiveness at the sectoral level could be taken to provide support for the view that non-price factors (such as finance constraints) may be important determinants of competitiveness at the firm and industry levels. Equally, it could also be due to the possibility that, notwithstanding the economic reforms of 1991, there remain severe distortions in the Indian economy, which are far too deep and in extent to enable the country to exploit its labour resources.[26]

Financial environment and finance constraints

In the restrictive policy environment prior to 1991, financial intermediaries were passive conduits of funds from the government and the banking sector to manufacturing firms. The 1991 reforms have empowered financial intermediaries to play an active role in resource allocation. We have argued that in a regime where resources are allocated according to government directives, the very concept of finance constraints is of little consequence (as all real plans are backed by a financial plan). Finance constraints (caused by informational and agency costs) are relevant when financial intermediaries screen projects. In our empirical work, we have demonstrated that in the new environment financial intermediaries seem to take export performance as an indicator of a firm's competitive strength. Thus, investments by exporters in general and, in particular, among exporting firms in winning industries are not restricted by the availability of internal funds. On the other hand, financial intermediaries seem to view firms that operate primarily in domestic markets as lacking in competitive strength and, consequently, investments by these firms are constrained by the availability of internal funds.

Notes

1 We gratefully acknowledge comments by Mustapha Nabli, José María Fanelli, Ari Kuncoro, Paolo Guerrieri and other participants in the Interim Workshop held at the Philippines Institute for Development Studies, Manila, during 21–23 April 1998, and in the Final Workshop held at the Trade and Industrial Policy Secretariat, Johannesburg, during 30 November–2 December 1998. Usual disclaimers apply.
2 As we shall see in Section 2, there was, in fact, an improvement in India's export performance since the mid-1980s, due in great part to the export-promotion policies followed during this period.
3 There was another mechanism by which the foreign exchange constraint would prove to be binding on domestic demand-driven growth in the Indian context. An increase in aggregate demand would lead to higher food prices and, hence, inflation. Given the aversion of Indian policy-makers to high inflation, this would invariably trigger off deflationary fiscal and monetary policies (as the lack of adequate foreign exchange reserves precluded the possibility of large-scale imports of food).
4 It should be noted that such a periodisation is widely accepted in the literature. For example, see Ahluwalia (1991) and Joshi and Little (1994).
5 Further details of these policies can be found in Ganesh-Kumar *et al.* (1998).
6 Openness as conventionally defined is the sum of exports and imports as a ratio of GDP.
7 A full discussion of the CMS methodology is available in Kumar, Sen and Vaidya (1999).
8 The definition of manufacturing used here is the SITC-based one and includes all commodities in the SITC categories 5 to 8 excluding 68. It should be pointed out that this definition differs from the definition of manufacturing exports used in Section 2 beginning with 'The real exchange rate and aggregate competitiveness'.
9 It should be noted that the CMS analysis ends in 1992 while the rest of the empirical results in this section are until 1996. The CMS analysis requires data on bilateral trade flows for all commodities and all countries. Such detailed data for the post-1992 period were not readily available at the time of the study.
10 The RCA measure expresses the share of country *i*'s export of product *j* in total world exports of product *j*, as a ratio to the share of country *i*'s total exports of manufactures in world total exports of manufactures. An RCA of unity would imply 'normal' export performance of product *j* relative to the size of country *i*, as an exporter, while a ratio of 2 would suggest that the product *j*'s share in country *i*'s exports is twice the corresponding world share, and so on. An RCA of more than unity is usually taken as an indicator of competitiveness, while an increase in the RCA supposedly suggests a strengthening of the competitiveness so revealed (see Balassa (1965) for further details).
11 Commodity-wise time series of RCAs are not presented here but will be made available upon request.
12 We use the Grubel and Lloyd (1975) measure of intra-industry trade (IIT), defined as

$$\text{IIT}_{it} = 1 - \frac{|X_{it} - M_{it}|}{(X_{it} + M_{it})},$$

where X_{it} is India's exports of commodity *i* at time *t*, and M_{it} is India's imports of commodity *i* at time *t*. The variable IIT_{it} can be between 0 and 1, with higher values indicating greater intra-industry trade.

13 Details available from the authors upon request.
14 We have excluded ISIC 3909 from the above list as it includes manufacturing industries not elsewhere classified. Therefore, by definition, ISIC 3909 would have a high volume of intra-industry trade.
15 We have used Lall's (1998) classification of the technological complexity of various exports, which is a refinement of OECD (1998).
16 See Lall (1998) for further details.
17 The presence of such domestic firms can be explained primarily in terms of the extremely restrictive trade and industrial policy regime that prevailed prior to 1985.
18 Recall that an Indian industry was classified as winner/loser by comparing its export performance with a world norm for that industry: winner if it outperformed the world norm; loser otherwise.
19 Note that RCA of an industry can rise/fall over time even when the world trade in that industry is falling over time. None of the industries (both winners and losers) chosen below in our analysis fall in such a category. Hence this case is not discussed further.
20 We have not reported the correlations matrix for brevity.
21 The figures for 1997 for both winners and losers seem to be influenced by some extreme values and thus need to be interpreted with caution.
22 We draw upon Hubbard (1997), Athey and Laumas (1994) and Harris *et al.* (1994) in this discussion.
23 Note that introducing a dummy variable for exporting firms and simultaneously allowing for firm-specific or time effects through relevant dummy variables would result in the equation being collinear. Hence, we ignore firm and time effects.
24 Note that the Government of India defines a small firm as one whose gross fixed asset is less than Rs 1 crore for its priority lending policies. Historically, this limit was much lower.
25 The small size of our sample in each of these four categories prevented us from estimating the investment function separately.
26 Two such distortions that may be relevant here are the lack of an exit policy in labour market and the widespread reservation of products for the small-scale sector.

References

Agrawal, P., Gokarn, S., Mishra, V., Parikh, K. S. and Sen, K. (1995) *Economic Restructuring in East Asia and India: Perspectives on Policy Reform*. Basingstoke: Macmillan.

Ahluwalia, I. J. (1991) *Productivity Growth in Indian Manufacturing*. New Delhi: Oxford University Press.

Athey, M. J. and Laumas, P. S. (1994) 'Internal Funds and Corporate Investment in India', *Journal of Development Economics* 45: 287–303.

Balassa, B. (1965) 'Trade Liberalisation and Revealed Comparative Advantage', *Manchester School* 33(2): 99–123.

Brockett, P. and Levine, A. (1984) *Statistics and Probability and Their Applications*. New York: CBS College Publishing/Saunders College Publishing.

Edwards, S. (1994) 'Real and Monetary Determinants of Real Exchange Rate Behaviour: Theory and Evidence from Developing Countries', in J. Williamson (ed.), *Estimating Equilibrium Exchange Rates*. Washington, DC: Institute for International Economics.

Elbadawi, I. A. (1994) 'Estimating Long-Run Equilibrium Real Exchange Rates', in J. Williamson (ed.), *Estimating Equilibrium Exchange Rates*. Washington, DC: Institute for International Economics.

Fagerberg, J. (1988) 'International Competitiveness', *The Economic Journal* 98: 355–74.

Feenstra, R. C., Lipsey, R. E. and Bowen, H. P. (1997) 'World Trade Flows, 1970–1992 with Production and Tariff Data', *National Bureau of Economic Research Working Paper*, No. 5910.

Ganesh-Kumar, A., Sen, A. K. and Vaidya, R. R. (1998) 'Finance and Changing Trade Patterns in Developing Countries: A Case-Study of India', *Indira Gandhi Institute of Development Research, Mumbai PP Series*, No. 38.

Grubel, H. and Lloyd, P. J. (1975) *Intra-Industry Trade*. London: Macmillan.

Hall, B. H. (1992) 'Investment and Research and Development at the Firm Level: Does the Source of Finance Matter?', *National Bureau of Economic Research Working Paper*, No. 4096.

Harris, J. R., Schiantarelli, F. and Siregar, M. G. (1994) 'The Effect of Financial Liberalization on the Capital Structure and Investment Decisions of Indonesian Manufacturing Establishments', *The World Bank Economic Review* 8(1): 17–47.

Helpman, E. and Krugman, P. (1989) *Trade Policy and Market Structure*. Cambridge, MA: MIT Press.

Hubbard, R. G. (1997) 'Capital Market Imperfections and Investment', *National Bureau of Economic Research Working Paper*, No. 5996.

Joshi, V. and Little, I. M. D. (1994) *India: Macroeconomics and Political Economy, 1964–1991*. New Delhi: Oxford University Press.

Kanji, G. K. (1993) *100 Statistical Tests*. New Delhi: Sage Publications (India) Private Ltd.

Lall, S. (1998) 'Technological Capabilities in Emerging Asia', *Oxford Development Studies* 26(2): 213–43.

Loertscher, R. and Wolter, F. (1980) 'Determinants of Intra-industry Trade: Among Countries and across Countries', *Weltwirtschaftliches Archiv* 116: 280–93.

Mayers, C. (1990) 'Financial Systems, Corporate Finance, and Economic Development', in R. G. Hubbard (ed.), *Asymmetric Information, Corporate Finance, and Investment*, National Bureau of Economic Research Project Report. Chicago: University of Chicago Press.

Modigliani, F. and Miller, M. H. (1958) 'The Cost of Capital, Corporation Finance, and the Theory of Investment', *American Economic Review* 48(3): 261–97.

Myers, S. C. and Majluf, N. (1984) 'Corporate Financing and Investment Decisions when Firms Have Information that Investors Do Not Have', *Journal of Financial Economics* 13: 187–221.

Singh, A. and Hamid, J. (1992) 'Corporate Financial Structures in Developing Countries', *International Finance Corporation Technical Paper*, No. 1.

Stiglitz, J. E. and Weiss, A. (1981) 'Credit Rationing in Markets with Imperfect Information', *American Economic Review* 71(3): 393–410.

5 International trade, productivity and competitiveness

The case of the Indonesian manufacturing sector

Ari Kuncoro

1. Introduction: Competitiveness, macroeconomic and financial problems

The growth path of the Indonesian economy from the late 1960s to the early 1990s was not always smooth. Indonesia experienced several economic crises, usually dictated by the development of external events, which resulted in the deterioration of the current account. The problem stemmed from the fact that throughout the 1970s, Indonesian exports depended heavily on oil, gas and primary products. From 1973 to 1980, the value of Indonesian exports was dominated by oil, gas and timber, which made up approximately 60 per cent of the total exports. As more and more processing plants developed domestically, the share of semi-processed goods in total exports rose steadily, and from the mid-1980s to the early 1990s became one of the most important foreign exchange earners.

According to Haque (1995), competitiveness is defined as an economy's ability to grow and to raise the general living standard of its population without being constrained by balance-of-payment difficulties. In other words, competitiveness is defined as the capacity to increase productivity without generating a balance-of-payment crisis. We use this definition of competitiveness to examine the evolution of economic growth and current account sustainability in Indonesia.

The structure of Indonesian exports (heavily dependent on oil and gas and natural resource products) made the current account very vulnerable to international price fluctuations. The increase in oil prices in 1973 helped the government finance its economic development plan.[1] On the negative side, the heavy dependence of the government on oil export revenues made the economy very vulnerable to the fluctuations in oil and other primary commodity prices on the international market. It is not too surprising that in an economy where government expenditures constitute most of the domestic purchasing power, any balance-of-payment crisis immediately translates into low or even negative economic growth. In the 1982–3 period, Indonesia was hit by the economic crisis that resulted from the drop in oil prices. The crisis worsened because of the fall in primary commodity prices in international markets as industrialized countries entered economic recession. The current account deficit suddenly soared from a mere 0.67 per cent of GDP in 1980 to 6.2 per cent of GDP in 1982 and 8.1 per cent of GDP in 1983.

This event brought strong impetus for a change in development strategy. It was acknowledged that export revenues from oil and primary commodities were unreliable and it was seen as urgent to develop and diversify non-oil sectors in the economy, particularly manufacturing and agriculture. As a first step, the government announced the Banking Deregulation in 1983, followed by an overhaul of the taxation system.

Another economic crisis taking place in 1986, once again caused by the sharp fall in oil price, caused the current account deficit to jump from 2.2 per cent of GDP in 1985 to 6.2 per cent in 1986. This crisis increased the need to speed up economic reforms. The government launched broad-based economic reforms in 1986, which covered all aspects of the economy: labor markets, the goods and services market and financial markets. The reforms also encompassed the improvement of market infrastructures, including administrative procedures, licensing systems and the legal system. The economic reforms marked changes in trade and industrial policies, from the import substitution industrial policy with emphasis on the development of capital-intensive manufacturing in the upstream and resource-based industries to labor-intensive export-oriented industries.

Foreign and domestic investors responded favorably to improvements in investment climate and the impact was felt in the structure of Indonesian exports. Foreign direct investment made a significant contribution to the diversification of exports, especially manufactured exports. Exports of manufactured goods produced by cheap labor such as textiles, processed woods, electronics and shoes started to rise. In 1991, the share of non-oil exports in the total exports surpassed oil and gas exports. The share of non-oil exports in 1985 was 32 per cent, of which 8 per cent consisted of manufactured exports. In 1991, the share of non-oil exports reached 62 per cent, of which 32 per cent was manufactured goods (Table 5.1). In the 1990s, Indonesia was no longer as dependent on oil exports. Oil exports are still important, however, since without them, the trade balance remains negative.

The emergence of unskilled labor-intensive industries as foreign exchange earners creates a new problem for the current account. These industries are very dependent on imported inputs, and this, as in the current economic crisis, makes them very vulnerable to exchange rate fluctuations. Their contribution to the trade balance in relation to their contribution to employment creation is still relatively small.[2] The problem of labor-intensive export-oriented industries' dependency on imported inputs comes, to a large extent, from a government policy to provide incentives to both export-oriented and import substitution industries. To offset negative incentives created by the structure of protection to export activities, the government has designed a so-called duty drawback scheme in which producers are eligible for reimbursement on the taxes paid on imported inputs, provided that the final products are destined for export markets. Obviously, with this scheme there is no incentive for export-oriented producers to use inputs from domestic suppliers since it will be more expensive and also it cannot qualify for the duty drawback scheme. As a result, there is minimal linkage between export-oriented producers and domestic suppliers of inputs.

Besides export-oriented producers, there are also domestically oriented industries. From a macroeconomic standpoint, the presence of domestic industries with heavy

Table 5.1 Structure of Indonesian exports (selected commodities, % of total exports)

	1985	1991	1993	1995	1997
Total exports					
Oil and gas	68.42	37.39	26.47	23.04	21.75
Non-oil exports	31.58	62.61	73.53	76.96	78.25
Unskilled labor intensive					
Shrimp	0.17	0.32	0.26	0.21	0.17
Fish	0.14	0.75	0.91	0.70	0.69
Coffee	1.52	1.28	0.89	0.50	0.58
Textiles	1.18	6.13	7.26	6.20	6.84
Garments	1.83	7.86	9.53	7.46	5.38
Resource intensive					
Rubber	3.68	3.29	2.89	4.82	3.72
Plywood	4.44	9.85	11.56	7.62	6.38
Sandwood	1.65	0.61	1.06	1.00	0.71
Palm oil	0.89	1.15	1.28	1.65	2.71
Paper and paper goods	0.11	0.92	1.36	2.23	1.76
Technology intensive					
Tin	0.11	0.10	0.05	0.09	0.12
Aluminum	1.21	2.35	1.42	0.58	0.41
Nickel	0.29	0.15	0.13	0.12	0.08
Fertilizer	0.43	1.02	0.42	0.61	0.58
Chemicals	0.31	0.51	0.71	1.14	1.35
Cement	0.12	0.15	0.18	0.02	0.07
Electronic	0.77	2.29	4.45	2.03	2.56

Source: Central Bureau of Statistics, Economic Indicator.

dependence on imported inputs and low exporting activity has burdened the current account. Why do these industries exist at all? The issue has something to do with the effective protection rate (EPR). The combination of an overvalued exchange rate, a high degree of protection given to final products and low tariffs imposed on industrial inputs has prevented the development of linkages between producers of final goods and domestic suppliers of inputs. Given the low backward linkages of these industries with domestic suppliers of inputs, the expansion of aggregate demand very soon resulted in the deterioration of the current account, with little multiplier effects in the Keynesian sense. As shown in Table 5.2, in 1995 and 1996, a new wave of deregulation measures spurred economic growth to around 8 per cent, leading to the worsening of the current account deficit to around 4 per cent of GDP.

High dependency on imported inputs is the main weakness of the Indonesian manufacturing industry. The sharp depreciation of the rupiah in the current economic crisis affects the manufacturing sector negatively across the board, including segments that are highly export orientated. Under normal conditions, exports would be expected to rise when the exchange rate depreciates. This does not seem to be the case, however, for Indonesia's labor-intensive export-oriented manufacturing

Table 5.2 Selected macroeconomic indicators, 1990–7

	1990	1991	1992	1993	1994	1995	1996	1997
Real GDP growth	9.0	8.9	7.2	7.3	7.5	8.1	7.8	4.7
Agriculture	2.3	2.9	6.3	1.7	0.6	4.2	1.9	0.6
Industry	13.2	11.6	8.2	9.8	11.1	10.2	10.4	6.2
Services	7.6	9.3	6.8	7.5	7.2	7.9	7.6	3.8
Inflation (CPI)	9.5	9.5	4.9	9.8	9.2	8.6	6.5	11.1
Fiscal balance (% of GDP)	0.4	0.4	−0.4	−0.6	0.1	0.8	0.2	
Current account balance	−2.8	−3.7	−2.2	−1.6	−1.7	−3.7	−4.0	−2.3
Net capital inflows	4.9	5.0	3.8	1.9	2.4	4.6	5.0	
Net portfolio investment	−0.1	0.0	−0.1	1.1	2.2	2.0		
Net direct investment	1.0	1.3	1.4	1.3	1.2	2.2		
Other capital	3.3	3.6	3.5	1.4	−0.9	1.3		
Net error and omissions	0.7	0.1	−1.0	−1.9	−0.1	−0.9		
Total external debt (% of exports)	222.0	236.9	221.8	211.9	195.8	205.0	194.0	
Short-term debt (% of total external debt)	15.9	17.9	20.5	20.1	17.7	20.9	24.8	
Short-term debt (billions of USD)	11.1	14.3	18.1	18.0	17.1	24.3	29.3	
Debt-service ratio (% of exports)	30.9	32.0	31.6	33.8	30.0	33.7	33.0	
Exports (% of GDP)	26.6	27.4	29.4	25.9	26.0	26.0	26.2	
Exports (% growth rate)	15.9	13.5	16.6	8.4	8.8	13.4	9.7	
Exchange rate (Rp/USD)	1,901	1,992	2,062	2,110	2,200	2,308	2,383	5,700

Sources: International Financial Statistics, various issues.

industry. Export-oriented industries are not able to capitalize on the depreciation of the rupiah, not only because of their high dependency on imported inputs, but also because they have difficulty obtaining trade finance due to the deterioration of the Indonesian banking system's creditworthiness. In addition, foreign importers are reluctant to import from Indonesia due to the general perception that Indonesian exporters are unable to guarantee continuity in supply.

In 1991, the good economic performance that marked the 1986–91 period began to show signs of leveling off.[3] Several macroeconomic indicators illustrated this slackening off. After managing to grow around 21 per cent a year during 1985–91, export growth fell to 12.4 per cent in 1993 and 8 per cent in 1994. This performance could be attributed to the disappointing performance of manufactured exports, which recorded 15 and 12 per cent growth in 1992 and 1993 respectively, in comparison with an average growth rate of 30 per cent per annum during 1985–91.[4] In the case of foreign investment, the economy also seemed to lose its attractiveness to foreign investors. Post-1992, the value of new foreign investment continued to fall. In the first half of 1994, for example, the number of approved foreign investments declined by 43 per cent when compared to 1992. In 1992 and 1993, the total value of approved foreign investments amounted to 10.32 billion USD and 8.4 billion, respectively.

In response to this situation, the government in 1994 announced a bold economic reform, including the abolition of the limitation on foreign ownership, a reduction in trade barriers in the form of tariff cuts, and the opening up of ten previously closed sectors to foreign investment. Foreign investors were allowed to have full ownership (i.e. a 100 per cent stake) of business entities in Indonesia. Investors responded favorably to these measures, reflected in the influx of foreign investment during the second half of 1994 such that, by the end of the year, the value of foreign investment projects reached an all time high of 23.7 billion USD.[5] The resurgence of flows of foreign investment continued well until the middle of 1997 when the currency crises hit Indonesia. In 1994, for the first time the value of approved new domestic investment projects exceeded approved foreign investment.

Various deregulatory measures announced in the middle of 1994 changed many aspects of economic incentives, including consumption, investment and exports. The government itself seemed to underestimate the impact of deregulation on the expansion of aggregate demand. Economic growth rebounded to 7 per cent, and even reached 8 per cent during the 1994–6 period. At first glance, the figures of economic growth are impressive. Looking more deeply however, the growth was hardly sustainable. Economic growth actually took place in non-tradable sectors like residential and non-residential construction and infrastructure (e.g. roads and telecommunications), contributing very little to foreign exchange generation as it was intended to meet domestic demand. To complicate matters, most of the expansion of the non-tradable sector was financed by short-term foreign commercial loans.[6] So Indonesia experienced not only a problem of currency mismatch, but also a maturity mismatch.

It soon became apparent that the domestic economy was overheating. The expansion of domestic aggregate demand was reflected in the ballooning of the current account deficit. The current account deficit rose from 2.9 billion USD in 1994 to 7.9 billion USD in 1995, approximately a two and a half times increase. This increase could be attributed to rising imports of intermediate goods due to the expansion of domestic demand. The flood of foreign direct investment also contributed to a soaring current account deficit as a result of a rise of capital good imports and rising demand for foreign consultants, especially for setting up plants.

To contain the economy from overheating, the monetary authority continued to pursue a tight monetary policy. At the same time, to maintain the competitiveness of non-oil exports the central bank adopted a policy to depreciate the currency at the rate of 5–6 per cent per annum. Within the targeted depreciation rate, the currency was allowed to fluctuate within a band. In the long run, however, these policies proved to be inconsistent. High interest rates attracted huge capital inflows that had to be bought or sterilized by the central bank if the currency depreciation was to be maintained. This operation injected new liquidity in the economy, which in turn had to be absorbed by a high interest rate. Thus, the central bank has been burdened by two conflicting tasks, namely to maintain a low inflation rate and to maintain a competitive exchange rate. As the purchasing power parity theorem tells us, the combination of a high domestic interest rate and a low expected currency depreciation produced an overvalued rupiah, making import activities and borrowing from abroad artificially cheaper in the domestic currency. Moreover, the high interest rate policy that led to the currency appreciation, as well as the policy to depreciate the rupiah, required timely interventions which were themselves susceptible to currency speculation.

The current account deficit reached approximately 4 per cent of GDP in 1996 and 1997, reflecting Indonesia's vulnerability to external events. In the past, soft loans and foreign direct investment mainly financed the deficit. Starting in 1991, portfolio investment that was lured by high domestic interest rates and the perception of Indonesia as a stable and booming economy was increasingly playing an important part in financing the deficit. Meanwhile, high domestic interest rates and an overvalued rupiah encouraged the private sector to borrow heavily from overseas to finance their domestic ventures, many of which were intended for the domestic market. For this reason, the deficit was also increasingly financed by short-term private loans. To make matters worse, the predictability of exchange rate movement with a steady depreciation of around 4–5 per cent provides very little incentive for borrowers to hedge their foreign debt.

Various macroeconomic conditions such as a huge current account deficit, a mounting foreign debt and a weak banking system with large non-performing loans put Indonesia in the same category of countries like Thailand and Korea, and to a lesser extent with Malaysia and the Philippines. The 1994–6 economic boom did not last very long, coming to an abrupt end in August 1997 when Indonesia sunk into the worst economic crisis in its history. The Indonesian crisis started as a currency crisis triggered by the economic crisis in Thailand. After the Thai crisis, suddenly there was doubt about Indonesia's economic stability that brought about a reversal in expectations. As the direction of capital inflows started to reverse, the external value of the rupiah plummeted – between June and November 1997, the external value of the rupiah depreciated by 35 per cent. It became apparent then that the monetary authority did not have sufficient reserves to defend the rupiah; instead after increasing interest rates it opted first to enlarge the band and finally to move to a free float system. Despite a high interest rate, capital outflows continued to accelerate and as a result the currency continued to weaken. The move towards a free float created a panic among domestic corporations with large exposure to overseas loans. Due to the stability of the rupiah in the past, these debts were largely unhedged. As they scrambled to buy US dollars, it put further pressure on the domestic currency. Worse still, as the crisis continued to deteriorate, the international banking community cut its credit line to Indonesian banks (including trade financing). The lack of credit financing, particularly for export-oriented sectors, was partially blamed for the failure of Indonesian exports to benefit from the currency depreciation.

In the short run, Indonesia's recovery will depend on its ability to regain market confidence. The economic stabilization program sponsored by the IMF is only the first step in this direction, and by itself does not guarantee a speedy recovery. The return of the private sector's money – foreign or domestic – is what Indonesia needs in the short run. In the long run, there is a need to change the strategy of economic development away from the current import substitution approach to a more export-oriented strategy, including in agro-business-related industries.

Based on the Indonesian experience, many researchers have largely accepted the notion that both competitiveness and external trade were key to its rapid growth and stability, and that to achieve this requires liberalizing the economy. It is true that important improvements in resource allocation were observed after the 1986 deregulation. Nonetheless, the last economic deregulation in 1994 seemed less successful than the 1986 economic deregulation, also because it culminates in the 1997 currency crisis. Some cite an overvalued exchange rate and a weakly supervised banking system as the main weaknesses of the Indonesian economy. Some claim that other factors such as a reversal of international expectation and corruption were the main causes behind the crisis. The 1994 economic deregulation, although at first appearing to spur economic growth between 1994 and 1996, also produced unsustainable trade account deficit in the following years, which was followed by the 1997 currency crisis.

The apparent failures of the 1994 deregulation measures, however, are not interpreted as flaws of traditional theory. Rather, the failures stem from the problem of sequencing market liberalization. It is hypothesized that the comparative static of the model is correct and that more research is necessary regarding the dynamic of the liberalization model.

At present, it seems researchers have reached some consensus on two issues. First, there is little disagreement over the crucial role of competitiveness and trade in fostering growth and avoiding recurrent balance-of-payment crises. Second, there is agreement that more research needs to be done to settle the question regarding the relationship between trade, competitiveness and macroeconomic stability.

Accordingly, this study will examine the linkages between international trade, productivity and competitiveness in Indonesia. Since comprehensive data is only readily available for the Indonesian manufacturing sector, the study will focus on this area. Two specific linkages will be the focus of this study: the relationship between trade specialization and productivity growth and, second, the linkages between productivity and current account sustainability. In order to achieve these ends, the research strategy will proceed in two steps. The first step is to analyze the country's trade specialization by examining the Indonesian export commodity base available from the Central Bureau of Statistics (CBS). Data from 1980 to 1994 is used to construct an index of revealed comparative advantage (RCA). The pattern of trade specialization emerging from the RCA analysis will then be used to examine the relationship between trade specialization, the evolution of competitiveness and the sustainability of the current account.

2. Trade specialization, productivity growth and current account sustainability

The effort to examine the linkage between trade and competitiveness can only be accomplished by examining the annual survey on manufacturing firms, which contains important information regarding export–import activities and production processes at the firm level. Based on the definition of competitiveness, we try to identify winner and loser sectors in the Indonesian economy. Competitiveness at the sectoral level is defined as the capacity to increase productivity as well as to contribute to the closing of the current account deficit. Indonesian manufacturing surveys are well suited for this purpose since they provide information on export strategy and imported inputs at the firm level which can easily be aggregated to the industry level. It is quite possible that a highly productive firm or sector does not meet the above definition of competitiveness due to a heavy dependence on imported inputs such that its net contribution to the current account is negative. The effort to assess the evolution of sectoral competitiveness necessitates the measurement of productivity. The manufacturing surveys provide information on the values of output and inputs, such that by assuming a specific functional form for production process, it is possible to construct the level of labor productivity and labor productivity growth at the sectoral level.

Trade specialization

RCA is one method to measure comparative advantage in a geographic area. The argument behind this approach is that the flow of goods between countries is the reflection of the comparative advantage of the nation. The pattern that emerges from this measure does not only reflect the cost to produce such commodities, but also the difference in other non-price factors.

Applying the RCA method to the Indonesian non-oil export data, twenty commodities (three-digit SITC) that have relatively constant comparative advantage during the period 1990–4 can be identified, and thus are supposed to be leading export commodities. Most of these consist of primary products, while the rest are manufactured goods. In the category of primary products, agricultural products such as coffee, coconut, tea, spices, rubber and vegetable oil (SITC 071–5, 121, 231, 422 and 431) dominate. Other primary products include minerals such as iron ore, non-ferrous metal, coal and tin (SITC 283, 284, 321 and 087). One primary product that dropped out from the leading commodities in the period 1990–4 was forestry goods (SITC 024), which in the 1980s still dominated primary product exports. Apparently, the government decree that banned the export of unprocessed timber as well as other products such as rattan was responsible for the disappearance of forestry products from the list of leading commodities.

Looking at manufactured goods, products that possessed comparative advantages were textiles (SITC 651, 652, 653 and 656), household appliances from metal (SITC 697), furniture (821), garments (841) and footwear (851). If we look at the growth of exports from 1985 to 1997, the conclusion drawn from the RCA exercise seems to be confirmed (Table 5.3). Textiles, garments, paper, chemicals and electronics showed high rates of growth. Although their shares in total exports are still relatively small, products that have good export potential are paper and electronic products. It would be interesting to know whether these products derived their competitiveness from productivity. To achieve this purpose, the manufacturing database is needed since the export database does not possess information on production processes and related items such as value added, output, number of workers, etc.

Table 5.3 Trend of Indonesian exports (selected commodities, million USD)

	1985	1991	1997	GR 85–91	GR 91–7	GR 85–97
Total exports	18,586.7	29,142.4	53,443	7.78	10.64	9.20
Oil and gas	12,717.9	10,894.9	11,622	−2.55	1.08	−0.75
Non-oil exports	5,868.8	18,247.5	41,821	20.81	14.82	17.78
Unskilled labor intensive						
Shrimp	30.8	93.6	92.1	20.35	−0.27	9.56
Fish	26.3	217.2	369.3	42.17	9.25	24.63
Coffee	282.7	371.7	307.9	4.67	−3.09	0.71
Textiles	219.7	1,785.1	3,658	41.79	12.70	26.41
Garments	339.6	2,289.9	2,875.6	37.45	3.87	19.49
Resource intensive						
Rubber	683.3	959.9	1,988	5.83	12.90	9.31
Plywood	824.7	2,871	3,410	23.11	2.91	12.56
Sandwood	307.2	177.3	380	−8.75	13.55	1.79
Palm oil	166.2	335.4	1,446	12.41	27.58	19.76
Paper and paper goods	20.9	267.6	938.5	52.95	23.26	37.31
Technology intensive						
Tin	21.1	29.2	64.1	5.56	14.00	9.70
Aluminum	225.2	683.7	221.4	20.33	−17.13	−0.14
Nickel	54	42.3	41.8	−3.99	−0.20	−2.11
Fertilizer	80	297.6	312.4	24.48	0.81	12.02
Chemicals	56.7	147.2	721.2	17.23	30.32	23.61
Cement	21.5	43.2	39.5	12.33	−1.48	5.20
Electronic	144	668.7	1,370.6	29.16	12.71	20.66

Sources: Economic Indicator, various issues.

The evolution of productivity

After looking at the figures of labor productivity (LP) at the three-digit level, one thing is certain: it is hard to make any generalizations (Table 5.4). There are three distinct high value-added industries: high physical capital intensity such as basic metal (371–2), basic chemicals (351) and cement (363); high-skill intensity sectors

Table 5.4 Index of labor productivity and productivity growth

ISIC	Industry	1986	1991	1995	GR 86–91	GR 91–5
311	Food	50.12	109.34	78.79	16.88	−6.34
312	Food	47.43	47.43	62.09	0.00	5.53
313	Beverages	152.59	161.68	224.95	1.16	6.83
314	Tobacco	113.30	56.23	214.09	−13.08	30.66
321	Textiles	95.54	60.41	115.25	−8.76	13.79
322	Garment	40.43	44.61	61.49	1.99	6.63
323	Leather products	111.45	73.29	88.80	−8.04	3.91
324	Footwear	112.27	30.46	65.06	−22.96	16.39
331	Wood products	87.79	83.93	107.56	−0.89	5.09
332	Furniture	30.17	64.93	42.12	16.56	−8.29
341	Paper and paper products	78.04	132.37	189.27	11.15	7.41
342	Printing and publishing	68.97	109.72	130.52	9.73	3.53
351	Industrial chemical	172.63	242.13	329.05	7.00	6.33
352	Other chemical	129.04	110.62	110.24	−3.03	−0.07
353	Petroleum refinery	N/A	N/A	627.54	N/A	N/A
354	Oil and gas processing	N/A	70.26	124.73	N/A	12.17
355	Rubber products	47.74	65.25	49.09	6.45	−5.53
356	Plastics	37.47	35.12	55.84	−1.29	9.72
361	Ceramics	40.22	62.04	69.22	9.05	2.21
362	Glass products	161.29	70.61	145.07	−15.23	15.49
363	Cement	171.74	229.53	173.30	5.97	−5.47
364	Structural clay	13.87	96.27	16.39	47.33	−29.82
369	Other non-metallic mineral	47.49	175.70	79.55	29.91	−14.66
371	Iron and steel	1,008.75	287.29	896.99	−22.21	25.57
372	Basic metal exc. iron and steel	N/A	721.94	1,021.92	N/A	7.20
381	Metal products	73.34	67.65	100.78	−1.60	8.30
382	Non-electrical machinery	46.82	140.49	186.62	24.58	5.84
383	Electrical equipment	108.88	106.83	192.52	−0.38	12.50
384	Transportation equipment	87.27	133.65	323.34	8.90	19.33
385	Professional equipment	22.00	55.43	98.19	20.30	12.11
390	Miscellaneous	41.97	38.65	57.86	−1.63	8.40
	Total	91.66	82.88	125.46	−1.99	8.65

Sources: Calculated from Industrial Surveys.

such as machinery (ISIC 381–4); and highly differentiated products such as beverages (313) and tobacco (314). Caution is needed when interpreting the high figures of value added for electronics (383), transportation equipment (384) and chemicals (ISIC 35) since they are influenced, to a certain extent, by the degree of protection given to these industries.

On the other hand, there are also labor-intensive industries with low productivity. Food (311–12), textiles (321), garments (322), leather (323), footwear (324), rubber products (355), plastics (356) and several non-metallic mineral industries (such as bricks, tiles and ceramics), professional equipment and miscellaneous industries can be considered as labor-intensive sectors with LP less than half of highly productive industries. Resource-based industries cover a wide range of factor intensities from relatively more labor-intensive wood and rubber products to relatively more capital-intensive ones such as basic metal and cement. In this category, LP is usually lower in the more capital-intensive ones.

An examination of the figures of LP growth at the three-digit level reveals that manufacturing productivity growth is very erratic (Table 5.4). The range of total factor productivity growth is very broad. The manufacturing sector as a whole experienced negative LP growth during the 1986–91 period. Manufacturing is one sector that benefited the most from a series of deregulation measures since 1986. Previously, we have seen that manufacturing export growth accelerated immediately once economic liberalization started. The impact on productivity growth, however, was only apparent almost five years later. Obviously there are many factors behind this fact. It is possible that a better investment climate did not produce an instant improvement in the productivity of capital and labor. For example, it takes time to produce better quality labor. Another explanation is also possible: the 1991–6 period were years of prosperity for Indonesia. In this period, flows of capital, foreign direct investment (FDI) and portfolio investment accelerated. Outward orientation created by the 1986 economic liberalization gave firms the opportunity to gain better access to the global market, which allowed the acquisition of technology, the import of capital goods, management and professional services and new products and process. This eventually led to improvements in firms' productivity.

Another interesting observation is that in the period 1991–5, the productivity gap among industries seemed to decrease. If we use the whole manufacturing LP growth as a benchmark, there is a huge gap between industries with high positive total factor productivity (TFP) growth and industries with negative ones. Between 1986 and 1991, for example, structural clay (364) recorded the highest positive TFP growth around 47 per cent, followed by other non-metallic minerals (369) in second place. The worst case is footwear (324) with almost 23 per cent negative LP growth. This is in contrast with the 1991–5 period where the productivity disparity narrowed. The highest LP growth is recorded by tobacco (314), while structural clay posted the lowest LP growth.

Even after the era of economic liberalization, there remains some of the legacy of the era of import substitution industrial policy. High valued-added industries usually enjoyed higher effective rates of protection compared to other industries.

In the period 1986–95, the performance of these industries varied. Cement (363), for example, showed better performance in 1986–91 with positive TFP growth. In the period 1991–5, the impact of the 1986 economic liberalization in terms of reduced trade barriers started to have a harmful impact on the cement industry as LP growth turned negative. The steel industry (371), on the other hand, recorded negative LP growth during the first half of the 1986–95 period, and then showed a dramatic improvement in the later period.

Machinery industries (ISIC 381–4) also enjoyed a high degree of protection during the era of import substitution policy. Judging from the figures of LP growth, however, these industries appeared to benefit from a better investment climate after the 1986 economic deregulation. Good performance of LP growth was also reflected in the strong growth of domestic demand and greater penetration of global markets. In the 1986–95 period, electrical machinery showed dramatic improvements in LP growth, from near zero initially to around 16 per cent in 1991–5. This proved that greater inflows of foreign investment had a favorable impact on this industry. The only shortcoming was that there is almost no linkage between local firms producing parts and export-oriented producers. This can be attributed, in part, to the present structure of protection along with the duty drawback scheme.

Garments (322) and footwear (324) are among the most important foreign exchange earners for the country. In the period 1986–91, footwear in particular showed negative LP growth that confirmed that these industries based their competitiveness on low labor costs rather than productivity gains. The pattern of productivity improvement observed earlier in the case of machinery industry seems to appear again – economic liberalization tended to have positive impact on LP growth later in the 1986–95 period rather than earlier. Aside from the improved investment climate discussed above, another explanation involved the expansion of domestic aggregate demand after 1991 as a result of the injection of capital inflows into the economy. These industries were able to capitalize on apparent increase in per capita income brought about by a booming domestic economy. In other words, the resurgence of LP growth might have come from an aggregate demand shock.

After comparing the RCA analysis with productivity in the manufacturing industry, it is clear that Indonesia is still specializing in products with low productivity. The base of Indonesian manufactured exports is still narrow and mainly consists of wood products, textiles, garments and footwear. The good thing is that these main export products continue to record at least positive LP growth. Performance in terms of LP growth, however, is not sufficient to determine competitiveness since we have to look at industry's contribution to the trade account.

Contribution to the trade balance and sectoral competitiveness

Using information from the manufacturing surveys, it is possible to distinguish export-oriented producers from domestically oriented ones. It is possible that highly productive firms or sectors do not meet the definition of competitiveness, which involves both the capacity to increase productivity and to contribute to the closure of the current account deficit. Production activity may require a lot of imported inputs, such that an attempt to increase productivity will put a heavy burden on the current account gap. It seems that the contribution of the manufacturing sector in Indonesia to foreign exchange generation is much less than its neighbors in Southeast Asia. For this reason, examining trends in export orientation is incomplete without examining firms' input structure (Tables 5.5–5.7).

The Indonesian manufacturing surveys provide information on imported inputs in terms of their dollar value and as a percentage of total inputs. Using the most recent data (1990–5), it can be observed that the entire manufacturing sector's contribution to the trade balance is positive, meaning it generates more foreign exchange through exports than it uses to purchase imported inputs, excluding capital goods. The net contribution of the manufacturing sector rose from merely 1.8 billion USD in 1990 to 7.7 billion USD in 1995. In general, multinational corporations (MNCs) are more dependent on imported inputs than their local counterparts. The portions of imported inputs for the manufacturing sector were between 29 per cent in 1990 and 27 per cent in 1995, while the figures for MNCs were almost twice as high (57 per cent in 1990 and 56 per cent in 1995). For this reason, in 1990 local industries made a net positive contribution of 590 million USD to the trade balance, while the deficit of MNCs amounted to 839 million USD (Table 5.6).

The same observation can be extended further in more detailed fashion to the three-digit ISIC code. First, we look at industries characterized by a very high export orientation (i.e. exported more than 50 per cent of total output). These industries include garments (322), footwear (324), wood products (331), furniture (332) and rubber products (355). Some of these industries have substantial import content (for 1995), notably textiles (31 per cent), garments (33.12 per cent) and footwear (58 per cent). Despite their high dependency on imported inputs, these industries are the top three foreign exchange contributors to the trade balance, with footwear the highest contributor, followed by garments and textiles. Industries with high or moderate export orientation made a positive contribution to the trade balance in 1995. These industries include food (311), beverages (313), tobacco (314), leather (323), furniture (332), paper products (342), basic chemicals (351), petrochemicals (354), rubber products (355), ceramics (361), glass products (362), structural clay products (364), non-ferrous basic metal (372), professional equipment (385) and miscellaneous industry (390). Electrical equipment is one exception since it has high export orientation (43 per cent) and thus has the ability to generate a substantial amount of foreign exchange. However, it is not high enough to offset its high dependency on imported inputs such that the contribution of electronic industry to the trade balance is still negative.[7] High dependence on imported inputs can also be found in low export-oriented industries. In general, these industries export less than 10 per cent of total output, although imported inputs are more than 30 per cent of output, and in some cases like machinery (ISIC 38) exceed 50 per cent.

Referring back to the definition of competitiveness, i.e. the ability to improve productivity without worsening balance of payments, it seems that few industries

Table 5.5a Net exports by industry (1990)

ISIC	Industry	Exports (%)	Exports ($000)	Imports (%)	Imports ($000)	Net exports ($000)
311	Food	11.39	487,046.90	9.39	225,932.00	261,114.90
312	Food	18.19	197,846.10	17.53	101,329.00	96,517.10
313	Beverages	1.94	4,595.61	25.38	17,617.00	−13,021.39
314	Tobacco	1.29	39,085.31	10.94	126,524.00	−87,438.69
321	Textiles	15.84	628,259.20	30.09	722,401.00	−94,141.80
322	Garment	40.85	485,568.50	32.04	224,513.00	261,055.50
323	Leather products	46.44	57,361.22	16.15	12,720.00	44,641.22
324	Footwear	53.08	188,261.60	44.16	67,114.00	121,147.60
331	Wood products	47.35	1,776,936.00	3.32	68,468.00	1,708,468.00
332	Furniture	49.19	143,633.10	2.29	3,606.00	140,027.10
341	Paper and paper products	10.03	128,458.80	38.88	231,608.00	−103,149.20
342	Printing and publishing	1.82	7,866.46	27.88	77,642.00	−69,775.54
351	Industrial chemical	10.50	220,156.20	54.22	640,495.00	−420,338.80
352	Other chemical	4.50	70,232.18	51.85	388,396.00	−318,163.82
353	Petroleum refinery	N/A	N/A	N/A	N/A	N/A
354	Oil and gas processing	0.00	0.00	27.75	3,801.00	−3,801.00
355	Rubber products	42.48	690,879.40	19.24	203,349.00	487,530.40
356	Plastics	9.31	68,743.32	44.71	209,288.00	−140,544.68

361	Ceramics	10.44	17,734.37	67.09	34,952.00	−17,217.63
362	Glass products	6.14	12,802.84	18.08	17,812.00	−5,009.16
363	Cement	10.00	74,727.53	17.67	33,281.00	41,446.53
364	Structural clay	0.60	226.44	54.66	6,781.00	−6,554.56
369	Other non-metallic mineral	8.67	8,871.50	45.32	17,004.00	−8,132.50
371	Iron and steel	8.90	201,966.70	43.77	447,529.00	−245,562.30
372	Basic metal exc. iron and steel	33.83	202,214.90	64.63	262,857.00	−60,642.10
381	Metal products	8.29	101,367.00	36.30	304,756.00	−203,389.00
382	Non-electrical machinery	1.32	5,868.33	65.52	180,325.00	−174,456.67
383	Electrical equipment	13.52	173,873.70	61.91	515,828.00	−341,954.30
384	Transportation equipment	1.36	31,191.91	54.92	684,560.00	−653,368.09
385	Professional equipment	8.16	2,089.64	61.92	8,164	−6,074.36
390	Miscellaneous	15.88	25,754.41	32.92	31,472	−5,717.59

Sources: Calculated from Industrial Surveys, CBS.

Table 5.5b Net exports by industry (1995)

ISIC	Industry	Exports (%)	Exports ($000)	Imports (%)	Imports ($000)	Net exports ($000)
311	Food	19.96	1,662,922.02	4.84	277,421.00	1,385,501.02
312	Food	16.12	384,797.01	26.63	401,383.00	−16,585.99
313	Beverages	10.77	63,201.17	22.97	40,651.00	22,550.17
314	Tobacco	36.81	1,949,429.78	8.33	97,592.00	1,851,837.78
321	Textiles	24.90	2,337,334.09	21.16	1,712,733.00	624,601.09
322	Garment	54.05	1,304,675.93	33.12	487,313.00	817,362.93
323	Leather products	33.08	91,782.22	24.53	42,592.00	49,190.22
324	Footwear	70.68	1,587,613.60	58.54	728,945.00	858,668.60
331	Wood products	65.78	4,007,056.24	2.79	96,207.00	3,910,849.24
332	Furniture	53.33	453,448.87	3.39	16,966.00	436,482.87
341	Paper and paper products	7.33	219,968.56	33.37	551,498.00	−331,529.44
342	Printing and publishing	23.81	242,206.51	16.65	87,013.00	155,193.51
351	Industrial chemical	24.58	868,285.04	44.91	730,133.00	138,152.04
352	Other chemical	5.74	187,737.54	48.34	776,398.00	−588,660.46
353	Petroleum refinery	0.00	0.00	6.51	357.00	−357.00

354	Oil and gas processing	24.03	8,377.36	17.18	2,380.00	5,997.36
355	Rubber products	61.23	1,688,168.55	8.91	184,592.00	1,503,576.55
356	Plastics	14.88	343,230.42	37.58	505,779.00	-162,548.58
361	Ceramics	13.57	59,387.41	44.63	49,658.00	9,729.41
362	Glass products	22.90	97,477.31	41.81	54,489.00	42,988.31
363	Cement	1.75	25,715.60	9.17	35,896.00	-10,180.40
364	Structural clay	11.21	9,713.36	34.38	8,191.00	1,522.36
369	Other non-metallic mineral	14.01	40,917.51	39.06	44,998.00	-4,080.49
371	Iron and steel	8.99	374,954.85	51.02	958,696.00	-583,741.15
372	Basic metal exc. iron and steel	45.53	498,959.15	83.62	494,500.00	4,459.15
381	Metal products	13.06	368,429.90	38.89	604,045.00	-235,615.10
382	Non-electrical machinery	8.53	106,445.69	58.59	469,722.00	-363,276.31
383	Electrical equipment	43.02	2,404,342.94	72.29	2,523,430.00	-119,087.06
384	Transportation equipment	2.41	155,459.53	52.32	1,990,615.00	-1,835,155.47
385	Professional equipment	47.65	97,847.13	75.84	84,389	13,458.13
390	Miscellaneous	44.59	230,799.61	31.76	102,229	128,570.61

Sources: Calculated from Industrial Surveys, CBS.

Table 5.6 Net exports according to ownership status

	Exports (%)	Exports ($000)	Imports (%)	Imports ($000)	Net exports ($000)
1990					
Local	19.03	3,601,927.08	29.94	3,011,151.00	590,776.08
MNC	16.91	1,210,319.25	57.58	2,049,369.00	−839,049.75
Other	13.02	1,241,373.12	15.36	809,602.00	431,771.12
1991					
Local	24.58	5,459,593.44	29.66	3,597,036.00	1,862,557.44
MNC	20.28	1,530,312.61	55.31	2,311,197.00	−780,884.39
Other	14.88	1,687,624.90	23.97	1,540,316.00	147,308.90
1993					
Local	22.96	5,530,395.91	24.28	3,185,139.00	2,345,256.91
MNC	29.52	3,455,223.21	54.74	3,309,260.00	145,963.21
Other	18.73	4,199,743.03	19.18	2,580,721.00	1,619,022.03
1995					
Local	28.96	9,676,576.78	27.18	4,818,921.00	4,857,655.78
MNC	33.70	7,019,409.90	56.12	6,310,679.00	708,730.90
Other	21.22	5,175,678.23	21.46	3,031,219.00	2,144,459.23

Sources: Manufacturing Surveys.

Table 5.7 Net exports according to firm size

	Exports (%)	Exports ($000)	Imports (%)	Imports ($000)	Net exports ($000)
1990					
Large	18.29	4,090,604.30	33.48	3,748,327.00	342,277.30
Medium	16.52	1,704,142.46	29.21	1,790,515.00	−86,372.54
Small	8.75	255,086.48	17.34	325,898.00	−70,811.52
Total		6,049,833.24		5,864,740.00	185,093.24
1995					
Large	31.81	16,508,543.07	38.59	10,228,534.00	6,280,009.07
Medium	22.79	4,774,463.38	25.78	3,417,420.00	1,357,043.38
Small	10.27	587,398.39	15.55	513,940.00	73,458.39
Total		21,870,404.84		14,159,894.00	7,710,510.84

Sources: Manufacturing Surveys.

can satisfy such a definition. According to 1991 data, some industries like paper (341), industrial chemicals (351), cement (364), non-electrical machinery (382) and transportation equipment (384) possess above-average LP growth but are not very export oriented and often negatively contribute to the trade balance. These industries generally enjoy a high degree of protection; therefore their value-added figures might be inflated by the degree of protection. The picture is not quite so different in 1995; although most industries have positive LP growth, many domestic-oriented industries such as paper products (341), plastic (356), iron and steel (371), metal products (381), non-electrical machinery (382) and transportation equipment (384) are negative contributors to the trade balance. Some industries such as textiles, garments, footwear and wood products emerge from the RCA analysis of the 1995 sample as the most competitive sectors since they recorded positive productivity as well as made a positive contribution to trade balance.

Overall competitiveness and the current account sustainability

The overall competitiveness of the Indonesian economy is measured by the evolution of real exchange rate (RER) (Table 5.8). RER is obtained by combining a measure of domestic inflation, as a proxy for the costs of domestic producers, with foreign inflation, as a measure of the change in world prices, and the nominal exchange rate. RER is calculated as nominal exchange rates times a measure of tradable prices (the attractiveness of export versus import substitutes) divided by a domestic price index, which serves as a proxy for domestic costs of production. RER can serve as an indicator of the domestic producer's competitiveness *vis-à-vis* the rest of the world. Operationally, RER is defined as a weighted average of the bilateral exchange rate of trading partners. It is common to use the value of trade (exports plus imports) as a weight. To measure the prices of tradables, three indexes are often used, industrial countries' consumer price index (CPI), industrial countries' wholesale price index (WPI) and import/export unit value indices, where CPI is used to measure domestic costs. In this study the United States, Japan, United Kingdom, Germany and France are chosen as trading partners because of the size of their bilateral trade with Indonesia.

Table 5.8 Nominal and real exchange rate

Year	IRER	IRERD	INER	INERD	INFL*	INFLDOM	CA/GDP
1988	80.19		88.30				−1.7
1989	86.80	8.24	90.50	2.49	3.43	6.42	−1.2
1990	100.00	15.21	100.00	10.50	3.97	7.76	−2.8
1991	99.18	−0.82	105.10	5.10	3.70	9.40	−3.7
1992	86.27	−13.02	103.56	−1.46	2.56	7.59	−2.2
1993	79.74	−7.57	104.89	1.28	2.07	9.60	−1.6
1994	76.60	−3.94	111.36	6.16	1.52	8.53	−1.7
1995	79.36	3.61	118.43	6.35	1.16	9.43	−3.7
1996	92.03	15.97	122.45	3.39	1.28	8.03	−4.0
1997	137.98	49.93	284.51	132.35	2.08	4.71	−2.3
1997:Q1	95.33		121.90		−1.31	−0.98	
1997:Q2	92.09		123.34		1.33	0.87	
1997:Q3	102.68		163.27		0.25	1.62	
1997:Q4	122.35		232.42		0.04	5.91	
1998:Q1	150.62		415.08		0.25	15.24	

Source: Calculated from Economic Indicator, Central Bureau of Statistics.

IRER: index of trade-weighted real exchange rate; IRERD: trade-weighted real exchange rate depreciation; INER: index of trade-weighted nominal exchange rate; INERD: trade-weighted nominal exchange rate depreciation; INFL*: inflation rate in six biggest trading partners; INFLDOM: domestic inflation rate based on CPI.

It is quite obvious that the appreciation of the RER in recent years has been significant. There was an indication that the Indonesian economy was experiencing gradual erosion of competitiveness. This phenomenon was a part of the wider trend taking place in Southeast and East Asian countries like Thailand, Malaysia, Philippines and Singapore (Wallace 1997). The reason behind this appreciation was higher inflation in Indonesia compared to its trading partners. The domestic inflation itself is the outcome of interaction between the domestic goods and services market, the labor market, and some function of domestic monetary and fiscal policies.

In the labor market, there was upward pressure on wages as the government continued to enforce the increase of minimum wages (i.e. since 1991). There was also an indication of a liquidity increase; the ratio of M2 to reserves which in the 1990–3 period was very close to five, rose to a little over six in the 1994–6 period. The source of this liquidity increase was mostly short-term capital inflows that were channeled to finance investment, mainly in non-traded goods sectors such as property and infrastructure. The worsening of the current account deficit also reflected the erosion of fiscal discipline that created excessive aggregate demand. In the goods and services market, the concentration of market power in the hands of a very few firms, particularly those producing essential commodities, resulted in upward price adjustments as they exercised their market power.

The slowdown of export growth in the 1991–6 period seems to support the assertion that Indonesia is losing competitiveness in its main manufactured exports such as footwear and garments which exploit the relative abundance of unskilled labor.[8] As shown before, these industries recorded positive LP growth, although apparently their productivity increase could not match the appreciation of the real exchange rate. There was also evidence that successive increases in minimum wages were not matched by increases in productivity (Kuncoro 1995).[9] The export growth in 1993 and in 1994 slowed to 8.4 and 8.6 percent, respectively, in contrast to an average of 15 per cent in the period 1986–91.

In the period 1991–6, the persistence of an interest rate differential between Indonesia and the rest of the world attracted huge capital inflows, most of which were sterilized by the central bank. Without such intervention, such inflows lead to the nominal appreciation of the rupiah, which would eventually hurt exporters. This would be in conflict with the central bank's policy to depreciate the rupiah at roughly 5 per cent per annum. Over the years, Indonesia has pursued a policy to maintain the competitiveness of non-oil exports. In fact, given the inability of the government to combat a high-cost economy resulting from bureaucratic red tape, corruption and inefficient regulation, currency depreciation remains the only workable alternative to maintain the competitiveness of the Indonesian economy. Substantial portions of the inflows were channeled directly and indirectly through the banking system to finance investments, including those in non-tradable sectors such as construction, real estate and financial services. As a result, overall investment jumped from approximately 28 to 32 per cent of GDP.

The combination of export slowdown and investment boom resulted in the deterioration of the current account, a deficit around 2 per cent of annual GDP in 1993 and 1994 increasing to 3.7 per cent in 1995 and 4 per cent in 1996.

The phenomena of real exchange rate appreciation and worsening current account deficits were also observed before the 1994 Mexican crisis, although for Indonesia these two factors do not sufficiently explain the spillover of the Thai currency crisis to Indonesia. In the Indonesian case, currency appreciation was also the result of capital inflows that were directed to finance excessive investment in non-traded good sectors such as property and infrastructure. The most important factor was the huge amount of short-term foreign borrowing, which due to the predictability of rupiah depreciation in the past was largely unhedged. The movement of the exchange rate from 2,500 to 4,000 between July and September was perhaps dictated by the amount of the current account deficit. Movement beyond 4,000 however, probably reflected attempts by foreign investors to avoid short-term capital losses and by domestic firms with large exposure to foreign debt to buy foreign exchange to service their future debt repayment.

3. The financial environment and portfolio decisions of firms

Financial characteristics: Winner and loser firms[10]

In this study, several variables are constructed to analyze the financial aspect of manufacturing firms. First, to measure firms' profitability or rates of return, we use the ratio of gross operating surplus before interest payment in relation to capital, which reflects the total returns to capital independent of financial structure. Second, the degree of leverage is measured by the ratio of debts to capital. Finally, to measure the average cost of borrowing funds, we use the ratio of total interest payments to total debt. The key summary statistics for manufacturing firms are given in Tables 5.9 and 5.10. These tables provide information on all manufacturing firms as well as on specific samples according to different categorization: (i) according to firm size – large, medium and small establishments; (ii) according to ownership status – MNC versus local firms; (iii) according to export orientation – exporter versus non-exporter. The observations are taken between 1990 and 1995.

A general observation suggests that in the last period of analysis (i.e. 1995), firms are more leveraged than in the first period (i.e. 1990). The ratio of total debt to capital stock for winner industries (e.g. garments, footwear and wood products) is higher in comparison to loser sectors (e.g. industrial chemicals and transportation equipment).[11] Interestingly, the domestically oriented cement industry (363), which is controlled by conglomerates, had the highest leverage in 1995. The data also shows that the average cost of borrowing (interest payment over the stock of debt) was generally higher than in 1991. In this respect however, winner industries generally paid lower interest rates.

High interest rates were the consequence of the tight monetary policy pursued by the government. Initially, this policy was originally intended to stop large capital flight in response to the rumor of devaluation in 1991. In subsequent years, the policy was maintained to sterilize large capital inflows in the form of commercial loans and portfolio investment which were coming to Indonesia in response to a booming domestic economy and more openness created by deregulation measures.

Table 5.9 Indonesia manufacturing sector: several financial indicators

	INV-STOCK	PROFIT	LEVERAGE	AVCOB	FLOAN
1987					
Large	0.3125	0.5313	0.4422	0.1070	0.0632
Medium	0.2250	0.3906	0.3534	0.1066	0.0161
Small	0.1187	0.1603	0.2884	0.0399	0.0025
1991					
Large	0.1055	0.1222	0.2648	0.0489	0.0253
Medium	0.6869	0.3348	0.0460	0.0767	0.0565
Small	0.3360	0.3384	0.0129	0.2200	0.3300
Exporters	0.1231	0.1762	0.2459	0.0815	0.0336
Non-exp.	0.3340	0.1342	0.0828	0.1566	0.0578
1995					
Large	0.2577	0.6703	0.3035	0.1554	0.0908
Medium	0.2837	0.4824	0.2810	0.1479	0.0738
Small	0.5210	0.4300	0.1124	0.3175	0.0603
Exporters	0.2954	0.6647	0.3159	0.1609	0.0997
Non-exp.	0.2670	0.5423	0.2256	0.1713	0.0169

Sources: Manufacturing Surveys, CBS.

INV-STOCK: ratio of investment to capital stock; PROFIT: ratio of gross operating surplus to capital stock; LEVERAGE: ratio of debt to capital stock; AVCOB: average cost of borrowing; FLOAN: ratio of foreign debt to total debt.

In this case, instead of letting the exchange rate appreciate, the monetary authority opted to sterilize the flows since an undervalued domestic currency was needed to keep exports competitive.

High domestic interest rates in 1991 caused a substantial rise in the interest rate burden (as illustrated in the 1995 figures) for all sizes of firms (Table 5.9). This high interest rate environment appears to have had an impact: comparing the 1987 data across all categories shows lower leverage than in 1991. After 1991, the interest rate falls slowly, although it has not yet come back to the 1990 level.[12] Predictably, this new development had some impact on firms' behavior; between 1991 and 1995 all categories show some increase in leverage. The environment faced by small establishments, however, is characterized by higher average costs of borrowing when compared to large and medium ones. In this period, we also started to observe substitution between domestic credit and foreign credit. Particularly in the category of large firms, there was indication of an increase in the portion of foreign debt. It appears that the booming domestic economy and easy access to offshore borrowing made it possible for firms to thrive in a high interest rate environment.

According to Table 5.9, exporters tend to be more leveraged. The average cost of borrowing is lower for exporters, not too surprising since exporters have better access to foreign loans. The only exception was in 1991, when domestic interest rates reached their highest level. Various deregulatory measures since the mid-1980s have positively impacted exporters. This situation was documented in profit

Table 5.10 Indonesian manufacturing sector: firm financial aspects at the sectoral level

ISIC	Industry	1987					1990				
		INV-ST	PROFIT	LEVER	AVCOB	FLOAN	INV-ST	PROFIT	LEVER	AVCOB	FLOAN
311	Food	0.2115	0.4821	0.1717	0.1472	0.0125	0.1574	0.6938	0.0144	0.2252	0.5523
321	Textiles	0.1436	0.3938	0.3844	0.1042	0.0464	0.1055	0.0225	0.0716	0.0478	0.0392
322	Garment	0.1016	0.2193	0.3069	0.0312	0.0007	0.6480	0.5459	0.0063	0.0926	0.2314
324	Footwear	0.0240	0.0760	0.1088	0.1680	0.0000	0.5405	0.8929	0.0369	0.1146	0.3832
351	Industrial chemical	0.6313	0.2738	0.5317	0.1023	0.1090	0.1755	0.3502	0.1015	0.0613	0.1983
352	Other chemical	0.6253	1.4179	0.3328	0.4049	0.1191	0.9244	1.3597	0.0106	0.1149	0.2303
362	Glass products	0.4218	1.5738	0.5548	0.0860	0.0000	0.2815	1.1398	0.0017	0.0479	0.1698
363	Cement	0.0467	0.3294	0.1807	0.0997	0.0000	0.1813	0.5415	0.0104	0.3314	0.1520
383	Electrical equipment	0.3351	0.6445	0.2393	0.2649	0.0107	0.0593	0.0115	0.0305	0.0437	0.0160
384	Transportation equipment	0.3958	0.3142	0.8030	0.0264	0.1474	0.9853	0.3617	0.0104	0.1314	0.2632
385	Professional equipment	0.3918	0.4525	0.2073	0.0867	0.0000	0.1572	0.6122	0.0722	0.0729	0.0000
390	Miscellaneous	0.4308	0.7027	0.3244	0.2221	0.0142	0.1875	0.8028	0.0023	0.5135	0.0000

ISIC	Industry	1991					1995				
		INV-ST	PROFIT	LEVER	AVCOB	FLOAN	INV-ST	PROFIT	LEVER	AVCOB	FLOAN
311	Food	0.0451	0.0607	0.0316	0.1213	0.0061	0.1436	0.3881	0.2621	0.0885	0.0217
321	Textiles	0.1654	0.1228	0.4110	0.0531	0.0363	0.2666	0.3573	0.4595	0.1001	0.0650
322	Garment	0.1914	0.0701	0.0650	0.1369	0.0214	0.4885	0.9095	0.4242	0.1813	0.0368
324	Footwear	0.9498	0.6840	0.0722	0.9143	0.2231	0.2820	0.6289	0.3967	0.1088	0.1912
351	Industrial chemical	0.8172	0.4860	0.1079	0.7287	0.7177	0.1701	0.5066	0.2707	0.2356	0.0970
352	Other chemical	0.6526	0.3335	0.0171	0.1449	0.0810	0.2361	0.9573	0.2970	0.1722	0.0780
362	Glass products	0.2280	0.8572	0.1694	0.4076	0.0461	0.4504	0.6138	0.1027	0.8300	0.0001
363	Cement	0.5348	0.4614	0.0096	0.1417	0.1237	0.1133	0.3981	0.5883	0.0348	0.0640
383	Electrical equipment	1.4194	0.5348	0.0572	0.1207	0.6380	0.4369	1.1696	0.4460	0.1282	0.3118
384	Transportation equipment	0.1171	0.0999	0.0580	0.1387	0.0247	0.6559	1.0919	0.0691	0.8008	0.1559
385	Professional equipment	0.0777	0.4476	0.3930	0.0542	0.0000	0.4971	0.4678	0.3698	0.0663	0.0038
390	Miscellaneous	0.4431	0.7391	0.0117	0.7750	0.4600	0.1681	0.2940	0.3361	0.0912	0.0242

Sources: Manufacturing Surveys, CBS.

INV-ST: ratio of investment to capital stock; PROFIT: ratio of gross operating surplus to capital stock; LEVER: ratio of total debt to capital stock; AVCOB: average cost of borrowing.

figures, where the rates of return were consistently higher for exporters. The rates of return gap between exporters and non-exporters was somewhat narrowed in 1995 in the context of a booming domestic economy. The profitability of non-exporters increased substantially, although it was still lower than for exporters.

Looking at the industry level, winning sectors (garments, footwear and wood products) are more leveraged than others (Table 5.10). Interestingly, some domestically oriented industries have higher leverage rates than winners, for example cement (363). Cement, which is controlled by politically well-connected conglomerates, in fact is the most leveraged industry at the three-digit level. With their political ties to the government, it is possible for conglomerates to have preferential access to credit from state banks at subsidized rates. This practice is a legacy of the past, although it is still prevalent for industries with very strong connections to the government. Conglomerates also have another advantage, namely their high profiles, which have enabled them to get better access to offshore credit markets.

If one looks at the data classified by firm size, large enterprises tend to have higher leverage than medium or small establishments. Also, large establishments are more likely to use offshore borrowing as a source of capital. Better access to foreign credit markets is also evident for export-oriented firms, particularly in recent years. Interestingly, in the past (1990) domestically oriented firms have been more likely to resort to foreign credit. This picture is rather difficult to interpret since the domestic interest rates climbed sharply in 1991, but the portion of foreign credit did not increase.

After observing the financial aspects of establishments, it can be concluded that the ability to obtain external funds in the domestic market differs among small and large firms, and between exporters and non-exporters. The credit market usually favors large firms, outward orientation and a good reputation. Firms not possessing such characteristics may have to assume higher costs of borrowing. This situation is nonetheless much better than during times of financial repression when credit is rationed and allocated according to a set of rules defined by the government. A liberal foreign exchange regime also provides additional advantages for certain firms to borrow funds from overseas markets. Unfortunately, there is a lack of information on the ethnicity of the owner of firms in general. It is common knowledge, however, that conglomerates and large Chinese firms with connections to financial markets in Singapore and Hong Kong, foreign firms and exporters all have better access to foreign loans. Also, even after the 1983 Banking Deregulation, state bank credit at below market rates is still available for people and large firms with strong political connections to the government. So, even after deregulation, credit market segmentation remains. The only difference with the past is that access is higher now for previously disadvantaged firms, albeit at a higher rate.

Trade specialization, productivity and finance: Econometric evidence

In this section we try to answer a fundamental question regarding the interactions between financial factors, trade specialization and international competitiveness.

The question asks what the important factors are in determining whether a firm specializes in winning or losing sectors. Perhaps financial factors such as the availability of credit are very important in determining the pattern of specialization. The pattern of specialization itself is very important in determining the country's competitiveness since a country might be locked into activities that contribute very little to the sustainability of the current account. To be able to answer the above question, we model the firm's specialization decision, that is, to specialize in one particular sector or another. After a firm chooses a sector, it will then choose its market orientation (i.e. whether to concentrate on export market or domestic market). Firms' choices will ultimately determine the pattern of specialization and current account sustainability.

Consider a manufacturing firm making a decision to choose a sector or activities. A firm will choose a particular sector when it offers the highest profit. Formally, from M activities firm t chooses sector k according to eqn (5.1):

$$\pi_{tk}^* = \max[\pi_{t1}, \pi_{t2}, \dots, \pi_{tN}], \quad N = 1, 2, \dots, n. \tag{5.1}$$

For simplicity, let $N=2$, so there are only two sectors in the economy: winning sectors (textiles, garments, footwear and wood products) and losers (other sectors). The observed variable π_{tk} is defined as $\pi_{tk}=1$ if a firm chooses a winning sector, and $\pi_{tk}=0$ otherwise. The probability of specializing in the winning or losing sectors is determined by several factors, including firm characteristics and financial characteristics. Specifically, the profit function is specified as a function of output price (p), input price (w) and 'financial' price (f) reflecting financial access or availability. This is illustrated in eqn (5.2):

$$\pi_{tk} = \pi[p, w, f, c, a], \tag{5.2}$$

where c represents various firm's characteristics and a refers to a productivity shock or productivity growth.

After examining the relationship between finance and patterns of specialization, the next task is to investigate the consequences of finance and pattern of specialization on the current account. For this, we need to model a firm's output decision. In standard microeconomics textbooks, profit maximization will result in an output supply function and input demand function. The firm's net exports, or contribution to the trade balance, are treated as the output supply function net of imported raw materials. Therefore, following eqn (5.1), the firm's exported output net of imported raw materials or net exports (nx) is specified in eqn (5.3):

$$nx_{tk} = nx[px, w, f, a], \tag{5.3}$$

where px is the price of exported output.

For the firm's specialization function, probit regressions are performed on eqn (5.1), while for the contribution to the trade balance we use ordinary least square (OLS) estimation. For financial availability, we use two proxies: the ratio of domestic credit to total capital and the ratio of overseas borrowing to total capital. The ratio of value added to intermediate inputs is used as a proxy for output price. This variable is also intended to capture the differences in effective rates of protection among industries. The basic result of firm-level regression for the entire 1991 and 1995 samples can be seen in Table 5.11.

In the first exercise, we examine the determinants of a firm's contribution to the trade balance or exported output net of imported raw materials (numerical columns 1 and 2 of Table 5.11). For the complete sample of manufacturing establishments

Table 5.11 Factors affecting contribution to trade balance and probability to specialize in leading RCA sectors

	Contribution to TB Whole sample		Leading RCA sector Whole sample	
	1991	*1995*	*1991*	*1995*
C	3.42E+04	4.61E+04	−9.31E−01	−1.02E+00
	[0.051]	[−0.696E+07]	[−9.487]	[−15.742]
PRICES	5.72E+06	−6.96E+06	27.379	23.023
	[2.312]	[−1.125]	[70.53]	[67.183]
WAGES	−8.554	−1.60E+02	1.77E−06	−2.57E−05
	[−0.606]	[−2.977]	[−1.121]	[−4.361]
LPG	−5,591	−17,621	−0.021	−0.046
	[−1.577]	[−1.472]	[−27.279]	[−36.898]
AGE	3,052.8	36,241	−0.015	−0.015
	[0.399]	[2.117]	[−12.363]	[−13.147]
DMNC	−2.47E+05	−5.84E+05	−0.401	−0.543
	[−0.547]	[−0.639]	[−6.278]	[−9.275]
DLARGE	1.58E+06	9.87E+06	7.28E−01	5.51E−01
	[2.149]	[8.148]	[6.898]	[7.333]
DMED	4.13E+05	1.05E+06	3.11E−01	1.73E−01
	[0.603]	[0.988]	[3.103]	[2.577]
DSMALL	81,965	1.20E+05	0.171	1.49E−01
	[0.123]	[0.120]	[1.755]	[2.325]
DMLOAN	−0.004	0.081	8.06E+08	1.36E−10
	[−1.431]	[4.264]	[2.075]	[0.114]
FRLOAN	−0.038	−0.162	9.74E−11	−1.67E−09
	[−5.233]	[−7.471]	[−0.087]	[−0.960]
N	16,494	21,559	16,494	211,551
F	6.11	26.29		
Rest-Log-*L*			−10,141.1	−1,318,980
Log-*L*			−6,466.66	−7,559.26

PRICES: price of exported output; LPG: labor productivity growth; DMNC: dummy for FDI firms; DLARGE: dummy for large firms; DMED: dummy for medium-sized firms; DSMALL: dummy for small firms; DMLOAN: domestic banks' credit; FRLOAN: overseas credit.

in the 1995 sample, we find a significant negative relationship between wages and contribution to the trade balance (TB) or net export. Thus in 1995, labor cost is still an important factor in determining the ability to compete in export markets. The later economic deregulation measures seem to make this pattern stronger, and thus confirm the result of the probit regressions.

We also find a negative relationship between TFP growth and contribution to TB, which means firms in industries with high TFP growth tend to not be export oriented. However, the coefficient is not significant at the 5 per cent confidence level. In the case of the age variable, there is a suggestion that older firms tend to generate surplus for the trade account. This result seems in conflict with the probit regressions, although if we take into account the possibility that older firms may have stronger linkages with domestic suppliers compared to younger ones, this result is plausible.

The impact of differences in firm type on foreign exchange contributions also present interesting results. In the 1991 sample, there is no significant difference between large, medium and small firms with regard to contribution to the TB. In the 1995 sample, however, large firms are more likely to contribute to the TB compared to medium and small ones. In another categorization, we test the behavior of MNC or FDI firms versus non-FDI firms. We find that in both samples, there is no significant difference between FDI firms and local firms in terms of contribution to the TB.

In the case of the impact of the availability of credit financing on contribution to the TB, we observe the phenomenon of currency mismatch. The availability of foreign credit does not guarantee that firms will be sufficiently export oriented. This is especially apparent in the 1995 sample, as more and more domestically oriented firms with negative contributions to the TB use foreign credit to finance their domestic activities. A booming domestic economy, an overvalued exchange rate and high domestic interest rates have made borrowing from abroad an attractive option. Obviously, this behavior puts pressure on the current account and is also one of the many factors that contributed to the crisis. Interestingly, firms with a positive contribution to the TB are more likely to use domestic credit as a source of finance.

In the second regression (numerical columns 3 and 4 of Table 5.11), the coefficient of exported output price is positive as expected. Meanwhile the coefficient of wages is negative as expected, although it is only significant in the 1995 sample. This means that low wages are still important in influencing Indonesia's pattern of specialization, which confirms an earlier assertion that Indonesia is still specializing in low-end products which base their competitiveness on cheap labor. The sign of the LP growth coefficient also supports this conclusion. The coefficients of LP growth are negative and significant in both samples. It becomes more negative and significant in the later period. Indonesia is locked into the pattern of specialization in the production of low-productivity goods with high dependency on imported raw materials. There was some indication that the economic liberalization that started in 1986 reinforced this pattern of specialization.

There is a sign that finance does affect the pattern of specialization, particularly if we look at the coefficient of domestic credit in the 1991 sample. The coefficient of domestic credit is positive and significant, indicating the role of domestic banking in financing activities in export-oriented sectors. The coefficient becomes insignificant in the 1995 sample, so it is possible that the booming activity in the non-tradable sectors such as property, infrastructure and other less export-oriented activities has shifted the banking sector's attention away from the tradable sector.

All the dummy variables for capturing differences in a firm's size are significant in both samples. The most significant variable, and at the same time the largest positive coefficient, is the dummy for large firms, followed by medium and small establishments. Therefore, larger-size firms have a higher probability of specializing in the leading RCA sectors. With regard to age difference, the regression results also reveal that young firms tend to specialize in the leading RCA sector. Perhaps young firms with newer technologies are more suited to export markets.

The MNC dummy variable capturing the differences between MNC and local firms is negative and significant, meaning MNC firms do not tend to specialize in the leading RCA sectors. The negative coefficient is stronger and more negative in the 1995 sample, which suggests that FDI firms in the later period tend to see Indonesia as a potential market to be exploited, rather than as a base for export expansion. This does not mean that the later deregulation policies seeking to open up the economy are misplaced. Rather, inconsistency in the government's trade and industrial policies in the form of non-trade barriers makes the rates of returns on domestically oriented economies artificially high, while at the same time lower trade barriers in input markets and an overvalued currency make the cost of imported inputs artificially cheaper.

Firms' portfolio decisions

The Indonesian Manufacturing Surveys provide information regarding the sources of capital. We use this information to address the question about firms' portfolio decisions. An overview of the sources of firm finance is presented in Table 5.12. In general, firms in winning sectors tend to have a higher proportion

Table 5.12 Sources of finance

	1991		1995	
	All	*Winner*	*All*	*Winner*
Own capital	31.46	34.81	23.15	17.37
Retained earnings	12.89	10.19	10.68	9.02
Stock	8.89	11.52	11.04	8.52
Domestic credit	28.47	29.43	33.14	36.43
Foreign credit	5.79	10.87	14.54	18.62
Foreign placement	9.47	20.07	4.07	4.60
Government equity	4.03	1.11	3.38	5.44

Sources: Calculated from the Industrial Surveys database.

of foreign loans when compared to the average manufacturing firm. In 1991, for example, the figure for foreign loans in the winning sectors was 10.87 per cent, while the corresponding figure for all manufacturing firms was 5.79 per cent. In 1991, on average a winner's other important financial sources were own capital (34.81 per cent), domestic banking credit (29.43 per cent), retained earnings (10.19 per cent), stocks (11.52 per cent) and foreign direct capital placements (20.07 per cent). Thus, winners are more leveraged and more likely to obtain foreign loans than average manufacturing firms.

In 1991, for winning sectors the portions of retained earnings, foreign direct capital placement and government equity participation were lower than the average manufacturing firm. So it could be concluded that winning sectors tend to have higher portions of domestic bank credits, foreign credits, their own capital and the stock market as sources of finance. In 1995, some portfolio shifts took place; for both winners and the average manufacturing firms a big decline of the share of own capital could be observed. Thus, all firms tended to raise capital externally, in particular in the domestic credit market and through overseas borrowing.

To model the portfolio decisions of firms, we employ a multinomial logit model in which the choice of sources of finance is specified as a function of firm characteristics including age, labor productivity growth, size differences, and MNC versus local firms. As in the above discussion, there are seven choices for financing: own-capital injection, retained earnings, stock market, domestic banking, overseas borrowing, foreign direct capital placement and government equity participation. As required by the multinomial logit procedure, the parameters of one choice need to be normalized to zero. In this case, we chose own-capital injection to be normalized. The reason behind this choice is that we are more interested in other sources of financing. The results of multinomial logit regressions are presented in Table 5.13. First, we look at the 1991 sample. At first glance, it can be seen that one variable which is always significant in all cases is labor productivity growth (LPG). Thus, productivity growth is always important in all choices of source of finance. Firm age has a negative coefficient in three choices: stock market, domestic bank credit and foreign credit. This means older firms are less likely to use these three sources of financing. For foreign direct capital placement, the sign of the coefficient is positive and significant, indicating that older firms are more likely to choose this source of finance. Another interesting variable is the dummy variable for large firms. The sign of this variable indicates that large firms have a high probability of using the stock market, bank credit, foreign borrowing and foreign direct capital placement to raise capital. Medium firms, with foreign direct capital placement as an exception, also showed similar preferences.

In the 1991 sample, the case of MNC firms is also interesting. The only positive and significant variable is foreign credit, indicating better access to overseas credit markets. MNC firms are also less likely to use domestic bank credit as a source of funds. Better access to overseas borrowing and higher domestic interest rates make it unnecessary to secure domestic credit. In the case of winner firms, retained earnings, foreign credit and foreign direct capital placement are chosen as sources of finance. Interestingly, they avoid government equity participation.

Table 5.13 Factors affecting firm portfolio decisions (multinomial logic estimation)

	Retained earnings		Stock		Domestic bank credit	
	1991	1995	1991	1995	1991	1995
C	-1.30857 (-21.1683)	-0.864072 (-16.6740)	-2.44869 (24.0431)	-3.29912 (-24.2278)	-0.861983 (-15.4582)	-0.669374 (-13.3598)
AGE	4.19E-03 (1.67229)	0.013078 (5.01024)	-0.14078 (3.03601)	-5.70E-03 (-0.873041)	-9.94E-03 (-3.94927)	-4.19E-03 (-1.54099)
PG	3.58E-06 (4.97147)	9.55E-06 (4.67062)	4.71E-06 (6.54513)	9.99E-06 (4.00521)	4.28E-06 (6.15864)	8.25E-06 (4.07938)
DMNC	0.136403 (0.918419)	0.798009 (3.94947)	0.27653 (1.46656)	0.604485 (1.90015)	-0.347212 (-2.40387)	0.50547 (2.63725)
DWIN	0.215943 (3.08950)	-0.151825 (-2.18725)	-0.204891 (-1.82397)	0.074109 (0.506668)	0.114795 (1.84872)	0.205713 (3.34649)
DLARGE	-0.61389 (-0.495102)	0.692944 (5.51038)	1.26361 (8.54642)	2.08893 (9.89206)	0.707507 (7.40571)	1.38599 (12.4313)
DMED	0.13216 (1.77613)	0.327876 (4.21228)	0.969101 (8.91211)	1.64711 (10.8018)	0.46621 (7.19578)	0.873283 (12.7565)

	Foreign credit		Foreign direct capital		Government equity	
	1991	*1995*	*1991*	*1995*	*1991*	*1995*
C	-3.42145 (-21.5331)	-4.36467 (-20.6467)	-3.36586 (-26.0583)	-4.74043 (17.1974)	-4.62034 (-13.9996)	-4.74043 (-17.1974)
AGE	-0.024471 (-3.39453)	-0.032728 (-2.97558)	0.022923 (5.94416)	-0.087641 (5.36597)	9.86E-03 (0.7288226)	-0.087641 (5.36597)
LPG	5.20E-06 (6.77664)	1.31E-05 (5.92772)	4.39E-06 (5.53726)	9.39E-06 (3.38700)	4.97E-06 (4.13023)	9.39E-06 (3.38700)
DMNC	1.54151 (8.55219)	3.57384 (15.4204)	-0.35744 (-1.04789)	5.76058 (18.6109)	-25.7244 (-0.799E-04)	5.76058 (18.6109)
DWIN	0.551413 (3.78128)	0.424417 (2.38965)	0.416206 (2.96919)	-0.451513 (-2.17890)	-1.54404 (-2.51481)	-0.451513 (-2.17890)
DLARGE	1.41212 (7.36451)	2.40685 (9.34578)	0.881273 (4.85236)	1.28005 (4.28290)	0.553575 (0.878425)	1.28005 (4.28290)
DMED	0.769345 (4.73044)	1.55227 (6.95577)	-0.46763 (-0.279974)	0.923312 (-25.4382)	0.438528 (1.02922)	0.923312 (3.74099)

Note: All *t*-statistics significant at the 5 per cent level.

The results for the 1995 sample differ from the 1991 sample, with some exceptions. Labor productivity is still important in all choices. With regard to age, older firms tend to choose retained earnings. The positive and significant coefficient for government equity participation must come from the presence of the substantial number of state-owned enterprises. Older firms are also less likely to use foreign credit and foreign direct capital placement.

The size factor is still important in the 1995 sample, as indicated by the coefficient of the dummy variable for large firms which is significant in all choices of financing. The same picture also applies to medium firms. MNC firms show different behavior. It is true that they still prefer to use foreign credit, and in 1995 also foreign direct capital placement. Unlike in the 1991 sample, MNC firms now are more supportive of the use of retained earnings and domestic bank credit. Winner firms also show a more favorable attitude towards the use of domestic bank credit, although the choice of foreign credit is still in favor. There is a shift in behavior, however, with regard to the use of retained earnings and foreign direct capital placement as they are now less likely to use these sources.

4. Conclusion

The structure of Indonesian exports in the 1970s and the early 1980s, with a heavy dependence on oil/gas and natural resource products, made the current account very vulnerable to international price fluctuations. The economic reforms initiated in response to the plummeting of oil prices marked a change in trade and industrial policy from import substitution, with its emphasis on the development of capital-intensive manufacturing in the upstream and resource-based industries, to labor-intensive export-oriented industries.

The impact of economic reforms after 1986 is very obvious in the structure of Indonesian exports. Exports of manufactured goods like textiles, processed woods, electronics and shoes started to rise. In 1991, the share of non-oil exports in total exports exceeded oil and gas exports. Until the mid-1990s however, Indonesia's manufactured export base was still very narrow, and mainly consisted of wood products, textiles, garments and footwear, industries exploiting low-cost labor rather than productivity as a source of competitiveness. There was an indication that the economic liberalization of 1986 seemed to reinforce this pattern of specialization. Indonesia is locked into a pattern of specialization that emphasizes the production of low-productivity goods with high dependency on imported raw materials. The emergence of unskilled labor-intensive industries as foreign exchange earners creates a new problem for the current account. As these industries are very dependent on imported inputs, this makes them very vulnerable to exchange rate fluctuations, as happened in the recent economic crisis.

There is an indication that finance does affect the pattern of specialization. In a 1991 sample, the domestic banking system had a very important role in financing activities in export-oriented sectors. In later periods, however, the booming activity of the non-tradable sectors (such as property, infrastructure and other less export-oriented activities) shifted the attention of the banking sector away from tradable sectors. The influx of capital inflows is also responsible for the expansion of the non-tradable sector during the 1991–5 period. As activities in non-tradables continued to expand, high growth was maintained until 1996, although the current account deficit continued to soar. This eventually triggered a reversal in expectations.

Notes

1　In terms of development strategy, the oil boom also produced a shift in the strategy of economic development. The availability of money and the expansion of domestic aggregate demand persuaded the government to pursue an import substitution policy. Many ambitious infrastructure and industrial projects were launched. The shift towards more inward-looking policies was also reflected through more protectionist industrial and trade policies.

2　See Section 2 on contribution to the trade balance and sectoral competitiveness.

3　Some (e.g. Iqbal 1995) argued that the reason behind the economic slowdown was a slowdown in pace of deregulation. For example, although the nominal tariff showed a decreasing trend in the pre-1991, it hardly changed during the 1991–4 period. The same pattern could also be observed for products subject to import licensing.

4　Although some argued that the dismal performance of several economic indicators was caused by the slowdown in the pace of economic deregulation, others suggested that this downward trend was part of a global phenomenon. This latter argument was based on the observation that other Asian tigers like Malaysia, Thailand and South Korea were also exhibiting a similar trend. Another reason behind the slowdown of manufactured exports was the nature of the products produced – basically destined for low end consumption and relying on low-cost labor. With the successive increases of national minimum wages, the competitiveness of Indonesian labor-intensive exports seemed to erode.

5　Unlike the previous investment boom in 1988–92 where textiles, garments and footwear made the bulk of total investments, the second investment boom was more diversified, ranging from electronic components, automotive parts, chemicals, to food and beverages. Also, most of the projects in the latter boom were destined for the Indonesian domestic market.

6　The reason for this is that an overvalued rupiah and high domestic interest rates made borrowing from abroad cheaper.

7　It is worthwhile to highlight the Indonesian electronics industry since it might become the great foreign exchange earner for the country in the future provided that the government alters the structure of protection. At present, the electronic industry has not moved much beyond assembly operations.

8　There are several explanations regarding Indonesia's loss of competitiveness in its main manufacturing exports. One explanation is that the competitiveness of Indonesia's labor-intensive industries had been eroded by the successive increases of minimum wages. Other factors, such as the boom in the domestic market, might have played a role as well. Finally, Indonesian producers also recently faced stiff competition from several emerging markets such as China, Vietnam and India that produce products of comparable quality at competitive prices.

9　A study by the World Bank (1996) found that productivity growth in Indonesia kept pace with the large increases in minimum wages untill 1993. Thereafter, the minimum wage became more binding.

10　Winners and losers have been defined from the point of view of international trade. Based on the previous analyses, winner industries include garments, footwear and wood products. All of these industries are characterized by a huge contribution to the balance of trade. Meanwhile, loser industries include industrial chemicals and transportation equipment.

11 This phenomenon is not limited to the chosen winner and loser industries. In general, industries with a net positive contribution to the trade account are more highly leveraged than industries with negative contributions.
12 Nominal interest rates in Indonesia are the highest among Southeast Asian countries, though inflation in Indonesia is also the highest in the region.

References

Chapman, R. (1992) 'Indonesian Trade Reform in Close-Up: The Steel and Footwear Experiences', *Bulletin of Indonesian Economic Studies* 28(1): 67–84.

Dowling, M. (1997) 'Industrialization, International Trade and Structural Change in Indonesia during the Suharto Era', Paper presented at the conference 'Sustaining Economic Growth of Indonesia: A Framework for the Twenty-First Century', organized by USAID, ACAES, and Institute of Economic and Social Research University of Indonesia.

Fane, G. and Philips, C. (1991) 'Effective Protection in Indonesia in 1987', *Bulletin of Indonesian Economic Studies* 27(1): 105–26.

Haque, I. (1995) *Trade, Technology, and International Competitiveness*. Washington, DC: World Bank.

Harris, J. R., Schiantarelli, F. and Siregar, M. G. (1994) 'The Effect of Financial Liberalization on the Capital Structure', *World Bank Economic Review* 8(1): 1–47.

Henderson, J. V. and Kuncoro, A. (1996) 'Industrial Centralization in Indonesia', *World Bank Economic Review* 10(3): 223–39.

Hill, H. (1995) 'Indonesia's Industrial Policy and Performance: Orthodoxy Vindicated', Paper presented at the conference 'Building on Success: Maximizing the Gains from Deregulation', organized by the Association of Indonesian Economists and the World Bank.

Iqbal, F. (1995) 'Deregulation and Development in Indonesia', Paper presented at the conference 'Building on Success: Maximizing the Gains from Deregulation', organized by the Association of Indonesian Economists and the World Bank.

Kuncoro, A. (1995) 'The Impact of Seller Concentration on Industrial Location', Paper presented at the conference 'Building on Success: Maximizing the Gains from Deregulation', organized by the Association of Indonesian Economists and the World Bank.

Kuncoro, A. (1997) 'Export Orientation, Productivity and Finance', Paper presented at the conference 'Sustaining Economic Growth of Indonesia: A Framework for the Twenty-First Century', organized by USAID, ACAES, and Institute of Economic and Social Research University of Indonesia.

Lall, S. (1998) 'Technology Policies in Indonesia', in H. Hill and T. Kian Wie (eds), *Indonesia's Technological Challenge*. Singapore: ANU and Institute of Southeast Asian Studies.

Nasution, A. and James, W. E. (1995) 'Future April 12, Direction for Economic Policy Reform: Where Are We and Where Do We Go from Here', Paper presented at the conference 'Building on Success: Maximizing the Gains from Deregulation', organized by the Association of Indonesian Economists and the World Bank.

Wallace, W. (1997) 'Prospect for the Indonesian Current Account Deficit', Paper presented at the conference 'Sustaining Economic Growth of Indonesia: A Framework for the Twenty-First Century', organized by USAID, ACAES, and Institute of Economic and Social Research University of Indonesia.

6 Trade, competitiveness and finance in the Philippine manufacturing sector, 1980–95[1]

Josef T. Yap

1. Introduction: The Philippine development experience

The East Asian miracle of the 1960s up to the mid-1990s and the East Asian debacle in 1997 put in perspective two crucial factors that affect sustainable economic growth and development. The first factor is outward orientation, which is a necessary ingredient for increasing the competitiveness of an economy, and the second is a sound financial structure that is required for efficient resource allocation and macroeconomic stability. The primary objective of this chapter, is to analyse how these two factors interact with each other, i.e. how the level of financial development affected the evolution of the Philippine current account. Of particular concern is the trade sector, with emphasis on the dynamics of competitiveness and the pattern of exports in the Philippine manufacturing sector.

The Philippines was pointedly left out of the list of High Powered Asian Economies (HPAEs) identified by the World Bank (1993) in its study of the East Asian miracle. This is due primarily to her erratic economic performance that has been characterized by boom-bust cycles. During the period 1970–97, for which data is presented in Table 6.1, the Philippines experienced three balance-of-payments (BOP) crises. The first and most acute was in 1983–5 following the onset of the international debt crisis, the second was in 1990–2 in the aftermath of Gulf War; and the last was in the second half of 1997 as the Philippines was drawn into the financial crisis. Even when the economy's performance was being considered exceptional by the international community, the peak GDP growth rate was only 5.7 per cent, which was recorded in 1996. Not surprisingly, this growth was the second lowest in Southeast Asia in that year.

The Orthodox view

The performance of the Philippine economy during the postwar period has been directly linked to the fortunes of its industrial sector. The various studies on this sector came up with the following major conclusions (Medalla *et al.* 1995):

1　That the more than three decades of protection had been very costly in terms of its inherent penalty on exports, its serious adverse impact on resource allocation, and dynamic efficiency losses arising from lack of competition.

Table 6.1 The Philippines, selected economic indicators

	1970–4	1975–9	1980–2	1983–5	1986–9	1990–2	1993–7
Income (*growth rates*)							
Real GDP	5.4	6.2	4.1	−4.3	5.2	0.9	4.4
Agriculture	2.8	4.5	2.8	−2.1	3.3	0.2	2.5
Industry	8.0	7.9	4.0	−8.9	5.8	−0.5	5.3
Manufacturing	7.9	5.2	2.6	−6.1	5.7	0.2	4.5
Services	5.0	5.4	4.9	−1.1	5.6	1.8	4.7
Real GDP (*% share*)							
Agriculture	27.4	24.5	23.3	23.2	23.9	22.6	21.6
Industry	35.3	39.6	40.7	38.0	35.2	34.9	35.2
Manufacturing	28.0	27.9	27.2	25.5	25.2	25.4	25.0
Services	37.4	35.9	36.0	38.8	40.9	42.5	43.2
External sector							
Degree of openness (% of GDP)[a]	40.5	41.6	53.7	48.7	58.7	70.3	97.2
Value of exports (USD)	1,583	3,209	5,510	5,008	6,364	8,950	17,615
Share of manufactured exports	8.6	24.4	41.0	51.1	60.7	72.1	80.7
Current balance/ GDP (%)	0.7	−5.3	−6.8	−4.1	−0.6	−3.3	−4.9
BOP/GDP (%)	1.8	−1.2	−2.4	0.6	1.9	1.8	0.8
Real Effective Exchange Rate Index[b]	98.9	96.8	102.5	86.4	68.8	71.2	83.6
Public Sector							
Public sector deficit/GDP[c]		−8.4	−13.6	−5.4	−3.9	−2.9	−0.6
Monetary Sector							
Money supply-M3 (growth rate)	23.2	18.9	18.6	11.8	14.6	15.0	22.6
M3/GNP	24.3	29.1	29.0	25.9	24.9	27.7	36.9
Labour Sector							
Unemployment rate (%)	5.6	7.5	8.9	11.2	10.4	9.5	9.1
Underemployment rate (%)[d]	13.4	11.6	26.3	30.8	24.6	21.8	21.2
Real wage (non-agricultural, pesos)	93.2	63.0	58.0	68.7	72.1	80.8	82.8
Sectoral employment (% share)							
Agriculture	52	52.1	51.6	50.0	47.6	45.3	43.3
Industry	15.8	15.3	14.7	14.5	14.7	15.8	16.0
Services	32.2	32.5	33.8	35.5	37.7	39.2	40.6
Prices							
Inflation rate (%)	18.8	9.9	13.4	26.8	5.9	13.1	9.4

Table 6.1 Continued

	1970–4	1975–9	1980–2	1983–5	1986–9	1990–2	1993–7
Internal terms of trade (% change)	5.4	−1.4	−5.4	−0.7	−0.2	−1.4	−1.4
Population							
Population growth rate (%)	2.8	2.7	2.6	2.5	2.4	2.6	1.8
GNP per capita (*USD*)	336	587	723	547	700	831	1,070
Real pesos of 1985	10,507	11,642	12,762	11,641	10,885	11,559	11,923

Sources: NSO, National Income Accounts; NSO, Philippine Statistical Yearbook; Central Bank, Annual Report.

Notes
a Defined as the ratio of the sum of imports and exports of goods and services to GDP; both terms at constant prices.
b Trade-weighted real exchange rate.
c Includes general government, state-monitored corporations and the Central Bank.
d Defined as workers working less than 40 hours per week.
e Ratio of implicit GDP deflator of agriculture to that of non-agriculture.

2   That a reform toward a more liberal and neutral trade policy is necessary to propel the economy to a higher level of industrialization.

This is the basic neoclassical view that revolves around the issue of comparative advantage. Economic protection in the past meant that the resources of the country flowed into sectors where the Philippines did not possess a comparative advantage. Hence, production, particularly in the industry sector, became highly inefficient. Moreover, such policies prevented export-led industrialization from taking root in the Philippine economy. Filipino entrepreneurs simply made profits behind the protective cover of tariff walls and non-tariff barriers to trade and did not aggressively seek to manufacture products where the Philippines had a distinct comparative advantage in the world market.

That the Philippine economy is largely inefficient is without question. This trend can be gleaned by comparing labour productivity across time and across countries in East Asia. Table 6.2 shows that labour productivity in the Philippines largely stagnated between the period 1975 and 1996. The overall labour productivity of Malaysia, Indonesia, Singapore and Thailand more than doubled in this period while the index for the Philippines even declined by one point. The agriculture and manufacturing sectors exhibited the same pattern.

Apart from reference to the neoclassical argument, the poor performance in terms of labour productivity can also be attributed to the low saving and investment rates in the Philippines (Table 6.3). A low rate of capital accumulation leads to a low marginal product of labour and low average labour productivity. The variance in the investment rate between the Philippines and the more developed Southeast Asian economies can be explained partly by the ability to attract

Table 6.2 Indices of average labour productivity overall, agriculture and manufacturing

		1975	*1980*	*1985*	*1990*	*1996*
China	Overall	100	122	131	140	—
Indonesia	Overall	100[a]	126	131	148	204[b]
(1993 prices)	Agri	100[a]	104	121	114	160[b]
	Mftg	100[a]	155	194	242	310[b]
Malaysia	Overall	100	125	138	161	216
(1978 prices)	Agri	100	133	158	201	281
	Mftg	100	104	118	143	181
Philippines	Overall	100	119	92	102	99
(1985 prices)	Agri	100	117	100	109	108
	Mftg	100	119	96	108	100
Singapore	Overall	100	116	137	171	233
(1985 prices)	Agri	100	114	194	177	288
	Mftg	100	115	128	171	272
Thailand	Overall	100	116	132	181	297
(1988 prices)	Agri	100	101	113	118	234
	Mftg	100	121	133	178	210

Sources: Intal and Basilio, 'The International Economic Environment and the Philippine Economy', PIDS Discussion Paper (1998) and ADB Key Indicators, 1988 and 1997.

Notes
a 1976.
b 1995.

foreign direct investment (FDI). In turn, both FDI and domestic investment are largely affected by the degree of macroeconomic stability in an economy.

The financial sector and macroeconomic stability

The dismal record of the Philippines in terms of macroeconomic stability is reflected in her higher inflation rate (Table 6.3). Econometric studies cite import costs and the money supply as the explanatory variables with the highest impact on Philippine inflation. Rapid monetary growth is usually related to a large public deficit, but a closer analysis of the Philippine financial system will reveal that the instability of the banking sector during the postwar period contributed heavily to macroeconomic imbalances.

The development of the financial system of the Philippines does not provide an exemplary case of smoothly operating financial markets fuelling investment and growth. On the contrary, structural features of the process of financial intermediation have been at the root of the recurring liquidity and solvency crises in various parts of the Philippine banking system and capital markets. Rather than providing channels to alleviate financial constraints, the malfunctioning of the financial system

Table 6.3 Selected indicators, East Asian economies

	1980	*1985*	*1990*	*1995*	*1997*
Indonesia					
M2/GNP	13.7	24.8	45.5	52.8	61.1
Inflation	18.0	4.7	7.4	9.5	6.1
Savings/GNP	30.5	31.1	33.8	31.5	32.0
Investment/GNP	21.8	29.2	32.2	32.9	32.6
FDI (million USD)			746[a]	4,348	5,350
Malaysia					
M2/GNP	53.4	67.9	69.3	95.1	111.8
Inflation	6.7	0.3	2.6	5.3	2.7
Savings/GNP	34.2	35.2	34.9	41.5	46.7
Investment/GNP	31.6	29.7	32.7	45.7	45.1
FDI (million USD)			1,605[a]	4,132	3,754
Philippines					
M2/GNP	22.8	26.8	34.2	49.0	59.0
Inflation	18.3	23.2	14.1	8.1	5.0
Savings/GNP	26.8	19.5	18.8	14.2	14.8
Investment/GNP	29.3	14.9	24.3	21.6	23.9
FDI (million USD)			501[a]	1,459	1,253
Thailand					
M2/GNP	38.5	59.6	70.7	80.6	92.7
Inflation	19.8	2.5	6.0	5.8	5.6
Savings/GNP	23.2	25.2	34.7	37.8	37.0
Investment/GNP	29.4	28.7	41.9	42.5	36.1
FDI (million USD)			1,325[a]	2,002	3,600
China					
M2/GNP	37.4	58.5	78.9	104.0	120.8
Inflation	7.5	11.9	3.1	16.9	2.8
Savings/GNP	35.2	37.7	34.6	41.5	
Investment/GNP	34.1	35.5	38.6	41.7	
FDI (million USD)			3,105[a]	35,849	45,300
Korea					
M2/GNP	34.1	36.6	38.5	44.1	48.9
Inflation	28.7	2.5	8.6	4.5	4.5
Savings/GNP	24.8	34.7	36.4	37.1	35.7
Investment/GNP	33.0	30.6	37.2	37.4	35.4
FDI (million USD)			863[a]	1,776	2,341
Singapore					
M2/GNP	66.4	69.8	90.5	83.7	84.0
Inflation	8.5	4.1	3.5	1.7	2.0
Savings/GNP	40.2	39.2	45.3	49.9	48.7
Investment/GNP	48.1	41.0	35.7	33.4	36.4
FDI (million USD)			3,592[a]	8,210	10,000

Sources: International Finance Statistics, IMF, World Investment Report 1998

Note
a Average of 1986–1991.

has been a source of macroeconomic problems. The structural problems relate to the segmented nature of the Philippine financial markets, the lack of competition among financial institutions, wide-ranging interlocking directorates and ownership patterns across the banking industry and other economic sectors, the shallowness of financial markets and the unresolved external debt overhang (Vos and Yap 1996).

The structure of the financial sector, specifically the banking industry, reflects the patrimonial nature of the Philippine state and the dominance of a predatory oligarchy which leads to an ineffective and inefficient bureaucracy.[2] Banks in the Philippines are largely familial in nature wherein family conglomerates milked the loan portfolios of their own banks, causing liquidity problems. The situation was exacerbated by the inability of the Philippine Central Bank to regulate and supervise banks effectively, creating instability in the banking system. The existence of a patrimonial oligarchic state (as opposed to a patrimonial administrative state as in Thailand and Indonesia) could also explain why the protectionist policies in the Philippines deteriorated into rent-seeking activity while similar measures were a means of capital accumulation in other countries.

As a result, the Philippine financial system has had a strong dualistic nature, in which an important informal financial market segment coexists with the formal banking system. Informal moneylenders fund, at relatively high cost, small businesses and household firms which have little or no access to the formal banking system. Large private corporations are the preferred borrowers of the highly concentrated formally banking system. The interlocking interests of banks and corporate enterprises strongly direct the allocation of funds, often overriding normal financial risk assessment. Over-leveraged firms and bad loans have been systemic problems which have required Central Bank (now known as the Bangko Sentral ng Pilipinas or BSP) and government intervention to bail out ailing financial institutions, often with substantial macroeconomic costs. At the same time, financial markets have remained rather thin. While financial deepening has proceeded at an accelerated pace in neighbouring Asian countries, the mobilization of savings through the financial system has stagnated in the Philippines. This is reflected in a lower M2/GNP ratio up to the 1980s (Tables 6.3 and 6.1 for M3/GNP).

Various attempts at financial reform and liberalization during the 1970s and 1980s succeeded in reducing some of the structural problems of the Philippine financial system (cf. Intal and Llanto 1998). Adjustment policies in the early 1990s, particularly the liberalization of the capital account, sought to resolve the economy's fiscal and foreign exchange constraints. This included the rehabilitation of the BSP wherein the national government took over its bad loans. The M2/GNP ratio of the Philippines increased sharply after 1992 although this is largely a result of the liberalization of the capital account. Some reforms, however, exacerbated weaknesses, such as the increased concentration of the banking sector after the financial liberalization measures of 1981. Moreover, emphasis has been placed on increasing competition in the financial sector – mainly by allowing the entry of more foreign banks – rather than strengthening the supervisory and regulatory role of the BSP.

Framework and objective

An objective of this chapter is to examine the linkage between trade patterns and competitiveness – or the lack thereof – in the Philippine manufacturing sector, using data between 1980 and 1995. The most popular and influential standard for competitiveness is related to unit labour costs whereby a country attempts to keep wage increases in line with productivity changes. By keeping wage costs under control, a country can make its exports competitive – a higher market share for exports invariably reflects greater competitiveness. Recent evidence, however, has shown that unit labour cost is a weak indicator of a country's competitiveness (Fagerberg 1988). A more reliable measure would be productivity performance associated with technological development. Hence, competitiveness will be directly associated with measures of productivity.

Even with improvements in the technological capability of an economy, however, its trade performance may not show a commensurate response, or else the trade specialization of an economy diverges from the pattern dictated by its technological capability. If there is a weak relationship between these two variables, the next step is to determine to what extent this can be explained by an unstable macroeconomic environment, particularly in terms of exchange rate volatility and inflation. These variables usually work their way through the investment rate. Related to this is an inappropriate level of the real effective exchange rate which reflects an overvalued currency.

Meanwhile, a poorly functioning financial system can contribute to macroeconomic instability or hamper the flow of resources to sectors with high productivity growth thus failing to take advantage of export opportunities. Another major objective of this chapter is to determine how the level of financial development has affected the trade pattern.

2. Productivity, competitiveness and trade patterns

Theoretical developments

International competitiveness in a macroeconomic sense is defined as the 'ability of a country to produce goods and services that meet the test of international markets and simultaneously to maintain and expand the real income of its citizens (Haque 1995). The concern with international competitiveness stems primarily from the view that the growth of the HPAEs was export oriented. While it is still debated whether exports were the engine or merely a handmaiden of growth, increasing the competitiveness of the economy is definitely associated with greater efficiency and hence greater opportunities for economic growth.

Two advances in economic theory have brought non-price competitiveness – referring mainly to technological capability – to the forefront. The development of the New Trade Theory represents attempts to relax the restrictive assumptions of the neoclassical framework which assumes the existence of competitive markets, factor substitutability and mobility, and profit maximization. The new theory seeks to extend and develop the traditional framework by incorporating in its analysis such issues as the treatment of economies of scale, externalities, technical progress, product differentiation, and monopolistic and oligopolistic situations (Haque 1995). In this framework, a link between international technological competition and international trade is established, showing that strategic R&D rivalry between countries can be crucial for explaining the evolution of trade flows (Magnier and Toujas-Bernate 1994).

A parallel development occurred in the theory of economic growth that likewise stressed the importance of human resource development and technological accumulation: the development of endogenous growth models which suggest the hypothesis that investment (either in physical capital, human capital, or R&D activities) generates externalities that offset the decreasing returns to inputs. The offshoot of the new trade theory and endogenous growth theory was to shift the focus on technology capability as the primary determinant of an economy's competitiveness.

Analytical framework: Determinants of export share

We use the framework of Fagerberg (1988) to show the interrelation among the variables under consideration. Both technological competitiveness and price competitiveness should play a key role in determining the export market share of an economy. Even if a country is very competitive in terms of technology and prices however, it is not always able to meet the demand for its products because of a capacity constraint.

The market share of exports $S(X)$ is expressed in multiplicative form in eqn 6.1 as

$$S(X) = AC^v \left(\frac{T}{T_w}\right)^e \left(\frac{P}{P_w}\right)^{-a},$$
(6.1)

where A, v, e and a are positive constants. T/T_w represents the technological competitiveness of a country, P/P_w is its price competitiveness, and C is its capacity to deliver. In this framework, export performance is affected by competitiveness and is not an indicator of competitiveness *per se*. Competitiveness is associated more with the concept of efficiency.

Fagerberg assumes that C depends on three factors: (a) the growth in technological capability and know-how that is made possible by the diffusion of technology from the countries on the world innovation frontier to the rest of the world (Q); (b) the growth in physical production equipment, buildings, equipment and infrastructure (K); and (c) the rate of growth of world demand (W). The latter could actually influence $S(X)$ in both directions. Without a capacity constraint growth in W would lead to an increase in $S(X)$. If demand outstrips the given level of capacity, exports will remain constant, but the market share of exports will decrease, because other countries will increase their exports.

Evolution of the Philippine manufacturing sector

The anti-protectionist neoclassical view became dominant among government technocrats starting in the late 1970s, and as a result a major trade reform programme was implemented in 1980. The objective was to make the Philippines more outwardly oriented by opening up its economy. After the trade reform process was disrupted because of the external debt crisis in 1984–5, major import liberalization programmes were implemented from 1986 to 1988. During this period, imports for more than 1,400 items were liberalized, bringing down the percentage of import-restricted items to less than 10 per cent.

This was followed by the second phase of the Tariff Reform Program that narrowed down the tariff range to mostly within 30 per cent. This was implemented by the Aquino administration under Executive Order (EO) 470 that covered the period 1991–5. Tariff reform was accelerated during the third phase of the programme this time under the Ramos administration. EO 264 called for a tariff range from 3 to 10 per cent by the year 2000 and a uniform 5 per cent tariff by the year 2004.

Partly because of the reforms in the trade sector, the overall efficiency of the manufacturing sector as measured by the effective protection rate (EPR) and the domestic resource cost (DRC) increased (Medalla 1998). In addition, total exports and the share of manufactured exports increased sharply. From only 4.8 billion USD in 1986, total exports surged to 20.5 billion USD in 1996. This represents an increase in the share of the Philippine exports in the world market from 0.24 per cent in 1986 to 0.40 per cent, although it is lower than the share of the developing HPAEs. The share of manufactured exports increased from 55 to 83 per cent (Table 6.1). Exports, however, are still concentrated in electronics and garments (at least up to 1993 for the latter), revealing a slow pace of change in the structure of the trade sector.

A more detailed exposition of the trade sector will show the evolution of the current account and the nature of structural problems of the Philippine economy. Table 6.4 presents data on revealed comparative advantage (RCA) for exports in the manufacturing sector.[3] During the period 1980–95, the economy lost comparative advantage in tobacco manufactures, wood and cork products, and basic metal industries. The Philippines gained comparative advantage in electrical machinery during this same period, mainly through the semiconductor industry. It maintained a comparative advantage in food manufactures, footwear and wearing apparel, and furniture and fixtures. The RCA index for these industries, however, declined between 1980 and 1995.

The index of a sector's contribution to the trade balance (ICTB) is generally consistent with the trend in RCA (Table 6.5). The value of the ICTB for tobacco and basic metals fell during the period 1980–95. In the case of the food sector, there was a sharp drop in its ICTB while the values of footwear, wearing apparel and furniture remained fairly constant. The ICTB of electrical machinery turned from negative to positive in this period.

The distribution of exports across the different categories using data from the International Trade Statistics also reveals a disturbing trend (Table 6.6). Electrical machinery and miscellaneous manufactures have been the sectors with the fastest growing shares. Despite this development, gross value added of electrical machinery was only 2 per cent of GDP in 1997. Meanwhile special transactions,

Table 6.4 Revealed comparative advantage: Philippine share/world share per industry

	1980	1981	1982	1983	1984	1985	1986	1987	1988	1989	1990	1991	1992	1993	1994	1995
Food manufactures	4.74	4.52	5.36	3.97	4.05	3.80	3.48	3.05	2.91	2.79	2.64	2.50	2.41	2.23	1.66	1.40
Beverage industries	0.00	0.00	0.00	0.00	0.00	0.00	0.00	0.00	0.00	0.00	0.00	0.00	0.00	0.00	0.00	0.00
Tobacco manufactures	1.39	2.05	1.88	1.58	1.34	1.29	1.07	0.72	0.62	0.57	1.14	1.41	0.60	0.42	0.31	0.25
Textile manufactures	0.49	0.47	0.47	0.32	0.37	0.33	0.35	0.32	0.29	0.22	0.14	0.24	0.23	0.21	0.28	0.27
Footwear and wearing app.	2.80	3.33	3.11	3.16	2.11	2.42	2.08	1.67	1.70	2.12	2.42	5.41	2.22	1.96	1.84	1.77
Wood and cork prod.	6.11	6.60	6.38	6.98	5.72	5.27	4.89	3.69	3.21	2.67	1.84	2.09	1.26	0.81	0.81	0.73
Furniture and fixtures	2.67	3.09	2.87	3.30	3.28	3.35	2.89	2.67	2.98	3.24	2.80	2.33	2.07	2.01	1.97	1.79
Paper and paper prod.	0.00	0.00	0.00	0.00	0.00	0.00	0.00	0.00	0.00	0.00	0.11	0.12	0.14	0.12	0.11	0.08
Publishing and printing	0.00	0.00	0.00	0.00	0.00	0.00	0.00	0.00	0.00	0.00	0.00	0.00	0.00	0.00	0.00	0.00
Leather and leather prod.	0.00	0.00	0.00	0.00	0.00	0.51	0.52	0.47	0.50	0.76	0.91	1.06	0.85	0.70	0.79	0.93
Rubber products	0.00	0.00	0.00	0.00	0.00	0.00	0.00	0.00	0.00	0.00	0.00	0.00	0.00	0.00	0.00	0.00
Chemical and chemical prod.	0.14	0.19	0.19	0.20	0.25	0.56	0.86	0.63	0.47	0.46	0.42	0.46	0.31	0.26	0.24	0.20
Petroleum and coal prod.	0.03	0.03	0.03	0.13	0.09	0.05	0.14	0.14	0.22	0.23	0.22	0.29	0.30	0.27	0.23	0.24
Non-metallic mineral prod.	0.36	0.28	0.34	0.00	0.00	0.00	0.00	0.00	0.00	0.00	0.17	0.20	0.22	0.22	0.20	0.17
Basic metal industries	3.21	2.62	2.05	1.95	1.44	2.01	1.96	1.28	1.53	1.35	1.45	1.23	1.10	0.86	0.77	0.74
Metal industries	0.00	0.00	0.00	0.00	0.00	0.00	0.00	0.00	0.00	0.00	0.04	0.05	0.03	0.36	0.04	0.04
Machinery exc. electrical	0.00	0.00	0.00	0.00	0.00	0.00	0.00	0.00	0.00	0.00	0.00	0.00	0.00	0.00	0.00	0.00
Electrical machinery	0.17	0.22	0.27	0.51	0.79	0.63	0.73	0.73	0.68	0.76	0.92	2.07	1.17	1.55	1.25	1.24
Transport equipment	0.07	0.08	0.05	0.05	0.06	0.05	0.06	0.09	0.02	0.02	0.06	0.03	0.05	0.08	0.12	0.13
Misc. manufactures	3.63	4.74	5.77	5.44	6.21	6.07	5.13	4.71	4.43	4.51	4.53	0.70	4.69	4.92	5.27	5.51

Source of basic data: UN International Trade Statistics, 1980–8, 1990–5. Figures for 1989 were obtained by taking the average of 1988 and 1990.

Table 6.5 Contribution to trade balance, 1980–95

	1980	1981	1982	1983	1984	1985	1986	1987	1988	1989	1990	1991	1992	1993	1994	1995
Food	0.294	0.272	0.307	0.231	0.232	0.184	0.186	0.180	0.141	0.118	0.097	0.118	0.101	0.083	0.057	0.070
Tobacco	0.001	0.003	0.002	-0.001	0.001	-0.007	-0.009	-0.012	-0.007	-0.004	0.001	0.001	-0.004	-0.003	-0.007	-0.003
Textile	-0.014	-0.018	-0.017	-0.029	-0.028	-0.035	-0.051	-0.051	-0.051	-0.052	-0.052	-0.089	-0.047	-0.040	-0.036	-0.033
Wearing apparel	0.048	0.061	0.055	0.063	0.046	0.057	0.060	0.066	0.063	0.074	0.085	0.226	0.088	0.073	0.069	0.062
Leather	0.000	0.000	0.000	0.000	0.000	0.002	0.003	0.003	0.003	0.001	0.003	0.000	0.001	0.001	0.003	0.004
Footwear	0.012	0.013	0.011	0.011	0.009	0.009	0.007	0.006	0.007	0.009	0.010	0.016	0.012	0.012	0.013	0.009
Wood	0.082	0.072	0.062	0.078	0.062	0.055	0.055	0.056	0.051	0.037	0.021	0.025	0.012	0.006	0.009	0.006
Furniture	0.014	0.016	0.013	0.017	0.017	0.019	0.020	0.024	0.028	0.026	0.024	0.021	0.019	0.017	0.018	0.016
Paper	-0.014	-0.013	-0.014	-0.014	-0.018	-0.019	-0.024	-0.022	-0.021	-0.018	-0.013	-0.015	-0.011	-0.012	-0.012	-0.015
Printing	-0.004	-0.003	-0.003	0.000	0.000	-0.002	-0.003	-0.004	-0.003	-0.003	-0.002	-0.005	-0.003	-0.003	-0.003	-0.003
Chemicals	-0.077	-0.075	-0.075	-0.075	-0.079	-0.080	-0.088	-0.083	-0.082	-0.069	-0.062	-0.064	-0.057	-0.054	-0.050	-0.050
Petroleum	-0.299	-0.319	-0.276	-0.268	-0.265	-0.289	-0.171	-0.184	-0.124	-0.132	-0.130	-0.131	-0.117	-0.097	-0.079	-0.079
Rubber	-0.003	-0.002	-0.004	0.000	0.000	0.000	0.000	0.000	0.000	-0.004	-0.003	-0.002	-0.004	-0.004	-0.004	-0.004
Plastics	-0.013	-0.013	-0.016	-0.022	-0.016	-0.013	-0.023	-0.024	-0.022	-0.022	-0.025	-0.030	-0.023	-0.024	-0.026	-0.026
Non-metals	0.001	0.003	0.003	0.000	0.000	0.000	0.000	0.000	0.000	-0.006	-0.001	0.003	-0.001	0.002	0.002	0.000
Basic metals	0.142	0.109	0.042	0.055	0.046	0.082	0.056	0.014	0.022	0.018	0.009	-0.017	-0.021	-0.034	-0.031	-0.043
Fabricated	-0.013	-0.015	-0.018	-0.016	-0.007	-0.011	-0.007	-0.005	-0.006	-0.006	-0.006	-0.008	-0.007	-0.013	-0.013	-0.006
Machinery	-0.125	-0.104	-0.123	-0.112	-0.065	-0.067	-0.073	-0.075	-0.082	-0.096	-0.102	-0.070	-0.101	-0.113	-0.109	-0.100
Electrical	-0.032	-0.035	-0.034	-0.014	-0.001	0.003	0.010	0.018	0.015	0.018	0.024	0.041	0.035	0.086	0.061	0.052
Transport	-0.061	-0.051	-0.034	-0.033	-0.035	-0.006	-0.006	-0.008	-0.039	-0.048	-0.062	-0.055	-0.058	-0.084	-0.074	-0.067
Prof. Scientific	-0.007	-0.006	-0.009	-0.010	-0.007	-0.009	-0.009	-0.008	-0.008	-0.008	-0.008	-0.001	-0.008	-0.010	-0.008	-0.009
Miscellaneous manufactures	0.067	0.105	0.127	0.137	0.106	0.127	0.067	0.109	0.116	0.167	0.193	0.036	0.194	0.211	0.221	0.220

Source of basic data: UN International Trade Statistics, 1980–8, 1990–5. Figures for 1989 were obtained by taking the average of 1988 and 1990.

Table 6.6 Share to total exports, 1980–95

	1980	1981	1982	1983	1984	1985	1986	1987	1988	1989	1990	1991	1992	1993	1994	1995
Food	34.78	33.23	41.96	29.16	29.30	25.64	25.24	22.73	21.10	19.07	17.32	16.90	15.94	14.40	10.65	12.14
Tobacco	0.50	0.84	0.93	0.67	0.53	0.52	0.43	0.32	0.27	0.26	0.60	0.79	0.34	0.23	0.17	0.12
Textile	1.30	1.22	1.24	0.84	0.98	0.85	0.97	1.11	0.95	0.67	0.43	0.78	0.74	0.65	0.87	0.82
Wearing apparel	4.68	5.90	5.89	6.14	4.36	5.39	5.68	6.21	5.92	6.93	8.32	21.25	8.59	7.50	6.66	6.06
Leather	0.00	0.00	0.00	0.00	0.00	0.21	0.24	0.28	0.30	0.42	0.53	0.62	0.54	0.47	0.56	0.63
Footwear	1.16	1.28	1.24	1.10	0.86	0.84	0.64	0.55	0.64	0.81	0.95	1.52	1.19	1.25	1.30	0.88
Wood	7.94	6.96	6.68	7.69	5.95	5.24	5.17	5.32	4.81	3.49	2.36	2.61	1.55	1.10	1.08	0.88
Furniture	1.33	1.53	1.43	1.67	1.64	1.81	1.85	2.28	2.60	2.45	2.31	2.02	1.84	1.79	1.78	1.58
Paper	0.00	0.00	0.00	0.00	0.00	0.00	0.00	0.00	0.00	0.00	0.26	0.29	0.31	0.25	0.23	0.19
Printing	0.00	0.00	0.00	0.00	0.00	0.00	0.00	0.00	0.00	0.00	0.00	0.00	0.00	0.00	0.00	0.00
Chemicals	0.42	0.50	0.60	0.72	1.00	2.33	4.12	3.35	2.64	2.45	2.28	2.56	1.59	1.32	1.28	1.13
Petroleum	0.63	0.55	0.64	2.21	1.53	0.74	1.27	1.65	2.04	2.13	2.21	2.63	2.42	2.01	1.59	1.50
Rubber	0.00	0.00	0.00	0.00	0.00	0.00	0.00	0.00	0.00	0.00	0.00	0.00	0.00	0.00	0.00	0.00
Plastics	0.19	0.32	0.19	0.19	0.17	0.59	0.63	0.69	0.71	0.63	0.57	0.67	0.71	0.63	0.58	0.62
Non-metals	0.65	0.41	0.50	0.00	0.00	0.00	0.00	0.00	0.00	0.00	0.31	0.37	0.41	0.42	0.38	0.32
Basic metals	20.99	15.37	11.87	10.80	7.82	10.99	10.13	7.32	10.18	9.04	8.06	6.72	5.37	4.03	3.63	3.82
Fabricated	0.00	0.00	0.00	0.00	0.00	0.00	0.00	0.00	0.00	0.00	0.04	0.06	0.04	0.43	0.05	0.04
Machinery	0.00	0.00	0.00	0.00	0.00	0.00	0.00	0.00	0.00	0.00	0.84	3.73	1.97	1.89	1.73	2.53
Electrical	0.92	1.44	1.83	3.90	6.85	5.62	7.30	8.38	8.39	8.89	10.08	22.41	13.35	20.29	17.42	17.39
Transport	0.52	0.57	0.38	0.46	0.49	0.46	0.63	0.99	0.20	0.23	0.59	0.31	0.55	0.85	1.23	1.20
Prof. Scientific	0.34	0.36	0.23	0.00	0.00	0.00	0.00	0.00	0.00	0.00	0.00	0.71	0.00	0.00	0.00	0.00
Misc. Manufactures	18.00	23.63	28.65	28.17	33.26	32.87	29.91	32.78	32.85	33.96	34.91	4.11	35.61	39.21	39.65	41.80

Source of basic data: UN International Trade Statistics, 1980–8, 1990–5. Figures for 1989 were obtained by taking the average of 1988 and 1990.

Note: Breakdown of misc. manufactures: toys, sporting goods, etc.; gold, silver ware, jewelry; musical instruments, pts.; other manufactured goods; special transactions; gold, non-monetary nes.

consisting mainly of re-exports, are the main component of miscellaneous manufactures.

The deceptive export configuration explains why despite the increasing share of manufactured exports, the share of value added of the manufacturing sector in total output has remained stagnant for the past twenty years and is even lower than the value in 1980 (Table 6.1). Estimates of total factor productivity (TFP) for the Philippine manufacturing sector show a steady decline in the period 1956–75 which became sharper from 1975 to 1980 (Hooley 1985). The trend continued into the 1980s up to 1992 (Cororaton *et al.* 1995). The year-on-year growth of value added in the manufacturing sector in real terms has actually declined for thirteen consecutive quarters – from 1995Q4 to 1998Q4.

Medalla (1998) attributes the conflicting trends – a rise in efficiency measures in the manufacturing sector and continuing structural problems – to three factors: (1) adjustment, often times painful, to a more open trade regime; (2) a persistently overvalued currency; and (3) the switch in relative protection between agriculture and manufacturing, this time in favour of the former. One could add to this list a relatively low investment rate in the Philippines and poor infrastructure.

An inevitable outcome of a more open trade regime is that inefficient local firms are weeded out almost immediately because of the deluge of imports. It will take some time before the resources are reinvested in more efficient sectors that are usually export oriented. The restructuring process is akin to the 'J-curve' effect of a currency devaluation. In this case, the manufacturing sector contracts because of the closure of non-competitive firms but it should start to grow rapidly once resources are used more efficiently. This explanation, however, conveniently ignores the fact that the bulk of trade liberalization took place in the late 1980s but the marked slowdown of the manufacturing sector occurred between 1995 and 1997 in spite of accelerated economic growth up to 1996.

The restructuring process would have been smoother if the currency had been allowed to depreciate in real terms following the increase in demand for imports. The lower value of the peso would have acted as a cover for import-competing industries. Because of the overvaluation of the peso, import-competing firms were hit with a double whammy: lower tariffs and an artificially strong peso, both of which made imports cheap. An overvalued currency could also explain why exports are heavily concentrated in commodities that are import dependent. Because it is relatively cheap to import, exporters focus on products whose inputs can be sourced from abroad, making labour the primary source of value added.

Overall, the Philippines has taken great strides to enhance its outward orientation and is bordering on being a completely open economy by the year 2004. This progression has dovetailed with the process of globalization. Despite the policy reforms, however, manufacturing growth has not performed up to expectations. Apart from the factors discussed in this section, the reasons may deal with the structural aspects related to macroeconomic stability and weaknesses in financial institutions.

Empirical results

Based on the analytical framework, the following general functions were estimated using data from 1980 to 1995:

$$\text{RCA}_{it} = \beta_1 + \beta_2 \rho_{it} + \beta_3 \frac{P_{it}}{P^*} + \beta_4 K_{it} + \varepsilon_{it}, \qquad (6.2)$$

$$\frac{I}{\text{GVA}_{it}} = \gamma_1 + \gamma_2 \sigma + \gamma_5 e + \gamma_4 \frac{M3}{\text{GNP}} + \gamma_7 \frac{\text{FDI}}{\text{GDP}} + \varepsilon_{it}. \qquad (6.3)$$

The index i refers to a particular manufacturing sector while t is an index for time.[4]

The RCA index for the various manufacturing sectors was computed and was used as the measure of trade performance and an indicator of the trade pattern in the Philippines. Competitiveness for each sector was determined using a productivity measure, ρ. The simplest would be growth in labour productivity.[5] A more complicated procedure would be to estimate the TFP for each sector.

TFP is a concept of efficiency where the economy's productive inputs like labour and capital are jointly used in production. It can be measured in two ways: (1) the deterministic approach, and (2) the stochastic approach. The deterministic approach is further divided into two categories: (a) index number approach, and (b) growth accounting approach. The latter two methodologies are simple and TFP estimates can be easily computed. A weakness of these approaches, however, is the residual treatment of TFP that could render biased estimates.

The stochastic approach, on the other hand, assumes the existence of an unobservable production frontier function and from this, the actual production frontier is compared. In doing so, the residual treatment is eliminated and all factors contributing to production are accounted for. This approach can be used both for time series and cross-section data. Cororaton (1998) applied both the growth accounting and stochastic approach to Philippine manufacturing sector data.

The implicit price index P_{it} for each sector i was used as an indicator of price competitiveness since unit labour costs are not available for the given sectoral breakdown. The price index was scaled by an import price index for non-fuel products, P^*, to get a measure of relative prices. The capability of an economy to deliver or its capacity is related to existing capital stock, K.

Estimates of K for each sector were obtained by Cororaton using the perpetual inventory method. These values of K, which were also used to obtain the productivity figures, were used for the econometric estimation.

Since K is generated by investment, it is through the latter variable that the link between trade and financial development can be established. The investment rate per sector (I/GVA), defined to be sectoral investment divided by sectoral gross value added, is modelled to be determined by volatility in the real effective exchange rate, σ, and the level of financial sector development which is captured by the ratio of broad money M3 to GNP. The technique employed by Schwert (1989) was used to estimate volatility of the real effective exchange rate.

The amount of FDI scaled by GDP should also affect investment. The experience of the developing HPAEs shows that the entry of foreign investment spurred an increase in domestic investment that was put in place to support the requirements of MNCs. The real effective exchange rate, e, is added to incorporate the effects of an overvalued currency.

In the various estimates of the first equation (see Table 6.7), the coefficients for the growth in labour productivity, TFP using the growth accounting approach and TFP using the stochastic are all insignificant.[6] As a matter of fact, the coefficient of labour productivity growth is negative and significant at the 10 per cent level. The results show unambiguously that there is no empirical support for a link between the productivity measures and export performance. Changes in technology and productivity in the domestic manufacturing sector did not influence the pattern of Philippine exports during the period 1980–95.

The variable representing relative prices carries the correct negative sign but the coefficient is not significant. What is troubling though is the consistent negative sign of the coefficient for capital stock, which is significant at the 10 per cent level. It seems that increased investment activity that augments the capital stock does not contribute to better export performance and may even hamper it. This result, combined with the earlier observation that technological competitiveness and export performance are not related, is a clear indication that the export sector has its own dynamics, independent of the developments in the local manufacturing sector. A dichotomy exists between the domestic manufacturing sector and the export sector.

Estimates on eqn (6.2) were also run with and FDI/GDP as explanatory variables. Real exchange rate volatility may affect export performance directly since it affects the rate of return of exporters and hence their profit risk (Medhora 1998). FDI affects export performance in two ways. First, it relaxes the capacity constraint by providing more capital inputs for production. And second, to the extent that the FDI is export oriented, it directly contributes to the level of exports, and hence a higher market share. The results, however, did not improve with the inclusion of these two variables in eqn (6.2). Perhaps the results would differ if FDI by sector were used. Unfortunately, such data is not readily available.

Table 6.7 Estimation of eqn (6.1)

Estimation of eqn (6.1) using growth rate of labour productivity
Dependent variable: RCA?; Method: GLS (cross-section weights); Sample: 1981, 1995; Included observations: 15; Total panel (balanced) observations: 165; Cross sections without valid observations dropped.

Variable	Coefficient	Std. error	t-statistic	Prob.
C	0.169304	0.073901	2.290947	0.0233
GLP?	−0.001219	0.000559	−2.180934	0.0306
RELP?	−3.826360	2.255614	−1.696372	0.0918
K?	−3.44E−05	1.77E−05	−1.947312	0.0532
RCA?(−1)	0.929035	0.016572	56.06052	0.0000

Table 6.7 Continued

Weighted statistics

R^2:	0.909251;	Mean dependent var.:	1.795564;
Adjusted R^2:	0.906983;	S.D. dependent var.:	1.396951;
S.E. of regression:	0.426053;	Sum squared resid.:	29.04335;
Log likelihood:	83.07333;	*F*-statistic:	400.7776;
Durbin–Watson stat.:	2.332512;	Prob (*F*-statistic):	0.000000.

Estimation of eqn (6.1) using growth rate of TFP (growth accounting approach)
Dependent variable: RCA?; Method: GLS (cross-section weights); Sample: 1981, 1995;
Included observations: 15; Total panel (balanced) observations: 180.

Variable	Coefficient	Std. error	t-statistic	Prob.
C	0.131304	0.084445	1.554896	0.1218
TG?	0.144839	0.095450	1.517425	0.1310
RELP?	−2.746532	2.570912	−1.068310	0.2869
K?	−3.64E−05	1.94E−05	−1.877880	0.0621
RCA?(−1)	0.931458	0.015758	59.11175	0.0000

Weighted statistics

R^2:	0.915674;	Mean dependent var.:	1.541699;
Adjusted R^2:	0.913746;	S.D. dependent var.:	1.272487;
S.E. of regression:	0.373717;	Sum squared resid.:	24.44122;
Log likelihood:	91.13248;	*F*-statistic:	475.0681;
Durbin–Watson stat.:	2.308555;	Prob(*F*-statistic)	0.000000.

Estimation of eqn (6.1) using growth rate of TFP (stochastic approach)
Dependent variable: RCA?; Method: GLS (cross-section weights); Date: 11/19/98;
Time: 11:36; Sample: 1981, 1995; Included observations: 15; Total panel (balanced)
observations: 180.

Variable	Coefficient	Std. error	t-statistic	Prob.
C	−0.060769	0.195637	−0.310623	0.7565
TS?	20.13391	17.27408	1.165556	0.2454
RELP?	−2.237510	2.451574	−0.912683	0.3627
K?	−3.31E−05	1.79E−05	−1.844362	0.0668
RCA?(−1)	0.927263	0.016447	56.38029	0.0000

Weighted statistics

R^2:	0.903338;	Mean dependent var.:	1.707719;
Adjusted R^2:	0.901128;	S.D. dependent var.:	1.330213;
S.E. of regression:	0.418271;	Sum squared resid.:	30.61633;
Log likelihood:	107.3332;	*F*-statistic	408.8559;
Durbin–Watson stat	2.285064;	Prob(*F*-statistic)	0.000000.

Variable definitions: RCA?: revealed comparative advantage by sector (indexed by?);
GLP?: growth rate of labour productivity by sector (indexed by?); TG?: growth rate of total
factor productivity by sector (indexed by?) using growth accounting; TS?: growth rate of total
factor productivity by sector (indexed by?) using stochastic approach; RELP?: relative price per sector; defined as P_i/P^*, where P_i is the implicit price index of sector i and P^* is the price index of non-oil imports. P^* is not available on a sectoral basis; K?: capital stock by sector.

Table 6.8 Estimation of eqn (6.2)

Estimate of eqn (6.2) using REER volatility
Dependent variable: INVA; Method: GLS (cross-section weights); Date: 11/19/98;
Time: 12:48; Sample: 1981, 1995; Included observations: 15;
Total panel (balanced) observations: 180.

Variable	Coefficient	Std. error	t-statistic	Prob.
C	0.006326	0.003867	1.635895	0.1037
SIGMA	−1.84E−05	0.000693	−0.026515	0.9789
M3GNP	0.000306	0.000121	2.524540	0.0125
FDIGDP	−0.002243	0.000979	−2.291524	0.0231
REER	−0.000137	5.01E−05	−2.729968	0.0070
INVA?(−1)	0.730557	0.053361	13.69080	0.0000

Weighted statistics

R^2:	0.534363;	Mean dependent var.:	0.016618;
Adjusted R^2:	0.520983;	S.D. dependent var.:	0.020799;
S.E. of regression:	0.014396;	Sum squared resid.:	0.036058;
Log likelihood:	816.4368;	F-statistic:	39.93638;
Durbin–Watson stat.:	2.509469	Prob(F-statistic):	0.000000.

Estimate of eqn (6.2) using inflation as volatility measure
Dependent variable: INVA?; Method: GLS (cross-section weights); Date: 04/29/99;
Time: 11:49; Sample: 1981, 1995; Included observations: 15;
Total panel (balanced) observations: 180.

Variable	Coefficient	Std. error	t-statistic	Prob.
C	0.007200	0.003515	2.048365	0.0420
INFL	−3.76E−05	3.63E−05	−1.034215	0.3025
M3GNP	0.000267	0.000126	2.120790	0.0354
FDIGDP	−0.002290	0.000914	−2.505885	0.0131
REER	−0.000127	4.97E−05	−2.558213	0.0114
INVA?(−1)	0.718011	0.054607	13.14881	0.0000

Weighted statistics

R^2:	0.490294;	Mean dependent var.:	0.016001;
Adjusted R^2:	0.475647;	S.D. dependent var.:	0.019529;
S.E. of regression:	0.014141;	Sum squared resid.:	0.034796;
Log likelihood:	816.6738;	F-statistic:	33.47463;
Durbin–Watson stat.:	2.512686;	Prob(F-statistic)	0.000000.

Variable definitions: INVA?: investment per sector as a ratio to sectoral value added (indexed by?); SIGMA: measure of exchange rate volatility; M3GNP: ratio of total domestic liquidity to GNP; FDIGDP: ratio of foreign direct investment to GDP; REER: real effective exchange rate (1980 = 100), an increase in REER implies an appreciation; INFL: inflation rate.

Estimates of eqn (6.3) (Table 6.8) show a significant positive relationship between the investment rate and the measure of financial development. Because of the adverse relationship between capital stock and RCA obtained in the first equation, a conclusive statement on the impact of financial development on export structure cannot be made. A different line of analysis will be adopted and discussed in the latter part of the chapter.

Another variable that is significant is FDI although it carries a negative coefficient. Apparently the entry of FDI displaces some local investment or else it leads to complacency among domestic entrepreneurs. This result, however, must be studied more carefully. Certainly, it does not imply that policies discouraging FDI should be implemented.

The measure of exchange rate volatility is not significant although the level of REER carries a significant negative coefficient. A higher REER implies an appreciating peso in real terms which hurts import-competing industries and exporters. This would of course discourage investment in these two important sectors. Other measures of exchange rate volatility could also be used to model more closely the extent of macroeconomic instability. If the inflation rate is used instead of exchange rate volatility, there is a minor improvement in the equation but the variable for macroeconomic instability remains insignificant.

3. Competitiveness, finance and macroeconomic stability

Major hypothesis

The dichotomy between the domestic manufacturing sector and the export sector is the reason why the share of manufacturing value added to GDP has been stagnant despite the dramatic rise in the share of manufactured exports. One possible reason for the dichotomy is that the more efficient sectors are not allocated enough credit. This section aims to provide empirical evidence to test this hypothesis.

In a world of perfect capital markets where the Modigliani and Miller and the Fisher separation theorems would be valid, the performance of firms and economic sectors could be explained without reference to the developments in the financial sector. But at the onset, it is observed that the financial sector of the Philippines is far from perfect. Apart from the usual problems of asymmetric information in financial markets, the Philippine financial system has been hampered by structural problems related mainly to the oligarchic banking system. Access to credit, thus, is a key determinant of economic performance.

The role of export finance

Export finance is another area that may offer an explanation for the weak link between productivity growth and export performance. A survey of exporters revealed that only a minority were covered by the BSP's rediscount window, which was the most important export financing scheme in the Philippines, at least in the 1980s. Only about 500 out of about 6,000 direct exporters had access to the export loan discount scheme. As a result, export loans outstanding declined from 14 per cent of export value in 1982 to just 1 per cent in 1986–8 (Rhee *et al.* 1990).

Indirect exporters were not eligible for the CB's pre-shipment export finance window even though they are several times more numerous than direct exporters. This failure to assure equal access to working capital financing for indirect exporters hindered the development of backward linkages as well as the development of trading companies (Rhee *et al*. 1990). One mechanism suggested to expand the coverage to indirect exporters is the introduction of the domestic letter of credit.

The underdevelopment of the export financial system was generally a product of the underdevelopment of the entire financial system. For example, heavy collateral requirements by commercial banks have been cited as the major impediment to wider access to export financing. A pre-shipment export finance guarantee could have been designed to overcome this constraint. Such a scheme existed in the Philippines, but had only a limited role, at least in the 1980s. This could be explained by a shallow financial base that prevented effective risk sharing among the various parties involved.

Framework and empirical results

In the absence of robust financial data at the firm level, the methodology of Rajan and Zingales (1998) will be adopted. In their study, the growth of a particular industry is linked to the external financial dependence of that industry and the degree of financial development of the economy. Their hypothesis is that industries that are more dependent on external finance grow faster in economies that are more financially developed.

To test this hypothesis, Rajan and Zingales estimate the technological demand for external finance that a firm operating in a specific industry would choose in a perfect capital market. Since the US comes closest to the criteria for a well-functioning capital market, the observed ratio of external finance (defined to be the difference between investment and cash generated from operations) in the US for a particular industry is used as a benchmark.

To test the relationship between the level of financial development on the one hand and competitiveness and trade pattern on the other, the EDR is compared with the growth rate of productivity – the measure of competitiveness – and RCA. In both cases, the sectors are ranked, first, by labour productivity growth and, then, by RCA. A rank correlation coefficient using the EDR ranking as a basis for comparison is then computed for both cases.

In the context of a financially underdeveloped economy like the Philippines, there should be a negative correlation between the ranking obtained from EDR and the ranking obtained from the growth rate of labour productivity. This implies that inadequate access to credit prevents firms with a high EDR from reaching their potential growth, leading to low productivity performance. A similar explanation could be made in the case of the RCA measure. A negative correlation would imply that the economy is unable to develop a comparative advantage in particular sectors because of lack of access to credit.

The estimates of the rank correlation coefficients are shown in Table 6.9. There is no general pattern for the sample period 1980–95 for both RCA and growth of labour productivity. Moreover, the values are closer to zero than to one. It would seem that access to credit plays no major role in determining competitiveness or the trade pattern.

Table 6.9 Estimates of Spearman rank
coefficient

Year	EDR, RCA	EDR, GLP
1981	0.121	0.046
1982	0.121	−0.380
1983	0.288	0.204
1984	0.288	−0.165
1985	0.099	−0.301
1986	0.099	0.200
1987	0.099	0.327
1988	0.110	0.429
1989	0.143	0.512
1990	−0.058	0.222
1991	−0.162	−0.301
1992	−0.102	0.442
1993	−0.052	−0.235
1994	0.080	0.077
1995	−0.190	0.209

EDR: external dependence ratio; RCA: revealed
comparative advantage; GLP: growth rate of
labour productivity.

Based on this evidence, the dichotomy between the export sector and the domestic manufacturing sector could be attributed more directly to real factors rather than financial constraints. What could be emphasized though is that the financial sector was a major source of macroeconomic instability leading to high inflation rates, an overvalued currency and a low investment rate.

4.   Micro–macro and real–financial interactions

General analysis

The dichotomy between the export sector and domestic manufacturing sector transcends the usual dualistic structure that exists between the traditional and modern sectors. A possible explanation for this structure in the manufacturing sector is provided by Dohner and Intal (1989). Philippine export promotion measures allowed producers to obtain imported inputs at world market prices, leading to the development of export processing based on imported materials and the low wages of Philippine labour. The retention and augmentation of the system of protection for manufacturing firms producing for the domestic market meant that value-added margins of these export producers would remain very thin; the higher cost and lower quality of domestic materials precluded the growth of domestic sourcing. The high degree of protection of the domestic markets also tended to limit export products to industries where the transport cost of materials was low and labour input requirements high. Garments and electronic components, which have been the top two export categories since 1982, fit these requirements perfectly. Dohner and Intal describe export growth as intensive rather than extensive.

This explanation – citing the highly protectionist system as the main factor behind the narrow export base – is largely consistent with the orthodox or neo-classical economic view. The natural policy recommendation would be a more open trade regime. A corollary to the orthodox position is the problem of an over-valued currency. An artificially cheap peso encouraged exports that are import intensive. Exporters offset the penalty of an uncompetitive exchange rate by rely-ing heavily on higher quality imports of raw materials and intermediate goods made relatively inexpensive by the overvalued peso.

The experience of the developed HPAEs provides a striking contrast to the neo-classical blueprint. Instead of working to get prices right, the economies of Japan, Korea and Taiwan implemented policies to get the fundamentals right. Among the major thrusts was to enhance their technology capability through the judicious use of policy interventions (Lall 1995). The developed HPAEs relied heavily on licensing agreements and reverse engineering and were selective with, even sometimes hostile to, FDI (Lall 1994).

Meanwhile, developing HPAEs and Singapore sourced the technological devel-opment of their export sector primarily from FDI. In this situation, the link between productivity growth in the manufacturing sector and export performance would depend on the level of FDI and degree of technology transfer. The evolu-tion of the Philippine export sector since 1975, and its contrast to the experience of the developing HPAEs, can largely be explained by the nature and extent of FDI flows into the economy.

Table 6.3 shows that the Philippines was a laggard in terms of attracting FDI mainly because of the adverse macroeconomic and political environment. The pattern of export growth in the Philippines in the last two decades was simply a response to the trend towards the internationalization of the division of labour where the industries which lost their comparative advantage in the more devel-oped countries found their way into economies characterized by a relatively low wage scale (Broad 1988). The inability of the export sector to effectively diver-sify into other commodities indicates that the Philippines was simply riding on the worldwide trend towards industry relocation rather than seriously implement-ing an industrial policy, particularly an export programme. Unlike Singapore and Malaysia, there was no coherent strategy implemented to ensure effective tech-nology transfer.

A key finding of Cororaton *et al.* (1995) is that FDI has not generally been con-tributing to the technical progress of the manufacturing sector. This conclusion is consistent with the survey results of Lindsey (1989) from the manufacturing sector where he finds that: (1) most of the equipment brought in by investors are already in use in the Philippines; (2) R&D activities are limited to quality control instead of basic research; (3) there is minimal diffusion of technology to local firms; and (4) the processes used are very simple, leaving little room for skills development.

Implications for policy

To bring about a more integrated economy, economic managers in the Philippines followed the standard response, adopting a programme akin to the Washington consensus. Several analysts have cautioned against strict adherence to this framework (Rodrik 1992; Guerrieri 1994; French-Davis 1994). Structural transformation has a major influence on the acquisition of comparative advantage and is a cause of economic growth. Guerrieri argues that the economic metamorphosis should not be considered as an automatic by-product of an outward-oriented strategy and sound macroeconomic policies, as free trade orthodoxy regards it. Neoliberal economics largely disregards the key role played by technology in changing trade patterns and hence misses the structural dimension of a country's competitiveness.

Echoing this sentiment, Lall (1995) argues that the more important and pervasive source of market failure is likely to be learning processes in production rather than scale economies or externalities. This fact is particularly important for developing countries, which are latecomers to industrialization and thus face established competitors that have already undergone the learning process.

Depending on the extent of the learning costs involved, as well as the efficiency of the relevant factor markets and supporting institutions, there may be a valid case for selective and variable infant industry protection, and for the gradual exposure of existing activities to import competition. Since protection itself reduces the incentive to invest in capability building, however, it has to be carefully designed, sparingly granted, strictly monitored, and offset by measures to force firms to aim for world standards of efficiency. The most effective way to offset the disincentives to develop capabilities that arise from protection seems to be strong pressures to enter export markets, as a commitment to exporting disciplines not only firms but also those who design and administer policy. In Lall's view, the true contribution of export orientation to industrialization is to provide the right framework for selective interventions.

The emerging external environment, however, constrains the available policy options. As Lall (1994) points out: '... the international scene, the GATT, and the pressures exerted by the developed Western countries, are inimical to selective intervention ... Many instruments of industrial policy are increasingly constrained in the name of liberalization.' (p. 652) He correctly asserts, however, that if there is a valid case for intervention, then a review of the international rules of the game is warranted.

The recent performance of the Philippine manufacturing sector supports the aforementioned concerns. Despite the reforms implemented in the late 1980s and accelerated in the early 1990s, the manufacturing sector experienced a deceleration even prior to the 1997 financial crisis.

Meanwhile, the liberalization of the financial system and the capital account in order to spur financial development also has its downside, as painfully revealed by the 1997 East Asian financial crisis. These twin liberalizations could fuel what is termed 'financierism', characterized by the growing supremacy of financial activity over productive activity (French-Davis 1994). The adverse effects of financierism could be attributed to the inadequate regulatory structure in place at the time of liberalizing the financial system. Some analysts put the blame squarely on the corrupt practices in some of the East Asian countries, citing behest loans in Korea and crony capitalism in Indonesia.

What is certain is that the situation is more complicated than this. Many of the East Asian economies that were buffeted by the crisis had relatively strong macro-economic fundamentals and were dragged into crisis by the financial panic of foreign investors. Krugman (1999), for instance, does not agree that Asian economies are being punished for crony capitalism since the 'the scale of punishment seems wholly disproportionate to the crime' (p. 22). He has joined the bandwagon of those calling for the reform of the international financial architecture.

The ideology of liberalization should not cloud the objective of policy reforms: the improvement of the technological capability of the manufacturing sector, the establishment of a dynamic link between the manufacturing and export sectors, and the development of a stable financial system. Given that globalization is an irreversible process, the Philippines must strive to attract FDI and achieve the success of the developing HPAEs in this regard. Simultaneously, economic managers must apply strategic interventions to facilitate the transfer of technology. These would include:

1 Encourage the practice of 'mirroring' similar to the case of Korea. An expatriate engineer would be assigned a local counterpart whom he should train. The local engineer would eventually assume the responsibility of the foreign engineer.
2 Encourage multinational corporations to link up with a domestic firm and develop the latter as a source of intermediate inputs. Such subcontracting was practised extensively in Singapore and Malaysia.
3 The government must set clear strategies and policies on technology development – whether adoption, modification, or generation – by industry.
4 Develop in parallel the human resource capital to cope with the requirements of technology transfer.

These recommendations are consistent with the findings of a recent PIDS study (Yap 1998) showing that the Philippines has many weak links at the microeconomic level preventing the benefits from macroeconomic reforms from being realized. This includes a low level of technological capability that hampers backward and forward linkages in industries; a poor record in human resource development that contributes to low labour productivity; extremely slow alleviation of poverty and income inequality that gnaws at the basic fabric of social cohesion; and inadequate infrastructure that discourages domestic and foreign investment. These shortcomings are at the root of coordination failures that threaten macroeconomic stability.

Policy recommendations for the financial sector have to be studied more carefully given the recent experience in East Asia. The study by Rhee *et al.* (1990) recommended the establishment of a foreign currency loan scheme for exporters to take advantage of the lower international interest rates. Presumably, this need was addressed when the capital market was liberalized. Unfortunately, the dollar-denominated loans were not limited to exporters and borrowers without a natural exchange rate hedge also availed of these loans. This situation was one of the primary causes of the downward economic spiral when the crisis struck.

There are, of course, the standardized proposals for reform of the banking sector. It has been recommended that prudential regulation and supervision be strengthened by implementing comprehensive risk-based assessment and supervision instead of focusing primarily on credit risk. In addition, there is a need for more stringent information disclosure requirements, adequate accounting and auditing standards, as well as clearer rules and greater transparency in asset classification and provisioning (Intal and Llanto 1998).

These reforms, however, must take into consideration political and institutional factors which are at the core of the problems in the banking sector. For example, no matter how comprehensive the risk assessment that is required, it is ineffective if bank supervisors fall prey to the pressures of special interests. While making reforms more difficult to implement, these factors are fundamental in nature and, if tackled, would definitely bring about a beneficial transformation of Philippine society.

Notes

1 Funding from IDRC and CEDES and the organizational support of the Policy and Development Foundation, Inc. (PDFI) are gratefully acknowledged. This chapter would not have been possible without the excellent research assistance of Ma. Teresa Dueñas-Caparas. The author would also like to gratefully acknowledge the vast contribution of Dr Caesar B. Cororaton to this chapter in terms of estimates of capital stock and productivity. The usual disclaimer applies.
2 Hutchcroft (1998) provides an excellent description and analysis of the political economy of the Philippine banking system and the overall Philippine development experience.
3 The RCA index is the ratio of the share of single countries in world exports of a given product group to the share of the same country in total world exports. An RCA greater than one indicates RCA for that particular product group.
4 In the actual estimation, only twelve manufacturing sectors were included. These sectors both had non-zero RCA and an available estimate of capital stock.
5 Labour productivity for a particular sector is simply value added in that sector divided by employment in that sector.
6 Other specifications, which are not reported, include a variable to control for the growth of world trade, which may affect RCA. This did not significantly change the results shown in Table 6.7.

References

Agenor, P. (1995) 'Competitiveness and External Trade Performance of the French Manufacturing Industry', *International Monetary Fund Working Paper*, No. 95(137).
Broad, R. (1988) *Unequal Alliance: The World Bank, the International Monetary Fund and the Philippines*. Berkeley: University of California Press.

Cororaton, C. B., Endriga, B., Ornedo, D. and Chua, C. (1995) 'Estimation of Total Factor Productivity of Philippine Manufacturing Industries: The Estimates', *Philippine Institute for Development Studies Discussion Paper,* No. 95(32).

Cororaton, C. B. (1998) 'Total Factor Productivity of the Philippine Manufacturing Sector: 1956–1995', Manuscript.

Dohner, R. S. and Intal, P. S. Jr (1989) 'The Marcos Legacy: Economic Policy and Foreign Debt in the Philippines', in *Developing Country Debt and Economic Performance,* Vol. 3. Chicago: University of Chicago Press.

Fagerberg, J. (1988) 'International Competitiveness', *Economic Journal* 98: 355–74.

Fanelli, J. M. and Frenkel, R. (1995) 'Micro–Macro Interaction in Economic Development', *UNCTAD Review.*

French-Davis, R. (1994) 'The Macroeconomic Framework for Investment and Development: The Links Between Financial and Trade Reforms', in *The New Paradigm of Systemic Competitiveness: Toward More Integrated Policies in Latin America.* Paris: OECD Development Centre.

Guerrieri, P. (1994) 'International Competitiveness, Trade Integration and Technological Interdependence', in *The New Paradigm of Systemic Competitiveness: Toward More Integrated Policies in Latin America.* Paris: OECD Development Centre.

Haque, I. (1995) 'Technology and Competitiveness', in I. Haque (ed.), *Trade, Technology and International Competitiveness.* Washington, DC: World Bank.

Hooley, R. (1985) 'Productivity Growth in Philippine Manufacturing: Retrospect and Future Prospects', *Philippines Institute for Development Studies Monograph Series,* No. 9.

Hutchcroft, P. D. (1998) *Booty Capitalism: The Politics of Banking in the Philippines.* Manila: Ateneo de Manila University Press.

Intal, P. S. Jr and Llanto, G. M. (1998) 'Financial Reform and Development in the Philippines, 1980–1997: Imperatives, Performance and Challenges', *Philippines Institute for Development Studies Discussion Paper Series,* No. 98(02).

Krugman, P. (1999) 'The Return of Depression Economics', *Foreign Affairs* 78(1): 56–74.

Lall, S. (1994) 'The East Asian Miracle: Does the Bell Toll for Industrial Strategy?', *World Development* 22(4): 645–61.

Lall, S. (1995) 'The Creation of Comparative Advantage: The Role of Industrial Policy', in I. ul Haque (ed.), *Trade, Technology and International Competitiveness.* Washington, DC: World Bank.

Levine, R. (1997) 'Financial Development and Economic Growth: Views and Agenda', *Journal of Economic Literature* XXXV: 688–726.

Lindsey, C. W. (1989) 'Commodities, Technology and Trade: Transnational Corporations and Philippine Economic Development', *Philippine Review of Economics and Business* 26(1): 67–108.

Magnier, A. and Toujas-Bernate, J. (1994) 'Technology and Trade: Empirical Evidences for the Major Five Industrialized Countries', *Weltwirtschaftliches Archiv.* 130(3): 494–520.

Medalla, E. M. (1998) 'Trade and Industrial Policy', *Philippines Institute for Development Studies Discussion Paper Series,* No. 98(05).

Medalla, E. M., Tecson, G., Bautista, R. M., Power, J. H. and Associates (1995) *Catching Up With Asia's Tigers.* Makati: Philippine Institute for Development Studies.

Medhora, R. (1998) 'Exchange Rates, Real–Financial and Micro–Macro linkages', Manuscript.

Rhee, Y. W., Young, K. and Galvez, E. (1990) 'Export Finance-Issues and Directions: Case Study of the Philippines', *World Bank Industry and Energy Department Series Paper,* No. 42.

Rajan, R. G. and Zingales, L. (1998) 'Financial Dependence and Growth', *American Economic Review* 88(3): 559–86.

Rodrik, D. (1992) 'The Limits of Trade Policy Reform in Developing Countries', *Journal of Economic Perspectives* 6(1): 87–105.

Schwert, G. W. (1989) 'Why Does Stock Market Volatility Change over Time?', *The Journal of Finance* XLIV(5): 1115–53.

Vos, R. and Yap, J. T. (1996) *The Philippine Economy: East Asia's Stray Cat? Structure, Finance and Adjustment*. London: Macmillan.

World Bank (1993) *The East Asian Miracle: Economic Growth and Public Policy*. New York: Oxford University Press.

Yap, J. T. (1998) 'Beyond 2000: Assessment of Economic Performance and an Agenda for Sustainable Growth, Integrative Report', *Philippines Institute for Development Studies Discussion Paper Series*, No. 98(28).

7   Competitiveness, international trade and finance in a minerals-rich economy

The case of South Africa[1]

Trevor Bell, Greg Farrell and Rashad Cassim

1. Introduction

The aim of this chapter is to consider the relationship between competitiveness, international trade and financial factors in the South African economy.

The term 'competitiveness' is used here in two closely related but distinct senses. One of these refers to a country's ability 'to realise central economic policy goals, especially growth in income and employment, without running into balance of payments difficulties' (Fagerberg 1988: 355). This may be thought of as competitiveness in the macroeconomic sense, or what we shall refer to as macro-competitiveness. Competitiveness, however, may also be defined as the ability of an economy, or sectors of it, to compete in world markets. Conventionally emphasised sources and indicators of competitiveness in this sense are movements in real exchange rates, productivity and unit labour costs, which are reflections of price competitiveness. As distinct from these, there are various sources of the ability to compete in world markets, such as product differentiation and innovation, and (of particular interest in the context of the present study) access to finance, which may be regarded as aspects of non-price competitiveness.

Section 2 considers the competitiveness of the South African economy in the macroeconomic sense, by examining the historical relationship between GDP growth and the ratio of the current account deficit to GDP. On this basis, it finds that there has apparently been a significant deterioration in the competitiveness of the South African economy.

The rest of the chapter is in effect an attempt to shed light on this problem. The rate of growth of exports is clearly one factor pertinent to South Africa's macro-competitiveness. One concern of the chapter, thus, is with explaining trade performance in recent years. A long historical view, however, is seen as indispensable for this purpose. The evolution of the growth and sectoral pattern of South Africa's exports in the period 1911–72 is therefore described briefly in Section 3.

Section 4, the longest in the chapter, discusses variations in the growth and sectoral pattern of South Africa's trade in 1972–97, divided into two subperiods: 1972–83, which includes the great gold-led, commodity price boom of that decade; and the period of adjustment from the onset of economic crisis in the mid-1980s, through to 1997, which is the main focus of attention. The emphasis is on changes in relative prices, in particular on real exchange rates, as the determinant of variations in the growth rate and composition of South Africa's exports, though some consideration is also given to productivity and unit labour costs. The problem of sustaining rapid growth of exports, and hence of increasing macro-competitiveness, is seen as lying in the sectoral pattern of South Africa's exports.

The effect of financial factors based on trade and competitiveness, one of the particular concerns of the studies in this volume, is the subject of Section 5. Matters considered there, in varying degrees of detail and in different subsections, are the effects of South Africa's relatively advanced stage of financial development; the availability of credit and economic instability as factors relevant to the level of investment; differences in the severity of financial constraints between groups of firms categorised according to trade orientation and trade performance, and hence relevant to competitiveness (in both senses stated above); and the question of whether the ownership of banks by South Africa's conglomerates has skewed the allocation of credit in suboptimal directions. Section 6 consists of concluding remarks.

2. The relationship between economic growth and the current account deficit

This section considers the competitiveness of the South African economy in the sense of its ability to grow without running into balance-of-payments difficulties (Fagerberg 1988: 355). That is, it deals with what we shall refer to as the macro-competitiveness of the South African economy.

Essential to this issue is the statement that:

> [W]hat is assumed is that countries do not wish, or are not able, to continually increase debts or claims to the rest of the world, so that the balance-of-payments, with the exception of short run fluctuations, will have to balance through its current account. This implies that, in the medium and long run, actual growth has to adjust to the balance-of-trade equilibrium growth rate, or the growth rate 'warranted' by the current account, to use a Harrodian term.
>
> (Fagerberg 1988: 361)

Figure 7.1 shows the relationship between the two-year moving average rate of growth of South Africa's actual GDP, as conventionally measured, and the current account/GDP ratio, in each year from 1960 to 1997.[2] The trend line through these points is shown in this figure. As indicated, and as would be expected, a higher growth rate is associated with a higher current account/GDP ratio. For instance, a current account deficit ratio of zero is associated with a growth rate of 2.5 per cent, and a 6 per cent growth rate with a deficit ratio of 2.3 per cent.

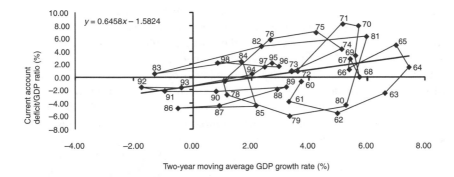

Figure 7.1 The relationship between the GDP growth rate and the current account deficit/GDP ratio, 1960–98.

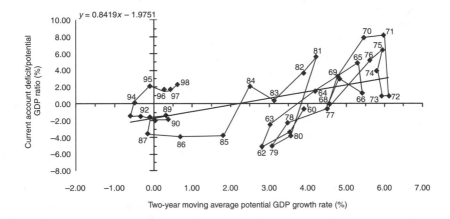

Figure 7.2 The relationship between the potential GDP growth rate and the current account deficit/potential GDP ratio, 1960–98.

It is noteworthy that, as the growth rate increased in 1992–4, the current account deficit increased gradually, close to the average for these growth rates in 1960–97. In 1995, however, when the two-year moving average reached 2.9 per cent, the current account deficit increased sharply to 2.1 per cent. As in earlier years, when the deficit ratio rose sharply above the regression line, both the growth rate and the deficit ratio were pulled back to more sustainable levels. The deficit ratio of 2.1 per cent in 1995, it should be noted, is one associated in the 1960s with a GDP growth rate close to 6 per cent. This suggests an unfavourable change in the relationship between the growth rate and the current account deficit ratio.

Figure 7.2 suggests even more strongly that there has been a substantial unfavourable change in the relationship between the growth rate and the current account deficit ratio. Following Ros (1995: 101–2), it shows the historical relationship between the current account deficit ratio and the two-year moving average rate of growth in potential GDP, rather than of GDP as conventionally measured.[3]

As Figure 7.2 shows, the potential GDP growth rate increased in every year from 1994 to 1998. However, it remained negative in 1994 and 1995, and, though positive in 1996, 1997 and 1998, was still very low, at 0.26 per cent, 0.43 per cent and 0.6 per cent, respectively. Despite these low growth rates of potential output, the current account deficit ratio, as noted above, was 2.1 per cent in 1995, and 1.4 per cent, 1.6 per cent and 2.2 per cent in 1996, 1997 and 1998, respectively. These are clearly current account deficit ratios such as would, on average, have been historically associated with much higher potential GDP growth rates.

Figure 7.2 probably gives a better indication than Figure 7.1 of the implications for the current account deficit ratio of some desired, higher average annual growth rate of, say, 4 or 5 per cent, sustained over a period of, say, five years. As the differences between the actual GDP growth rates in 1994–7, shown in Figure 7.1, and the negative or very low potential output growth rates in those years, shown in Figure 7.2, suggest, a large part of the growth in actual output in recent years has been due to increases in capacity utilisation rather than to increases in the stock of productive capital, and hence in output capacity.[4] Once capacity utilisation reaches a sufficiently high level, the rate of capital accumulation required to achieve any particular GDP growth rate will tend to increase, with probably adverse consequences for the current account. Even at the low potential output growth rates of recent years, the investment to GDP ratio (I/Y) increased considerably in 1993–7 (Figure 7.3).

As noted earlier, much of the rest of the chapter is in effect an attempt to shed light on this apparently significant deterioration in the macro-competitiveness of the South African economy. The rate of growth and sectoral pattern of South Africa's exports is clearly one factor that would be expected to be pertinent to this problem. Given our view that a long historical perspective is necessary for understanding the problems of the South African economy today, we turn now to

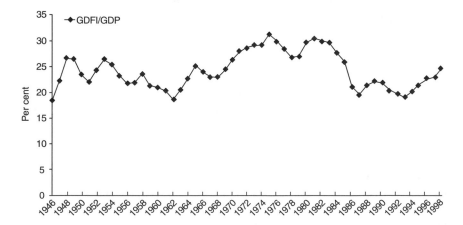

Figure 7.3 GDFI to GDP ratio (both in 1990 prices) (%).

consider briefly, in Section 3, the evolution of South Africa's export trade in earlier decades, from 1911 to 1972.

3. The evolution of South Africa's trade specialisation, 1911–72

1911/12–1956/7: The drive to industrialisation through import substitution

In 1911/12, minerals comprised 81.8 per cent of South Africa's total exports (gold and diamonds alone contributing 63.5 per cent and 15.1 per cent, respectively), with agriculture's 17.6 per cent accounting for virtually all of the rest (Frankel 1938: 108, table 16).

Thereafter, through to the Second World War, gold output and exports grew slowly, and the drive to industrialisation began in earnest in the years between the First and Second World Wars. Manufacturing value-added grew rapidly in these interwar years, and through to the mid-1950s, largely on the basis of substantial import substitution. The ratio of imports to domestic supply (that is, imports to gross output plus imports) for manufacturing in the aggregate fell from 57.2 per cent in 1926/7 to 28.7 per cent in 1956/7 (Bell and Farrell 1997: 596–600, 603, table 3).

The forty-year period from 1916/17 to 1956/7 thus saw substantial diversification of production in the economy as a whole, and, within manufacturing, a considerable shift away from consumer non-durables (Bell and Farrell 1997: 598, table 2).[5] Exports also became more diversified. The export share of primary products fell from 86.6 per cent in 1916/17 to 64.6 per cent in 1956/7, and that of manufactures increased from 8.2 to 26.3 per cent.

There was also considerable diversification of manufactured exports. The share of non-durable consumer goods in manufactured exports halved from 80.2 to 40.6 per cent between 1926/7 and 1956/7. Of particular interest here and throughout the rest of the chapter, however, is the distinction between natural resource-based manufactured exports and the exports of more downstream manufacturing sectors, and variations in the export growth rates of each of these categories and their shares in total manufactured exports. Here, and in subsequent tables, the natural resource-based category includes the chemicals, iron and steel, non-ferrous basic metals, and pulp and paper sectors; while downstream sectors are represented by the fabricated metal products, machinery, electrical machinery, motor vehicles and parts, and other transportation equipment sectors, which together we shall refer to as the 'metal products group of sectors'.

Between 1926/7 and 1956/7, the share of the natural resource-based sectors in manufactured exports increased from 16.2 to 26.2 per cent, and that of the more downstream metal products group of industries rose even more sharply from 2.0 to 18.9 per cent over the same period. As this implies, during these four decades the exports of the more downstream sectors grew considerably faster than those of the natural resource-based sectors. The rate of growth of manufactured exports in the aggregate increased from each subperiod to the next, reaching a rate of 10.1 per cent per year in 1946/7–1956/7.

1956–72: The resurgence and decline of gold, and the spectre of a foreign exchange constraint

With the opening of the Orange Free State gold fields, gold output increased almost uninterruptedly from 358 thousand kilograms in 1951 to a peak of 1 million kilograms in 1970, but at a declining rate (Figure 7.4). Given the fixed gold price of 35 USD per fine ounce (which prevailed from 1933 to about 1970), gold exports in current US dollars increased in a similarly uninterrupted fashion. In constant US dollars, however, gold exports reached their peak in 1965 and declined (at a rate of 0.9 per cent a year) in 1965–70, compared to an average annual increase in 1960–5 of 6.9 per cent (Table 7.1).

What is particularly noteworthy, however, is that the rate of growth of manufactured exports behaves in a contrary fashion. Having increased at 6.1 per cent per annum in 1960–5, that is, slower than gold exports, the growth of manufactured exports accelerated to 9.9 per cent in 1965–70, as gold exports declined in absolute terms (Table 7.1). The result was that manufactured exports (as defined in the Standard Industrial Classification) came to exceed gold exports for the first

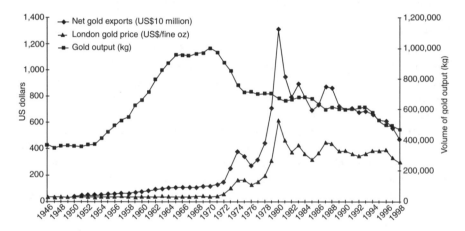

Figure 7.4 Gold output, exports and price.

Table 7.1 Average annual exports growth rates in constant USD (%)

	1960–5	1965–70	1960–70
Agriculture, forestry and fishing	3.9	−1.4	1.2
Mining (excluding gold)	4.6	−1.9	1.3
Manufacturing	6.1	9.9	8.0
Total exports (excluding gold)	5.3	4.9	5.1
Gold exports	6.9	−0.9	3.0
Total exports (including gold)	6.0	2.6	4.3

Sources: Central Statistical Services. South African Statistics (various issues).

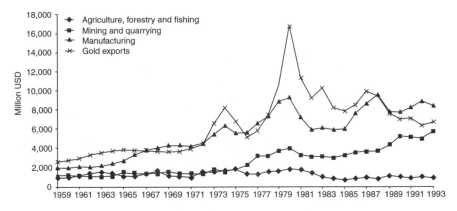

Figure 7.5 Exports by main economic sector (constant 1990 USD), 1959–93.

time in 1967, and continued to do so right through to the eve of the first oil crisis and the commodity price boom of the 1970s (Figure 7.5).

Despite the accelerated growth of manufactured exports, the average annual rate of growth of South Africa's total exports declined substantially, from 6.0 per cent in 1960–5 to 2.6 per cent in 1965–70 (Table 7.1). This problem, of sustaining export growth in the face of declining gold exports (which was to return with a vengeance in the 1980s), was a matter of increasing concern in official circles. The Reynders Commission was appointed in 1969 to inquire into South Africa's export trade. Its report, published in 1972, emphasised the need for diversification into non-gold exports, and proposed the use of direct export promotion measures.[6]

For a moment, thus, there was the possibility of South Africa making the transition to export-oriented industrialisation. The ink had hardly dried on the Reynders Commission report, however, when it was overtaken by events, and, for the time being at least, rendered largely superfluous by the natural resource boom of the 1970s.

4. The gold-led natural resource boom and its aftermath

1972–83: The natural resource boom and its effect on South Africa's exports

Though interrupted by declines in the mid-1970s, the price of gold increased dramatically from a yearly average of about 52 USD in 1972 to 613 USD in 1980, before beginning its descent to 376 USD in 1982 (Figure 7.4). Commodity prices in general, which are shown in Figure 7.6 against the backdrop of downward and upward phases in the South African business cycle, followed a roughly similar pattern, with a large upswing from 1972 to 1980, interrupted by declines from late 1974 through to 1976–7.

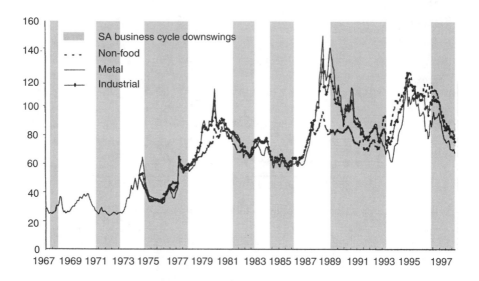

Figure 7.6 Monthly commodity price indices.

Table 7.2 Shares in total exports excluding services (%)

	1972	1975	1980	1985	1990	1993
Agriculture	9.7	8.5	5.9	2.9	2.7	3.9
Gold mining	34.7	41.1	51.1	43.3	29.9	27.7
Other mining (coal, diamonds and other)	16.1	15.4	15.3	20.3	24.2	28.9
Manufacturing	39.6	35.1	27.8	33.5	43.1	39.5

Source: Calculated from IDC (1995) current price database.

As would be expected, the effect on the sectoral composition and growth of South Africa's exports was dramatic (Tables 7.2 and 7.3). Whereas total visible exports, in constant US dollars, had increased at 2.6 per cent a year in 1965–70 (Table 7.1), the export growth rate in 1972–80 was 12.7 per cent per annum. Exports of gold and 'other mining' (coal, diamonds, iron ore, etc.) grew at 18.3 and 12.0 per cent a year in 1972–80 (Table 7.3).

In this context of massive growth of total exports, it is striking, and significant, that manufactured exports grew no faster, indeed slightly slower, in 1972–80 than in 1960–70. This is especially noteworthy given that exports of natural resource-based manufactures, which even in 1972, before the commodity price upswing, contributed 26.4 per cent of manufactured exports (Table 7.4), increased at 15.9 per cent per annum (Table 7.5). By 1980, these sectors accounted for no less than 46.9 per cent of manufactured exports.

Table 7.3 Average annual export growth rates in constant USD (%)

	1972–5	1975–80	1972–80	1980–5	1985–90	1990–3	1985–93
Agriculture	5.1	6.4	5.9	−22.7	4.1	12.3	7.1
Gold mining	16.3	19.5	18.3	−13.9	−2.2	−2.3	−2.3
Other mining (coal, diamonds and other)	8.3	14.3	12.0	−5.8	9.1	6.4	8.0
Total manufacturing	5.6	9.2	7.8	−7.7	10.8	−2.6	5.6
Total exports excluding services	9.9	14.4	12.7	−11.0	5.3	0.3	3.4

Source: Calculated from IDC (1995) current price database.

Table 7.4 Shares in manufacturing exports (%)

ISIC	Sector	1972	1975	1980	1985	1990	1993
351–4	Chemical products	11.7	14.1	19.7	18.8	16.3	14.7
371	Iron and steel basic industries	9.2	11.6	17.5	21.2	24.5	23.0
372	Non-ferrous metal basic industries	2.8	2.2	7.4	11.3	8.6	8.4
341	Paper and paper products	2.7	1.9	2.4	4.2	4.4	6.5
	Sub-total: natural resource based	26.4	29.7	6.9	55.5	53.7	52.5
381	Fabricated metal products	3.9	3.6	2.7	2.1	3.5	4.1
382	Machinery	7.4	5.3	4.5	4.2	5.7	5.8
383	Electrical machinery	2.4	1.7	1.5	1.5	2.3	2.6
384	Motor vehicles and parts	2.0	2.0	1.7	2.2	4.3	7.3
385	Other transport equipment	2.5	2.1	1.6	1.2	1.7	2.8
	Sub-total: metal products group	18.2	14.7	12.1	11.1	17.5	22.7

Source: Calculated from IDC (1995) current price database.

As the above clearly implies, the exports of manufacturing sectors other than those in the natural resource-based category grew very slowly. In particular, the export growth rate of the downstream, metal products group of sectors was only 2.4 per cent per year in 1972–80 (Table 7.5) compared to an estimated 8.0 per cent for these sectors in 1960–70. Their share in total manufactured exports (which had been strongly on the increase before 1956 and held steady in the 1960s) fell from about 18.2 per cent in 1972 to 12.1 per cent in 1980.

Table 7.5 Average annual growth rates of natural resource based and downstream manufactured exports in constant 1990 USD (%)

ISIC	Sector	1972–5	1975–80	1972–80	1980–5	1985–90	1990–3	1985–93
351–4	Chemical products	12.2	16.8	15.0	−8.5	7.7	−6.0	2.4
371	Iron and steel basic industries	13.7	18.7	16.8	−4.0	14.0	−4.7	6.6
372	Non-ferrous metal basic industries	−2.2	39.1	21.9	0.6	4.8	−3.4	1.6
341	Paper and paper products	−5.6	13.9	6.2	3.6	11.7	11.6	11.6
	Sub-total: natural resource based	9.8	19.6	15.9	−4.5	10.1	−3.3	4.8
381	Fabricated metal products	2.7	3.1	2.9	−12.7	22.8	3.1	15.0
382	Machinery	−5.7	5.8	1.3	−9.1	17.9	−1.6	10.1
383	Electrical machinery	−6.5	6.9	1.7	−8.3	21.0	2.2	13.6
384	Motor vehicles and parts	5.0	6.6	6.0	−3.6	27.3	16.2	23.0
385	Other transport equipment	0.7	3.0	2.2	−12.1	18.4	14.2	16.8
	Sub-total: metal products group	−1.8	5.0	2.4	−9.2	21.3	6.3	15.5
	Total Manufacturing	5.6	9.2	7.8	−7.7	10.8	−2.6	5.6

Source: Calculated from IDC (1995) current price database.

Relative prices and the competitiveness of manufactured exports

The variations in the rate of growth and in the sectoral pattern of South Africa's trade described above, seem to be largely explicable in terms of changes in relative prices.

As is well known, the major relative price change which normally accompanies a natural resource boom in a natural resource abundant country is an appreciation in the real exchange rate. This represents a deterioration in the price competitiveness of domestic producers relative to foreign ones in international trade.

The most commonly used measure of such changes in price competitiveness is the trade-weighted real effective exchange rate (REER), movements in which are shown in Figure 7.7. In the case of South Africa, an increase in the REER represents a real appreciation of the rand, and signifies a loss of competitiveness.[7] As is generally the case in a natural resource abundant economy experiencing a significant commodity price boom, there was a substantial increase in South Africa's REER in the 1970s. Relative to its level in 1970–2, the REER was 9.4 per cent higher in 1974–8, 24.8 per cent higher in 1979–81 and 28.2 per cent higher in 1982–3. In terms of this standard indicator thus, there was a substantial deterioration in the price competitiveness of South African producers, including producers of both exports and import-competing goods, between 1970–2 and 1982–3.

The REER, however, is an unsatisfactory indicator of competitiveness for various reasons. In the case of exports, which are the particular focus of our attention, exporters of agricultural products and minerals were clearly insulated from any adverse effects of the increase in the REER on their competitiveness by rising world prices.[8] The REER, thus, is not a good indicator of changes in competitiveness for such primary commodity exports. Furthermore, as we have seen, a large proportion of South Africa's manufactured exports consists of natural resource-based products like steel, non-ferrous basic metals, basic industrial chemicals, and pulp and paper, whose prices are also subject to fluctuations in the

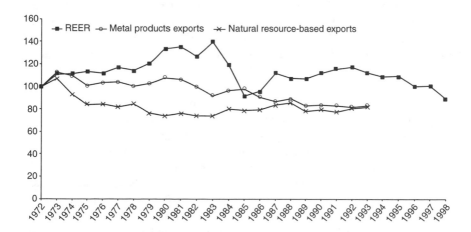

Figure 7.7 Real exchange rates (1972 = 100).

commodity price cycle. For this reason alone, the REER is a poor indicator of changes in competitiveness, even for manufactured exports, in the aggregate.

In an attempt to overcome this problem, and so to obtain a better indicator of the effect of the commodity price boom of the 1970s on the competitiveness of manufactured exports, two separate measures of the real exchange rate facing exporters of manufactures have been calculated, one for natural resource-based sectors, and another for the more downstream, non-commodity sectors in the metal products group of industries. These real exchange rates are defined as the ratio of the domestic manufacturing component of the South African PPI to the trade-weighted export unit values of the sectors in the natural resource-based and metal products categories respectively.[9] They are therefore estimates of the ratio of the price of non-tradables to the price of tradables, and thus of the real exchange rate facing exporters, in each of these categories of manufacturing industries.

The real exchange rate for exporters in the metal products group of industries, after rising sharply in 1973, falls through to 1975, but thereafter shows a tendency to increase to levels higher in 1980–1 than in 1972. It is noteworthy too that, from 1975–82, there is an almost invariable tendency for the real exchange rate of this group and the REER to rise and fall in unison, but the REER suggests a much greater real appreciation than the real exchange rate applicable specifically to exporters in the metal products category. There is evidently a general tendency for the REER to overstate significantly in the short term the adverse impact of a natural resource boom on the competitiveness of the non-commodity exports of a natural resource abundant economy (Warr 1986: 293–304). The REER thus is not a good indicator of variations in competitiveness even for non-commodity exports, as is evident in Figure 7.7. There was nevertheless a noticeable tendency for the metal products group of sectors to lose competitiveness during the 1970s, though to a lesser extent than suggested by the increase in the REER.

By contrast, the real exchange rate of South Africa's natural resource-based manufactured exports fell sharply during the initial burst of commodity price increases, then levelled off, but declined further during the next strong commodity price upswing of 1979–80. This is hardly surprising and is only to be expected given that rising world prices of natural resource-based manufactured products increase the denominator in the formula for calculating the real exchange rate for such products.

There was, thus, a substantial decline in the competitiveness of the more downstream industries, relative to the natural resource-based manufacturing sectors, between 1972 and 1981. What is particularly noteworthy, and perhaps significant, is the relationship of the year-on-year movements in the real exchange rates of the downstream and natural resource-based sectors to one another. From 1975 right through to 1981, movements in the respective real exchange rates of these two categories invariably bear an adverse relationship to one another. When the competitiveness of natural resource-based manufactured exports improves (worsens), the competitiveness of non-commodity manufactured exports worsens (improves).

Considered together, these observations on the most striking features of Figure 7.7 suggest that the variations in the real exchange rates depicted contributed significantly both to the slowdown in export growth of downstream manufactured exports in the 1970s, compared to the 1960s, and to the substantial decline in the growth rate of such exports relative to the exports of natural resource-based manufactures. In particular, the inverse relationship between movements in the respective real exchange rates of these categories of exporting sectors, as noted above, seems to suggest strongly that, to some extent at least, the absolute and relative decline in the export growth rate of the downstream manufacturing sectors was caused by the effects of higher world commodity prices (including the prices of commodity-type manufactures) on the real exchange rates applicable to exporters of downstream manufactures.

As suggested earlier, the natural resource boom of the 1970s put paid to the possibility, which began to emerge in the late 1960s, of a decisive shift from import substituting to export-oriented industrialisation. The effect of the rise in commodity prices, especially the price of gold, was to render this both unnecessary and, because of its impact on the real exchange rate for exports of non-commodity manufactures, unsustainable.[10]

1983–97: The onset of economic crisis and the shift to export-oriented industrialisation

The exports of all the main sectors of the economy declined drastically in 1980–5 (Table 7.3). The rand began to depreciate in late 1983, and fell precipitously from mid-1984 (Figure 7.7), culminating in the debt crisis of August 1985, and the rescheduling of foreign debt. As in many other countries, which had been subjected to such debt shocks in the early 1980s, the immediate effect was a sharp reduction in gross domestic expenditure, particularly investment, which declined by 20 per cent between 1984 and 1986. The most urgent requirement for recovery was accelerated growth of exports including, especially, manufactured exports, to compensate for the decline of gold. The effect of these events was an abrupt, involuntary shift to export-oriented industrialisation (EOI), in conditions of economic crisis.

A more deliberate, voluntary liberalisation had in fact begun before the debt crisis, involving a substantial reduction in quantitative restrictions (QRs) in 1983–5. The real depreciation of the rand in this period, together with domestic recession, however, were the decisive factors in the shift towards a system of incentives more neutral as between production for the domestic market and for export. Following the debt crisis, in 1985–90, QRs were relaxed further; systems of duty free imports for exports were introduced in the motor vehicles, textiles and clothing industries in 1989; and export subsidies in the form of the General Export Incentive Scheme were introduced in April 1990. By the early 1990s only tariff reductions had been neglected. Between 1990 and 1995, import surcharges, which had been imposed earlier in response to the foreign exchange crisis, were removed. Comprehensive tariff reductions began with the commencement of the Uruguay Round implementation period in January 1995.[11]

Adjustment, export performance and price competitiveness

During the first five years of adjustment following the debt crisis, the substantial depreciation of the real exchange rate, depressed domestic economic conditions, and an improvement in the world economy gave a strong stimulus to manufactured exports. Whereas gold exports continued to decline in 1985–90, manufactured exports, in constant US dollars, grew at 10.8 per cent, and 'other mining' exports at 9.1 per cent, giving an overall export growth rate of 5.3 per cent (Table 7.3).

The sectoral pattern of the growth of manufactured exports, in 1985–90, is very different from the 1970s. Whereas the export growth rate of the natural resource-based manufacturing sectors together was 10.1 per cent per year in 1985–90, compared to 15.9 per cent in 1972–80, the exports of non-commodity manufactures, represented by the metal products group of industries, increased at 21.3 per cent a year, compared to 2.4 per cent in 1972–80 (Table 7.5). The much faster growth of non-commodity compared to natural resource-based manufactured exports in 1985–90 is particularly remarkable since this period included an upswing in the commodity price cycle from about mid-1986 to late 1988 (Figure 7.6).[12]

The effect of these differences in growth rates was that the share in manufactured exports of the downstream, metal products sectors increased from 11.1 per cent in 1985 to 17.5 per cent in 1990, i.e., close to the level of about 18 per cent which prevailed in 1972 (and indeed as far back as 1956/7), before the aberration from long-term trends produced by the natural resource boom of the 1970s (Table 7.4).

As shown in Figure 7.7, the real exchange rate applicable to exporters in the metal products group of industries declined substantially, and virtually without interruption, between 1985 and 1990, whereas the real exchange rate for exporters of natural resource-based products, having risen quite significantly in 1983–5, was at about the same level in 1990 as in 1985.[13] These trends in relative prices probably account to a significant extent for the much faster export growth of the downstream, metal products sectors relative to the natural resource-based sectors, in 1985–90.

The period from 1990 to 1993 was one of slow growth in the world economy and a downswing in the commodity price cycle. Rather than increasing, the index of industrial country imports showed a slight decline (Tsikata 1998: 15, table 1.2). Unsurprisingly, therefore, there was virtually zero growth in South Africa's total exports in this period, and manufactured exports fell at 2.6 per cent per annum (Table 7.3). This was, however, due mainly to the decline in the exports of natural resource-based manufacturing sectors, with the only exception of significant size being pulp and paper which continued to grow strongly. Apart from this sector, the only other significant three-digit SIC sectors to achieve positive growth were four of the five sectors comprising the metal products group of industries, two of which had export growth rates of 14.2 per cent and 16.2 percent, respectively (Table 7.6). Collectively, the export growth rate of this group of industries, 6.3 per cent per annum, though much lower than in 1985–90, was outstandingly good in the context of generalised export decline (Table 7.5). Their share of manufactured exports, thus, increased from 17.5 per cent in 1990 to 22.7 per cent in 1993 (Table 7.4).[14]

Table 7.6 Average annual growth rates of South African manufacturing exports in constant 1990 USD (%)

ISIC	Sector	1972–5	1975–80	1980–5	1985–90	1990–3	1972–80	1985–93
311–2	Food	5.9	-0.7	-12.8	3.6	-6.6	1.7	-0.3
313	Beverages	-0.2	9.5	-6.5	19.3	-4.4	5.7	9.8
314	Tobacco products	66.1	-2.8	5.9	11.7	-18.1	18.8	-0.5
321	Textiles	-3.3	5.1	-9.2	14.4	-10.2	1.9	4.5
322	Clothing	10.5	11.4	-7.6	-3.5	-4.9	11.1	-4.1
323	Leather products	-8.8	14.6	2.7	3.0	-6.6	5.2	-0.7
324	Footwear	6.9	20.1	-7.0	3.9	-26.7	15.0	-8.8
331	Wood and wood products	16.8	34.8	-9.4	13.1	-3.5	27.7	6.6
332	Furniture	8.2	28.4	-5.5	22.9	-6.5	20.4	10.9
341	Pulp and paper products	-5.6	13.9	3.6	11.7	11.6	6.2	11.6
342	Printing and publishing	25.7	-14.2	-8.7	6.3	-15.0	-1.0	-2.2
351–4	Chemical products	13.8	16.9	-11.8	2.0	-1.1	15.0	0.8
355	Rubber products	-7.8	10.4	-8.1	22.3	-5.1	3.2	11.2
356	Plastic products	-19.3	11.8	-1.4	30.5	2.3	-1.1	19.1
361	Pottery china and earthenware	26.2	-48.6	33.2	29.8	19.6	-28.0	25.9
362	Glass and glass products	-7.2	26.5	-9.3	21.8	-10.5	12.7	8.5
369	Non-metallic mineral products	21.2	1.8	-27.0	30.4	0.8	8.7	18.4
371	Iron and steel basic industries	13.7	18.7	-4.0	14.0	-4.7	16.8	6.6
372	Non-ferrous metal basic industries	-2.2	39.1	0.6	4.8	-3.4	21.9	1.6
381	Metal products	2.7	3.1	-12.7	22.8	3.1	2.9	15.0
382	Machinery	-5.7	5.8	-9.1	17.9	-1.6	1.3	10.1
383	Electrical machinery	-6.5	6.9	-8.3	21.0	2.2	1.7	13.6
384	Motor vehicles and parts	5.0	6.6	-3.6	27.3	16.2	6.0	23.0
385	Other transport equipment	0.7	3.0	-12.1	18.4	14.2	2.2	16.8
386–90	Other manufacturing industries	8.8	4.0	-13.0	1.0	-12.6	5.8	-4.4
	Total manufacturing	5.6	9.2	-7.7	10.8	-2.6	7.8	5.6

Source: IDC (1995).

Table 7.7 Shares in manufacturing exports of SACU (%)

Sector	1990	1991	1992	1993	1994	1995	1996	1997
Paper and paper products	6.2	5.4	5.8	5.9	7.1	8.9	5.3	4.7
Basic iron and steel products	29.3	25.3	24.8	24.2	23.8	21.0	19.6	18.2
Non-ferrous metal basic products	14.3	12.5	13.1	10.7	7.3	6.9	9.6	10.0
Chemicals	10.7	11.8	14.6	13.4	15.2	19.8	21.6	20.3
Sub-total: natural resource based	60.4	55.0	58.2	54.2	53.4	56.6	56.2	53.1
Metal products, excluding machinery	5.0	4.6	3.5	3.8	4.8	5.7	5.8	5.4
Machinery and equipment, exc. electrical	3.2	3.7	4.5	5.3	5.4	7.1	6.6	7.7
Electrical machinery	1.6	1.4	1.7	2.3	2.2	2.5	2.5	2.6
Motor vehicles, parts and accessories	2.6	3.6	5.4	5.9	4.8	4.3	4.4	5.2
Transport equipment, exc. motor vehicles, parts and accessories	1.3	0.6	1.5	1.6	2.4	0.7	0.9	2.5
Sub-total: metal products group	13.6	13.9	16.6	18.9	19.5	20.4	20.1	23.5

Source: Calculated from Industrial Development Corporation current price data.

Table 7.8 Average annual growth rates of manufactured exports of SACU, constant 1990 USD (%)

Sector	1990–3	1993–5	1993–7	1990–7
Paper and paper products	0.3	49.4	6.5	3.8
Basic iron and steel products	−3.9	12.9	4.6	0.9
Non-ferrous metal basic products	−7.1	−2.8	10.5	2.6
Chemicals	10.4	46.8	24.5	18.3
Sub-total: natural resource based	−1.3	23.8	11.8	6.0
Metal products, excluding machinery	−6.6	47.2	22.8	9.2
Machinery and equipment, exc. electrical	21.7	40.4	23.5	22.7
Electrical machinery	16.8	25.9	16.0	16.3
Motor vehicles, parts and accessories	34.4	3.8	9.2	19.3
Transport equipment, exc. motor vehicles, parts and accessories	10.0	−17.4	25.6	18.6
Sub-total: metal products group	14.2	25.6	18.7	16.7
Total manufacturing	2.3	21.1	12.4	8.0

Source: Calculated from Industrial Development Corporation current price data.

In the period 1985–93 as a whole, thus, there was significant diversification of South Africa's manufactured exports, towards more downstream sectors. Data for South Africa alone, such as those used above, are not available for the years since 1993. Data on the manufactured exports of the Southern African Customs Union (SACU) as a whole (i.e. for South Africa, Botswana, Lesotho, Namibia and Swaziland together), however, suggest that the trends in the sectoral pattern of manufactured exports described above continued through to 1997.[15]

As in the case of South Africa alone (Table 7.4), the SACU data (Table 7.7) show a decline in the share of the natural resource-based sectors in manufactured exports, and an increase in the share of the metal products group of industries over 1990–3. As also indicated for South Africa alone (Table 7.5), SACU's natural resource-based exports in constant US dollars declined in absolute terms (at 1.3 per cent per annum), while the exports of the metal products group of industries increased strongly (at 14.2 per cent a year), giving a growth rate for manufactured exports as a whole of 2.3 per cent (Table 7.8).

After several years of stagnation, however, the industrial countries and their demands for imports grew rapidly in 1993–5, in the context of a commodity price upswing.[16] The average annual rate of growth of SACU's total manufactured exports increased sharply to 21.1 per cent in 1993–5, with a particularly marked increase in the case of natural resource-based manufactures to 23.8 per cent. Nevertheless, despite the commodity price upswing, and a return to positive GDP growth in South Africa, the export growth rate of the downstream, metal product sectors (25.6 per cent per year) continued to exceed that of the natural resource-based sectors (Table 7.8). Even in 1995–7, as the commodity price upswing petered out, and the average annual rates of growth of total manufactured exports and of the natural resource-based sectors fell sharply (to 4.3 per cent and 1.1 per cent, respectively), the exports of the downstream sectors grew at a lower but still respectable, rate of 12.2 per cent per annum.

In the adjustment period, 1985–97, thus, there was a return to the tendency evident in earlier decades, but interrupted by the natural resource boom of the 1970s, for manufactured exports to diversify increasingly towards more downstream manufacturing sectors. Exports of the downstream manufacturing sectors grew faster than natural resource-based manufactured exports in every subperiod throughout 1985–97, irrespective of the phase of the commodity price cycle. As this, and trends in real exchange rates since 1985 shown in Figure 7.7 suggest, since 1985 there has been a substantial, persistent increase in the competitiveness of downstream manufactured exports. Diversification towards more downstream exports is now apparently beginning to include exports of high technology products (Hodge 1997). Despite some claims to the contrary (Tsikata 1998: 17), it is questionable whether import liberalisation through tariff cuts has been a significant cause of the increased competitiveness of manufactured exports.

Productivity, unit labour costs and trade performance

It has been suggested above that variations in the rate of growth, and in the sectoral pattern of South Africa's manufactured exports are largely explicable in terms of two variables conventionally regarded as key determinants of trade performance: real exchange rates, as indicators of price competitiveness, and world demand. Other possibly relevant determinants of price competitiveness, and hence trade performance, which must be considered, however, are productivity growth and movements in unit labour costs.

Figure 7.8 shows real average earnings per worker, labour productivity (defined as value-added per worker) and, from these two measures, unit labour costs, for manufacturing industry in the aggregate. Unit labour costs decline in the 1970s, particularly from 1976 to 1980, and, as we have seen, manufactured exports in the aggregate grew strongly in the 1970s, especially in 1975–80. Similarly, in the 1980s, the levelling off and then decline of unit labour costs, from 1983 to 1989 was also accompanied by rapid growth of manufactured exports. In neither case, however, does it seem plausible to attribute the rapid growth of manufactured exports to declining unit labour costs.

In the 1970s, it was the rapid export growth of natural resource-based manufactures that produced the rapid growth of manufactured exports in the aggregate. This clearly was due predominantly to the commodity price boom, beside which the effect of any decrease in unit labour costs would have been completely insignificant. Non-commodity manufactures might perhaps be expected to have been more sensitive to the apparent tendency for unit labour costs to decline, but as we have seen, exports of non-commodity manufacturers grew very slowly in this period, both relative to the 1960s, and to natural resource-based products. It seems more likely that the increase in productivity, which produced the decline in unit labour costs, was due to the increase in capacity utilisation, which was a

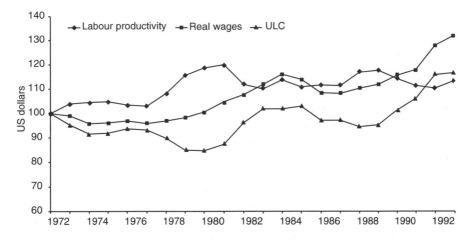

Figure 7.8 Labour productivity, real wages and unit labour costs (1972 = 100).

feature of the latter half of the 1970s, and so was a consequence rather than a cause of the export boom.

The movement in unit labour costs in the 1980s, described above, resulted from the combination of zero productivity growth and a tendency for real wage rates to fall. These in turn were probably mainly due to the decline in capacity utilisation and in the price of non-tradable goods and services (of which labour services are an important case), which characterised the period.[17] Thus, rather than the decline in unit labour costs and export growth being causally related directly, both were probably caused by a third set of forces (namely, the external shocks described earlier), which reduced the level of capacity utilisation and the real exchange rate.

Furthermore, for the period 1985–93, regressions were run across the twenty-five three-digit SIC sectors, of labour productivity growth and the rate of increase in unit labour costs, respectively, on export growth rates and changes in sectoral contributions to the trade balance (CTBs). In each case it was found that the productivity and unit labour cost variables were statistically insignificant, so that there was no apparent explanatory relationship between them and either export growth or change in CTB.[18]

In the case of South Africa, there are a number of reasons why productivity growth and unit labour costs are not likely to be significant determinants of trade performance across manufacturing subsectors. The bulk of manufactured exports are natural resource-based, capital-intensive products, which are relatively insensitive to variations in productivity and unit labour costs, and depend mainly on fluctuations in world commodity prices.[19] Non-commodity manufactured exports are mainly of only intermediate capital-intensity, and relatively high tech. They probably depend to a relatively large extent on product differentiation and innovation. Unlike more labour abundant developing countries, South Africa has never had a comparative advantage in very labour-intensive sectors such as textiles, clothing and footwear, where labour productivity and unit labour costs are more likely to be important determinants of trade performance.

Conclusion

The discussion above in this section suggests various ways in which the sectoral mix of South Africa's trade specialisation has affected the country's macroeconomic performance. These macroeconomic effects, in turn, have had significant sectoral, or micro-level, consequences. Indeed, there is constant interaction between micro-level and macroeconomic forces, which to a large extent occur concurrently.

As the discussion suggests, one way in which South Africa's trade pattern affects its macroeconomic performance is through the Dutch disease effects of a natural resource boom. The natural resource boom of 1972–81 produced a massive foreign exchange and fiscal windfall and high levels of investment. As is well known, however, the essence of the Dutch disease effects is that 'there are some adversely affected sectors and some relative price changes which accompany the boom' (Corden 1975: 324). One of the expected sectoral effects of a temporary natural resource boom, as in the case of a minerals-rich economy like South Africa, is a reduction in the rate of growth of non-mining GDP (Gelb 1986: 79–80).

Whether strictly attributable to such expected Dutch disease effects or not, it is noteworthy that despite the massive foreign exchange and fiscal windfalls, South Africa's non-mining GDP growth rate fell from 5.9 per cent in 1967–72 to 4.4 per cent in 1972–81; and the growth rate of GDP as a whole fell from 4.8 per cent to 3.7 per cent. This was significantly larger than the proportionate decline in the GDP growth rate of middle income, oil-importing countries in general, from 5.8 to 5.1 per cent (Gelb 1986: 78–80). Though the connection is not conclusively established, this is consistent with the expected effects of the Dutch disease.[20] The other, closely related, feature of the period at a sectoral level, the slow growth of non-commodity manufactured exports noted above, was clearly due to the change in relative prices, produced by the natural resource boom.

As we have seen, the collapse of the boom brought a substantial absolute decline in exports, and a precipitous real depreciation of the rand, which culminated in the debt crisis of August 1985, and the rescheduling of foreign debt. Though many other developing countries experienced similar foreign exchange and debt crises in the first half of the 1980s, in the case of South Africa, these crises, and the consequent fall of the rand, were intimately related to the sectoral pattern of its trade, and the sharp decline in commodity prices, especially the price of gold.[21] As noted above, these external shocks plunged the economy into deep recession, and created an urgent need for accelerated export growth.

South Africa, however, has evidently had great difficulty sustaining rapid export growth. As the discussion above indicates, this has largely been due to the preponderance of primary commodities and natural resource-based manufactures in South Africa's exports, which have either been declining (as in the case of gold) or growing slowly.

As Table 7.9 shows, since 1950–70 there has been a tendency for the rate of growth of total exports to decline. With the exception of 1980–5 when exports collapsed, the export growth rate of 1.3 per cent per annum in 1990–8 was lower than in any other subperiod before 1990 shown in Table 7.9, including 1965–70, when gold exports first began to fall. A major (but not only) part of the problem in 1990–8 was the decline in gold exports at 5.7 per cent per annum.

The rate of growth of manufactured exports in particular has also been impeded by a preponderance of natural resource-based products and their relatively poor export performance. Despite the high average annual export growth rate of the downstream metal products sectors (15.5 per cent), because of the slow export growth of natural resource-based sectors (4.8 per cent), manufactured exports in the aggregate grew at only 5.6 per cent a year in 1985–93 (Table 7.5).[22] Similarly, in 1990–7, as noted earlier, the average annual percentage export growth rates of the metal products and natural resource-based sectors, and of manufactures in the aggregate were 16.7, 6.0 and 8.0, respectively.[23]

Contrary to widely held views, the growth of South Africa's exports has not been limited primarily by the lack of an 'export culture', or the 'anti-export bias' created by protection, or by an inherently uncompetitive manufacturing sector. Since the mid-1980s the price competitiveness of non-commodity manufactures as indicated by real exchange rates has increased, and the export growth rate of such products has been high both relative to the past, especially relative to natural resource-based manufactures. This may augur well for the future, but at

Table 7.9 Average annual growth rates of South Africa's exports and imports in constant 1990 USD, 1950–98 (%)

	Merchandise exports	Net gold exports	Total exports	Merchandise imports
1950–5	9.4	2.9	6.9	8.1
1955–60	2.9	6.2	4.0	1.5
1960–5	2.8	7.5	4.6	9.5
1965–70	3.8	−1.1	1.8	4.7
1970–5	9.6	13.1	11.0	9.6
1975–80	9.9	19.8	14.3	5.4
1980–5	−8.9	−14.2	−11.5	−13.1
1985–90	10.6	−2.1	5.7	7.4
1990–5	5.0	−3.8	2.7	8.6
1990–3	0.8	−1.5	0.1	2.2
1993–5	11.7	−7.2	6.7	18.8
1995–8	1.1	−8.9	-0.9	−0.1
1950–70	4.7	3.8	4.3	5.9
1970–98	4.5	0.6	3.5	2.8
1985–98	6.2	−4.4	3.0	6.0
1990–8	3.5	−5.7	1.3	5.2

Sources: SARB Quarterly Bulletin (various).

Note: Excluding non-factor services.

present natural resource-based products still account for over 50 per cent of South Africa's manufactured exports, and these are exercising a significant braking effect on the growth of manufactured exports in the aggregate.

The case of South Africa, thus, provides a striking illustration of the fact that the sectoral mix of trade specialisation, through its effects on export expansion, can have a significant impact on a country's current account deficit at any particular growth rate, and hence on its macro-competitiveness.

It also seems to exemplify Chenery and Syrquin's (1975: 90) finding that primary orientation of exports makes for slow export growth and impedes the transformation of production; and to suggest one possible reason for Sachs and Warner's finding that natural resource abundant economies, reflected in a 'high ratio of natural resource exports to GDP in 1971, tended to have low growth rates ... in 1971–89' (1995: 1). Orientation to natural resource exports clearly does not necessarily make for slow export growth. Numerous countries with such an orientation, including South Africa, have achieved relatively rapid export and GDP growth over extended periods of time. Eventually, however, in world market conditions such as those in the early 1980s, it will give rise to difficulty in sustaining rapid export growth, and hence in avoiding a deterioration in macro-competitiveness.

It is arguable that what has happened, in essence, is that the weighted average income elasticity of demand for South Africa's exports has declined, and that, in accordance with the thesis of Thirlwall (1979), this has contributed to a deterioration in the ability of the South African economy to grow without running into balance of payments difficulties.[24] Furthermore, for reasons also related to differences in income elasticities of demand, Spraos (1991) argues that success in the expansion of visible exports, in adjusting to the external shocks of the early 1980s, depended crucially on the division between commodities and manufactures. Individual countries and regions heavily dependent on natural resource exports tended to experience greater difficulty in adjusting. The sectoral pattern of South Africa's exports, thus, was probably a significant obstacle to an improvement in macro-competitiveness.

So far as trade performance is concerned, the discussion above emphasises the inability to sustain export growth as a reason for the evident deterioration in the macro-competitiveness of the South African economy. Developments affecting the import side of the trade account (which can only be touched on briefly here) may also have contributed to this.

One striking difference between earlier and more recent decades is a significant decline in the rate of import substitution (Bell and Farrell 1997: 595–9).[25] In earlier decades, the effect of GDP growth on import growth was contained in some measure by rapid import replacement.[26] Since the early 1980s, it seems that there has rather been a tendency towards import de-substitution, as indicated by increases in import penetration ratios.[27] Trade liberalisation may well have contributed to this in recent years.[28]

Another factor which might have increased the income elasticity of demand for imports, and so impacted adversely on the macro-competitiveness of the South African economy, is that the output/capital (Y/K) ratio for the economy as a whole was more than one-third higher in 1960–5 than in 1995–7. Given the complementarity between domestic resources and imported capital goods in gross domestic fixed investment (GDFI), this seems to imply that the increase in capital goods imports as a proportion of GDP required to support a 1 percentage point increase in potential output, was about one-third smaller in the 1960s than it is today.[29] In terms of the ability to increase capacity output, it appears that a GDFI/GDP ratio of about 30 per cent today would be equivalent to the ratio of 22.8 per cent which prevailed in 1964 (Figure 7.3). A GDFI/GDF ratio of 30 per cent however, would involve a substantial increase in imports, which would impact adversely on the current account and render unattainable potential output growth rates such as those of the mid-1960s.

5. Finance, trade and competitiveness

Introduction

This section considers whether financial factors have had an effect on the competitiveness of the South African economy in the sense of its ability to grow without running into balance of payments difficulties.

In terms of some of the standard macroeconomic measures, South Africa evidently has a well-developed financial system, compared to other middle-income countries, and indeed even compared to a number of advanced industrial countries (Rajan and Zingales 1998: 570–1, table 7.2). One reason for this may be South Africa's historical connection with Great Britain and its effect on the country's financial and legal system, which may have made, *inter alia*, for a sophisticated accounting system (see La Porta *et al.* (1996), as reported by Rajan and Zingales 1998: 576). Whether due to this or not, it seems that South Africa's legal system does facilitate the extension of bank credit to private borrowers. For instance, a World Bank study notes that '[r]elative to other developing countries, South Africa's banking system is unusually flexible as to what it accepts as collateral', and states that this 'reflects the high level of development of South Africa's legal institutions' (Levy 1996: 12).

South Africa's relatively well-developed financial system may also be related to the importance of mining. By contrast with countries which have developed initially mainly on the basis of agriculture, investment in mining, especially deep-level gold mining, necessitated the raising of capital for large-scale private sector projects. It is clear, for instance, that major developments in South Africa's money and capital markets in the 1950s, particularly the development of merchant banking, were directly related to investment in the newly opened Orange Free State gold fields (Fine and Rustomjee 1996: 154–6). It is noteworthy that in their comparison of Australia and Argentina, Duncan and Fogarty say of Australia: 'Gold – provided the foundations for a sophisticated banking and financial system with close connections in London' (1984: 10).

As is well known, a number of studies, of which Levine and Zervos (1998) is a notable recent example, find a significant positive link between financial development and economic growth. There are a number of arguments against attributing causality to financial development in such studies. Nonetheless, such studies, as well as Rajan and Zingales (1998) who use an entirely different methodology, suggest that the relatively advanced stage of South Africa's financial development would have tended to be conducive to economic growth or, at least, would not have impeded it. It would be surprising, therefore, to find that South Africa's financial system, as such, accounted for the evident deterioration in the competitiveness of the South African economy, as defined and described in Section 2 above.

We must nevertheless consider the effect that financial factors may have had on the competitiveness of the South African economy. The next subsection subtitled 'Investment, finance and economic instability' touches on the problem of isolating the effects of variations in the availability of credit in the economy as a whole, on the aggregate level of investment. It considers, in particular, changes in the stability of the South African economy as one possibly significant influence on investment. The main part of the discussion follows this subsection. Here, we test for differences in the severity of financial constraints among firms and sectors categorised on various trade-related bases seemingly relevant to the competitiveness of the South African economy, through the estimation of an investment function, along the lines of Fazzari *et al.* (1998). The final subsection considers, more briefly, the argument that the oligopolistic position of South Africa's conglomerates in the financial system has skewed the allocation of financial resources in an economically suboptimal direction.

Investment, finance and economic instability

Investment is clearly an important source of economic growth, and the sharp decline in the investment rate since the early 1980s may well be a significant cause of the deterioration in South Africa's growth performance, as it apparently has been in Latin America (Agosin 1995: 173).[30] This raises the question, however, of the determinants of the level of investment and of its allocation amongst sectors.

The availability of finance is one factor that might be expected to play a significant role in explaining variations in the level and sectoral pattern of investment, as is implied for instance, by the credit-rationing literature. In contrast with factors such as real exchange rates and unit labour costs, discussed in Section 4, access to credit may perhaps be seen as a non-price determinant of competitiveness.

Isolating the effect of the availability of credit, as such, on investment at the aggregate level is no easy matter, however. Though we shall not present any data here to show this, the period 1972–81 was one of low (indeed negative) interest rates, and a general increase in the availability of credit, whereas the period from about 1983 was characterised by severely restrictive monetary and credit conditions. It would clearly be misleading, however, to regard the decline in investment levels in the 1980s, compared to the 1970s, as due to the change in the cost or availability of credit as such. The fundamental causes were real forces: the natural resource boom of the 1970s; and the ensuing external shocks of the early to mid-1980s. Investment in the 1980s declined because of foreign exchange scarcity, which reduced South Africa's capacity to import capital goods essential for domestic investment. Similarly, the more recent positive shocks of renewed capital inflows from 1993 to 1994 and the upswing in the commodity cycle which coincided with these probably contributed to the noticeable increase in the investment rate in 1993–8 (Figure 7.3) largely by alleviating the foreign exchange constraint.[31] Other real forces at work in the 1990s in South Africa are import liberalisation and the dismantling of export incentives, which, as in Latin America (Agosin 1995: 159), may have discouraged investment in tradable goods, and in this way, and through their direct effects on the balance of trade, contributed to the evident deterioration in the macro-competitiveness of the South African economy.

As the above indicates, separating financial factors, in particular the availability of credit as such, from other possible determinants of the aggregate level of investment is exceedingly difficult.[32] One macroeconomic factor, however, which does seem to be separable, which is generally regarded as having a significant negative effect on the level of investment, and which in some respects may be seen as a financial factor, is economic instability.

On the grounds that macroeconomic instability is associated with instability in relative prices, the volatility of the real exchange rate is sometimes taken as a proxy for economic instability in general (see, for instance, Agosin 1995: 168). In addition to its effect on investment in its role as a proxy for economic instability in general, exchange rate volatility may also have a direct effect on a country's foreign trade. Though the general empirical literature on the connection between exchange rate volatility and the volume of trade is inconclusive, it may well be, as some contend, that there is a link between the volatility of the REER and trade.

Recently, the family of autoregressive conditional heteroschedastic (ARCH) models have been used to estimate the conditional variance as a proxy for exchange rate volatility. Based on this approach, Figure 7.9 shows that 1980–6 was a period of relatively significant economic instability, whereas the 1970s and the nine years from early 1987 through to early 1996 were periods of relatively little instability.[33]

These variations in the volatility of the REER from one subperiod to another may well be found in a thorough econometric analysis to have affected the investment rate and trade in each subperiod. Given the other powerful real forces mentioned above however, the effect of economic instability on the investment rate is likely to have been relatively insignificant; and in the case of trade it is the level of the real exchange rates emphasised in Section 4, rather than their short-term volatility which has doubtless been the predominant influence.

Nevertheless, one question which does arise, and which is of particular interest in the context of our consideration of the effect of financial factors, is whether South Africa's liberalisation of the capital account in March 1995 has contributed to the significant increase in the volatility of the exchange rate in recent years, evident in Figure 7.9.[34]

Clearly there has been an increase in the volatility of real exchange rates in emerging markets in general since the Mexican crisis of 1994/5, and the increase in the volatility of South Africa's REER therefore cannot be attributed simply to

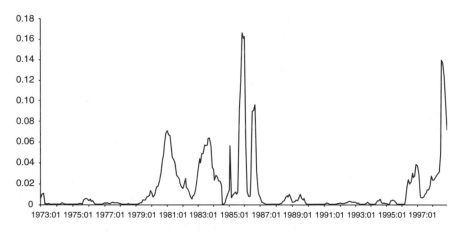

Figure 7.9 Monthly conditional variance of the REER.

the liberalisation of its capital account. Though a link has not been established econometrically, it is quite possible that the liberalisation of the capital account, by increasing the mobility of capital and the effect of capital flows on the balance of payments has contributed to the increased exchange rate volatility in recent years. This particular financial factor, thus, may well have impacted in some measure on South Africa's economic performance since 1985.

Financial constraints and competitiveness

For the reasons stated above, isolation of the effects of availability of credit on the aggregate level of investment is problematic. It may nevertheless be possible to establish differences in the severity of financial constraints, which are applicable to different categories of firms or sectors, resulting from capital market imperfections. In keeping with the approach adopted by other studies in this volume, this involves the estimation of investment functions, along the lines set out in Fazzari *et al.* (1988).

The investment model of choice is rooted in the sales accelerator theory, where the firm's investment decision is determined primarily by changes in sales. In addition, cash flow and the level of debt are included in the model as variables, which capture financing constraints of the firm. The specification to be tested (Harris *et al.* 1994: 38) is stated in eqn (7.1):

$$\frac{I_{i,t}}{K_{i,t-1}} = \alpha_1 + \alpha_2\left(\frac{\Delta S_{i,t}}{K_{i,t-1}}\right) + \alpha_3\left(\frac{CF_{i,t}}{K_{i,t-1}}\right) + \alpha_4\left(\frac{D_{i,t}}{K_{i,t-1}}\right) + \varepsilon_{i,t}, \tag{7.1}$$

where I is investment, K is capital stock, S is sales, CF is cash flow, D is debt, ε is the error term, i is the firm subscript and t is the time subscript. The coefficient α_2 is expected to be positive. The coefficient α_3 captures the firm's ability to raise finance internally and, if significant and positive, indicates that the firm is credit constrained. The α_4 coefficient reflects the premium above the safe rate that must be paid as the debt-to-capital ratio increases and is expected to differ across firms and between periods.

The capital stock variable was estimated using the perpetual inventory method as described by Hall *et al.* (1998) and stated in eqn (7.2):

$$K_t = \frac{1-\delta}{K_t - 1} + \frac{I_t}{P_t} \tag{7.2}$$

where δ is the rate of depreciation ($\delta = 8$ per cent), P_t is the equipment goods price deflator, and the base year capital stock is proxied by net fixed assets of the firm. All the variables have been deflated into constant 1995 rand. S, CF and D were deflated by sectoral production price indices, while P_t, the equipment goods deflator, is common to all sectors.

Financial data was provided by the Bureau for Financial Analysis (BFA), University of Pretoria, for companies listed on the Johannesburg Stock Exchange. Yearly data were obtained from this source for companies whose main business was apparently in manufacturing, for the period 1985–98, but was incomplete for a large number of firms. Therefore, in order to increase the number of observations and include a greater number of firms, the sample period chosen was 1990–7. Twenty-eight manufacturing firms were included in the sample.

A crucial step in the analysis is the categorisation of firms on an a priori basis, according to whether they would be expected to be subject to high or low information costs in the raising of external funds in the capital market. In the general literature, criteria commonly used in this process have been size of dividend payout, firm size and the age of firms. In the context of the present study, however, we are concerned with categories relevant to the competitiveness of the South African economy as defined above. Clearly categories related to trade performance are crucial for this purpose. Furthermore, if the various parts of the chapter are to be properly integrated, the discussion of finance must be related to the other major aspects of the study, trade and competitiveness.

Each firm in our sample has been categorised on each of three trade-related bases as follows:

1 *Trade orientation.* Export-oriented and domestically oriented firms. Export-oriented sectors were those whose percentage of production sold in world markets was above the sample median.[35]
2 *The rate of growth of exports.* This was based on export data for the Southern African Customs Union (SACU) for the period 1990–7. High export growth firms were those belonging to sectors with export growth rates above the median growth rate for sectors in the sample.
3 *The change in the contribution to trade balance (CTB).* Sectors with high rates of change in CTB were those with changes in CTB above the median for sectors in the sample, based on SACU export and import data for the period 1990–7.

The assumption made is that firms successful in international trade, in terms of one or another of these measures, will be in the low information cost category and thus less subject to financial constraints. We leave aside the question whether a convincing case can be made for this assumption on a priori grounds.

We test for the significance of financial constraints in one category relative to the other, in each of the three cases listed above, in two different ways. Table 7.10 presents the results of the full sample regressions, which include dummy variables for export orientation, high export growth and change in CTB. The investment equation is estimated using dummy variables for both intercept and slope coefficients, which are attached to the cash flow and debt variables, in order to account for the differences in trade-related characteristics.

The first column in Table 7.10 shows that the dummy is positive, indicating that investment is affected positively by export orientation. The cash flow slope dummy is negative and significant, indicating that export-oriented sectors are less financially constrained than domestically oriented sectors, as would perhaps be expected.

The second column shows that the export growth dummy is negative and significant, indicating that the level of investment is negatively impacted by high export growth. The cash flow dummy is positive and significant, indicating that high export growth firms are more financially constrained than low export growth firms, contrary to our assumption.

Table 7.10 Empirical results of investment function, 1990–7; all firms with dummy variables

	Exporters	Export growth	ΔCTB
Constant	−0.666	−0.157	−0.360
	(−10.138)	(−4.546)	(−29.439)
$\Delta S/K_{t-1}$	0.0272	0.071	0.017
	(2.642)	(5.834)	(2.010)
CF/K_{t-1}	0.560	0.185	0.233
	(8.926)	(3.846)	(15.727)
D/K_{t-1}	0.371	0.184	0.413
	(8.322)	(4.684)	(25.314)
AR(1)	0.527	0.372	0.618
	(14.322)	(9.909)	(30.162)
Dummy	0.356	−0.444	−0.125
	(5.198)	(−6.570)	(−0.757)
$(CF/K_{t-1})*$Dummy	−0.419	0.247	0.008
	(−5.998)	(3.629)	(0.375)
$(D/K_{t-1})*$Dummy	0.060	0.234	0.120
	(1.121)	(4.652)	(2.662)
Method	GLS	GLS	GLS
R^2	0.780	0.798	0.697
No. of observations	196	196	196

Notes: *t*-statistics in parentheses. Dummy variables differ in each of the three regressions that include dummies for sectors that are export oriented, sectors with high growth in exports, sectors with high change in CTB. Classifications of the export growth and change in CTB dummies are based on SACU trade data for the period of 1990–7, while the export orientation dummy was based on data from the IDC from the period of 1985–93.

The final column shows that the change in CTB dummy is negative but insignificant, suggesting that CTB performance has no significant effect on investment. The cash flow dummy is positive but insignificant, indicating, in accordance with our assumption, that high CTB-change firms are less financially constrained than low CTB-change firms.

Equation (7.1) was also estimated using divided samples. The divided samples are based on the same classifications used for the dummy variables, that is, on export orientation, growth of exports and change in CTB. The results of these regressions, presented in Table 7.11, offer support for those found in the previous regressions presented above.

As the first two columns in Table 7.11 show, for both the export-oriented and domestically oriented samples, the cash flow variable is positive and statistically significant. The cash flow coefficient is larger for the domestic sectors however, indicating that they are more financially constrained.

The third and fourth columns show that for both the high and low export growth samples, all the variables are positive and statistically significant. Therefore, both categories are financially constrained, but the cash flow coefficient is larger for the high export growth sectors, indicating that they are more financially constrained.

The fifth and sixth columns show that for the high CTB-change sample, all the explanatory variables are positive and statistically significant. For the low CTB-change sample, the sales variable is negative and insignificant while the cash flow and debt variables are positive and statistically significant. The results suggest that while both high and low CTB-change sectors are financially constrained, low CTB-change sectors are more financially constrained, as indicated by the larger cash flow coefficient.

What are the implications of these findings for the competitiveness of South African manufacturing? The finding on the effect of trade orientation suggests that

Table 7.11 Empirical results of investment function, 1990–7; using sectoral classifications

	Domestic	Exporting	High export growth	Low export growth	High CTB change	Low CTB change
Constant	−0.656	−0.381	−0.574	−0.160	−0.149	−0.401
	(7.764)	(−9.460)	(−8.216)	(−3.968)	(−2.028)	(−13.634)
$\Delta S/K_{t-1}$	0.029	0.021	0.043	0.112	0.189	−0.009
	(1.807)	(1.432)	(2.714)	(6.609)	(24.022)	(−0.420)
CF/K_{t-1}	0.545	0.146	0.393	0.200	0.154	0.258
	(7.020)	(3.123)	(7.032)	(3.989)	(2.462)	(6.016)
D/K_{t-1}	0.368	0.533	0.427	0.167	0.167	0.466
	(6.902)	(13.318)	(9.837)	(4.113)	(7.678)	(9.837)
AR(1)	0.509	0.665	0.371	0.418	0.052	0.695
	(7.837)	(15.555	(7.270)	(7.130)	(0.964)	(17.749)
Method	GLS	GLS	GLS	GLS	GLS	GLS
R^2	0.881	0.687	0.781	0.799	0.831	0.693
No. of obs.	49	147	77	119	98	98

the financial system is at least not unfavourable to export-oriented firms, in accordance with what might be expected, and may thus have been conducive to export and GDP growth. In fact, however, as we have seen, high export growth firms were found to be more financially constrained than low export growth firms.

The difference between the results based on trade orientation, and those based on export growth rates, suggests that firms which exhibited rapid export growth in 1990–7 tended to be those which in 1985–93 were more oriented to production for the domestic market. There was, in fact, a negative correlation across sectors between the export/gross output ratio and the export growth rate of 0.4 in 1990–7. (The presence of such a tendency in 1985–90, and the reasons for it, are discussed in Bell 1993a: 108–10). Thus, while rapid export growth in 1990–7 may, on its own, have been favourable for access to credit, this may have been outweighed by the relatively severe financial constraints associated with an initially low degree of export orientation.

The fact that the results on trade performance are mixed (with high export growth firms more financially constrained than low export growth firms; but high CTB-change firms less financially constrained than low CTB-change firms), seems to limit our ability to draw inferences on the effects of capital market imperfections on trade performance, and hence on competitiveness, in general. Nevertheless, the question remains whether the findings on export growth mean that financial constraints have been an obstacle to yet faster export growth in the high export growth sectors, and hence to competitiveness, in both senses described above.

Despite the evident financial constraints, the high export growth sectors were by definition those that exhibited superior export performance. One reason for this is the fact that the availability of finance is not the only, or, indeed, may not even be the most important, determinant of investment. Furthermore, in conditions of significant excess productive capacity, such as have prevailed for much of the period since 1985, significant investment is not necessary for sustained, rapid export expansion over an extended period of time.[36] The very fact that low export growth firms were less financially constrained than high export growth firms seems to suggest that financial constraints due to capital market imperfections were a relatively unimportant determinant of export growth, and hence via this channel, of the competitiveness of the South African economy.

Furthermore, the performance of high export growth firms in terms of certain other indicators also creates uncertainty about the significance of the finding above that high export growth firms were relatively more severely financially constrained than low export growth firms. In general, it is not unusual for firms subject to more severe financial constraints, as indicated by the sensitivity of investment to the cash flow variable, to outperform in some respect or other, less severely financially constrained firms. For instance, Fazzari *et al.* (1988: 159) find that though their 'class 1' (low dividend payout) firms were the most financially constrained; they 'experienced much more rapid growth in fixed capital stock than the mature firms in class 3'. Similarly, we find for South Africa that though domestically oriented and high export growth firms were more financially constrained, they exhibited faster growth of both fixed assets and net assets in 1990–7 than export-oriented and low export growth firms. An apparently more severe financial constraint thus did not prevent high export growth firms out-performing low export growth firms in these terms too.

Also contributing to uncertainty about the significance of the result on the export growth variable reported above, is the finding of Fazzari *et al.* (1988: 161) that their financially constrained 'class 1 and 2' (low and medium dividend pay-out) firms have higher debt-to-capital ratios than their 'class 3' firms. This finding, they say, is 'consistent with a financing hierarchy' and supports 'the idea that constrained firms borrow up to their debt capacity'. Apparently thus, Fazzari *et al.* expect that relatively more financially constrained firms would have higher debt–capacity ratios. This seems to hold for our financially constrained domestically oriented and low CTB-change firms, but not for our financially constrained high export growth firms. Assuming that the reasoning of Fazzari *et al.* is sound, and that a relatively low debt-to-capital ratio is indicative of a relatively less severe financial constraint, our finding that high export growth firms had a smaller debt-to-capital ratio than low export growth firms, seems to suggest that it is not clear after all that high export growth firms were relatively more constrained financially.

A further implication of the above, it might be noted, is that none of the variables discussed in the preceding two paragraphs seem to provide a reliable indicator for deciding a priori which category of firms, classified on the basis of trade orientation, export growth or change in CTB, will be more financially constrained.

The argument of Rajan and Zingales (1988) referred to earlier may perhaps be interpreted as implying that sectors with higher dependence on external finance would be subject to more severe financial constraints.[37] However, using Rajan and Zingales' (1998: 566–7, table 1) estimated external dependence ratios (EDRs) for the sectors included in our sample, and once again using eqn (7.1), we find for both our full and split samples that high EDR sectors are less credit constrained than low EDR sectors.

As noted earlier, though, Rajan and Zingales' argument implies that high EDR sectors will tend to grow faster *relative* to low EDR sectors, the more developed a country's financial system. This clearly does not necessarily mean that high EDR sectors will grow faster than low EDR sectors within a relatively financially developed economy, even controlling for other determinants of sectoral growth. It is nevertheless noteworthy that, of Rajan and Zingales' (1998: 566–7, table 1) thirty-six sectors, there are nine which fall in what we have called the metal products group of industries. These nine sectors are all amongst the seventeen sectors most dependent on external finance in Rajan and Zingales' table, and as we saw earlier, they were consistently the sectors with high export growth rates in 1985–97. It seems that South Africa's relatively advanced financial system may have tended to reinforce the effects of real exchange rates in making for relatively rapid export growth in the downstream metal products group of industries.[38]

South Africa's conglomerates and the financial system

The evidence considered above seems to give no reason to think that the financial system as such has had a detrimental effect on the competitiveness of the South African economy. If anything, South Africa's relatively advanced financial system might be expected to have had a favourable effect. It is held that capital market imperfections related to problems of asymmetric information, which underlie much of the discussion above, are 'marginal'. What is really damaging, however, is the oligopolistic power of the conglomerates in South Africa's financial markets (Fine 1996: 26–39).

This argument clearly cannot be dismissed out of hand, and it calls for serious attention. To date, however, no proper evidence has been adduced in support of the contention that the ownership by conglomerates of commercial banks, as such, has made for a suboptimal allocation of credit. Apparently, as evidence for this view, Fine (1996: 33) states that the 'core businesses [of the conglomerates] remain in and around mining and energy', and that they have failed to diversify to the extent warranted by opportunities for 'vertical and horizontal integration'.

There has been a tendency to understate the extent to which the South African economy has been diversified, and this probably applies to the conglomerates in particular.[39] Furthermore, insofar as natural resource-based activities have been and remain important, it obviously does not follow that this is due to the financial system. Indeed, as the present study suggests, it seems to be largely explicable in terms of South Africa's natural resource endowment. In any event, there is no evidence that the ownership by conglomerates of commercial banks has been a significant determinant of the growth and structure of South Africa's production and trade.

Such evidence as there is suggests that it has had little effect. A World Bank study of small and medium enterprises (SMEs) states:

> Lack of access to finance scores strikingly low – as a constraint on enterprise expansion. This result is surprising in light of the common view that, since South Africa's dominant banks [are] owned by the country's major business groups, they skew their activities to large enterprises within their own business stable and neglect small firms .... Banks (appropriately) evaluate loan requests in relation to their riskiness and transaction costs.
>
> (Levy 1996: 11)

It is found that the results on access to finance according to the size and age of firms simply follow 'the expected pattern for a well-functioning banking system'.

For instance, the relative importance of financial constraints declines with firm age and size; and both collateral required as a proportion of loan value, and immovable assets required as a proportion of total collateral, fall with firm size. Perhaps contrary to expectations, younger firms, Levy (1996: 12) finds, 'were at least as likely to be able to use moveables as collateral as were their other counterparts'. Only 'once ethnic variables are incorporated' do they find that the performance of the financial system 'seems more problematic'. The study finds that collateral requirements were more of an obstacle to borrowing by Africans, but there 'was no evidence of discriminatory ethnic variations in the type of collateral required, with moveables widely accepted regardless of their ethnic origin' (Levy 1996: 13).

The investment levels of the conglomerates themselves may well be found to be relatively unconstrained by access to finance. This would be hardly surprising, given their size and maturity. It would not signify that their relationship with the commercial banks is not one at arm's-length. Our clear impression from extensive discussions with South African financial institutions is that it is an arm's-length relationship. The relationship is quite unlike that in Japan, as described, for instance, by Hubbard (1998: 205).

6. Conclusion

The principal aim of the chapter has been to shed some light on the apparently significant deterioration in the ability of the South African economy to grow without running into balance-of-payments difficulties.

One obviously relevant, and significant, factor is the rate of growth of South Africa's exports. It is argued that given South Africa's natural resource endowment, which largely accounts for the sectoral mix of its trade specialisation, variations in the pattern and rate of growth of South Africa's exports have been determined to a major extent by cyclical and longer-term trends in the world prices of the country's primary commodity and natural resource-based manufactured exports, and the variations in real exchange rates which they have produced.

The natural resource boom of the 1970s, which resulted in a substantial real appreciation of the rand, had major adverse effects on the price competitiveness, and hence on the export growth rate of non-commodity manufactures. It produced an aberration from longer-term manufacturing export growth trends and put paid temporarily to the possibility, which was emerging in the latter half of the 1960s, of a shift to export-oriented industrialisation.

In the period since the collapse of the natural resource boom and other ensuing external shocks, which resulted in the real depreciation of the rand in the mid-1980s, the price competitiveness of non-commodity manufactures, especially of the downstream metal products group of industries, has increased significantly. Exports of these downstream manufacturing sectors have grown rapidly, indeed considerably faster than natural resource-based manufactured exports throughout the period 1985–97.

Nevertheless, the rate of growth of South Africa's total exports, which has shown a long-term tendency to decline, was lower in 1990–8 than in any other subperiod before 1990 shown in Figure 7.9, excepting only 1980–5 at the end of the commodity boom, when exports collapsed. This evident decline in the export growth rate has probably contributed significantly to the deterioration in the macro-competitiveness of the South African economy. It has been largely due to the preponderance of primary commodities and natural resource-based manufactures in South Africa's exports, which have either been declining (as in the case of gold) or growing slowly, rather than to any inherent lack of competitiveness. The case of South Africa thus provides a striking illustration of the fact that the sectoral mix of trade specialisation can have significant effects on a country's macroeconomic performance, including in particular on its ability to grow without running into balance-of-payments difficulties.

Other trade-related factors relevant to the decline in macro-competitiveness concern developments on the import side of the trade account, including the decline in the rate of import substitution and in the output/capital ratio.

The other main focus of the chapter is on the effects of financial factors on the macro-competitiveness of the South African economy. By contrast with its negative effect on the export growth rate in recent years, the country's natural resource endowment, in particular its specialisation in gold mining, probably accounts to a significant extent for South Africa's relatively advanced stage of financial development. This would be expected to have had a positive effect on the macro-competitiveness of the South African economy.

By estimating the coefficient on the cash flow variable in an investment function, it is found that in the period 1990–7, export-oriented firms were subject to a less severe financial constraint than domestically oriented firms. This suggests that the financial system is at least not unfavourable to exporters, and may thus have been conducive to macro-competitiveness. However, the results on trade performance are mixed (with high export growth firms more financially constrained than low export growth firms, but high CTB-change firms less financially constrained than low CTB-change firms). This seems to prevent clear-cut conclusions on the effect of the financial system on trade performance, but it is argued that, in any event, the interpretation of the findings on the export growth variable is subject to considerable uncertainty.

This uncertainty arises from doubts about the significance of differences in access to finance as a determinant of investment, and about the necessity of investment for rapid export growth. Also pertinent to this is that, though high export growth firms were relatively more financially constrained, they exhibited faster growth of both fixed assets and net assets, and had lower debt-to-capital ratios (associated by Fazzari *et al.* (1988) with a less severe financial constraint), than low export growth firms. Furthermore, the analysis of Rajan and Zingales (1998) seems to suggest that South Africa's financial system may have reinforced the effects of real exchange rates in making for relatively rapid export growth in the downstream metal products industries, and so enhanced the competitiveness of the South African economy.

In attempting above to shed light on the apparent deterioration in the macro-competitiveness of the South African economy, only the effects of certain trade-related and financial factors have been considered, in keeping with the subject of this volume. A more comprehensive analysis of the problem would need to take into account various other possibilities as well. Some of these, including inadequate levels of educational and skills attainment in South Africa's population at large, may also be related to some extent to the country's natural resource abundance.[40] South Africa's natural resource endowment has clearly had a major determining influence on the country's path of development. Without its mineral wealth, South Africa would probably have remained a relatively poor, industrially backward country. However, in the past few decades, South Africa's natural resource abundance has apparently not been an unmixed blessing.

Notes

1 We benefitted greatly from the discussions with the other participants in this project and from access to the earlier drafts of their papers. Valuable assistance was provided by the Industrial Development Corporation, including access to its database. Professor Leon Brümmer of the Bureau for Financial Analysis, University of Pretoria, kindly provided the data for companies listed on the Johannesburg Stock Exchange for analysis in Section V, under 'Investment, finance and economic instability'. Senior members of ABSA Bank, First National Bank, Nedbank and Standard Bank gave generously of their time to discuss some of the financial aspects of the paper. Troy Elyea, who provided outstanding research assistance, produced Figure 7.8, performed the regression analysis for Section V, 'Investment, finance and economic instability', and gave considerable help in the final stages of the production of the chapter. A major part of the research expenses incurred by Trevor Bell was funded by a research grant from the Liberty Life Foundation for a project that includes the subject of this chapter. To all of the above, none of whom bears any responsibility for the views expressed in this chapter, we are most grateful. Greg Farrel hasa contributed to the study in his personal capacity and the views expressed are not necessarily those of the South African Reserve Bank.

2 In Figure 7.1, the growth rate for 1975, for instance, is the average GDP growth rate for 1974 and 1975.

3 The method used there in estimating potential or capacity output is an adaptation of Panic (1978), as described by Christiano (1981: 151–4). Capacity output is obtained by multiplying the estimated output/capital ratio (Y/K) (derived from a shifted regression of Y/K), for each year, by the actual capital stock in that year. The capital stock data used in the estimation of capacity GDP are from the South African Reserve Bank. The two-year moving average is calculated in the same way as for Figure 7.1 described above.

4 The index of capacity utilisation (the ratio of actual to potential GDP, calculated as described above, with 1969 = 100) increased substantially from 86.5 in 1993 to 95.1 in 1997, that is, at a rate of 2.4 per cent a year. Capacity output grew at an average annual rate of only 0.17 per cent. The greater part of the 2.55 per cent per annum increase in actual output in 1993–7, thus was apparently accounted for by increased capacity utilisation. In 1998, however, the increase in actual GDP was lower than the increase in potential output, due to a decline in capacity utilisation as the economy went into recession.

5 Measured in constant (1956/7) rands, the GDP share of mining declined from 24.0 per cent in 1916/17 to 11.1 per cent in 1956/7, while that of manufacturing increased from 6.2 per cent to 19.4 per cent. These figures, as well as export shares and growth rates in the period 1916/17–1956/7 have been calculated from data in constant (1956/7) rands from T. A. du Plessis (1965).

6 See also the prescient study by J. C. du Plessis (1965), at the time an economist at the South African Reserve Bank.

7 South Africa's REER is defined as equal to $e \cdot P/P^*$, where e is the trade-weighted nominal exchange rate, expressed as the number of units of foreign currency per rand, P is the South African producer price index (PPI), and P^* is a trade-weighted measure of the PPIs of South Africa's trading partners.

8 That is, the increase in e was offset, indeed more than offset, by the increase in P^*, defined now as the foreign currency price of such products, so that the real exchange rate applicable to them fell.

9 The export unit values are calculated from the IDC (1995) Sectoral Data series. The weights in these cases are the shares of the constituent subsectors of each category in the total exports of the category. Data availability does not allow calculation of these real exchange rates for years after 1993.

10 In keeping with the views of the Reynders Commission (1972), a new export incentive scheme was introduced in 1972. Also, under pressure from GATT and the IMF, quantitative restrictions were gradually relaxed in the period 1972–6. This was accompanied

by some compensating increases in tariffs but the net effect was a reduction in levels of protection in this period. Though there was a nominal depreciation of the rand in 1975, the increase in the real exchange rate effectively ended this attempt at trade liberalisation in about 1976.

11 For more detail on South Africa's trade policy reforms, see Bell (1993a, 1997).

12 Even in 1985–8, before the downswing in the commodity price cycle, the exports of the metal products group of industries grew at an average annual rate of 27.7 per cent, and natural resource-based manufactures at 17.8 per cent. In 1988–90, natural resource-based manufactured exports grew at only 0.5 per cent a year, whereas the export growth rate of the metal products group, 12.4 per cent, remained relatively high.

13 It is indeed noteworthy too that, by contrast with 1975–82, there was no tendency in 1985–90 for the REER and the real exchange rate for the metal products group of industries to rise and fall in unison. They had apparently become de-linked, and there was a persistent tendency for the competitiveness of the metal products sectors to improve, whether the REER was rising or falling.

14 The description above of variations in the growth rates of manufactured exports is based on exports valued in constant (1990) USD. In estimating export demand functions, including the effect of variations in real exchange rates, however, the dependent variable is generally the physical volume of exports. It is noteworthy, therefore, as comparison of Tables 7.5 and 7.12 shows, that the growth rates of exports measured in constant rands (which gives a better indication of changes in export volumes) and in constant USD, respectively, move up and down in unison. The constant rand growth rate also varies significantly, so that the variations in export growth rates are not due simply to changes in world prices. The discussion above, thus, would not have been significantly different had the export growth rates reported been based on constant rand, rather than constant US dollar values.

15 Though the sectoral shares of the manufactured exports of South Africa and SACU differ, as comparison of Tables 7.4 and 7.7 show, the data on SACU manufactured exports, which are dominated by South Africa, may reasonably be taken to reflect trends in the sectoral composition and growth rates of the manufactured exports of South Africa alone in the period 1990–97.

16 The index of industrial country imports increased at 15.6 per cent per year in 1993–5, but by only 3.3 per cent in 1996 (Tsikata 1998: 15, table 1.2).

17 See Wright (1993: 58–60) on the significance of capacity utilisation as a determinant of total factor productivity growth in the 1980s.

18 A simple bivariate analysis such as this, however, is clearly in this case both statistically and theoretically unsatisfactory and there is no apparent reason to expect significant results. To establish whether productivity growth or changes in unit labour costs are significant influences on trade performance, a much more sophisticated analysis is required.

19 According to Wright (1993: 17, table 1.3), in 1981–90, industrial chemicals, iron and steel and non-ferrous basic metals, the three natural resource-based manufacturing sectors with relatively low export growth rates, had higher TFP growth rates than any other manufacturing sectors, and were three of only eight sectors (out of 26) with positive TFP growth rates in this period. Despite this, as we have seen, these sectors had relatively slow export growth.

20 It should be noted that South Africa's GDP growth rate was declining even before 1972.

21 See Bell (1993b: 2–5) for a fuller discussion of the causes of South Africa's debt crisis and the role played in it by the price of gold.

22 This was despite the fact that 1985–90 was a special period of export recovery following several years of absolute decline.

23 This included an exceptional discontinuous increase in 1993–5.

Table 7.12 Average annual export growth rates in constant 1993 rands (%)

ISIC	Sector	1972–5	1975–80	1972–80	1980–5	1985–90	1990–3	1985–93
341	Pulp and paper products	−6.36	13.71	5.72	9.96	−1.22	13.74	4.14
351–4	Chemical products	4.79	4.41	4.55	−1.07	12.05	−3.52	5.94
371	Iron and steel basic industries	−0.16	20.55	12.32	4.35	10.46	−1.49	5.82
372	Non-ferrous metal basic industries	−4.26	34.79	18.56	6.32	−1.94	4.41	0.39
	Sub-total: natural resource based	1.18	14.52	9.32	3.69	7.40	0.11	4.61
381	Metal products	−0.15	4.88	2.96	−11.22	10.53	−0.63	6.20
382	Machinery	−7.62	0.71	−2.49	−7.67	10.42	3.86	7.91
383	Electrical machinery	−7.72	9.32	2.59	−2.17	18.58	5.86	13.64
384	Motor vehicles and parts	−0.16	11.26	6.83	−2.54	21.15	19.45	20.51
385	Other transport equipment	3.19	2.98	3.06	−7.14	17.65	16.00	17.03
	Sub-total: metal products group	−3.83	4.22	1.13	−7.18	14.60	9.20	12.54
	Total manufacturing	3.50	7.23	5.81	−1.20	6.64	1.80	4.80

Source: IDC (1995).

24 The combined export share of 'agriculture, forestry and fishing', 'other mining' and the four natural resource-based manufacturing sectors, for which world demand would be expected to be relatively income inelastic, increased from 31.7 per cent in 1970–1, before the commodity price boom, to 53.5 per cent in 1993. Furthermore, gold, whose export share in 1993 was 27.7 per cent, no longer faces a perfectly elastic export demand at a fixed price.

25 The exceptions in the 1970s, in the context of the natural resource boom, were import substitution in the natural resource-based iron and steel and chemical industries, and the motor vehicle industry.

26 See Krugman (1995: 47) on the possible beneficial effects of growth which is biased towards import-competing production.

27 See Bell (1993: 97–8) and Bell and Cattaneo (1997: 14, table 11).

28 Simulations by the IDC in 1994 of the effects of the reforms scheduled for 1995–9 implied a larger percentage increase in imports than exports, and that the largest increases in imports occur in consumer goods industries (Bell and Cattaneo 1997: 21–3). Also the S. A. Reserve Bank (1996: 21–3) argues that the increase in the ratio of imports to gross domestic expenditure has partly been due to 'the reform initiated – to open up the economy more to international competition'.

29 It is estimated that the ratio of imported capital goods to gross domestic fixed investment in South Africa in 1975–90 averaged about 20 per cent.

30 As Rodrik (1995: 94) states, 'the causal relationship between investment and growth should be one of the least controversial in economics'; and Rodrik (1997: 13), in arguing for the importance of capital accumulation, as distinct from productivity growth, states that the best single predictor of the growth of any economy remains its investment rate: hence 'capital accumulation is the proximate source of growth'.

31 Indeed, as in Latin America (Agosin 1995: 159), credit conditions have remained relatively tight, partly because of the ever-present danger of the capital flows going into reverse.

32 It does not seem to us that Agosin's (1995: 166) use of bank credit to the private sector as a proportion of GDP, as a proxy for the availability of finance, overcomes these difficulties.

33 Initially, various ARCH-type specifications of the return-generating process were estimated over this sample period. Of the valid models, an ARCH(2) specification was selected on the basis of information criteria (the restriction that the sum of the coefficients of the lagged values in the conditional variance equation not exceed unity was not met in the case of the benchmark generalised ARCH or GARCH(1,1) model).

34 The abolition of South Africa's dual exchange rate (financial rand) system in March 1995 effectively removed exchange controls on non-residents. There has also been considerable relaxation of exchange controls on permanent residents of South Africa.

35 As no data were available for this purpose for years since 1993, trade orientation was based on IDC data for 1985–93.

36 See Bell (1993a: 108–9) on South African export expansion in 1985–90; and Rodrik (1995: 66–7) with reference to the case of Turkey from the early 1980s.

37 Whether this is an implication of their argument, however, is questionable. In their model, dependence on external finance is technologically determined, rather than being related to constraints on access to credit due to capital market imperfections and associated high information costs. Financial development, it seems, has its beneficial effect on sectors with high external dependence, not by alleviating capital market imperfections, but by increasing the supply of external finance.

38 In general however, we do not find a significant relationship between export growth rates and EDRs, in a regression involving all thirty-six of Rajan and Zingales, sectors. Also, Rajan and Zingales' (1998: 568–9) base their findings on real value-added growth rates rather than export growth rates.

39 See Bell and Farrell (1997: 600–9). Also, Fine's (1996: 33) remark that the conglomerates 'are responsible for the ownership of the vast majority of South African manufacturing' seems to conflict with the notion that the conglomerates are inadequately diversified.

40 See, for instance, Crafts and Thomas (1986: 643) on 'a favourable endowment of natural resources' as the source of Britain's industrial leadership in the nineteenth century, and Britain's consequent difficulty because of a scarcity of human capital 'in adjusting to the technologically progressive product cycle industries that dominated the Second Industrial Revolution'.

References

Agosin, M. R. (1995) 'Savings and Investment in Latin America', *UNCTAD Review 1995*. Geneva: UNCTAD.

Ariovich, G. (1979) 'The Comparative Advantage of South Africa as Revealed by Export Shares', *South African Journal of Economics* 47(2): 188–97.

Bell, T. (1983) 'The Growth and Structure of Manufacturing Employment in Natal', *Institute for Social and Economic Research, University of Durban-Westville, Occasional Paper*, No. 7.

Bell, T. (1993a) 'Should South Africa Further Liberalise its Foreign Trade?', in M. Lipton and C. Simkins (eds), *State and Market in Post Apartheid South Africa*. Boulder, San Francisco and Oxford: Witwatersrand University Press, Johannesburg and Westview Press.

Bell, T. (1993b) 'The Impact of Sanctions on South Africa', *Journal of Contemporary African Studies* 12(1): 1–28.

Bell, T. (1997) 'Trade Policy', in J. Michie and V. Padayachee (eds), *The Political Economy of South Africa's Transition*. London: The Dryden Press.

Bell, T. and Cattaneo, N. (1997) 'Foreign Trade and Employment in South African Manufacturing Industry', *International Labour Office Occasional Report*, No. 4.

Bell, T. and Farrell, G. (1997) 'The Minerals-Energy Complex and South African Industrialisation', *Development Southern Africa* 14(4): 591–613.

Central Statistical Services (CSS), *South African Statistics* (various issues), Pretoria.

Chenery, H. and Syrquin, M. (1975) *Patterns of Development, 1950–1970*. London: Oxford University Press for the World Bank.

Christiano, L. J. (1981) 'A Survey of Measures of Capacity Utilization', *International Monetary Fund Staff Papers* 28(1): 144–98.

Corden, W. M. (1986) 'Round-Table Discussion', in J. P. Neary and S. Van Wijnbergen (eds), *Natural Resources and the Macroeconomy*. Cambridge, MA: The MIT Press.

Crafts, N. F. R. and Thomas, M. (1986) 'Comparative Advantage in UK Manufacturing Trade, 1910–1935', *Economic Journal* 96: 629–45.

Duncan, T. and Fogarty, J. (1984) *Australia and Argentina: On Parallel Paths*. Carlton: Melbourne University Press.

Du Plessis, J. C. (1965) 'Investment and the Balance of Payments in South Africa', *South African Journal of Economics* 33: 311–40.

Du Plessis, T. A. (1965) *The Industrial Growth Pattern and the Real Forces of Economic Expansion in South Africa, 1916/17–1956/57*, unpublished D.Com thesis, University of South Africa, Pretoria.

Fagerberg, J. (1988) 'International Competitiveness', *Economic Journal* 98: 355–74.

Fazzari, S., Hubbard, G. and Petersen, B. (1988) 'Financing Constraints and Corporate Investment', *Brookings Papers on Economic Activity*, No. 1.

Fine, B. (1996) 'Industrial Policy and South Africa: A Strategic View', Mimeo, National Institute for Economic Policy, Johannesburg.

Fine, B. and Rustomjee, Z. (1996) *The Political Economy of South Africa: From Minerals-Energy Complex to Industrialisation*. Johannesburg: Witwatersrand University Press.

Frankel, S. H. (1938) *Capital Investment in Africa: Its Course and Effects*. London: Oxford University Press.

Gelb, A. H. (1986) 'Adjustment to Windfall Gains: A Comparative Analysis of Oil-Exporting Countries', in J. P. Neary and S. Van Wijnbergen (eds), *Natural Resources and the Macroeconomy*. Cambridge, MA: MIT Press.

Hall, B., Mairesse, J. and Mulkay, B. (1998) 'Firm Level Investment in France and the United States: An Exploitation of What We Have Learned in Twenty Years', Mimeo.

Harris, J. R., Schiantarelli, F. and Siregar, M. G. (1994) 'The Effect of Financial Liberalisation on the Capital Structure and Investment Decisions of Indonesian Manufacturing Establishments', *World Bank Economic Review* 8(1): 17–47.

Hodge, J. (1997) 'South African Trade in High Technology Products', *Trade and Industry Monitor* 3: 1–7.

Hubbard, R. G. (1998) 'Capital Market Imperfections and Investment', *Journal of Economic Literature* 36(1): 193–225.

Industrial Development Corporation (IDC) (1995) *Sectoral Data Series for Manufacturing*. Johannesburg: IDC.

Krugman, P. R. (1995) *Currencies and Crises*. Cambridge, MA: The MIT Press.

La Porta, R., Lopez de Silanes, F., Shleifer, A. and Vishny, R. (1996) 'Law and Finance', *National Bureau of Economic Research Working Paper*, No. 5661.

Levine, R. and Zervos, S. (1998) 'Stock Markets, Banks and Economic Growth', *American Economic Review* 88(3): 537–58.

Levy, B. (1996) 'South Africa: The Business Environment for Industrial Small and Medium Enterprises', *The World Bank Southern Africa Department, Informal Discussion Papers on Aspects of the Economy of South Africa*, No. 11.

Rajan, R. G. and Zingales, L. (1998) 'Financial Dependence and Growth', *American Economic Review* 88(3): 559–86.

Reynders Commission (1972) *Report of the Commission of Inquiry into the Export Trade of the Republic of South Africa*, RP. 69/1972. Pretoria: Government Printer.

Rodrik, D. (1995) 'Getting Interventions Right: How Taiwan and Korea Grew Rich', *Economic Policy* 20: 53–108.

Rodrik, D. (1997) 'TFPG Controversies, Institutions and Economic Performance in East Asia', *National Bureau of Economic Research Working Paper*, No. 5914.

Ros, J. (1995) 'Trade Liberalization with Real Appreciation and Slow Growth: Sustainability Issues in Mexico's Trade Policy Reform', in G. K. Helleiner (ed.), *Manufacturing for Export in the Developing World: Problems and Possibilities*. London: Routledge.

Sachs, J. D. and Warner, A. (1995) 'Natural Resource Abundance and Economic Growth', *National Bureau of Economic Research Working Paper Series*, No. 5398.

South African Reserve Bank (SARB) (1996) *Annual Economic Report 1996*. Pretoria: SARB.

Spraos, J. (1981) 'Sub-optimal Market-Led Adjustment to External Shock in Developing Countries', *South African Journal of Economics* 59(3): 352–64.

Thirlwall, A. P. (1979) 'The Balance of Payments Constraint as an Explanation of International Growth Rate Differences', *Banca Nazionale del Lavoro* 32(128): 45–53.

Tsikata, Y. (1998) 'Liberalization and Trade Performance in South Africa', *Informal Draft*, Macroeconomics Division, Southern Africa Department, World Bank.

Warr, P. G. (1986) 'Indonesia's other Dutch Disease: Economic Effects of the Petroleum Boom', in J. P. Neary and S. Van Wijnbergen (eds), *Natural Resources and the Macroeconomy*. Cambridge, MA: MIT Press.

Wright, A. J. (1993) 'Productivity Growth in the South African Manufacturing Sector: Deriving and Assessing Neoclassical TFP Measures', in K. Kruger (ed.), *Papers Submitted for the Competition to Promote Academic Research into Industrial Policy and Development in South Africa*. Sandton: Industrial Development Corporation.

8 Trade, finance and competitiveness in Tunisia[1]

Mustapha K. Nabli, Mejda Bahlous,
Mohamed Bechri, Marouane El Abbassi,
Riadh El Ferktaji and Bechir Talbi

1. Growth and current account sustainability: an overview

Tunisia's total GDP growth of 5.1 per cent per year during 1965–97 was significantly higher than the average of 3.9 per cent for low- and middle-income countries (World Bank 1999, table 1.4). Its performance in terms of average annual GNP per capita growth of 2.7 per cent per year ranked seventh among non-industrial and non-East Asian countries (World Bank 1998, figure 1.4a). In this chapter, we focus on the experience since the early 1970s, when a major switch and reversal in policy occurred towards a more open and liberal economy. We analyze the factors explaining this experience of a sustained relatively high growth (5.1 per cent per year also during 1972–97) and a large current account deficit averaging 6 per cent of GDP (Table 8.1).

GDP growth fluctuated widely, however, with major swings in the current account balance (Figure 8.1). Agricultural production fluctuations, due to variability in rainfall and terms of trade changes, account for a major part of GDP growth fluctuations, with their effect declining with increased diversification of the economy. Different patterns in growth and the current account are discernable over the periods 1972–80, 1981–6, 1987–9 and 1990–7 (Table 8.1). After a surge in the 1970s, growth declined and the current account deficit increased. A major episode was the balance-of-payments crisis in 1985–6 which followed a period of large current account deficit (8.4 per cent of GDP during 1981–6), a significant decline in terms of trade because of the sharp decline in oil prices and poor productivity growth.

Tunisia mobilized significant external finance for its development. The growth performance and 'creditworthiness' of the country helped sustain this high level of capital inflows. Medium- and long-term gross debt inflows, mainly from official sources, averaged about 8 per cent of GDP and were quite stable (Table 8.1). It was only in the mid-1980s, and more recently in the mid-1990s, that private debt flows were significant. Equity flows, mainly foreign direct investment, were also an important source of external finance. Short-term and portfolio flows were tightly controlled and were not of any importance in external finance, and Tunisia did not experience significant effects from the volatility of private capital inflows.

Table 8.1 Growth and the current account (% growth, or % of GDP)

	1972–80	1981–6	1987–9	1990–7	1972–97
Real GDP growth	7.1	3.3	3.5	4.9	5.1
Investment rate	26.3	29.7	20.1	23.6	25.5
Saving rate	22.5	20.4	19.3	20.0	20.8
Financial saving	2.3	2.1	5.4	4.6	3.3
Fiscal deficit (net)	2.8	2.5	3.5	3.6	3.1
Fiscal deficit (primary)	1.6	0.6	1.2	0.1	0.9
Inflation	6.1	8.9	7.7	5.3	6.7
Terms of trade	2.4	−2.6	0.3	−0.8	0.1
(average annual rate of change)					
Trade balance	−5.1	−8.8	−1.5	−6.1	−5.9
Current account balance	−5.6	−8.4	−1.1	−6.6	−6.0
Capital inflows	10.1	12.0	9.8	11.3	10.9
Equity	2.0	3.5	1.4	2.6	2.5
Medium and long-term debt	7.0	8.2	7.8	8.2	7.6
Capital outflows	3.5	4.3	6.7	5.6	4.7
Capital account balance	6.5	7.7	3.1	5.7	6.1

Sources: Banque Centrale de Tunisie and Ministère du Développement Economique.

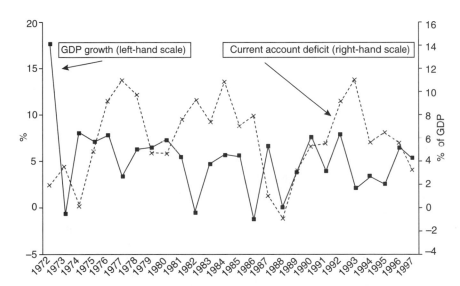

Figure 8.1 GDP growth and current account deficit.

Long-term growth performance and current account sustainability, or long-term competitiveness, have been associated with increased openness and strong export performance.[2] Export volume growth averaged 6.3 per cent during 1973–97 (Table 8.2), and led to an increase in the export to GDP ratio from 34 per cent in 1972 to 44 per cent in 1997.[3] Tunisia's exports structure underwent a dramatic shift: it changed from being dominated by natural resource-based

Table 8.2 Foreign trade indicators (%)

	1972	1980	1986	1989	1997
Exports (*X*)/GDP	34.2	37.8	33.9	44.2	44.2
Imports (*M*)/GDP	36.2	50.4	41.7	48.4	47.8
(*X* + *M*)/GDP	70.4	88.1	75.6	92.6	92.0
Export shares					
Agr., fishing, foods	22.7	5.9	8.0	6.7	7.1
Manufacturing (excl. foods and chemicals)	8.4	20.7	28.1	32.7	40.6
Non-manuf. industry (incl. chemicals)	38.5	37.1	31.3	26.0	15.0
Services	30.4	36.3	32.7	34.5	37.3
	1973–97	1973–80	1981–6	1987–9	1990–7
Import growth	5.8	10.3	0.8	9.1	3.8
Export growth	6.3	7.4	3.0	13.2	5.0
Agr., fishing, foods	4.7	−7.2	9.9	7.4	11.8
Manufacturing (excl. foods and chemical)	13.6	20.7	8.8	19.0	7.9
Non-manuf. Industry (incl. chemical)	2.5	6.8	0.5	6.6	−1.7
Services	7.8	9.9	1.3	17.8	6.9

Source: Ministère du Développement Economique (Budget Economique).

Note: Calculations are based on trade volume data (constant 1990 prices).

products with large oil export revenues in the 1970s to being more diversified in manufacturing and services exports as the country became a net importer of energy products in the 1990s.

In Section 2 we provide a detailed analysis of the trade specialization pattern and its change over time, and the resulting export diversification and improved market shares. The following sections explore factors explaining competitiveness, focusing more specifically on the macro–micro linkages or interactions between financial and macroeconomic factors and competitiveness. In Section 3, we investigate the role of price factors in determining long-term competitiveness including trade policy incentives, the real exchange rate and the links between export orientation and productivity growth. In Section 4 we consider the role of financial factors as determinant of competitiveness. These factors may affect trade specialization and competitiveness through price effects and productivity growth. But non-price effects may be even more important through increased capital accumulation, flexibility in reallocating resources, development and expansion of new activities and products for which there is comparative advantage, research and development inducing changes in comparative advantage and entrepreneurship development. Section 5 summarizes the results of the chapter about micro–macro and trade–finance interactions and competitiveness.

Table 8.3 Exportables (net export products, %)

Products	1984	1990	1995
Tourism	−329.9	−279.2	−557.4
Clothing	−104.7	−268.0	−332.0
Fertilizers	−50.3	−81.3	−73.9
Oil and gas	−40.8	−10.4	
Hosiery	−34.2	−77.9	−67.0
Canned foods	−30.2	−81.1	−27.5
Transportation	−27.7	−26.1	−29.5
Carpets	−27.2	−22.3	−8.8
Minerals	−25.1	−7.9	−37.0
Fruits	−7.6	−10.8	−10.4
Fish products	−6.9	−22.7	−4.3
Leather and shoes	−3.5	−15.3	−25.0
Services to firms		−22.9	
Cement and products		−19.2	−14.0
Vegetable oils and fats		−9.2	−42.1
Telecommunications		−8.0	−5.9
Drinks		−3.4	
Ceramic products		−2.9	−1.7
Transformation of grains		−2.4	−3.5
Animal products			−0.9
Financial services			−0.3

Source: Data from INS. Computations by El Abbassi *et al.* (1999).

Note: Ratio of net exports to domestic demand $t = (m - x)/(y + m - x)$.

2. Shifts in trade specialization and competitiveness

Tunisia's pattern of specialization shifted dramatically with an increase in manufacturing's share in total exports of goods and services (when we exclude foodstuffs and chemicals, which are mainly fertilizers based on rock phosphates) from 8.4 per cent in 1972 to 41 per cent in 1997 (Table 8.2). Similarly, services' (including tourism) share increased from 30 to 37 per cent over the same time period.[4] The share of non-food manufacturing and tourism in GDP increased from 8.6 to 19.5 per cent. It has been a major feature of the country's competitiveness performance.

Trade specialization

The evolution of the broad patterns of trade specialization is also evident from an analysis based on categories of tradables. Using a sixty-product classification, net imports to domestic demand ratio t is computed for each product $t = (m - x)/(y + m - x)$, where y, m and x are production, imports and exports of the product, respectively. Products are classified into four categories: (a) exportable if t is negative and greater than 2 per cent in absolute value; (b) import competing if t is positive, greater than 2 per cent and smaller than 75 per cent; (c) non-tradable if t is smaller than 2 per cent in absolute value; and (d) non-import competing for other values of t.[5]

Table 8.4 Categories of tradables and specialization

	Share in exports (%)	Contribution to trade balance (%)	Intra-industry trade index
Exportables			
1984	85.5	63.6	49.1
1990	84.6	60.2	49.7
1995	73.5	57.8	37.6
Exportables – natural resource based			
1984	42.4	29.6	56.0
1990	24.9	15.2	61.8
1995	12.0	9.7	34.7
Exportables – non-natural resource based			
1984	43.1	34.0	41.5
1990	59.7	45.0	44.0
1995	61.5	48.1	38.1
Import competing			
1984	11.4	−41.3	26.8
1990	11.7	−39.7	32.7
1995	23.5	−43.2	49.0
Non-import competing			
1984	2.4	−22.5	12.7
1990	2.8	−20.4	18.5
1995	1.8	−14.8	17.9

Sources: Données INS et Calculs effectués par El Abbassi *et al.* (1999).

Notes: Contribution of product category i to trade balance: $CTB_i = [(X_i - M_i) - (X - M)* (X_i - M_i)/(X + M)]/[(X + M)/2]$, where M_i and X_i are imports and exports of category i and M and X are total imports and exports. The intra-industry trade index is the Grubel–Lloyd index: $GL_i = [(X_i + M_i) - abs(X_i - M_i)]/(X_i + M_i)$.

A first group of exportables includes traditional and natural resource-based exports: fertilizers, oil and gas, minerals, vegetable oils and fats (olive oil) and fruits (oranges, dates) (Table 8.3). Oil and gas products have become, however, a net import category during the 1990s. The second group includes new product exports already significant during the 1980s: tourism (and transportation), clothing, hosiery, leather and shoes, and fish and products.[6]

Products classified as exportables constitute the bulk of exports, their share averaging 85 per cent during the 1980s (Table 8.4). By 1995 however, the share of exportables declined to 74 per cent and that of import-competing products increased from 12 to 24 per cent. This resulted from both increased exports by a number of import-competing activities, and the contraction of the list of exportables in favor of the import-competing group following trade liberalization. The indicator of contribution to trade balance gives the same result, with a smaller contribution of exportables to trade balance in 1995.

Calculations for the index of comparative advantage (based on European import data) also broadly give the same results, in terms of the characterization of Tunisia's pattern of specialization (Table 8.5). Some products however, that are important net exports (Table 8.3), do not show a high index of comparative advantage, because they are mainly exported to neighboring countries and do not appear in European trade (animal products, transformation of grains and canned foods). Also some products, which are significant net exports, have low index of revealed comparative advantage: hosiery, drinks, minerals and ceramic products.

Export diversification

The share of natural resource-based exports fell from 42 per cent in 1984 to about 12 per cent in 1997 (Table 8.4). But, the share of non-resource-based exports increased from 43 per cent in 1984 to 62 per cent in 1997. Their contribution to the trade balance increased from 34 to 48 per cent. The expanding exports are light manufacturing, mainly clothing and hosiery, and tourism services. This category of new exports broadened since the mid-1980s with the addition of a number of other products: leather and shoes, cement products, ceramic products, transformation of grains and a number of services (Table 8.3).

The index of intra-industry trade for exportables declined, however, in the 1990s (reflecting import liberalization of these products), and increased for import-competing products. The latter means that for many of these products there is a significant increase of exports. It is also noteworthy that a number of products, classified in the import-competing category, such as electrical and electronic products, metal products, and rubber products, are emerging in the 1990s as significant exports. All these products, however, do not yet show a revealed comparative advantage (Table 8.5), and Tunisia has not diversified into higher value-added and more technology-intensive sectors (Guerrieri 1998).

Export shares and competitiveness

The results for export performance and competitiveness are confirmed using constant market share analysis for the period after the crisis in the mid-1980s. Between 1988 (beginning year 0) and 1996 (end year t), the change in Tunisia's exports to its main trading partner, the European Union (EU), is decomposed into three components as shown in eqn (8.1).

$$\Delta X = s_0 \Delta M + \left[\sum_{i=1}^{n} s_{i0} \Delta M_i - s_0 \Delta M \right] + \sum_{i=1}^{n} \Delta s_i M_i, \tag{8.1}$$

where ΔX is the change in total exports of Tunisia to the EU over the period, ΔM is the change in total imports of the EU, M_i is imports of product i by the EU at the end of period, $s_0 = X_0/M_0$ is the share of Tunisia's total exports to the EU in total EU imports at the beginning of period, and $s_i = X_i/M_i$ is the share of Tunisia's exports of product i in total imports of the EU of product at the end of period.

Table 8.5 Revealed comparative advantage

Products	1988	1992	1996
Fruits	0.27	0.28	0.12
Animal products	0.08	0.02	0.00
Fish and products	7.22	3.05	2.32
Transformation of grains	0.01	0.04	0.07
Vegetable oils and fats	10.46	12.61	7.75
Canned foods	0.21	0.06	0.09
Drinks	0.54	0.24	0.14
Cement and products	2.91	0.76	1.04
Ceramic products	0.40	0.42	0.57
Electrical products	0.74	0.95	0.80
Fertilizers	22.05	13.62	14.92
Carpets	2.20	1.57	1.01
Hosiery	1.02	0.47	0.18
Clothing	11.31	12.17	14.01
Leather and products	1.42	2.19	3.25
Minerals	0.39	0.16	0.78
Oil and gas	2.02	1.46	1.40

Source: Data from Eurostat. Computations by El Abbassi *et al.* (1999).

Notes: (a) Index of revealed comparative advantage: $(x/X)/(m/M)$ based on European Union imports from Tunisia (x, X) and total (m, M) imports, (b) The products listed are those with an index higher than 1 and a few other products which are listed in Table 8.3.

The first component is the standard growth effect, which measures the increase in Tunisian exports under the assumption of maintained total constant share in the EU market. The second component measures the change in exports due to changes in EU demand structure for various products, if Tunisia maintained its initial share in the various EU product markets. The last term captures the 'competitiveness' effect, or increase in exports due to gains in market shares.

Tunisia's exports to the EU increased 11.8 per cent per year over the period 1989–96, while total EU imports increased by 7 per cent. The decomposition of this export growth to the EU during this period shows that the product structure effect is negligible (-0.2 per cent): changes in EU import demand structure had a neutral effect on Tunisia's export growth. The standard growth effect accounts for 55 per cent of the increase in exports. There are also significant gains in export shares and competitiveness effects during this period, which account for 45 per cent of the change in exports to the EU. The share of Tunisia in EU imports increased from 0.16 to 0.23 per cent, with the most significant gains in clothing and leather (0.78 to 1.7 per cent).

3. Productivity growth and the price determinants of competitiveness

Export performance and productivity growth have interacted in a virtuous cycle, enhancing competitiveness in Tunisia. In this section we show that trade policy, the real exchange rate and unit labor costs have been major price determinants of export performance.

Productivity growth and export performance

Total factor productivity (TFP) growth contributed about 25 per cent to the 5.1 per cent GDP growth in Tunisia over 1972–96 (Table 8.6), but varied considerably over time. Changes in TFP can be partly explained by exogenous shocks, such as rainfall and terms of trade, but policy also played a significant role. Moussa (1995) argues also that Tunisia had lower productivity growth than East Asian countries which started with similar conditions because of protectionist trade and industrial policies and limited competition, even despite some liberalization since the early 1970s and the reversal of the socialist experiment.

There is a large amount of evidence pointing to a positive link between export performance or trade openness and productivity growth.[7] But, there is little agreement on the direction of causality (Edwards 1993; Fagerberg 1996). The Tunisian experience shows such a link between export performance and productivity growth.[8] The total factor productivity growth surge in the 1970s and in the 1990s followed significant increases in trade openness (Table 8.2). During the 1972–80 period, TFP grew at 2.1 per cent on average, then declined significantly and was negative during the period and the run-up to the balance-of-payments crisis. With the implementation of the structural adjustment program, productivity growth

Table 8.6 GDP and TFP growth (annual growth rates in %)

	1972–80		1981–6		1987–9		1990–6		1972–96	
	VA	TFP	VA	TFP	VA	TFP	VA	TFP	VA	TFP
Agr. and fishing	4.6	2.3	2.8	0.5	0.1	−1.2	7.0	5.9	4.3	2.4
Manufacturing	11.3	2.4	6.5	1.0	5.6	2.7	6.0	3.3	8.0	2.3
Foods	6.9	−5.3	5.5	−1.7	0.0	−2.4	5.0	1.8	5.2	−2.4
Construction materials	20.4	3.7	7.1	2.0	6.7	4.2	3.9	1.5	10.9	2.8
Mech. and electr.	13.1	4.1	7.9	1.7	3.7	−0.7	4.6	1.1	8.3	2.0
Chemicals	10.8	1.6	7.8	1.3	8.3	6.3	5.4	3.5	8.3	2.5
Textiles and cloth.	14.3	7.2	5.1	1.2	9.7	4.8	8.2	4.5	9.8	4.7
Miscellaneous	11.1	4.0	9.4	2.9	5.9	2.2	6.3	2.4	8.8	2.9
Non-manuf. Industry	8.2	2.3	0.5	−1.7	0.0	0.0	2.4	0.8	3.7	0.6
Prod. services	7.9	2.0	3.6	−1.2	7.1	2.7	5.3	−0.1	6.1	0.7
Transp. and telecom.	9.4	2.2	2.8	−1.3	7.1	5.3	6.0	2.1	6.6	1.6
Tourism	10.0	2.2	1.4	−4.8	15.4	10.6	6.0	−1.0	7.5	0.7
Total	7.1	2.1	3.3	−0.7	3.5	1.0	4.9	1.9	5.1	1.3

Source: Ministère du Développement Economique.

VA: Value-added growth; TFP: total factor productivity growth.

recovered during 1987–9 in most sectors, except agriculture and foods, because of drought years. This recovery accelerated after 1990, and TFP growth averaged 1.9 per cent.

That TFP growth and export performance interacted in a virtuous cycle is also evident from comparing their evolution at the sectoral level. Non-traditional manufacturing has been the most dynamic export sector with 14 per cent annual growth over 1973–97. Growth was fastest during the 1970s and end of the 1980s, but slowed down somewhat in the 1990s (Table 8.2). TFP growth was also highest for manufacturing activities (excluding foods), with the most dynamic export activities, such as textiles and clothing, showing the largest rate of productivity growth. Even during the 1981–6 period when total export volume growth was weakest (non-food non-chemicals), manufacturing exports increased by 9 per cent per year and TFP grew at high rates in non-food manufacturing activities, ranging from 1.6 to 7.2 per cent per year.

The lagging sectors, in terms of productivity growth, were traditional exports of foods and agricultural products and non-manufacturing industries including oil and minerals. Their export performance was also the weakest. The performance of service exports was mixed. Export growth, led by tourism, was strong despite a setback in the early 1980s and slowdown in the 1990s, but productivity growth remained weak despite strong recovery in 1987–9.

Trade policy and export performance

Trade policy has been suggested as a main factor explaining the link between export performance and productivity growth. Recent empirical evidence has provided support for a positive effect of more open trade policy on productivity growth (Dollar 1992; Sachs and Warner 1995; Edwards 1998), but the findings remain controversial due to measurement and conceptual problems (Edwards 1993; Rodriguez and Rodrik 1999).[9]

In the early 1960s, Tunisia developed one of the most restrictive foreign trade regimes in the developing world.[10] Almost all imports required some kind of licensing and/or administrative approval with varying degrees of restrictiveness according to type of product. Exports were generally free, with some products restricted and all subject to foreign exchange control. It was a standard and excessive import-substitution policy with high nominal and effective protection rates.

The 1970s witnessed a reversal of the most controversial aspects of the previous policy orientation. This decade was also strongly influenced by the development of oil production, as well as the large increases in oil and other minerals (phosphates and derived fertilizer products, a main export) prices. Despite several attempts, especially in 1976, to simplify and make the import trade regime more flexible or more liberalized, it remained very restrictive, with a high level and dispersion of rates of protection, a high degree of complexity and a plethora of exemptions and product specific regimes. The import substitution strategy initiated in the 1960s was deepened, with the public sector continuing to expand rapidly. Government controls remained pervasive in all areas: prices, investment, credit, foreign trade and exchange. There was, however, the emergence of a private sector as well as a non-traditional exports sector, based on export processing zones.[11] Manufacturing exports increased 21 per cent per year during the period.

During the early 1980s, an expansionary macroeconomic policy was pursued in the context of improving terms of trade. But in the face of a sharp deterioration in the terms of trade since 1984 (a decline of about 20 per cent over 1984–6), there was a decline in the volume of oil exports, which were still a significant component of exports, and fiscal policy was not adjusted, even becoming expansionary in 1985–6. By early 1986, the situation had clearly become unsustainable. A major stabilization-cum-structural adjustment program was initiated in 1986, and was strongly deepened following a change in political regime at the end of 1987. It included a large currency devaluation as well as wide-ranging structural reform programs. The stabilization program that was implemented rapidly was successful and resulted, over a relatively short time, in a restoration of macrobalances by the early 1990s. A strong export surge helped achieve these gains with the main export sectors leading in terms of productivity gains.

Trade reform initiated during this period led to a reduction of nominal tariffs from a range of 10 per cent to 236 per cent to 15 per cent to 43 per cent, and the average nominal rate of protection declined from 41 per cent in 1986 to 29 per cent in 1988.[12] The average effective rate of protection declined from 70 per cent to 42 per cent, but remained high for most manufacturing activities, averaging 78 per cent.[13] Quantitative restrictions on imports were lifted gradually, as shown in Table 8.7.

The process of liberalization of the economy continued during the 1990–7 period.[14] The reforms affected all aspects of the domestic policy: investment, credit and the financial sector and prices. A major fiscal reform was implemented resulting in a simplification of the tax system, and a reduction in direct income taxes. A privatization program was initiated aiming at reducing the direct role of the state in economic activity. The trade regime was liberalized, and current account convertibility achieved in 1993. The opening of the trade regime led to Tunisia becoming a member of GATT in 1990, and later of the World Trade Organization. Further liberalization has been taking place since 1996 in the context of the Free Trade Area Agreement signed with the European Union. Complete implementation of the Agreement would lead to free trade in industrial products by 2010. Agricultural products and services are to be the subject of further negotiation for liberalization.

Table 8.7 Indicators of liberalization

Indicator (%)	1987	1990	1995
Tariff lines	20	48	87
Value of imports	32	46	93
Import-competing domestic production	N/A	10	89

Table 8.8 Share of 'off-shore' in total exports (%)

Export sector	1994	1996
Energy, mining and derived products	0.0	0.0
Foodstuffs	11.5	21.8
Textiles, clothing, leather	95.3	96.2
Mechanical and electrical	76.3	84.2
Other manufacturing	37.5	40.4
Total	59.6	64.2

Source: Institut National de la Statistique.

The 'normal' trade regime remained highly protectionist throughout the period, with a strong import substitution bias not supportive of exports. This did not contribute to enhancing competitiveness. In order to allow exporters to overcome the import restrictive regime and compensate for the incentive bias in favor of import-competing activities however, a new 'export processing zones' regime was introduced in the early 1970s.[15] According to this system, enterprises that exclusively specialize in production for export get a number of significant incentives. They have free access to intermediate inputs and capital goods, and 'suspension' of tariffs and duties on these imported products. They also benefit from an unlimited tax holiday on corporate taxes (for other enterprises, these had been reduced in 1994 to ten years with taxation on a reduced rate, i.e. by over a half). A number of other tax incentives were also provided.

This 'off-shore' production system is not limited to any specific geographical location, but is applied to any firm that meets the requirements and is subject to a special customs control system. It attracted a significant amount of entrepreneurial activity both domestic and foreign, and was the main channel of the manufacturing export drive. The export performance reflects the performance mainly of this 'warehouse production' system, especially for clothing products. In 1996, 64 per cent of total exports were made by these activities, especially in non-traditional non-natural resource-based activities (Table 8.8).

The 'off-shore' export regime and its tax incentives, as well as additional export incentives in the form of subsidies and export promotion, helped correct (at least partially) the import substitution bias and were effective in supporting the export performance of Tunisia. It also resulted in the development of a 'dual' economy, one for production for the domestic market and the other for exports only. Production linkages between the two remained weak or non-existent, which may constitute the biggest challenge to Tunisia's competitiveness in the future.

The real exchange rate

The 'off-shore' export regime is not sufficient to explain the export performance in the context of highly protectionist import-substitution biased trade regime.

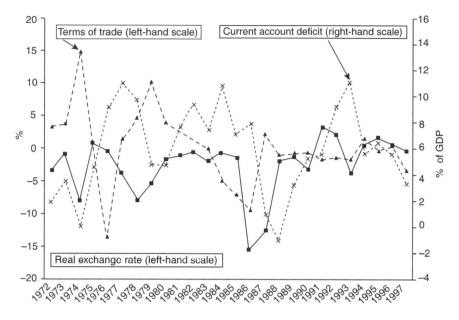

Figure 8.2 Terms of trade, real exchange rate and current account deficit.

Exchange rate policy and movements in the real exchange rate (RER) are a factor explaining the sustainability of the current account. RER changes have only short- to medium-term effects on competitiveness (Dornbusch 1996). But RER misalignments can also have long-term implications if hysteresis is present in an economy (Boltho 1996). Temporary overvaluations may cause permanent or long-lasting losses in market shares and shortfalls in the capital stock in the tradables sector.

In Tunisia, the RER has been depreciating throughout the 1972–97 period, with two major declines: 15 per cent in 1977–9 and 27 per cent in 1987–9 (Figure 8.2).[16] The medium- and long-term movements of the real exchange rate did not have negative effects on competitiveness. The movements in the RER, however, have not always been consistent with changes in the 'equilibrium exchange rate'. Sekkat and Varoudakis (1998) compute a measure of RER 'misalignment' from 'fundamentals' using a model-based approach suggested by Edwards (1988). They estimate an empirical model of the 'equilibrium exchange rate', which accounts for a number of fundamentals: terms of trade, sustainable capital inflows and domestic credit expansion, and trade policy orientation.[17] They find significant real exchange 'misalignment' of the order of 30–5 per cent in 1970–3, which was quickly corrected with the improved terms of trade in 1974–5 (increasing the equilibrium RER) and depreciation of the observed RER.

The most significant episodes of RER 'misalignment' are the 1977–9 and 1984–6 period. The first period started from a situation of a 15 per cent overvaluation of

RER and a large negative shock in terms of trade in 1976. A depreciation of the RER by 10 per cent in 1976–8, even after a reversal in terms of trade with a large positive shock, led to an adjustment in the current deficit from an unsustainable level of about 10 per cent in 1976–8 to 5 per cent in 1979–80. But, during the second period, the failure of the RER to depreciate despite the sharp decline in terms of trade (by about 20 per cent) led to significant misalignment over the period 1984–6 and the balance of payments crisis of 1986.[18] Even though manufacturing exports continued to increase significantly over this period, it was not sufficient to compensate for the low (even negative) volume growth of other exports and the decline in terms of trade. The devaluation of the currency and the sharp RER depreciation in 1986–7 along with a stabilization program, led to a sharp adjustment in the current account balance, to a more sustainable level in the 1990s, even achieving a surplus in 1988.

Unit labor costs and manufacturing exports

The non-traditional (non-food non-chemicals) manufacturing exports increase since 1985 followed a significant decline in unit labor costs since 1983 (Figure 8.3). The fall in unit labor costs is especially important when measured in terms of export prices (ULC2).[19] While labor productivity stagnated, the decline in real wages, after large increases in the previous years, induced strong export growth and restored competitiveness. The decline in unit labor costs since 1992 reflects, however, increased productivity while real wages were increasing.

4. Finance and competitiveness

Trade performance and competitiveness depend also on a number of non-price factors such as technological innovation which affects quality and diversity of

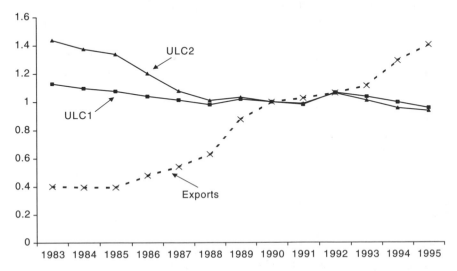

Figure 8.3 Manufacturing exports and unit labor costs.

products, responsiveness to customer's needs, delivery time, marketing and distribution networks and quality of physical infrastructure, public services and human capital. One factor that has not received much attention is the role of finance in determining trade specialization and competitiveness. In this section, we explore a number of such financial channels: overall financial development, development of long-term credit, sectoral allocation of credit and patterns of finance, and imperfections in the financial markets (and policies and institutions to deal with them). These factors influence competitiveness through improved efficiency, higher productivity and reduced costs. But non-price effects may be even more important through increased capital accumulation, flexibility in reallocating resources, development and expansion of new activities and products for which there is comparative advantage, research and development inducing changes in comparative advantage and entrepreneurship development.

Financial sector development

Despite a policy of financial repression from the early 1970s to the mid-1980s, there was a significant process of financial deepening in Tunisia comparable to that of the most advanced of the developing countries (Table 8.9).[20] The overall stability of the macroeconomic environment and economic growth were likely the main contributing factors.

The financial sector has developed under the close 'management' and supervision of the Central Bank, and barriers to entry made it very difficult to create new banks.[21] Competition has been restricted. Development banks created with

Table 8.9 Financial sector development

Indicator	1972	1980	1986	1989	1997
M2/GDP (%)	32.7	40.7	46.6	51.2	45.4
Financial sector assets/GDP (%)	63.8	73.9	104.4	125.5	118.7
Average interest rates (%) *Nominal (first row),* *real (second row)*		*1971–80*	*1981–6*	*1987–9*	*1990–7*
Money market		6.6	9.0	9.5	9.6
		0.4	0.1	1.8	5.1
Loan rate		7.2	8.7	11.9	12.5
		1.1	3.2	4.8	7.2
Time deposit rate		3.4	4.9	7.9	7.6
		−3.3	−4.0	0.2	2.6
Inflation rate		6.2	8.9	7.7	5.3

Source: Bechri (1999).

Notes: Financial sector assets include banking sector assets (Central Bank, domestic commercial and development banks, 'off-shore' banks) and leasing companies assets.

foreign parties in the early 1980s were not supposed to be a threat, since they were public in nature and offered medium- and long-term financing as opposed to short-term financing of commercial banks. Foreign entry was strictly limited. A number of 'off-shore' banks were created since the 1980s, but they are not a threat to the system since they do not directly compete with local banks.[22]

Financial development accelerated after financial liberalization, which was part of the structural adjustment program since 1987. Regulations on administrative allocation of credit were lifted and interest rates were liberalized, although with a cap on the margin between the money market rate and loan rates. Real time deposit rates remained negative until 1987–8, but real loan rates, which remained negative or close to zero during financial repression, became significantly positive since 1985. Also, the money market rate remained under tight Central Bank control. Interest rates margins were liberalized in 1994, but competition remains limited in the credit market. The ratio of financial saving to GDP more than doubled from 2.1 per cent in 1981–6 to 5.4 per cent during 1987–9 (Table 8.1), and the financial sector assets/GDP ratio, which was already fairly high, increased more than 20 per cent during 1986–9.[23]

Real loan rates became very high during the 1990s, exceeding 7 per cent on average. High interest rates for loans, combined with low deposit rates, reflected a large increase in bank margins, which were kept low during the financial repression. The predominance of public banks and limited competition resulted in significant inefficiency of the banking system, and an assessment by the business community, according to a recent survey, that banks are the third most important obstacle they face. Five out of the twelve commercial banks are public and they represent 68 per cent of total loans. According to a recent study, Tunisia's public commercial banks have lower return on assets, lower profitability and higher borrowing costs due to poor resource mobilization, compared to privately owned banks (World Bank 1995). The higher cost–income ratios demonstrate lower productivity, lower fee income as a percentage of total assets, and much lower quality of portfolio, which has been recently improving at a slower rate than in private banks. For example, in 1993 non-performing loans were approximately 14–25 per cent of total assets and off-balance sheet items for some private banks, compared to 36 and 72 per cent for the two main public banks. Similar weaknesses are also observed for development banks, especially in terms of low profitability and quality of portfolio. All of the eight development banks are public in character. Indeed, development banks seem to be withdrawing from the market with their commitments decreasing.

While in existence since 1969, the Tunis Stock Exchange remained completely marginal until the reforms of the late 1980s and early 1990s. The stock market capitalization to GDP ratio increased dramatically from 4 per cent in 1990 to 23 per cent in 1995, but declined to 13 per cent in 1997 after the burst of the 1994–5 price bubble.

Overall financial development and competitiveness

While causality remains controversial, a number of recent studies have found a significant positive link between financial development and growth (Levine

1997; Levine and Zervos 1998). Rajan and Zingales (1998) provide additional evidence for a significant impact of financial development on investment and growth, and argue for the existence of causality. By reducing the cost of external finance, and allowing for the rise of new firms and enhancing innovation, financial development supports economic growth. Levine *et al.* (1999) use country cross-sectional and panel data and present evidence that causality runs from financial development to growth.

The evidence about this link for Tunisia is mixed. The initial, relatively high level of financial intermediation in the early 1970s, and the strong process of financial deepening, have surely contributed to TFP growth over the long run. But limitations on the protection of creditor rights, accounting standards and enforcement of contracts may have limited the efficiency and performance of the financial system.[24] Table 8.10 shows no clear association between changes in level of financial development and TFP growth and export performance over the different periods. The strong TFP and export growth during the 1970s took place at the same time as financial development indicators increased. During the first half of the 1980s, the weak or negative performance, both in terms of competitiveness, with negative TFP, and total export growth (but high manufacturing export growth), have also occurred in the context of strong financial deepening. In the 1990s, while TFP growth was strong there was a negative change in the financial development indicators. The change in these indicators, however, does not reflect a reversal of financial deepening but rather, the development of capital markets and a switch of assets away from the banking system.

Long-term debt

The theoretical arguments about the effects of long-term debt on economic performance are inconclusive. Long-term debt may be less efficient because it allows less managerial discipline and provides opportunity for owners and managers to benefit from projects at the expense of external investors. It also allows management to delay taking decisions in the face of deteriorating conditions. On the other hand, lack of long-term finance may cause profitable projects with

Table 8.10 Competitiveness and overall financial development (%)

	1972–80	*1981–6*	*1987–9*	*1990–7*
TFP growth	2.1	−0.7	1.0	1.9[a]
Change in exports/GDP ratio	3.6	−2.9	10.3	0.0
Total export volume growth	7.4	3.0	13.2	5.0
Manuf. (non-food, non-chemicals) export volume growth	20.7	8.8	19.0	7.9
Change in M2/GDP ratio	8.0	5.9	4.6	−5.8
Change in financial sector assets/GDP ratio	10.1	30.5	21.1	−6.8

Source: From various tables in this chapter.

Note

a For period 1990–6.

long-term returns not to be undertaken, and innovative technologies not to be introduced. Firms with long-term asset structure need to have a long-term maturity debt structure.

Empirical evidence, however, from developed and developing country experience has shown that long-term finance contributes to increased efficiency and growth but that it is scarce in developing countries compared to industrial countries (Caprio and Demirgüç-Kunt 1998). Demirgüç-Kunt and Maksimovic (1996a) use data for thirty industrialized and developing countries and conclude that large firms in industrialized countries use much more long-term debt compared to total assets than large firms in the developing countries. For example, a German firm finances 35 per cent of its total assets using long-term debt while a firm from Brazil or Zimbabwe finances less than 10 per cent of its assets using long-term debt.

In Table 8.11, we investigate the financial structure and behavior of firms at the micro-level in Tunisia based on a sample of 163 manufacturing firms over the

Table 8.11 Long-term debt

	1984–6	1987–9	1990–2	1993–4
Total sample				
DT/*A*	0.524	0.457	0.421	0.392
DLT/*K*	0.200	0.156	0.157	0.142
DLT/*A*	0.191	0.138	0.138	0.132
DLT/DT	0.349	0.302	0.303	0.316
Public sector				
DT/*A*	0.638	0.555	0.494	0.547
DLT/*K*	0.364	0.322	0.273	0.306
DLT/*A*	0.294	0.227	0.258	0.313
DLT/DT	0.470	0.477	0.460	0.484
Private sector				
DT/*A*	0.512	0.447	0.414	0.377
DLT/*K*	0.183	0.139	0.145	0.125
DLT/*A*	0.181	0.129	0.126	0.113
DLT/DT	0.337	0.284	0.287	0.299
Growth firms				
DT/*A*	0.500	0.484	0.436	0.399
DLT/*K*	0.186	0.201	0.257	0.234
DLT/*A*	0.178	0.154	0.184	0.177
DLT/DT	0.316	0.299	0.381	0.414
Non-growth firms				
DT/*A*	0.519	0.428	0.403	0.365
DLT/*K*	0.182	0.106	0.086	0.067
DLT/*A*	0.182	0.115	0.096	0.079
DLT/DT	0.348	0.276	0.237	0.238

Source: Bahlous (1999).

DT/*A*: total debt (DT) to net worth (*A*) ratio; DLT/*K*: long-term debt (DLT) to capital stock (*K*) ratio; DLT/*A*: long-term debt (DLT) to net worth (*A*) ratio; DLT/DT: long-term debt (DLT) to total debt (DT) ratio.

period 1984–94.[25] The results show that the ratio of long-term debt to assets is in the upper range of the developing countries, as found by Demirguç-Kunt and Maksimovic (1996a), but in the lower range of developed countries. It averaged 19 per cent during 1984–6, then declined to around 13–14 per cent after liberalization. This ratio on average was twice as large for public sector firms than for the private sector (27 per cent compared to 14 per cent on average over 1984–94). It has been declining for the private sector over the period 1984–94.[26] The long-term debt to capital stock ratio and share of long-term to total debt ratios show similar results.

In Tunisia, long-term finance has developed with financial deepening. The share of medium- and long-term loans in total loans of the banking system increased significantly from less than 30 per cent in the 1970s to 41–42 per cent in the early 1980s. It remained at this level, despite some decline at the end of the 1980s and early 1990s. Macroeconomic stability and financial and institutional development have clearly allowed the growth of long-term finance. Nevertheless, the government also played a significant role.

The government used five instruments to enhance long-term finance. One, is a requirement of commercial banks to allocate a minimum of 10 per cent of deposits to medium- and long-term credit for priority activities. Second, there is provision of subsidized credit through lower interest rate or/and direct subsidies to some activities with long-term maturity of assets such as tourism and agriculture. A number of publicly financed development banks were used to channel such credits, some of which were specialized by sector (housing, tourism, agriculture). By the mid-1980s, development banks accounted for 20–5 per cent of total bank credit. A third instrument is the use of external lines of credit from bilateral or multilateral sources to finance priority activities such as agriculture, tourism and mining, these credits being guaranteed by the government. Finally, direct government direction of credit either through state-owned banks or Central Bank approval procedures is another instrument. Financial liberalization led to reduced intervention by the government with abandonment of the first two instruments, and lesser direct government intervention. But, development banks remain active, although their share of total bank credit has been declining.

While government intervention may have increased availability of long-term finance, it may also have reduced its efficiency. Demirguç-Kunt and Maksomovic (1996b) found that subsidizing long-term credit, for instance through public development banks, may reduce the efficiency gains from long-term finance. Our results from a sample of manufacturing firms show that allocation of credit tended to favor state-owned enterprises (SOEs), which have ratios of long-term debt to capital stock at least twice as large as private firms (Table 8.11). To the extent that public enterprises are less efficient and their expansion does not only reflect efficiency criteria, there may have been a general loss of efficiency. The reduction of long-term credit to some activities dominated by SOEs, as well as the general relative decline of long-term finance during the adjustment period 1987–9 and the beginning of the financial liberalization, supports this conclusion.

Access to long-term debt was associated with growth within the private sector. For the subsample of 'growth firms', which includes firms with assets growing by more than 15 per cent per year, the ratio of long-term debt to capital stock increased from 19 per cent before liberalization to 23–5 per cent in the 1990s, while it declined sharply for the 'non-growth' group (Table 8.11). Also for the growth group, the share of long-term to total debt increased significantly from 31 per cent in 1984–6 to 41 per cent in 1993–4. While overall leverage declined, long-term finance is strengthened. The financial and economic performance indicators worsen for the non-growth group throughout the period compared to the growth group, possibly indicating the capacity of the banking sector to screen better performing projects and firms (Bahlous 1999).

The development of long-term finance allowed firms to match the maturity of their assets and debts, contributing to increased efficiency and better performance. For instance, tourism, with assets of very long-term maturity, has a relatively larger share of long-term credit compared to total investment and is classified as a winner in credit allocation (see below, and Table 8.12). Manufacturing also had a share of

Table 8.12 Winners and losers in the credit market

Activity	1981–6	1981–6	1987–9	1990–6
Winner +, ratio > 2				
Mining	X	X		
Foods	X		X	X
Electrical and mechanical	X	X	X	
Chemicals and rubber	X	X		X
Textiles, clothing, leather	X		X	
Wood and paper	X	X		
Construction materials		X		
Tourism	X	X	X	X
Winner, ratio: 1.0–2.0				
Construction		X		X
Construction materials	X			X
Foods		X		
Textiles, clothing, leather		X		X
Wood and paper				X
Electrical and mechanical				X
Agriculture			X	
Wood and paper			X	
Loser, ratio: 0.5–0.9				
Agriculture	X	X		
Construction	X		X	
Mining			X	X
Loser −, ratio < 0.5				
Electricity–water,	X	X	X	X
Transport and telecom.	X	X	X	X
Construction materials			X	
Chemicals and rubber			X	
Agriculture				X

Source: Bechri (1999).

Note: 'Ratio' indicates the ratio of shares in credit (total, medium and long term and short term) to relevant share in economic activity (investment, value-added).

medium- and long-term credit twice as large as its share in investment, with relatively larger ratios for construction materials, mechanical industries and wood and paper all classified as winners. On the other hand, textiles and clothing had a lower ratio that is consistent with shorter maturity of assets in an activity dominated by apparel. Large adjustments took place in 1987–9 with long-term credit curtailed significantly for many activities which had benefited largely from long-term debt (construction materials, chemicals, mining), while clothing's share increased.[27]

Sectoral credit allocation: winners and losers in the credit market

Until the start of structural adjustment reforms, the allocation of credit was closely controlled by the authorities with a major role played by the Central Bank. The first general mechanism used was that of the compulsory allocation credit ratios. In addition to the minimum requirement for holding government paper (20 per cent of deposits), and housing bonds (5 per cent), banks are required to allocate 18 per cent of deposits to the private sector. Within the latter ratio, 10 per cent of deposits had to be allocated to medium- and long-term credit 'priority activities': agriculture, export activities, small- and medium-sized enterprises and energy saving industries. While effective allocation was not always in line with regulations, particularly depending on the requirements of budget financing, the system was generally enforced. The second mechanism was that of prior authorization by the Central Bank for short-term, as well as medium- and long-term credit, exceeding some minimum value. The third was that of preferential interest rates on credit for some activities. But all of these mechanisms of control were gradually lifted in 1987, and by the early 1990s the allocation mechanism for credit was almost completely liberalized.

In order to evaluate the 'success' of economic activities in obtaining bank credit, we calculate the 'ratio' of their share in medium- to long-term credit to their share in total investment, and the 'ratios' of the shares in short-term credit and total credit to their share in total value-added. The three calculated 'ratios' are used to obtain a qualitative classification of activities into five categories going from highly successful or 'winner' to great 'loser' in the allocation of credit. The results show a slight pro-tradables bias in the allocation of credit throughout the period (Table 8.12).[28] This bias was even quite strong during 1987–9. Most of the export activities identified above, for which Tunisia had a comparative advantage, were at the top of the list of 'winners' in the credit allocation process. This includes in particular the manufacturing activities, tourism and mining. Agriculture was a 'loser' in most periods, particularly for short-term credit, despite priority and success in obtaining medium- to long-term credit. Most non-tradable activities were 'losers', in particular the utilities and transportation and telecommunications. This result has to be interpreted with caution however, since these were mainly state-owned and operated activities, which either relied on the budget for finance or on government guaranteed foreign direct credit.

A number of specific activities are interesting to look into more carefully, in view of their situation in terms of credit allocation as compared to comparative advantage. Mechanical–electrical–electronics and wood–paper activities were very 'successful' in their access to credit, while they did not appear as successful export activities. The performance of 'chemicals and rubber' is influenced by the inclusion of the traditional fertilizers activity (a public sector operated activity) which went through a strong restructuring during the late 1980s to early 1990s. So, its share of credit collapsed during 1987–9. This applies to mining also with the related rock phosphate (which is also the main primary product for fertilizers) extraction being the main activity. Tourism received high priority in the allocation of medium- and long-term credit and had high allocation ratios, but fared low for short-term credit.

Financial structure and market imperfections

The sectoral allocation of credit was significantly affected, but not completely determined, by government direct intervention during the period of financial repression. It was also a result of the internal functioning of financial markets and their inherent imperfections. In this subsection, we investigate the financial behavior of firms at the micro-level and the effects of financial markets imperfections on competitiveness using our sample of manufacturing firms. The balanced panel data sample of 163 firms also allows an analysis of the effects of financial liberalization on firm finance and performance.

Financial structure of firms

The financial structure of firms and its change after financial liberalization is described in Table 8.13. The results provide a fairly good picture of firm finance in Tunisia, and the effects of financial liberalization. A first distinction is according to ownership. The sample includes fifteen public sector firms, some of which are fully SOEs, while the rest have more than 34 per cent government share of capital. The private sector comprises a few firms with partial foreign ownership, but most are domestically owned firms. Public sector firms have better 'access' to bank credit than the private sector, with debt ratios significantly higher and cost of credit lower. During the period 1984–6, the cost of credit for the private sector was on average twice (16.6 per cent) as large as for the public sector (8 per cent). Comparing the periods before (1984–6) and after financial liberalization and stabilization (1990–2), debt ratios (DT/K or DT/A) declined significantly for all categories of firms, but generally remained higher for the public sector. In contrast, while interest rate charges increased for all firms, the interest charges gap between public and private sector increased from about 8 percentage points to 10–11 percentage points. The public sector has also better access to long-term credit, with the share of short-term credit much higher for the private sector.

The performance indicators for the public sector, however, are much worse than for the private sector. The gross returns on capital (EBE/K) and productivity of capital (VA/K) indicators are higher for the private sector across periods. In addition, while the private sector maintains its efficiency indicators after liberalization, the performance of the public sector deteriorates significantly as the rate of capital accumulation increases.[29]

Table 8.13 Financial structure and liberalization

Firms	Period	I/K	EBE/K	VA/K	EBG/AB	DT/K	DT/A	R	DCT/DT
Total (163)	1984–6	0.059	0.246	0.563	0.111	0.641	0.524	0.158	0.651
	1990–2	0.078	0.237	0.504	0.096	0.510	0.421	0.215	0.697
Public sector									
SOEs (8)	1984–6	0.060	0.210	0.469	0.096	0.759	0.604	0.077	0.557
	1990–2	0.119	0.169	0.403	0.083	0.530	0.442	0.116	0.519
Mixed	1984–6	0.077	0.202	0.480	0.117	0.831	0.676	0.083	0.499
public–private (7)	1990–2	0.094	0.175	0.418	0.086	0.527	0.553	0.133	0.565
Exporting (4)	1984–6	0.034	0.120	0.347	0.049	1.224	0.814	0.048	0.312
	1990–2	0.084	0.123	0.270	0.051	1.079	0.825	0.046	0.392
Non-exporting (11)	1984–6	0.080	0.238	0.521	0.126	0.636	0.573	0.092	0.609
	1990–2	0.116	0.190	0.461	0.097	0.328	0.374	0.152	0.594
Private sector									
Private-domestic (142)	1984–6	0.057	0.247	0.566	0.111	0.624	0.509	0.166	0.665
	1990–2	0.074	0.244	0.514	0.097	0.512	0.414	0.223	0.714
Private with	1984–6	0.079	0.311	0.722	0.127	0.663	0.585	0.172	0.631
foreign partner (6)	1990–2	0.088	0.227	0.515	0.096	0.415	0.412	0.244	0.696
Large-size	1984–6	0.096	0.215	0.374	0.121	0.615	0.559	0.105	0.591
domestic (13)	1990–2	0.075	0.189	0.312	0.097	0.449	0.500	0.155	0.527
Medium-size domestic (48)	1984–6	0.042	0.244	0.475	0.116	0.532	0.512	0.175	0.656
	1990–2	0.069	0.215	0.401	0.089	0.477	0.403	0.213	0.690
Small-size domestic (83)	1984–6	0.060	0.254	0.647	0.106	0.677	0.500	0.171	0.681
	1990–2	0.077	0.269	0.608	0.101	0.542	0.407	0.239	0.757

Table 8.13 Continued

Firms	Period	I/K	EBE/K	VA/K	EBG/AB	DT/K	DT/A	R	DCT/DT
Exporting (18)	1984–6	0.060	0.308	0.688	0.139	0.670	0.527	0.171	0.684
	1990–2	0.058	0.200	0.474	0.071	0.673	0.529	0.182	0.612
Non-exporting (134)	1984–6	0.058	0.242	0.556	0.108	0.620	0.510	0.165	0.660
	1990–2	0.077	0.250	0.519	0.100	0.486	0.398	0.230	0.727

Source: Bahlous (1999).

I/K: ratio of gross fixed investment expenditures (I, which includes replacement and expansion for construction, equipment, furniture, land) to stock of capital (K, gross value at acquisition prices); EBE/K: gross rate of return on capital assets, EBE is gross income; VA/K: value-added to capital ratio; EBG/AB: ratio of total income net of interest and financial costs (EBG) to gross assets (AB); DT/K: total debt (DT) to capital stock ratio; DT/A: total debt to net worth (A) ratio; R: average financial cost of debt, or ratio of total interest and financial charges to total debt (at mid year); DCT/DT: ratio of short-term debt (DCT) to total debt.

Within the domestic private sector there are significant differences according to size of firm. Three categories of firms are considered according to size: small firms include those with total assets of less than 1 million dinars in 1984, medium-sized firms include those with assets with between 1 and 5 million dinars and large firms have assets greater than 5 million dinars.[30] The cost of credit is significantly lower for large-sized firms than for small- and medium-sized firms. The differential in cost of credit increased somewhat for the smaller sized firms after liberalization, but declined afterwards. Debt ratios declined for all firms after liberalization. But, it is interesting to note that the debt to capital stock ratio (DT/K) is larger for the smaller than the medium-sized firms. Indicators of economic and financial performance are negatively correlated with size. The smaller-sized firms show higher rates of return on capital as well as a higher productivity of capital.

Another distinction is according to export orientation: firms are classified as exporters if (over the period) the average ratio of exports to total sales is greater than 10 per cent. The sample includes only a limited number of exporting firms. The largest share of exports in Tunisia is by 'off-shore' export processing regime firms, which are not included in the sample. The limited information, reflected in Table 8.13, shows better access of exporting firms to credit, at lower rates, particularly for the public sector. A surprising result is the declining economic and financial performance of the exporting firms since 1984–6. One possible explanation is that these firms, which were initially import competing, had to face increased competition from imports after trade liberalization.[31] It is the loss of domestic market share and profitability, which induced them to become exporters.

Taking the 1990–2 period we observe also that the cost of credit (R) is positively correlated with the rate of return on capital EBE/K (Table 8.14). Assuming

Table 8.14 Debt allocation and efficiency, 1990–2

	R	EBE/K	DT/A	Share in total debt	Share in value-added	Share in total investment
				In total (%)		
Public sector	0.124	0.172	0.494	55.2	41.9	47.5
SOE	0.116	0.169	0.442	33.8	26.9	31.2
Mixed	0.133	0.175	0.553	21.4	15.0	16.3
Exporting	0.046	0.123	0.825	46.7	23.0	26.0
Private sector	0.224	0.244	0.414	44.8	60.0	52.5
Exporting	0.182	0.200	0.529	20.3	20.5	22.9
Private domestic	0.223	0.244	0.414	28.5	40.3	35.8
				In private domestic (%)		
Large	0.155	0.189	0.500	33.7	32.3	38.1
Medium	0.213	0.215	0.403	46.6	45.6	44.2
Small	0.239	0.269	0.407	19.7	22.1	17.7

Source: Bahlous (1999).

that higher rates of return are associated with greater risk, this may be interpreted as charging higher interest when projects are more risky. The higher cost of financing would lead managers to choose those projects with an internal rate of return higher than the cost of financing, which of course will improve the rate of return before interest charges of the firm. But, the ratio of debt to net assets (DT/A) is also negatively correlated with rates of return on capital. We observe also that the share of total debt allocated to the public sector is much larger than its share in value-added or investment. The public exporting sector captures twice as much debt as its share in value-added and investment. This may indicate that the banking system is not allocating credit only on efficiency grounds, and that other constraints and considerations are involved.

Investment decisions of firms

The preceding analysis shows that three main factors appear to determine access to credit and financial structure, i.e. state ownership, size of firm and market orientation. We conclude also that the banking system is not allocating credit only on efficiency grounds. The first explanation of the inefficient credit allocation is the lack of skill and experience in identifying those managers with the most promising projects. Problems of asymmetric information may also lead to inefficient credit allocation. Both of these reasons explain why possessing collateral is an important determinant of the firm's ability to raise new financing. In addition, government intervention was important in credit allocation.

Since the Modigliani and Miller (1958, 1961) irrelevance theorem of financial structure, asymmetries of information (Akerlof 1970), the signaling content of financial structure (Myers and Majluf 1984) and agency costs (Jensen and Meckling 1976) have been used to understand departures from the perfect world described by the Modigliani and Miller theorem. The choice of corporate financial structure should be considered as a result of these financial market imperfections, in addition to the general financial environment and public credit allocation policies.

One approach to investigate the role of financial market imperfections in the determination of financial structure is to test for the presence and importance of financing constraints using an investment function (Hubbard 1998). One methodology proposed by Fazzari, Hubbard and Peterson (FHP 1988), using data on US firms, compares cash flow sensitivities of different groups of firms and interprets the higher sensitivity as evidence of facing more financial constraints. Kaplan and Zingales (1997) recently questioned the underlying assumption of a monotonic increase of cash flow sensitivity with the degree of financing constraints. They argue that 'there is no strong theoretical reason to expect a monotonic relationship' and show for example that, some of the firms classified by FHP as financially constrained firms are healthy firms and 'could have increased their investment without tapping external sources of capital' (Kaplan and Zingales 1997: 170, 184). Keeping this possible caveat in mind, we follow the FHP approach and broaden it to focus on the significance of structural change in the cash flow sensitivities before and after the liberalization process for different groups of firms. This methodology was also used by Harris *et al.* (1994), Hermes (1996) and Gelos and Werner (1999) for Indonesian, Chilean and Mexican firms, respectively.

The following model is tested in eqn (8.1):

$$I_{i,t}/K_{i,t-1} = \beta_1(\Delta Y_{i,t-1}/K_{i,t-1}) + \beta_2(CF_{i,t-1}/K_{i,t-1}) + \beta_3(GA_{i,t}/K_{i,t-1}),$$
(8.1)

where $I_{i,t}/K_{i,t-1}$ is the ratio of investment to capital stock at the beginning of period (or rate of growth of the capital stock), $\Delta Y_{i,t-1}/K_{i,t-1}$ is the change in sales to capital stock ratio, $CF_{i,t-1}/K_{i,t-1}$ is the cash flow variable (net of tax profits + depreciation allowances + provisions), which represents the internal finance possibilities of the firm, and $GA_{i,t}/K_{i,t-1}$ is the ratio of value of land and construction (real estate) to capital stock which is a measure of guarantees or collateral the firm can provide to banks.

The results using panel data for 195 private sector firms for the period 1985–94 are presented in Table 8.15, where EX is a dummy for exporting firms.[32] We also test for the effects of financial liberalization using a multiplicative dummy variable (DU) for the period 1990–4 on the cash flow and collateral variables. The results confirm that the determinants of investment differ significantly according to size and trade orientation, supporting the existence of significant market imperfections.[33]

Whether a firm is exporting is clearly a significant factor for investment. The investment equation is different for this group from the non-exporting firms, and the coefficient of the dummy for exporting firms (EX) in the equations by size of firms is significant for the small- and medium-sized firms. Informational advantages of export firms include the fact that they have less scope for concealment

Table 8.15 Firm characteristics and investment determinants

Firms/group	$\Delta Y/K$	CF/K	$DU \times CF/K$	GA/K	$DU \times GA/K$	EX
Whole (195)	0.006** (6.89)	0.064** (9.47)	0.053** (2.70)	0.245** (19.44)	−0.050** (3.58)	0.030** (19.02)
Exporting (44)	0.015** (7.92)	0.080 (0.84)	0.134 (0.83)	0.590** (3.44)	−0.300 (1.75)	
Non (151)	0.002** (2.37)	0.036** (7.77)	−0.011 (1.38)	0.138** (18.76)	0.050** (5.30)	
Small size (120)	0.005** (4.96)	0.024** (3.16)	0.081** (3.57)	0.250** (13.68)	−0.070** (3.52)	0.030** (20.76)
Medium size (57)	0.012** (6.96)	0.146** (10.01)	−0.009 (0.34)	0.171** (10.69)	0.028 (1.50)	0.022** (5.33)
Large size (18)	−0.007 (0.40)	0.118 (1.07)	0.123 (0.99)	0.260* (2.55)	−0.060 (0.66)	0.018 (1.64)

Notes: Estimation using Feasible GLS, providing White heteroskedasticity consistent estimates. *t* ratios in parenthesis. * indicates significance at 5 per cent, and ** at 1 per cent.

of sales, because export receipts are mostly through their banks. In addition, they have benefited from preferential policies which induced access to credit.

The accelerator variable is expected to have a positive coefficient, and is significant in all equations. The cash flow variable represents the internal finance possibilities of the firms, and signals the willingness of the firm to risk its resources. It is expected to exert a more significant positive effect on investment the tighter are credit constraints.[34] The medium-sized firms appear to be the most finance constrained with the largest cash flow coefficient. As expected, for the large size and exporting firms, the coefficient of the cash flow variable is insignificant. These firms have informational advantages, which make them less subject to credit constraints. The coefficient for the small-sized firms is significant, but contrary to expectation it is very low and much smaller than for medium-size firms. This is consistent with our earlier finding that small-sized firms are highly leveraged and appear not to be constrained. This may be due to government intervention, which has supported credit allocation to smaller firms by banks as well as by direct government finance.

After liberalization the cash flow variable coefficient changes significantly only for the small-sized firms, making them more constrained. Since these firms have probably grown into medium-sized firms by this time (compared to the beginning of the period when classification into size groups is made), they became subject to the same constraints as the medium-sized group. Based on the cash flow variable, the overall conclusion is that financial liberalization does not seem to have significantly affected credit constraints.

The coefficient of the collateral variable depends on how valuable collateral is for credit decisions. For instance, collateral may be irrelevant and its effect on the debt ratio low, either because the collateral is not enforceable due to difficulties and high costs to foreclose, or because the firm has other characteristics of creditworthiness which compensate the need for collateral. The collateral variable has a highly significant effect on investment for all groups of firms, again supporting the significance of informational problems in financial markets. A smaller coefficient indicates a lower ability to leverage more (and invest more) for a given collateral, indicating enforceability may be too costly and problematic. Exporting firms have the largest coefficient on collateral due to better creditworthiness and less moral hazard. For medium-sized firms, on the other hand, collateral has a lower coefficient than larger-sized firms, indicating higher costs of enforcement and lower value of collateral.

The effect of collateral for small-sized firms is, however, similar to that of the large-sized firms, but decreases after liberalization. This is also consistent with the change of the cash flow variable coefficient, reflecting more difficult access to credit by the small-sized firms.

Firm characteristics and competitiveness

Our preceding analysis identified three main firm characteristics, which influence financial structure, and may have implications for trade: trade orientation, state ownership and firm size.

Trade orientation

Government intervention has favored export activities, but exporting firms may have also been able to better access domestic credit because of the informational advantages they have, given that their banks can better monitor their activities. Exporting also provides a signal about the efficiency of the firm and allows easier access to credit. Exporting public firms also had access to preferential credit. After liberalization, private sector exporting firms increased the share of long-term debt in total debt and increased their leverage. The tradables sector had a share of total credit greater than value-added throughout.

More importantly, manufacturing exports have been mainly by the 'off-shore' sector or the so-called 'bonded factories'. These firms are often affiliates of foreign firms or owned by foreigners, and have 'non-resident' status. The 'resident' firms are often subcontracting to some main foreign customer. These firms may be less constrained in the credit market, because they may be seen as less risky and more transparent. Since these firms are exempt from taxes, they do not have incentives to distort their accounts, and banks may have better information to assess risks and capacity to reimburse debt. They are also partially financed by their suppliers/customers. For instance, there is some evidence that apparel manufacturers have up to two-thirds of their working capital financed by the foreign firms for which they are outsourcing.[35] There is also an 'off-shore' financial sector in Tunisia, which mainly caters to these exporting firms. This gives improved services and financing opportunities to this exporting sector.

State ownership

State-owned firms had preferential access to credit through direct government intervention as well as implicit government guarantees, particularly to state-owned banks. A number of activities where state-owned firms are dominant had such preferential access: mining, fertilizers, metallurgy and construction materials. But, the weight of state-owned enterprises is also important in almost all other activities.

Exporting by public enterprises, mostly monopolies, was almost completely in natural resources: mining, oil and gas, fertilizers and cement. Public enterprises are not to be found exporting in activities with comparative advantage. Tourism is a notable exception where public enterprises played a significant role, at the initial stages, but were later privatized.

The preferential access of public enterprises to resources from the state and to credit may have helped develop some activities where the private sector would not have ventured, at least initially, because of the risks involved and the long-term maturity or size of investments. But, the extent of the involvement of the public sector in economic activity and its persistence may have contributed to lower efficiency. In fact, the financial crisis of 1985–6 may be seen as the result of loss of competitiveness, in part due to the weak performance of the expanding public enterprise sector. We actually find that the performance indicators of public enterprises are much worse than for private firms. The former also contributed little to the diversification and expansion of exports, which are associated with productivity growth, and may have diverted resources from other activities with comparative advantage.

Size of firm

Asymmetric information considerations and financial market imperfections make firm size a factor determining the ability of firms to obtain external finance, particularly long-term finance. We find that the financial structure of firms varies considerably according to size. There are a number of ways this may affect trade specialization and competitiveness. First, if the country has a comparative advantage in light manufactures, such as clothing or other activities, the development of such activities may be hampered by lack of external finance. Rajan and Zingales (1998) actually find that financial development has a particularly beneficial role in the rise of new firms. If the optimal scale of such firms is small, this limits the ability of the country to develop such export activities. Second, if some of these activities exhibit significant economies of scale, small firms with little access to external finance may be unable to develop and reap the benefits. Our findings suggest, however, that small-sized firms were not less able to increase their indebtedness. While they had to pay higher interest charges, their leverage ratios were not lower than the larger-sized firms. Nonetheless, their debt is of more short-term maturity, the long-term debt to asset ratio is much lower for the smaller-sized firms. This, however, may only reflect the nature of the maturity of their assets.

Export activity in the most dynamic sectors with revealed comparative advantage, such as clothing, is by small- and medium-sized enterprises (SMEs). The 'off-shore' nature of these firms may have contributed to offset their asymmetric information costs disadvantages. Banks may also have compensated for these costs by charging higher interest, particularly since financial liberalization. Higher rates of return are associated with higher interest costs.

Government intervention has also contributed to the development of the SMEs. In addition to the inclusion of these firms in the required ratio of medium- and long-term credit to the private sector, the government has also provided government resources (through the banking system) to finance new SMEs, including cash subsidies and long-term credit at subsidized, very low interest rates and guaranties.[36] Government intervention may have helped SMEs access external finance, but adverse selection as to the choice of firms benefiting may also have limited its effectiveness.

5. Stylized facts on micro–macro and trade–finance interactions

The analysis in this chapter underlined a number of micro–macro and trade–finance interactions with significant implications for competitiveness. Macroeconomic factors contributed to enhancing Tunisian long-run competitiveness. A stable macroeconomic environment with low level and variability of inflation, and policies which avoided major overvaluations of the real exchange rate provided a favorable environment for high saving and investment rates and improved productivity. They helped avoid severe Dutch disease effects of the oil windfall and commodity booms in the 1970s. Foreign capital inflows did not constitute a source of volatility and uncertainty. The current account deficit was financed mainly with medium-to-long-term official capital inflows and equity. Short-term debt and portfolio flows remained subject to restrictions. The significant overall financial deepening and development of long-term finance helped develop activities with long-term maturity of assets such as tourism, and allowed the reallocation of resources towards those with comparative advantage and helped achieve diversification of the economy and of exports.

A number of microeconomic factors have contributed also, on the other hand, to growth and current account sustainability. They supported consolidation of macroeconomic stability. The changes in the specialization pattern in Tunisia, with a significant shift from natural-resource-based exports to manufactures and services exports have contributed to an improved export performance and sustainability of the current account. The very active role of the government in trade and industrial policy and in the financial sector helped achieve these results. But, because of these interventions, the effects of microeconomic factors did not always enhance competitiveness. The distortions and inefficiencies reduced productivity growth since the early 1980s and resulted in lower growth in Tunisia than in countries such as in East Asia, which had similar rates of investment and macroeconomic environments. The much higher growth rate achieved during the 1970s was not sustained, and GDP growth averaged only 3.3 per cent during 1981–9, with a higher current account deficit of 6 per cent. The progressive elimination of these distortions since the end of the 1980s led to improved productivity growth and a higher average growth rate of GDP of 5 per cent in the 1990s.

Trade and industrial policy under the import substitution regime, with high levels of protection and active involvement of government in investment and credit allocation, supported the diversification of the economy and the development of a number of new activities including tourism, irrigated agriculture and manufacturing. But such interventions often created inefficiencies, and resulted in lower or even negative productivity growth. Despite the bias of the trade regime towards import substitution, significant export growth and diversification occurred in the context of a parallel 'off-shore' exports regime. The strong system of incentives provided export activities helped correct the bias and led to strong export growth mostly by the private sector. The development of this 'dual' economy of import-competing and exports sectors contributed to current account sustainability, but probably at the cost of significant distortions and negative long-term implications for future diversification and upgrading of exports into more technology intensive activities.

This chapter investigated at some length the role of non-price micro-financial effects on competitiveness. While it is not possible to quantify their relative importance, the analysis identified a number of channels. The well-developed financial structure and various government interventions to deal with market imperfections supported the diversification of economic activities. Winning sectors were able to obtain credit and expand. Banks were generally effective in selecting projects and pricing risk. Exporting firms have been able to better access domestic credit because of their informational advantages. Small-sized firms were not less able to increase their indebtedness than larger-sized firms, even though they had to pay a higher cost. Their debt was more short-term maturity, but this may be more of a reflection of the nature of the maturity of their assets. Entrepreneurs with limited own-resources were able to finance their projects and expand in existing and new activities, contributing to flexibility in reallocating resources and innovation in export activities. Financial liberalization since 1987 enhanced the capability of the financial system in all these dimensions. Long-term credit was available for firms to match their assets and liabilities. Medium-sized firms were most subject to financial constraints and limitations to access external finance. But evidence on the better access to credit on the growth of firms suggests that this effect is not likely to have restrained internal growth of medium-sized firms.

But government intervention in the financial sector may have also hampered performance. It directed credit to the state-owned sector, which was much more highly leveraged and benefited from lower cost of credit, despite lower performance. The financial crisis of 1985–6 may be seen as a result of loss of competitiveness, in part due to the weak performance of the expanding public enterprise sector. The public sector contributed little to the diversification and expansion of exports, which are associated with productivity growth. It may have diverted resources from other activities with better comparative advantage. Even for activities with comparative advantage, such as tourism, extensive government subsidies and priority allocation of credit may have resulted in weaker performance and low productivity growth. The direct financing from government resources of SMEs, even though screened by banks, was not always effective in selecting the most efficient projects or activities.

Notes

1 Financial support by the IDRC is gratefully acknowledged. We are also grateful to the Institut National de la Statistique (INS) for help in obtaining some of the statistical information.
2 In this chapter, our focus is on long-term competitiveness, as contrasted with short-term competitiveness as usually measured by the real exchange rate. For a discussion of the concept of competitiveness and controversy surrounding it, see Boltho (1996) and Krugman (1996).
3 Figures are based on trade volumes. The increase in the export ratio is even greater if expressed in current prices, and went from 25 per cent in 1972 to 43 per cent in 1997, but the oil price decline in the mid-1980s induced a decline from 40 per cent in 1980 to 31 per cent in 1986.
4 These numbers which measure gross values of exports overstate, however, the role of manufactures which are to a large extent based on processing imported inputs and low value-added.
5 A more detailed analysis and presentation of results discussed in this section is in El Abbassi *et al.* (1999).
6 A similar analysis of trade specialization in Tunisia for the 1970s is in Nabli (1981).

7 See for instance Balassa (1982, 1985) and Edwards (1993).

8 The following regression for the period 1972–96 shows that export orientation has significantly positive effect on productivity growth in Tunisia where EP and IS measure the contribution of exports and of import substitution, respectively, to growth:

$$TFP = -0.004 + 1.11\,EP + 0.60\,IS \quad R2 = 0.34.$$
$$(0.51) \quad (3.29) \quad (2.09)$$

While the estimated coefficients may be biased, because the causality runs in both directions, this estimation shows a strong relation between productivity growth and export orientation.

9 The links from trade policy to productivity growth are still not well understood. Wacziarg (1998) identifies and empirically investigates six channels of impact of trade policy on growth: improved macroeconomic policy, size of government, more efficient allocation of resources, factor accumulation, technological transmission and foreign direct investment. He finds that the most important linkages are increased capital accumulation, foreign direct investment and improved macro-policies.

10 During the 1960s there was implementation of socialist experiment with heavy state intervention. GDP growth averaged 5 per cent although TFP growth was negative (Morrisson and Talbi 1996). A description of the trade regime during the 1960s and 1970s is in Nabli (1981).

11 See below for more details.

12 The collected tariff rate declined from 13.5 per cent in 1987 to 10.2 per cent in 1990.

13 Effective rate of protection is based on nominal tariff rates.

14 The current account deficit peaked at over 9 per cent and 11 per cent of GDP in 1992 and 1993, respectively, with the realization of two major foreign direct investment 'offshore' energy: the Algeria–Italy gas pipeline and the Miskar project of gas extraction.

15 This is the so-called 'Law 72-38 of April 1972' or 'off-shore' regime.

16 The REER is computed using the IMF method and trade weights, and is based on consumer price indices.

17 The empirical model is similar to Cottani *et al.* (1990), Elbadawi (1994) and Devarajan (1997).

18 The exchange rate misalignment is also reflected by the black market premium on the official exchange rate which reached over 8 per cent in 1980–4, compared to 5 per cent in the preceding and ensuing periods (Sekkat and Varoudakis 1998).

19 The two indicators of unit labor costs are: $ULC1 = (W/(Y/L))/PC$ and $ULC2 = (W/(Y/L))/PX$, where Y, L, W and PX are indices for real output, labor, nominal wages and export prices in the non-food non-chemicals manufacturing sector, and PC is the consumer price index.

20 A detailed description of the evolution of the financial system is in Bechri (1999).

21 Central Bank regulations and collusion facilitated by the banks' professional association also play a crucial role in protecting the sector. The success of the Tunisian banks in collective action has been analyzed in Bechri (1989). In 1987, when interest rates were liberalized and a cap was placed on margins, a 'gentleman's agreement' prevented competition, with interest rates collectively set under the aegis of their association, the Association Professionnelle des Banques.

22 By 1986, the financial sector was well diversified comprising eleven commercial banks, eight development banks, one leasing company and seven off-shore banks. The commercial banking system, however, remained the backbone of the system.

23 From 1986 to 1996, the financial system was enriched mainly by the development of leasing finance (six companies) and of the capital market. Only one commercial bank has been created since 1986. The decline in the M2/GDP and financial assets/GDP ratios since 1989 is due mainly to substitution within the private sector's portfolio from bank deposits to bond and treasury bills assets, which developed considerably over this period.

24 See Levine *et al.* (1999).

25 A complete description of the sample and results are in Bahlous (1999). Data are from the industrial survey by the Institut National de la Statistique. From an initial sample of 229 firms, 163 were selected after checks on quality of data and availability for all years. The sample firms' value-added was about 14.5 per cent of the total manufacturing sector value-added in 1984.

26 This decline corresponds also to that of the share of medium- and long-term credit in total bank credit from 1985 to 1993 (from 42 to 33 per cent). But this ratio recovered since 1994. See more discussion below.

27 More detailed analysis is in Bechri (1999).

28 Detailed calculations are found in Bechri (1999).

29 Even though rates of return on equity deteriorate somewhat, due to the increase in interest rate charges.

30 One Tunisian dinar was 1.3 USD in 1984 and 1.0 USD in 1994.

31 The criterion for classification being based on the average for the period 1984–94, most firms had low rates of exports during the first period, and higher ones for 1990–2.

32 The sample includes an unbalanced panel of 195 private firms, more than the 148 firms of the balanced panel of private firms. In the econometric estimation, exporting firms considered are, those with an average ratio of exports to total sales greater than 5 per cent during 1984–94, which is different from the 10 per cent criterion used above.

33 F ratios for testing differences between groups of firms are: $F = 120.58$ for export and non-export firms, and $F = 6.52$ for firm size groups.

34 A basic problem with the methodology is that it assumes that changes in cash flows are not related to investment opportunities. If other relevant variables accounting for investment opportunities (such as Tobin's q) are not included and/or if the cash flow variable reflects such opportunities, the coefficient of CF may not measure the extent of financial constraints.

35 From preliminary results of a survey of exporting firms.

36 Over 1976–90, the program in question (FOPRODI) financed 1,353 projects.

References

Akerlof, G. A. (1970) 'The Market for "Lemons": Quality Uncertainty and the Market Mechanism', *Quarterly Journal of Economics* 84(3): 488–500.

Bahlous, M. (1999) 'Structure du Capital, Performance, Croissance et Investissement: Cas des Entreprises Tunisiennes', Background paper for this project, April.

Bahlous, M. and Nabli, M. K. (1999) 'Financial Liberalization and Financing Constraints on the Corporate Sector in Tunisia', Background paper for this project, April.

Balassa, B. (1982) *Development Strategies in Semi-Industrial Countries*. Oxford: Oxford University Press.

Balassa, B. (1985) 'Exports, Policy Choices and Economic Growth in the Developing Countries after the 1973 Oil Shock', *Journal of Development Economics* 18(2): 23–35.

Bechri, M. Z. (1989) 'The Political Economy of Interest Rate Determination in Tunisia', in M. K. Nabli and J. B. Nugent (eds), *The New Institutional Economics and Development: Theory and Applications to Tunisia*. Amsterdam and New York: North Holland.

Bechri, M. Z. (1999) 'Le Système Financier et l'Allocation Sectorielle du Crédit en Tunisie', Background paper for this project, February.

Boltho, A. (1996) 'The Assessment: International Competitiveness', *Oxford Review of Economic Policy* 12(3): 1–16.

Caprio, G. and Demirguç-Kunt, A. (1998) 'The Role of Long-Term Finance: Theory and Evidence', *The World Bank Research Observer* 13(2): 171–89.

Cottani, J. A., Cavallo, D. F. and Shahbaz Khan, M. (1990) 'Real Exchange Rate Behavior and Economic Performance in LDCs', *Economic Development and Cultural Change* 39: 61–72.

Demirguç-Kunt, A. and Maksimovic, V. (1996a) 'Institutions, Financial Markets, and Firm Debt Maturity', *World Bank Policy Research Working Paper*, No. 1686.

Demirguç-Kunt, A. and Maksimovic, V. (1996b) 'Financial Constraints, Uses of Funds, and Firm Growth: An International Comparison', *World Bank Policy Research Working Paper*, No. 1671.

Devarajan, S. (1997) 'Real Exchange Rate Misalignment in the CFA Zone', *Journal of African Economies* 6(1): 35–53.

Dollar, D. (1992) 'Outward-Oriented Developing Economies Really Do Grow More Rapidly: Evidence from 95 LDCs, 1976–85', *Economic Development and Cultural Change* 40(3): 523–44.

Dornbusch, R. (1996) 'The Effectiveness of Exchange Rate Changes', *Oxford Review of Economic Policy* 12(3): 28–38.

Edwards, S. (1988) *Exchange Rate Misalignment in Developing Countries*. Baltimore: The Johns Hopkins University Press.

Edwards, S. (1993) 'Openness, Trade Liberalization and Growth in developing Countries', *Journal of Economic Literature* 31: 1358–93.

Edwards, S. (1998) 'Openness, Productivity and Growth: What Do We Really Know?', *The Economic Journal* 108: 383–98.

El Abbassi, M., El Ferktaji, R. and Talbi, B. (1999) 'Avantage Comparatif, Spécialisation Commerciale et Compétitivié en Tunisie', Background paper for this project, April.

Elbadawi, I. A. (1994) 'Estimating Long-Run Equilibrium Exchange Rates', in J. Williamson (ed.), *Estimating Equilibrium Exchange Rates*. Washington, DC: Institute of International economics.

Fagerberg, J. (1996) 'Technology and Competitiveness', *Oxford Review of Economic Policy* 12(3): 39–51.

Fazzari, S. M., Hubbard, R. G. and Petersen, B. (1988) 'Financing Constraints and Corporate Investment', *Brookings Papers on Economic Activity*, No. 1: 141–95.

Fry, M. (1997) 'In Favor of Financial Liberalization', *The Economic Journal* 107(442): 754–70.

Gelos, R. G., A. M. Werner (1999) 'Financial Liberalization, Credit Constraints and Collateral: Investment in the Mexican Manufacturing Sector', *IMF Working Paper*, No. 99/25.

Guerrieri, P. (1998) 'Trade Specialization, Industrial Change and Economic Development', Technical Workshop on Trade, Competitiveness and Finance, Johannesburg, South Africa, December.

Harris, J. R., Schiantarelli, F. and Siregar, M. G. (1994) 'The Effect of Financial Liberalization on the Capital Structure and Investment Decisions of Indonesian Manufacturing Establishments', *The World Bank Economic Review* 8: 17–47.

Hermes, N. (1996) 'Financial Reform and Financial Intermediation in Chile, 1983–1992', in N. Hermes and R. Lensink (eds), *Financial Development and Economic Growth: Theory and Experiences from Developing Countries*. London: Routledge.

Jensen, M. C. and Meckling, W. H. (1976) 'Theory of the Firm: Managerial Behavior, Agency Costs and Ownership Structure', *Journal of Financial Economics* 3(4): 305–60.

Kaplan, S. N. and Zingales, L. (1997) 'Do Investment Cash Flow Sensitivities Provide Useful Measures of Financing Constraints', *The Quarterly Journal of Economics* 112(1): 169–215.

Krugman, P. R. (1996) 'Making Sense of the International Competitiveness Debate', *Oxford Review of Economic Policy* 12(3): 17–25.

Levine, R. (1997) 'Financial Development and Economic Growth: Views and Agenda', *Journal of Economic Literature* 35(2): 688–726.

Levine, R. and Zervos, S. (1998) 'Stock Markets and Economic Growth', *American Economic Review* 88(3): 537–58.

Levine, R., Loayza, N. and Beck, T. (1999) 'Financial Intermediation and Growth: Causality and Causes', *World Bank Policy Research Working Paper*, No. 2059.

Modigliani, F. and Miller, M. H. (1958) 'The Cost of Capital, Corporate Finance, and the Theory of Investment', *American Economic Review* 48(3): 261–97.

Modigliani, F. and Miller, M. H. (1961) 'Dividend Policy, Growth, and the Valuation of Shares', *Journal of Business* 34(4): 411–33.

Modigliani, F. and Miller, M. H. (1963) 'Corporate Income, Tax and the Cost of Capital: A Correction', *American Economic Review* 53(3): 433–43.

Morrisson, C. and Talbi, B. (1996) *La Croissance de l'Economie Tunisienne en Longue Période*. OECD Series Etudes du Centre de Developpement.

Moussa, H. (1995) 'Economic Policy and Economic Development in Tunisia', Paper presented at the International Economic Association World Congress, Tunis, Tunisia, December.

Myers, S. C. (1984) 'The Capital Structure Puzzle', *Journal of Finance* 39(3): 575–92.

Myers, S. C. and Majluf, N. N. (1984) 'Corporate Financing and Investment Decisions when Firms Have Information that Investors Do not Have', *Journal of Financial Economics* 13(2): 187–221.

Nabli, M. K. (1981) 'Trade Strategies and Employment in Tunisia', in A. O. Kreuger, T. Monson and N. Akrasanee (eds), *Trade and Employment in Developing Countries: Individual Studies*. Chicago: University of Chicago Press.

Rajan, B. G. and Zingales, L. (1998) 'Financial Dependence and Growth', *American Economic Review* 88(3): 559–86.

Rodriguez, F. and Rodrik, D. (1999) 'Trade Policy and Economic Growth: A Skeptic's Guide to the Cross-National Evidence', *National Bureau of Economic Research Working Paper Series*, No. 7081.

Sachs, J. D. and Warner, A. (1995) 'Economic Reform and the Process of Global Integration', *Brookings Papers on Economic Activity*, No. 1: 1–118.

Sekkat, K. and Varoudakis, A. (1998) 'Incentive Policies, Exchange Rate and Manufactured Exports in North Africa', Economic Research Forum Fifth Annual Conference: Regional Trade, Finance and Labor Markets. Gammarth, Tunisia, 31 August to 2 September.

Wacziarg, R. (1998) 'Measuring the Dynamic Gains from Trade', *World Bank Policy Research Working Paper*, 2001.

World Bank (1998) *World Development Indicators 1998*. Washington DC: World Bank.

World Bank (1999) *World Development Indicators 1999*. Washington DC: World Bank.

9 Trade openness, industrial change and economic development

Paolo Guerrieri

1. Introduction

This chapter analyzes the relationship between trade openness, the industrialization process and economic development. An evolutionist-structuralist approach, based on the more prominent and recent theoretical and empirical studies on the role of technology in international trade and economic growth, is used here. It stresses the importance of dynamic efficiency, technical infrastructure and the generation and diffusion of technology to achieving long-term growth. In this framework technological change and capability are considered key factors driving countries' trade specializations and economic performances.

Section 2 of the chapter surveys the most significant developments in the economic literature on trade openness and growth performances both at the theoretical and empirical levels. Section 3 analyzes the development experiences of three groups of countries in Latin America, East Asia and Mediterranean. Even though very different one to another, they have all been characterized by trade liberalization processes over the past two decades. A highly disaggregated analysis of trade specialization patterns of each individual economy is carried out in this section, emphasizing industrial changes and the main inter-industry linkages at each country level. Section 4 provides some interpretation of the main linkages between trade openness, industrialization and economic growth performance, drawing out some policy implications of our findings. A final section summarizes the main conclusions.

2. A survey of the literature on trade and growth performance

The economic literature on the influence of trade openness and liberalization on the industrialization and development process has been recently enriched by many contributions. Significant relationships between key variables, such as trade performance, international specialization and long-run growth, have been defined and/or redefined and new policy implications have also been offered. A few of them are outlined here.

As is well known, in the standard neoclassical model trade openness and liberalization produce substantial benefits in terms of a more efficient static resource allocation. Trade specialization, as long as markets are open and relative prices can freely change, does not represent a problem for a country because there is always something it can profitably produce and trade according to its comparative advantages based on its 'factor endowments'.

It follows that a country's positive economic adjustment requires measures to liberalize trade, minimize government intervention in the domestic economy, and getting prices right. Furthermore, a sound macroeconomic policy is considered an important corollary to trade openness. So, in the standard approach macroeconomic stability and trade liberalization are the two fundamental ingredients of a good economic performance. Once the government dealt with these issues, private markets would allocate resources efficiently and generate robust growth.

This linkage between trade openness and growth performance, however, has been challenged – even recently – on theoretical and empirical grounds. First, it has been outlined that gains from trade, as in the standard approach, can be only obtained now and then due to the reallocation of resources that trade openness is able to guarantee. Second, with regards to long-run growth, the standard model does not assign any significant role to international trade. In other words, trade openness and liberalization could affect the level and composition of output and welfare, but is not able to accelerate economy's long-run growth path. Furthermore, the predicted size of static gains from trade is usually very small. Empirical data do confirm, on this front, the small impact of trade openness upon aggregate income (Baldwin 1992).

In general terms, critics have emphasized that the standard model is based on very restrictive assumptions, and therefore largely neglects the key role played by important variables such as economies of scale (external or internal), learning by doing or technological differences across countries (Dosi *et al.* 1990).

In this regard, many contributions from the new trade and growth models have shown that in the presence of imperfect competition, economies of scale, technological spillovers and external economies, countries' trade performance and competitiveness is much less dependent on factor endowments and static comparative advantages. On the contrary, it is based upon dynamic gains, technology transfer, intangible capital, and complex trade and industrial strategies at the level of firms and nations (Verspagen 1992).

So, attempts have been made to relax the most restrictive assumptions either remaining within the neoclassical traditional approach or using other alternative conceptual frameworks.

First, a significant linkage between international trade and growth can be found at the macroeconomic level on the demand side of an open economy, given that export demand could represent an important source for countries' economic growth (Beckerman 1962; Kaldor 1970). The determinants of the rate of growth of exports could also significantly affect countries' economic growth. In this perspective, a country's balance of payments is an important constraint to economic growth, given that to sustain the growth path import requirement there should be an adequate flow of exports.

The relation between growth competitiveness and the balance of payments has been also studied in a long-run perspective. Conditions have been derived (Johnson 1958; Thirlwall 1979) that set the maximum rate of growth of an economy consistent with balance of trade equilibrium. Such conditions relate the equilibrium rate of growth to income elasticites of exports and imports (Krugman 1992) or, in other specifications, with income and price elasticities of trade volumes (Johnson 1958).

In this area, Thirlwall (1979) made an important contribution by showing that the rate of growth of an open economy depends on trade increase, on changes in relative prices, in other words on price competitiveness, and on the ratio of income elasticities of export and imports. *Ceteris paribus*, higher (lower) rates of growth correspond to higher ratios (lower) of these elasticities.

The problem with such contributions is that it is difficult to interpret satisfactorily the meaning of income elasticities. Some authors have suggested that these elasticities reflect the so-called non-price factors, while others (Krugman 1992) outlined that they reflect the influence, if any, of increasing returns in world trade. The problem is how to measure these non-price factors since their values could change, and do change, over time. In this regard, they can be considered only a useful first approximation to the concept of 'structural competitiveness', defined as a country's ability to maximize its real growth in the international economic environment. It remains difficult, however, to obtain useful information on the concept of structural competitiveness with such limited information.

To move forward, income elasticities of a country have been considered variables and not exogenously given parameters in other contributions. In this perspective, a promising approach (Fagerberg 1988) linked economic growth to a more detailed specification of international competitiveness. The latter is determined by three main factors: (a) price competitiveness, measured in terms of relative labor costs; (b) technological competitiveness, represented by both innovation capability and imitation potential of technological change from other countries; and (c) capacity growth, measured by a proxy that is the gross investment in physical capital stock. Within this approach each of these factors can be given a highly detailed specification and embedded in a more general framework that links growth to balance-of-payments behavior.

This represents an improvement towards understanding the relationship between growth, trade liberalization and the structure of the economy. Different factors affecting competitiveness may reflect the relative weight of different sectors and activities of the economy. Fagerberg's model has been estimated empirically with encouraging results that have generally confirmed the significance of the growth of production and technological capabilities to enhance competitiveness. In contrast, the impact of factor cost turned out to be rather marginal.

One should add immediately that the fact that accumulation processes and differences in technological capabilities represent important determining factors of countries' trade and growth performances is far from a novelty. It has been, however, supported recently by new contributions at both the theoretical and empirical levels (Dowrick 1997).

First, it has been done in the area of the so-called 'new growth models' or 'theory of endogenous growth', which stresses the importance of human resources development and technological accumulation (for a survey, see Verspagen 1992).

Two groups of contributions from this area are useful to quote here. The first group emphasizes the role of trade in favoring countries' specialization, since the latter leads to increases in productivity through learning by doing effect and/or R&D investments. Economic growth is thus enhanced by the opportunities to specialize that trade gives to a country. Specialization is important *per se*, irrespective of the kind of economic activities chosen by each country to be specialized. In this perspective an interesting contribution stems from the models that emphasize the role of R&D and its fallouts upon international trade and economic growth (Grossman and Helpman 1991). The results of these models, however, are very much dependent on the geographical diffusion of fallouts. If they have only national impact, one could have a lock-in situation, in which original differences in trade specializations, even marginal ones, are able to lead towards very different specialization and growth patterns across countries. Under these conditions international trade is able to favorably support countries' economic growth (Coe and Helpman 1995; Young 1991).

The second class of models emphasizes the role of trade in favoring countries' specializations in specific activities and sectors. Those countries specializing in activities characterized by higher rates of productivity growth tended to grow faster than countries locked into more traditional lower value-added activities. To give an example, the classical contribution of Lucas (1988) assumes significant differences in terms of technological change (learning) across sectoral activities. Therefore, those countries that are able to specialize in technologically advanced (high-tech) industrial sectors can achieve faster growth rates than others locked into traditional (low-tech) specialization. Furthermore, because of the cumulative nature of technological progress, current specialization patterns tend to be reinforced over time. Market forces could thus strengthen specialization trends in both directions, contributing to raising (lowering) countries' growth potentials. In this case, a country could find it convenient to change its specialization pattern through different interventionist policies (Lucas 1988).

Although all these contributions confirm a significant relation between trade specialization, technology and economic performance, the causation linkage between international trade and economic growth is still an ambiguous one (Edwards 1993; Dowrick 1997). Empirical literature in this field has not been able to disentangle it. At the empirical level over the last decade or so, a wide range of studies have indicated a positive correlation between trade openness and growth (Edwards 1998). Non-price factors appear to have had a major impact on countries trade performance, and within these factors technology plays a very important role. There is however little consistent evidence as yet on the mechanism by which trade stimulates growth. Many contributions show that there is no simple mechanical translation from trade to growth (Fagerberg 1996; Rodriguez and Rodrik 1999). There are many countries with a strong outward orientation which have nevertheless experienced relatively slow rates of economic growth.

There are also many examples of developing economies that have grown significantly despite temporary trade restrictions.

To sum up, the broad conclusions that emerge from these theoretical and empirical contributions can be listed in the following way:

1   Trade liberalization can indeed be expected to stimulate growth at world level, but it is not true that every country must benefit.
2   Benefits at country level are variable and depend on a set of heterogeneous endogenous factors (absorption capability).
3   The pattern of specialization could play an important role, since countries can experience Kaldorian vicious (virtuous) circles and be locked into a pattern of specialization in low(high)-skill, low(high)-growth activities characterized by tight (loose) external constraints.
4   To avoid the low growth trap, it is important to provide macroeconomic stability and trade liberalization, but it requires more than just low inflation and getting price right; it requires technological up-grading and policies to facilitate industrialization and structural change, to cite some fundamental issues neglected by the traditional approach.

3. Trade openness, industrialization and structural change in Latin American, South-East Asian and Mediterranean NICs

In this section, the long-term trade performances of three groups of countries in Latin America, East Asia and Mediterranean area are analyzed. The aim is to provide empirical evidence for the underlying long-term linkage between trade openness and trade performance-specialization of the three groups of countries. The analysis relies upon an original trade data base (SIE World Trade) comprising UN and OECD statistical sources (400 product classes, 98 sectors and 25 commodity groups) for more than 80 countries (OECDs, NICs, ex-CMEA and LDCs).

To take into account the industrialization process and structural transformations in the development path followed by each group of countries, a specific sectoral taxonomy is used here following the work of the OECD (1992), Pavitt (1984, 1988) and Guerrieri (1992, 1993). This taxonomy highlights the relation between technological capability and international trade performance at the level of individual countries and is consistent with recent theoretical literature on technological change and trade specialization (see above).

In this taxonomy, the linkages between different industrial sectors assume great importance (Rosenberg 1982; Pavitt 1988), i.e. in terms of innovation and user–producer relationships (Scherer 1982; Lundvall 1988). In other words, the industrial system could be viewed as national networks of inter-firm, intra-industry and inter-industry linkages that affect the ability of nations to transform opportunities for innovation into actual technological change (Lundvall 1988; Von Hippel 1988). These innovation linkages occur within and between industries and to a large extent they constitute externalities which increase the opportunity for technological spillovers across firms and sectors, generating a cycle of positive feedback and self-reinforcing growth (Arthur 1990; Kaldor 1981). The competitive advantages of individual countries are commonly concentrated in these clusters of sectors connected through vertical and horizontal relationships at the technological and production levels (Porter 1990; OECD 1992; Guerrieri and Tylecote 1997).

Five types of industries are identified, primarily through a combination of technology sources, technology user requirements and means of technology appropriation: *natural-resource-intensive, supplier-dominated or traditional sectors, science-based, scale-intensive* and *specialized supplier*. In the first two categories, factor endowments have a major influence on the generation of comparative advantage, since technology is easily accessible and firms' competitiveness is notably sensitive to price factors. In the last three categories (*science-based, scale-intensive, specialized suppliers*), comparative and absolute advantages are dominated by technological change and capability, as shown by various empirical studies (Soete 1987; Fagerberg 1988; Amendola *et al.* 1992). All other non-industrial goods are grouped into three remaining categories, namely agricultural products, fuels and other raw materials.

Trade and technological patterns of the Latin American NICs

The three Latin American NICs (Argentina, Brazil and Mexico) (LAN) together account for more than 80 per cent of the Latin American exports and have dominated the region's trade flows over the past two decades.

Three main phases characterized the trade patterns of the LAN over the past three decades: in the first period – from the early 1970s to 1982 – rapid growth and industrialization supported by either import-substitution or export promotion policies were the distinctive features; the second period, up to the late 1980s, was dominated by the debt crisis, gradual trade liberalization and high adjustment costs to serve the foreign debt; and the third phase covered all the first half in the 1990s and comprised increasing trade openness and anti-inflationary strategies.

The share of world exports of Latin American NICs as a group was relatively stable in the first two periods, from the early 1970s to the late 1980s, and increased significantly in the more recent phase (i.e. +39 per cent). This increase was entirely due, however, to the progress of Mexican exports (Table 9.1). The Latin American trade balances (standardized) showed no unequivocal trends but only cyclical ups and downs: decreasing deficits throughout the 1970s and significant surpluses during the adjustment period in the 1980s, with alternating trade deficits and surpluses over the first half of the 1990s (Table 9.2).

To evaluate patterns of trade specialization of the LAN, the indicator used here takes into consideration both exports and imports of a country by measuring the relative contribution to the trade balance of the various product groups. Note that positive values indicate countries' comparative (competitive) advantage in a given product group, whereas a negative value represents a comparative (competitive) disadvantage. This index is calculated with respect to the product categories included in the taxonomy presented above.

Table 9.1 Shares in world exports of selected groups of countries

	1970	1979	1989	1992	1995
Argentina					
Agricultural prod.	2.87	2.74	1.25	2.03	2.23
Fuels	0.00	0.00	0.03	0.17	0.68
Other raw materials	0.08	0.07	0.07	0.05	0.07
Food industries	3.32	2.58	2.13	1.86	2.16
Traditional ind.	0.20	0.38	0.19	0.15	0.26
Resource-intensive ind.	0.04	0.10	0.27	0.38	0.32
Scale-intensive ind.	0.14	0.18	0.24	0.15	0.27
Specialized suppliers ind.	0.10	0.18	0.09	0.08	0.10
Science-based ind.	0.12	0.09	0.08	0.07	0.09
Total trade	0.62	0.51	0.33	0.33	0.42
Mexico					
Agricultural prod.	1.10	1.28	1.31	1.28	2.01
Fuels	0.04	1.69	4.15	3.21	3.11
Other raw materials	1.14	1.12	1.59	1.16	1.18
Food industries	0.96	0.45	0.51	0.43	0.65
Traditional ind.	0.33	0.26	0.37	0.35	1.20
Resource-intensive ind.	0.47	0.17	0.66	0.61	0.80
Scale-intensive ind.	0.24	0.27	0.64	0.81	2.06
Specialized suppliers ind.	0.04	0.12	0.34	0.32	1.81
Science-based ind.	0.20	0.10	0.56	0.46	1.53
Total trade	0.42	0.58	0.80	0.74	1.58
Brazil					
Agricultural prod.	1.87	1.19	2.41	1.84	1.93
Fuels	0.00	0.01	0.00	0.00	0.02
Other raw materials	0.04	1.69	4.15	3.21	3.11
Food industries	2.35	4.11	3.48	2.76	3.29
Traditional ind.	0.49	0.89	0.81	0.78	0.74
Resource-intensive ind.	0.10	0.47	1.68	1.60	1.54
Scale-intensive ind.	0.22	0.66	1.23	1.06	0.90
Specialized suppliers ind.	0.18	0.54	0.69	0.57	0.60
Science-based ind.	0.11	0.46	0.54	0.37	0.29
Total trade	0.95	1.00	1.18	0.98	0.93

First, to take a glance at the world trade patterns over the past two decades one should note that the weight of manufactured products increased substantially in total trade and the share of agricultural products and raw materials symmetrically decreased (Table 9.3). Within the manufactured exports, the shares of *scale-intensive* and *specialized suppliers* held stable values, while that of *science-based* export increased more than twice, from 9.5 percentage points by 1970 to more than 21 percentage points by 1995. Since *science-based* goods embody relatively intensive R&D inputs, either directly or indirectly through the intermediate goods that are used in their production, this increased the importance of those industrial sectors with a higher technological content (Scherer 1992).

Table 9.2 Standardized trade balances of selected groups of countries

	1970	1979	1989	1992	1995
East Asian NICs					
Agricultural prod.	−1.982	−3.367	−4.200	−4.444	−4.900
Fuels	−0.732	−2.292	−6.120	−7.757	−8.857
Other raw materials	0.297	−1.341	−5.758	−6.637	−6.032
Food industries	−1.046	−1.088	−1.709	−2.376	−2.680
Traditional ind.	2.337	7.257	10.025	7.750	5.090
Resource-intensive ind.	−0.397	0.012	−1.842	−3.026	−4.326
Scale-intensive ind.	−1.646	−0.707	0.199	−0.014	−0.218
Specialized suppliers ind.	−2.870	−3.742	−3.490	−3.390	−2.703
Science-based ind.	−2.279	−2.107	0.827	0.943	1.851
Total trade	−0.886	−0.290	0.649	0.007	−0.286
Mediterranean NICs					
Agricultural prod.	2.965	0.793	0.391	0.157	−1.003
Fuels	−0.585	−1.073	−2.106	−2.047	−2.415
Other raw materials	2.608	3.262	1.980	0.617	0.824
Food industries	−0.354	−0.508	−1.270	−0.700	−0.615
Traditional ind.	−0.276	0.140	0.728	0.647	0.629
Resource-intensive ind.	−0.832	−0.547	−0.416	−0.664	−0.755
Scale-intensive ind.	−1.931	−1.871	−1.197	−1.367	−1.320
Specialized suppliers ind.	−2.214	−2.406	−1.842	−2.110	−1.781
Science-based ind.	−1.675	−1.093	−1.003	−1.195	−0.993
Total trade	−0.684	−0.872	−0.729	−0.888	−0.869
Latin American NICs					
Agricultural prod.	3.924	2.911	3.619	3.676	4.413
Fuels	−2.224	−2.142	1.362	0.809	1.486
Other raw materials	4.608	5.762	8.514	10.313	10.070
Food industries	5.584	6.070	4.549	2.958	3.895
Traditional ind.	−0.345	0.574	0.522	−0.197	−0.286
Resource-intensive ind.	1.394	0.340	2.585	1.669	1.282
Scale-intensive ind.	−2.641	−1.998	0.386	−1.064	−0.227
Specialized suppliers ind.	−4.680	−3.826	−1.639	−3.213	−2.279
Science-based ind.	−4.023	−2.362	−0.477	−1.316	−1.134
Total trade	−0.339	−0.471	0.804	−0.271	0.002

In the course of the 1970s and the first part of the 1980s, the trade specialization patterns of the LAN, as a whole, revealed intersectoral shifts towards manufactured goods due to an industrialization process led by traditional, scale-intensive and resource-intensive goods, although with different roles.[1] But during the second part of the 1980s, constrained by the high adjustment costs of servicing the foreign debt, the LAN experienced an industrial restructuring in quite the opposite direction (Table 9.4). As shown by trade patterns of the LAN in this period, all primary commodities, food products and, especially raw material processing industries increased their role. In all non-manufactured products, Latin American NICs maintained high

Table 9.3 Weights of the sectoral groups in world exports[a]

	1970	1973	1979	1985	1988	1991	1993	1995	70–95
Food items	9.8	10.5	8.0	6.6	6.2	5.2	4.6	4.6	−5.30
Fuels	6.5	7.8	14.8	13.1	5.8	6.8	6.0	4.7	−1.73
Other raw materials	2.9	2.0	1.8	1.5	1.1	1.0	0.8	0.9	−2.01
Food industries	7.2	7.6	6.2	5.4	5.8	5.7	5.6	5.5	−1.70
Resource intensive	10.1	8.6	9.2	9.4	7.8	7.2	6.4	6.6	−3.48
Agricultural products and raw materials	**36.5**	**36.5**	**40.0**	**36.0**	**26.6**	**25.8**	**23.4**	**22.2**	**−14.22**
Traditional	14.9	16.0	14.5	14.0	16.5	16.9	17.4	16.8	1.89
Scale intensive	24.7	24.9	23.0	24.6	26.2	25.2	25.0	25.0	0.35
Specialized suppliers	10.9	10.2	9.2	8.6	10.0	10.4	10.1	10.5	−0.43
Science based	9.5	9.4	10.9	14.4	17.5	18.9	19.9	21.5	12.07
Manufactures	**60.0**	**60.5**	**57.6**	**61.6**	**70.1**	**71.4**	**72.4**	**73.8**	**13.88**
Others	3.6	3.0	2.4	2.4	3.2	2.8	4.1	3.7	0.09

Source: SIE-World Trade Data Base.

Note

a Average value in each subperiod (in percentage).

Table 9.4 Trade specialization patterns of selected groups of countries

	1970	1979	1989	1992	1995
East Asian NICs					
Agricultural prod.	−2.28	−5.53	−3.29	−2.31	−1.96
Fuels	−0.91	−7.31	−4.76	−5.17	−3.86
Other raw materials	0.59	−0.51	−0.88	−0.61	−0.45
Food industries	−0.57	−1.24	−1.40	−1.45	−1.28
Traditional ind.	21.41	25.99	18.26	14.16	8.29
Resource-intensive ind.	0.91	0.49	−2.26	−2.10	−2.49
Scale-intensive ind.	−9.28	−2.50	−0.96	−0.05	0.02
Specialized suppliers ind.	−8.36	−7.39	−4.90	−3.66	−2.33
Science-based ind.	−5.34	−4.26	−0.09	1.87	4.46
Mediterranean NICs					
Agricultural prod.	36.09	15.29	7.93	6.49	2.92
Fuels	−0.94	−2.95	−5.41	−4.20	−4.78
Other raw materials	8.17	7.58	3.19	1.40	1.45
Food industries	2.35	2.76	−0.37	2.61	3.12
Traditional ind.	2.77	11.54	20.70	22.36	22.72
Resource-intensive ind.	−3.42	2.10	1.40	0.60	0.67
Scale-intensive ind.	−24.35	−19.15	−9.66	−10.12	−8.90
Specialized suppliers ind.	−13.84	−11.38	−9.44	−9.42	−7.96
Science-based ind.	−8.97	−5.79	−8.74	−9.96	−9.37
Latin American NICs					
Agricultural prod.	16.90	11.14	5.86	8.40	6.19
Fuels	−5.18	−9.32	0.22	2.95	2.23
Other raw materials	5.64	4.68	3.00	4.04	2.61
Food industries	16.94	16.17	7.43	8.13	6.66
Traditional ind.	−1.05	4.52	0.63	−0.25	−1.48
Resource-intensive ind.	7.11	2.75	5.33	5.49	2.65
Scale-intensive ind.	−22.70	−14.15	−3.89	−8.09	−1.76
Specialized suppliers ind.	−18.28	−11.75	−10.75	−12.32	−7.38
Science-based ind.	−13.54	−8.42	−8.04	−8.93	−7.49

market shares, trade surpluses and comparative advantages, such as in raw materials, agricultural primary resources and food products.

Only recently, the industrial exports of the LAN seem to have partially regained their strength. In many industrial groups, both imports and exports have been rapidly increasing, leading towards a parallel and significant increase in the index of intra-industry trade of the LAN. Although the latter could be interpreted as the first sign of a shift of trade composition towards more technologically intensive goods, LAN trade patterns do not yet show any significant changes in this direction. In fact, during the first part of the 1990s despecialization trends and significant trade deficits have continued to be a feature of all main industrial product groups, apart from resource-intensive products, of the LAN (Tables 9.4 and 9.5). This overall evolution in Latin America's trade performance, however, has been sharply differentiated according to country.

Table 9.5 Standardized trade balances of selected groups of countries

	1970	1979	1989	1992	1995
East Asian NICs					
Agricultural prod.	−1.982	−3.367	−4.200	−4.444	−4.900
Fuels	−0.732	−2.292	−6.120	−7.757	−8.857
Other raw materials	0.297	−1.341	−5.758	−6.637	−6.032
Food industries	−1.046	−1.088	−1.709	−2.376	−2.680
Traditional ind.	2.337	7.257	10.025	7.750	5.090
Resource-intensive ind.	−0.397	0.012	−1.842	−3.026	−4.326
Scale-intensive ind.	−1.646	−0.707	0.199	−0.014	−0.218
Specialized suppliers ind.	−2.870	−3.742	−3.490	−3.390	−2.703
Science-based ind.	−2.279	−2.107	0.827	0.943	1.851
Total trade	−0.886	−0.290	0.649	0.007	−0.286
Mediterranean NICs					
Agricultural prod.	2.965	0.793	0.391	0.157	−1.003
Fuels	−0.585	−1.073	−2.106	−2.047	−2.415
Other raw materials	2.608	3.262	1.980	0.617	0.824
Food industries	−0.354	−0.508	−1.270	−0.700	−0.615
Traditional ind.	−0.276	0.140	0.728	0.647	0.629
Resource-intensive ind.	−0.832	−0.547	−0.416	−0.664	−0.755
Scale-intensive ind.	−1.931	−1.871	−1.197	−1.367	−1.320
Specialized suppliers ind.	−2.214	−2.406	−1.842	−2.110	−1.781
Science-based ind.	−1.675	−1.093	−1.003	−1.195	−0.993
Total trade	−0.684	−0.872	−0.729	−0.888	−0.869
Latin American NICs					
Agricultural prod.	3.924	2.911	3.619	3.676	4.413
Fuels	−2.224	−2.142	1.362	0.809	1.486
Other raw materials	4.608	5.762	8.514	10.313	10.070
Food industries	5.584	6.070	4.549	2.958	3.895
Traditional ind.	−0.345	0.574	0.522	−0.197	−0.286
Resource-intensive ind.	1.394	0.340	2.585	1.669	1.282
Scale-intensive ind.	−2.641	−1.998	0.386	−1.064	−0.227
Specialized suppliers ind.	−4.680	−3.826	−1.639	−3.213	−2.279
Science-based ind.	−4.023	−2.362	−0.477	−1.316	−1.134
Total trade	−0.339	−0.471	0.804	−0.271	0.002

By the mid-1990s, Argentina's trade specialization was mostly based on agricultural products and food industry (Table 9.6). Trade composition, however, has been changing substantially over the past three decades, thanks to a larger role of industrial sectors and a related increased weight of industrial products in total Argentinean exports.

These changes in trade patterns, however, featured very differently in each of the three periods considered here (Tables 9.1, 9.6 and 9.7). Over the 1970s, resource-intensive, scale-intensive (such as automobiles, electrical equipment) and, to a lesser extent, specialized supplier (machine tools) categories contributed as a

Table 9.6 Trade specialization patterns of selected countries

	1970	*1979*	*1989*	*1992*	*1995*
Argentina					
Agricultural prod.	41.27	38.95	15.01	27.74	21.79
Fuels	−3.04	−9.64	−5.42	1.82	6.63
Other raw materials	−2.04	−2.09	−5.41	−1.42	−1.34
Food industries	37.01	27.29	29.49	27.95	24.82
Traditional ind.	−5.72	1.47	4.22	−4.78	−1.50
Resource-intensive ind.	−12.74	−10.47	−0.35	1.81	−2.09
Scale-intensive ind.	−26.53	−18.76	−14.95	−25.16	−17.61
Specialized suppliers ind.	−17.79	−12.38	−10.46	−11.51	−13.80
Science-based ind.	−8.60	−12.84	−11.85	−16.04	−16.31
Mexico					
Agricultural prod.	16.75	8.93	0.28	2.48	1.87
Fuels	−0.60	41.05	31.37	24.76	9.00
Other raw materials	5.32	1.55	0.75	0.73	−0.01
Food industries	11.88	2.10	−5.35	−3.14	−1.15
Traditional ind.	3.07	0.55	−3.89	−3.49	−3.91
Resource-intensive ind.	3.37	−3.88	−1.75	−0.52	−2.02
Scale-intensive ind.	−14.38	−23.66	−3.89	−5.01	9.59
Specialized suppliers ind.	−18.40	−18.68	−13.75	−12.60	−4.17
Science-based ind.	−12.48	−11.41	−3.42	−3.35	−2.78
Brazil					
Agricultural prod.	11.04	1.65	6.11	4.67	4.67
Fuels	−10.55	−35.10	−18.75	−18.43	−7.13
Other raw materials	8.89	7.69	3.91	4.82	4.81
Food industries	14.29	22.32	8.97	9.55	12.05
Traditional ind.	3.00	10.24	5.40	8.47	3.89
Resource-intensive ind.	−9.68	−2.55	2.85	2.64	2.09
Scale-intensive ind.	−20.83	−3.39	4.92	6.05	−5.04
Specialized suppliers ind.	−16.14	−6.98	−5.31	−9.10	−7.10
Science-based ind.	−14.90	−4.99	−8.91	−9.49	−10.23

group to a deep restructuring of Argentina's industry which seemed able to provide a more articulated industrial base for comparative advantages in Argentina. In the course of the 1980s, the debt crisis put a halt to this phase and, together with the recessionary adjustment policies, produced a deep impact on Argentina's industrial and trade structure (Bisang and Kosakoff 1995). Manufactured products continued to increase their share in total export, mostly thanks to natural-resource-intensive industries (e.g. pulp and paper, non-ferrous metal products) and a few scale- and capital-intensive industries (e.g. iron and steel, and basic chemicals) favored by generous fiscal incentive policies. So did, even to a lesser extent, the traditional sectors (such as clothing, textiles and shoes). On the other hand, specialized supplier (machine tools and agricultural equipment) and science-based products showed increasing comparative disadvantages.

Table 9.7 Standardized trade balances of selected countries

	1970	1979	1989	1992	1995
Argentina					
Agricultural prod.	2.605	2.550	1.146	1.842	2.009
Fuels	−0.276	−0.288	−0.136	0.018	0.574
Other raw materials	−0.416	−0.503	−0.735	−0.669	−0.637
Food industries	3.187	2.335	2.105	1.551	1.881
Traditional ind.	−0.217	0.099	0.148	−0.144	−0.025
Resource-intensive ind.	−0.743	−0.492	0.145	0.031	−0.112
Scale-intensive ind.	−0.626	−0.336	0.032	−0.433	−0.272
Specialized suppliers ind.	−0.953	−0.569	−0.129	−0.471	−0.523
Science-based ind.	−0.529	−0.511	−0.072	−0.355	−0.302
Total trade	0.029	0.074	0.185	−0.071	0.017
Mexico					
Agricultural prod.	0.510	0.408	0.091	−0.272	0.746
Fuels	−0.130	1.646	4.063	3.031	2.947
Other raw materials	0.617	0.253	0.545	0.278	0.071
Food industries	0.606	0.100	−0.714	−1.082	−0.261
Traditional ind.	−0.147	−0.081	−0.160	−0.548	−0.263
Resource-intensive ind.	−0.163	−0.436	−0.140	−0.573	−0.389
Scale-intensive ind.	−0.821	−0.998	−0.090	−0.892	0.710
Specialized suppliers ind.	−1.676	−1.784	−1.034	−1.958	−0.461
Science-based ind.	−1.483	−0.942	−0.125	−0.597	−0.086
Total trade	−0.437	−0.248	0.033	−0.561	0.109
Brazil					
Agricultural prod.	1.039	−0.078	1.824	1.278	0.804
Fuels	−1.616	−3.130	−2.192	−1.906	−1.581
Other raw materials	2.949	4.086	5.740	6.561	5.074
Food industries	1.879	3.584	2.695	2.065	1.825
Traditional ind.	0.181	0.669	0.587	0.597	0.136
Resource-intensive ind.	−0.957	−0.507	0.999	0.835	0.096
Scale-intensive ind.	−0.846	−0.389	0.680	0.533	−0.357
Specialized suppliers ind.	−1.470	−1.158	−0.075	−0.377	−0.821
Science-based ind.	−1.564	−0.744	−0.124	−0.196	−0.560
Total trade	−0.037	−0.296	0.522	0.3491	−0.144

This trend has been only partially mitigated in more recent years with the introduction of economic reforms and greater trade openness. It should have been followed by higher rates of growth of exports, together with a parallel increase in imports. Both trade composition and specialization, however, have not shown any substantial change yet with respect to its industrial content. On the contrary, only fuel products have significantly increased their contribution to trade balance and their share in total Argentina's exports during the first half of the 1990s.

Among the LAN, Brazil experienced the deepest industrialization restructuring over the past two decades. In the early 1970s, Brazil's comparative advantages were mostly concentrated in primary commodities, such as agricultural products, food industry and other raw materials; a few traditional industrial sectors (such as textile and leather products) were the only exceptions. Over the course of the 1970s and until the early 1980s, manufactured output and export growth was very high. An import substitution strategy together with export incentives led to strong diversification of Brazil's industrial base and trade structure in the same period (Fritsch and Franco 1991). A confirmation of this is the huge increase in the share of manufactures in total Brazilian exports in this period, from 20 per cent in the early 1970s to 63 per cent in the late 1980s.

In the course of the 1980s, the debt crisis and growing macroeconomic imbalances to a rather different pattern. The Brazilian economy, forced to generate huge trade surpluses, greatly increased the level of industrial protection. The Brazilian industry's competitive position also significantly deteriorated, with a sectoral trade composition shifting towards natural-resource-intensive and scale-intensive product goods. Most of Brazil's comparative advantages were concentrated in these two categories (basic chemicals, steel manufacturing, non-metallic minerals sectors, electrical machinery and autoparts).[2]

In the third period – covering the first half of the 1990s – a liberalization process was implemented in order to reduce the average level of protection of the Brazilian economy. Furthermore, the anti-inflationary strategy of 1994–5 increased the implementation of tariff reductions, although the Mexican crisis and the more recent Asian crisis led to a partial reversal of this liberalization trend.

In the course of this period, trade industrial diversification slowed down and was partially reversed. The share of industrial goods on overall exports did not increase for the first time in three decades, and Brazil's world export share and trade balance deteriorated in the same period. If we take the sum of the share of scale-intensive, specialized supplier and science-based sectors in total Brazilian exports (as a proxy for the overall technological content of the trade pattern), it increased significantly during the 1970s and up to the late 1980s, whereas in the second half of the 1990s it did not change at all. Clearly all this suggests that, due also to a real exchange rate appreciation, Brazilian industrialization process paid high adjustment costs in recent years. One should also note, however, that the index in intra-industry trade increased in the same period, suggesting that the production integration of the Brazilian firms into the international markets has been also gradually increasing.

Mexico distinguishes its position from the other two Latin American countries by its peculiar specialization patterns over the period considered. It was dominated by external shocks and events which led to different phases of domestic adjustments with regard to trade and industrial restructuring (Tables 9.1, 9.6 and 9.7).

Up to the early 1980s the trade pattern of Mexico was dominated by oil events. Since the first oil shock, fuels rapidly became the dominant item of Mexico's exports and specialization; as a consequence, the weight of manufactured goods in Mexican exports drastically decreased. A sort of 'Dutch disease', in terms of an advanced deindustrialization pattern, thus characterized the Mexican economy in this phase. From 1982 up to the early 1990s, a second major change took place in Mexico's trade pattern with its first openness initiative. In this second phase, the debt crisis forced Mexico to increase its exports rapidly, so that raw materials and natural-resource-intensive products achieved a greater role in overall export. In this respect, agricultural products also increased its share in Mexico's exports and specialization. This second period culminated with the signature of the NAFTA agreement and the financial crisis of the mid-1990s.

In very recent years, industrial exports have rapidly regained strength while fuel exports decreased their importance. There is no doubt that in this period Mexico has started a deep industrial restructuring process, driven by a consistent inflow of FDI and increasing opportunities stemming from NAFTA. The ICTB indicators in scale-intensive, specialized suppliers and science-based sectors showed significant improvements. The rapid increase in Mexican imports in those product groups that experienced the positive export performances emphasizes the intra-industry vertical type of new trade flows, mostly related to the maquiladora industries. As is well known, the industrial local impact and spillover effects of this type of industries are far from being assured. As a matter of fact, in the mid-1990s, Mexico's specialization pattern seemed still characterized by comparative advantages in primary commodities (fuels).

Trade and technological patterns of the East Asian NICs

In the past two and half decades, trade and technological patterns of East Asian NICs (EAN) seem to have been characterized, to a certain extent, by quite opposite features with respect to Latin American economies.

First, it is important to note the positive trade performances of South-East Asian countries – Hong Kong, Singapore, South Korea and Taiwan – over the entire period considered here (1970–95), in terms of rapidly increasing market shares (Table 9.8).[3] Although the financial crises in East Asia have attracted much attention recently, we should not forget the amazing achievements of the EAN in the past three decades.

Sound evidence of the positive trade performance of East Asia can be drawn from the competitive patterns in single product groups related to the taxonomy previously adopted (Table 9.9). Indicators show a sharp strengthening of the Asian NIC competitive positions on international markets in all the main industrial categories in terms of a rapidly rising share in world exports and positive trade balances. This is especially true in traditional industries up to the second half of the 1980s, and in science-based goods over the past decade. Within the latter group, the significant achievements of the EAN in many electronics sectors is emblematic (Guerrieri 1995). Finally, in specialized supplier sectors, and particularly in mechanical engineering, EAN have been able to register rising export shares in recent years.

The EAN experienced the highest rates of growth and accumulation among the three groups of economies here considered in the past two decades and a half. Such remarkable performance may be connected with the common

Table 9.8 Shares in world exports of selected groups of countries

	1970	1979	1989	1992	1995
Singapore					
Agricultural prod.	1.67	1.62	1.17	0.96	0.99
Fuels	0.01	0.02	0.03	0.04	0.06
Other raw materials	0.16	0.38	0.20	0.25	0.26
Food industries	0.72	0.91	1.14	1.22	1.20
Traditional ind.	0.47	0.79	0.94	0.91	0.93
Resource-intensive ind.	1.32	2.61	3.60	3.92	3.27
Scale-intensive ind.	0.17	0.53	1.10	1.26	1.52
Specialized suppliers ind.	0.26	0.59	1.24	1.27	1.81
Science-based ind.	0.16	1.34	3.01	3.66	5.78
Total trade	0.54	0.94	1.54	1.72	2.35
Taiwan					
Agricultural prod.	0.39	0.42	0.72	0.77	0.88
Fuels	0.00	0.00	0.00	0.00	0.01
Other raw materials	0.05	0.05	0.15	0.10	0.21
Food industries	0.76	0.80	1.03	1.00	0.99
Traditional ind.	1.06	2.66	4.20	3.07	3.80
Resource-intensive ind.	0.04	0.12	0.23	0.18	1.09
Scale-intensive ind.	0.28	0.68	1.26	0.88	1.39
Specialized suppliers ind.	0.12	0.44	1.36	1.11	2.56
Science-based ind.	0.14	0.80	2.33	2.51	4.27
Total trade	0.36	0.79	1.74	1.50	2.38
South Korea					
Agricultural Prod.	0.29	0.81	1.07	0.88	0.77
Fuels	0.02	0.00	0.00	0.00	0.02
Other raw materials	0.48	0.31	0.37	0.33	0.20
Food industries	0.07	0.36	0.54	0.42	0.52
Traditional ind.	1.09	3.34	4.87	3.67	3.12
Resource-intensive ind.	0.04	0.12	0.72	1.13	1.30
Scale-intensive ind.	0.08	1.14	2.61	2.71	3.19
Specialized suppliers ind.	0.04	0.28	0.87	1.03	2.37
Science-based ind.	0.17	0.94	2.28	2.45	3.31
Total trade	0.29	0.99	2.15	2.08	2.49

export-oriented growth strategies followed by East Asian countries since the late 1960s, after a relatively short period with import-substitution policies in the 1950s.

A massive reallocation of productive resources in those industrial sectors with highest export potential was the main goal of these strategies. To pursue this goal either state interventions or incentive and subsidy policies, as well known, were used on a large scale and in very different forms (Amsden 1989; Wade 1990).

The industrial development of the EAN was initially supported by the production and export of consumer goods requiring large amounts of unskilled labor, for which they benefited by the highest comparative (and absolute) advantages (Table 9.4). After increasing significantly up to the mid-1980s, however, the

Table 9.9 Shares in world exports of selected groups of countries

	1970	*1979*	*1989*	*1992*	*1995*
East Asian NICs					
Agricultural prod.	3.22	3.71	4.66	4.56	4.11
Fuels	0.71	1.03	0.96	1.08	0.98
Other raw materials	1.03	1.10	1.40	1.30	1.37
Food industries	2.08	2.59	4.07	4.41	4.33
Traditional ind.	6.53	11.56	18.53	18.01	16.45
Resource-intensive ind.	1.85	3.30	5.66	7.13	7.47
Scale-intensive ind.	1.05	3.16	6.67	7.45	8.59
Specialized suppliers ind.	0.87	1.92	5.66	6.83	8.76
Science-based ind.	1.07	4.94	11.56	13.41	17.75
Total trade	2.36	4.21	8.63	9.57	10.84
Mediterranean NICs					
Agricultural prod.	4.62	2.49	2.83	2.76	2.42
Fuels	0.45	0.62	0.65	0.75	0.48
Other raw materials	3.19	4.12	3.90	2.90	2.77
Food industries	1.25	1.20	1.52	1.77	1.84
Traditional ind.	0.81	1.20	2.02	2.16	2.20
Resource-intensive ind.	0.33	0.87	0.98	0.93	1.01
Scale-intensive ind.	0.29	0.26	0.66	0.60	0.64
Specialized suppliers ind.	0.02	0.07	0.15	0.25	0.28
Science-based ind.	0.04	0.08	0.12	0.13	0.13
Total trade	0.93	0.77	0.97	0.97	0.92
Latin American NICs					
Agricultural prod.	5.98	5.50	5.62	6.14	7.23
Fuels	0.05	1.70	4.18	3.38	3.82
Other raw materials	6.05	8.40	12.45	13.73	14.20
Food industries	6.76	7.45	6.68	5.65	6.79
Traditional ind.	1.06	1.61	1.46	1.37	2.30
Resource-intensive ind.	4.04	2.63	4.34	4.14	4.58
Scale-intensive ind.	0.64	1.16	2.16	2.08	3.30
Specialized suppliers ind.	0.33	0.85	1.12	0.98	2.53
Science-based ind.	0.43	0.68	1.19	0.90	1.92
Total trade	2.42	2.38	2.59	2.32	3.24

contribution of traditional goods to the trade balance decreased throughout the past decade. A diversification of manufacturing output and radical changes in trade patterns of the EAN have been taking place in the period considered here, although in very different forms. Actually, this overall trend masks sharp differences within East Asian countries. They are so huge that it is very difficult to define a common 'East Asian Pattern' (Tables 9.8, 9.10 and 9.11).

First of all, Singapore and Taiwan achieved the best results within the East Asian group, in terms of increasing market shares and upgrading their trade specialization towards science-based goods, especially electronic activities. This was due to deep structural changes in the two countries' trade patterns since the early 1970s, when comparative advantages were concentrated in traditional goods

Table 9.10 Standardized trade balances of selected countries

	1970	1979	1989	1992	1995
Singapore					
Agricultural prod.	0.303	0.217	−0.082	−0.240	−0.156
Fuels	−0.712	−1.677	−2.590	−2.669	−2.595
Other raw materials	−0.006	0.059	−0.196	−0.290	−0.207
Food industries	−0.332	−0.245	−0.169	−0.153	−0.163
Traditional ind.	−0.602	−0.149	−0.183	−0.294	−0.427
Resource-intensive ind.	0.408	1.889	1.584	1.271	0.682
Scale-intensive ind.	−0.410	−0.274	−0.194	−0.211	−0.271
Specialized suppliers ind.	−0.731	−0.663	−0.650	−0.901	−0.872
Science-based ind.	−0.454	−0.508	0.172	0.375	0.839
Total trade	−0.316	−0.224	−0.173	−0.236	−0.124
Taiwan					
Agricultural prod.	−0.211	−0.487	−0.611	−0.545	−1.027
Fuels	−0.005	−0.009	−0.283	−0.220	−0.748
Other raw materials	−0.035	−0.147	−0.575	−0.706	−0.923
Food industries	0.644	0.608	0.365	0.354	−0.018
Traditional ind.	0.799	2.406	3.687	2.477	2.752
Resource-intensive ind.	−0.178	−0.280	−1.003	−1.264	−1.104
Scale-intensive ind.	−0.314	−0.141	−0.183	−0.554	−0.273
Specialized suppliers ind.	−0.647	−0.628	−0.616	−0.920	0.408
Science-based ind.	−0.521	−0.348	0.649	0.696	1.522
Total trade	−0.071	0.202	0.518	0.220	0.578
South Korea					
Agricultural prod.	−0.924	−1.808	−2.515	−2.452	−2.699
Fuels	−0.643	−1.532	−3.798	−5.242	−6.137
Other raw materials	0.108	−1.133	−4.472	−5.128	−4.918
Food industries	−0.302	−0.295	−0.394	−0.656	−0.820
Traditional ind.	0.657	2.767	3.792	2.507	1.625
Resource-intensive ind.	−0.240	−0.707	−1.400	−1.726	−2.643
Scale-intensive ind.	−0.615	−0.018	0.912	1.262	1.190
Specialized suppliers ind.	−0.906	−1.914	−2.342	−2.090	−1.510
Science-based ind.	−0.566	−0.855	−0.282	−0.168	0.376
Total trade	−0.400	−0.346	0.032	−0.140	−0.200

and the food industry in the case of Taiwan, and in agricultural products and resource-intensive industries in the case of Singapore (Guerrieri 1995).

Taiwan adopted an industrial development strategy based initially on some competitive clusters comprising labor-intensive consumer goods. From the second part of the 1980s up to the mid-1990s, Taiwan gradually carried out a process of diversification and upgrading of industrial structure toward a strengthening of technology-intensive products, such as science-based goods (e.g. electronics components and investment goods). This is confirmed by the decreasing contribution to trade balance of traditional goods and the recent increasing contribution of science-based goods (Table 9.11).

Table 9.11 Trade specialization patterns of selected countries

	1970	1979	1989	1992	1995
Singapore					
Agricultural prod.	13.96	4.12	0.16	−0.27	−0.19
Fuels	−5.07	−21.09	−9.25	−8.62	−5.08
Other raw materials	0.27	0.23	−0.12	−0.11	−0.07
Food industries	0.71	−0.15	−0.13	0.04	−0.22
Traditional ind.	−5.43	0.48	−0.76	−1.51	−2.54
Resource-intensive ind.	13.11	19.61	9.21	6.08	2.31
Scale-intensive ind.	−8.51	−2.88	−1.05	−0.49	−1.92
Specialized suppliers ind.	−7.00	−4.09	−2.97	−3.81	−3.28
Science-based ind.	−3.80	−1.73	5.21	8.53	9.86
Taiwan					
Agricultural prod.	−3.06	−7.93	−3.79	−2.54	−3.08
Fuels	−0.07	−0.23	−1.38	−1.09	−1.99
Other raw materials	−0.17	−0.48	−0.59	−0.49	−0.45
Food industries	13.16	4.14	0.26	0.93	0.79
Traditional ind.	34.52	41.76	32.70	27.54	16.65
Resource-intensive ind.	−3.96	−4.73	−6.79	−6.63	−5.01
Scale-intensive ind.	−14.70	−12.07	−11.29	−13.57	−8.31
Specialized suppliers ind.	−15.71	−11.39	−8.12	−8.67	−1.23
Science-based ind.	−10.79	−9.99	−0.63	4.87	5.62
South Korea					
Agricultural prod.	−6.29	−8.93	−6.90	−5.34	−4.45
Other raw materials	−4.79	−16.60	−11.01	−15.02	−11.07
Fuels	2.64	−1.36	−2.52	−2.02	−1.53
Food industries	−1.74	−0.76	−1.05	−1.65	−1.60
Traditional ind.	38.60	41.82	29.64	21.69	11.63
Resource-intensive ind.	−2.28	−4.47	−5.30	−4.91	−6.31
Scale-intensive ind.	−15.02	6.40	10.47	16.63	13.39
Specialized suppliers ind.	−11.31	−12.26	−11.10	−9.38	−5.13
Science-based ind.	−3.87	−4.19	−2.62	−0.03	5.09

This process of diversification has been accompanied by a selective industrial policy comprising of a variety of measures like import protection, directed credit, technological support and strong export promotion. This support played a significant role, especially in helping those Taiwanese SME firms that dominate the domestic industrial structure to upgrade and diversify their technological bases.

Whereas FDI played a secondary role in the case of Taiwan, Singapore has relied heavily on FDI and MNCs (Urata 1993). As shown by specialization pattern, Singapore started with resource-intensive industries (ship servicing and petroleum refining) and moved into export-oriented industrialization, based on light industrial activity in the late 1970s. But it was in the course of the 1980s, after heavy interventions of Singapore's government, that trade specialization shifted heavily towards science-based goods (especially electronics industries), guided by higher openness, MNC foreign investments and global structure of their operations. A clear confirmation of this is the huge increase in the share of science-based goods in total Singapore exports in this period (from 14 per cent in the early 1980s to 52 per cent in the mid-1990s).

The electronics sector was the central pillar of Singapore's industrial and technological development in the past decade, as well as of many other East Asian countries' recent industrialization stories (Borrus 1993). As well known, electronics products are complex systems based on a number of critical components and therefore are particularly favorable to a network firm organization spread across countries (Ernst 1994). As many studies have shown, FDI and production networks based on strong intra-regional interdependencies as regards inputs and sales and often part of global production strategies of US and Japanese medium–large firms, have played a very important role in East Asia's overall competitiveness and intra-regional trade (see Doherty et al. 1997). Part of East Asian FDI, as shown in the 'product cycle' model, has aimed at taking advantage of local natural resources, skills and relatively low wage cost. But interest in the region has not been motivated only by the search for new low-wage localization costs. The same multinational companies that set up as 'footloose' industries pursued a more lasting involvement in the region (Guerrieri 1995). Therefore, other important inputs related to both economics and technology have played a dominant role in the network firm organization, such as the expansion of East Asian FDI, subcontracting and outsourcing (Borrus 1993). The increasing importance of intra-industry trade in the region, as shown in the cases of Singapore and Taiwan, could be also attributable to an increasing division of labor within multinational companies.

Thus, very often, foreign direct investment in the East Asian region has generated trade and trade opportunities and, in turn, has attracted new foreign investment (Ernst and Guerrieri 1998). Such specialization, however, seem to have, in many cases, greatly reduced the need for domestic technological efforts and contributed to keeping technological levels of the affiliates of MNCs relatively low in many countries.

South Korea exhibited a very different pattern from the other two Asian NICs. Korean industrial development relied primarily on labor-intensive traditional goods and raw materials. As shown by the trade specialization pattern, between the mid-1970s and late 1980s, Korea diversified its exports mainly toward scale-intensive, heavy industry by promoting giant private conglomerates (chaebol). In the few years between the early 1970s and the early 1980s, there was a huge increase in the share of scale-intensive goods in total Korean exports (from 7 per cent in the early 1970s to 36 per cent in the mid-1980s). The trade specialization pattern also showed this dramatic increase of the contribution to the Korean trade balance from scale-intensive industries in the same period.

For this purpose, Korea adopted far more interventionist strategies on trade and domestic resource allocation than Taiwan and Singapore. The chaebol were heavily subsidized and MNCs' entry into domestic markets severely restricted, pushing domestic enterprises to set up local technological capabilities and capital-intensive activities geared to export markets. To access technology, it relied primarily on capital-goods imports, technology licensing and other technology agreements.

In the course of the past decade, along with a gradual process of trade and capital liberalization, Korea tried to firmly upgrade their industrial structure, this time towards science-based activities. But this attempt was only a partial success. Science-based goods actually increased their share in total exports and their contribution to the trade balance, but at the price of a much higher technological dependence of Korean industry from external sources, especially from Japan's technology. As a consequence, Korea's trade balance severely deteriorated in the past three years, paving the way to the recent dramatic crisis.

Trade and technological patterns of the Mediterranean NICs

The Mediterranean NICs (MeN) experienced a peculiar pattern of trade, growth and openness in these years in comparison to the other two groups of countries previously considered (Tables 9.2, 9.4 and 9.9).

By the early 1970s, trade performance and specialization of the three Mediterranean NICs were still largely based on agricultural products and raw materials, and were geographically concentrated into European markets. But in the course of the 1980s, the Mediterranean specialization has been shifting towards industrial goods, especially traditional consumer goods, so that by the late 1980s industrial goods comprised about 67 per cent of exports, while non-industrial products comprised 30 per cent. These structural changes have been favoured, on the one hand, by a trade liberalization process implemented gradually and low labor costs in labor-intensive sectors, mostly textile-apparel, on the other. Trade liberalization, however, was combined, in the same period, with very intense support measures for export activities.

In the course of the 1990s, trade performance of the MeN has significantly deteriorated. Their modest share in world exports decreased further; their high trade deficit in industrial products did not improve; and their trade specialization remained locked into traditional and raw material sectors. Furthermore, the MeN intra-industry trade index, already very low in comparison to those of Latin American and Asian NICs, held stable values even in the more recent period. Besides these common features, however, the MeN show very distinct individual patterns of export growth, technological capability, industrial changes, reliance on FDI and policy interventions. Let us review three of them, amongst the most significant ones, that is Turkey, Tunisia and Greece.

Turkey has showed two distinctive trade patterns over the period considered (Tables 9.12, 9.13, 9.14 and 9.15). In the period from the late 1970s up to the second part of the 1980s, the Turkish share of world exports increased substantially, i.e. by around 100 per cent, whereas in the more recent phase the competitive position of Turkey did not show any improvement (1990–5). The trade balance pattern was very similar: small deficits in the course of the 1980s and a deteriorating external position, combined with a rapidly increasing total external debt, over the first half of the 1990s.

The positive trade performance in the 1980s followed the gradual opening up of the Turkish economy, after a prolonged period of protectionist import-substitution policy and heavy state intervention.

Table 9.12 Shares in world exports of selected groups of countries

	1970	1979	1989	1992	1995
Greece					
Agricultural prod.	0.88	0.59	0.81	0.90	0.73
Fuels	0.00	0.00	0.03	0.03	0.03
Other raw materials	0.54	0.81	0.74	0.62	0.56
Food industries	0.37	0.58	0.73	0.84	0.71
Traditional ind.	0.19	0.51	0.51	0.53	0.38
Resource-intensive ind.	0.18	0.49	0.38	0.43	0.43
Scale-intensive ind.	0.17	0.11	0.11	0.10	0.09
Specialized suppliers ind.	0.01	0.05	0.04	0.06	0.06
Science-based ind.	0.03	0.05	0.03	0.04	0.05
Total trade	0.22	0.25	0.26	0.27	0.22
Tunisia					
Agricultural prod.	0.08	0.07	0.10	0.09	0.09
Fuels	0.24	0.36	0.30	0.22	0.16
Other raw materials	0.33	0.19	0.16	0.14	0.16
Food industries	0.17	0.17	0.08	0.12	0.12
Traditional ind.	0.02	0.17	0.22	0.30	0.36
Resource-intensive ind.	0.05	0.06	0.04	0.05	0.04
Scale-intensive ind.	0.04	0.06	0.09	0.07	0.06
Specialized suppliers ind.	0.00	0.01	0.02	0.05	0.05
Science-based ind.	0.00	0.01	0.02	0.02	0.02
Total trade	0.06	0.12	0.10	0.11	0.11
Turkey					
Agricultural prod.	1.57	1.10	1.27	1.21	0.97
Fuels	0.02	0.00	0.01	0.01	0.00
Other raw materials	0.44	0.47	1.27	0.85	0.98
Food industries	0.19	0.16	0.48	0.59	0.77
Traditional ind.	0.09	0.24	0.94	1.04	1.20
Resource-intensive ind.	0.03	0.01	0.24	0.19	0.22
Scale-intensive ind.	0.02	0.03	0.35	0.31	0.37
Specialized suppliers ind.	0.00	0.01	0.07	0.12	0.15
Science-based ind.	0.00	0.00	0.05	0.05	0.05
Total trade	0.21	0.15	0.40	0.40	0.43

The various rounds of import liberalization, combined with a variety of export supports to Turkish firms, led to a massive export boom and decreasing import penetration in some sectors due to increasing domestic production. The major gains were achieved in the traditional labor-intensive industries (especially textile and clothing). Exports of raw materials and scale-intensive products (basic metals) also registered significant gains.

In the first half of the 1990s, the trade liberalization process progressed even further with the dismantling of most forms of export support policies. But export flows slowed down this time, barely keeping pace with world export growth.

Table 9.13 Standarized trade balances of selected countries

	1970	*1979*	*1989*	*1992*	*1995*
Greece					
Agricultural prod.	0.556	0.068	0.342	0.389	0.187
Fuels	−0.438	−0.819	−0.434	−0.736	−0.547
Other raw materials	0.209	0.628	0.522	0.446	0.399
Food industries	−0.409	−0.047	−0.563	−0.413	−0.416
Traditional ind.	−0.260	0.149	−0.079	−0.123	−0.173
Resource-intensive ind.	−0.265	0.149	−0.068	−0.117	−0.141
Scale-intensive ind.	−0.969	−0.877	−0.562	−0.702	−0.552
Specialized suppliers ind.	−0.885	−0.750	−0.546	−0.525	−0.366
Science-based ind.	−0.581	−0.338	−0.290	−0.306	−0.218
Total trade	−0.459	−0.381	−0.296	−0.368	−0.298
Tunisia					
Agricultural prod.	−0.111	−0.135	−0.153	−0.068	−0.210
Fuels	0.203	0.261	0.204	0.138	0.024
Other raw materials	0.248	−0.016	−0.350	−0.294	−0.177
Food industries	−0.005	−0.040	−0.105	−0.029	−0.026
Traditional ind.	−0.097	−0.057	0.013	0.028	0.079
Resource-intensive ind.	−0.010	−0.184	−0.138	−0.153	−0.113
Scale-intensive ind.	−0.047	−0.114	−0.023	−0.075	−0.054
Specialized suppliers ind.	−0.141	−0.293	−0.167	−0.200	−0.132
Science-based ind.	−0.083	−0.131	−0.055	−0.099	−0.063
Total trade	−0.043	−0.069	−0.050	−0.065	−0.048
Turkey					
Agricultural prod.	1.264	1.056	0.642	0.550	−0.160
Fuels	−0.263	−0.469	−1.677	−1.462	−1.720
Other raw materials	0.396	0.247	0.749	0.344	0.410
Food industries	0.178	0.080	0.083	0.188	0.328
Traditional ind.	−0.016	0.176	0.775	0.761	0.770
Resource-intensive ind.	−0.181	−0.598	−0.208	−0.283	−0.430
Scale-intensive ind.	−0.412	−0.365	−0.297	−0.365	−0.452
Specialized suppliers ind.	−0.621	−0.628	−0.603	−0.838	−0.830
Science-based ind.	−0.468	−0.264	−0.392	−0.531	−0.511
Total trade	−0.105	−0.177	−0.144	−0.221	−0.281

At the same time, imports increased dramatically, especially of consumption and intermediate goods.

Macroeconomic instability can account for a great part of this disappointing pattern. It is sufficient to point out the existence of chronic fiscal deficits, punitive high interest rates and appreciating real exchange rates in the first part of the 1990s. Long-term structural factors, however, also seem to have significantly contributed to this performance, as shown by the Turkey's trade specialization pattern over the past two decades. In the 1980s, the trade specialization pattern of Turkey displayed significant changes by showing rapid industrialization and deep restructuring over time. Traditional labor-intensive goods, especially textile and clothing, greatly

Table 9.14 Trade specialization patterns of selected countries

	1970	1979	1989	1992	1995
Greece					
Agricultural prod.	25.32	9.82	11.36	10.60	8.71
Fuels	−3.09	−15.57	−3.89	−5.84	−4.02
Other raw materials	4.12	4.29	2.54	1.50	1.59
Food industries	2.77	6.48	2.26	5.75	5.02
Traditional ind.	2.22	17.21	13.25	13.79	9.52
Resource-intensive ind.	1.24	10.38	4.51	4.08	4.91
Scale-intensive ind.	−16.54	−20.89	−17.23	−19.01	−17.23
Specialized suppliers ind.	−10.36	−8.04	−7.76	−6.04	−4.72
Science-based ind.	−5.28	−3.57	−7.08	−6.25	−5.23
Tunisia					
Agricultural prod.	−4.84	−3.89	−3.76	−0.41	−4.81
Fuels	20.79	35.37	13.78	9.28	2.78
Other raw materials	11.81	0.88	−2.07	−1.02	−0.55
Food industries	6.88	1.85	−2.38	1.27	0.99
Traditional ind.	−11.00	3.14	13.24	19.59	24.56
Resource-intensive ind.	2.33	−6.86	−6.05	−4.42	−3.91
Scale-intensive ind.	−4.56	−9.40	3.18	−4.96	−3.82
Specialized suppliers ind.	−13.57	−13.48	−9.99	−9.51	−7.10
Science-based ind.	−6.84	−6.78	−4.85	−8.83	−6.97
Turkey					
Agricultural prod.	62.88	49.91	11.39	9.27	2.83
Fuels	−5.09	−18.32	−18.46	−14.25	−11.03
Other raw materials	5.50	3.88	2.57	1.10	1.16
Food industries	6.14	4.38	2.52	4.62	6.08
Traditional ind.	1.44	17.55	33.75	35.97	34.29
Resource-intensive ind.	−5.13	−14.19	−1.74	−1.78	−2.53
Scale-intensive ind.	−30.52	−20.20	−7.74	−7.48	−6.87
Specialized suppliers ind.	−20.91	−15.17	−10.37	−12.24	−10.17
Science-based ind.	−13.67	−7.48	−11.76	−14.81	−13.49

increased their contribution to the trade balance. In contrast, agricultural products, the leading export sector in the 1970s, dramatically reduced its role, both in terms of specialization and share in total exports. The trade performance and specialization of scale-intensive goods (especially the basic metal and automotive sectors) also improved sharply during the 1980s.[4] High comparative disadvantages and trade deficits characterized the specialized supplier and science-based sectors over both decades, although slight improvements occurred in the former.

In more recent periods, the disappointing Turkish trade performance has been accompanied by a relatively stable trade specialization pattern, locked into traditional goods and sectors. If we take the sum of the shares of scale-intensive, specialized supplier and science-based sectors in total Turkish exports (as a proxy for the overall technological content of the trade pattern), it increased significantly during the late 1970s to the second half of the 1980s (7.3 per cent in 1979 to 27.6 per cent in 1987). Thereafter, it has remained almost stable, suggesting that technological capability of Turkey has not improved significantly in the last period.

Table 9.15 Intra-industry trade: index of Gruber Lloyd

	1970	1979	1989	1992	1995
Greece					
Agricultural prod.	0.54	0.94	0.73	0.72	0.85
Fuels	0.00	0.00	0.11	0.07	0.09
Other raw materials	0.76	0.37	0.45	0.44	0.45
Food industries	0.65	0.96	0.72	0.80	0.77
Traditional ind.	0.60	0.83	0.93	0.89	0.82
Resource-intensive ind.	0.58	0.82	0.92	0.88	0.86
Scale-intensive ind.	0.26	0.20	0.29	0.22	0.25
Specialized suppliers ind.	0.02	0.11	0.14	0.18	0.26
Science-based ind.	0.10	0.25	0.17	0.21	0.31
Total	0.36	0.45	0.56	0.53	0.55
Tunisia					
Agricultural prod.	0.60	0.49	0.58	0.73	0.45
Fuels	0.27	0.43	0.49	0.55	0.92
Other raw materials	0.39	0.96	0.48	0.48	0.64
Food industries	0.98	0.89	0.60	0.89	0.90
Traditional ind.	0.28	0.86	0.97	0.95	0.88
Resource-intensive ind.	0.91	0.40	0.36	0.40	0.41
Scale-intensive ind.	0.62	0.50	0.88	0.64	0.71
Specialized suppliers ind.	0.01	0.05	0.21	0.34	0.43
Science-based ind.	0.04	0.17	0.47	0.32	0.41
Total	0.51	0.52	0.69	0.68	0.71
Turkey					
Agricultural prod.	0.33	0.08	0.66	0.70	0.92
Fuels	0.11	0.00	0.01	0.01	0.01
Other raw materials	0.18	0.65	0.58	0.75	0.73
Food industries	0.14	0.67	0.90	0.81	0.73
Traditional ind.	0.92	0.40	0.30	0.42	0.53
Resource-intensive ind.	0.26	0.03	0.70	0.58	0.51
Scale-intensive ind.	0.10	0.13	0.70	0.63	0.62
Specialized suppliers ind.	0.01	0.02	0.19	0.22	0.26
Science-based ind.	0.00	0.02	0.22	0.15	0.17
Total	0.22	0.12	0.46	0.44	0.49

One should note, however, that in the cases of traditional goods (such as textile and clothing) and scale-intensive goods (basic metals), there was an upgrading of Turkish exports, through the increase of their average unitary values. This upgrading, however, should not be overemphasized, since by the mid-1990s the average unit values of the Turkish exports were still well below those of many developing economies in Europe and Asia (Landesmann and Burgstaller 1997).

In the case of Tunisia, trade patterns have also been characterized by significant changes over the period considered. By the early 1970s, Tunisia's trade specialization was still largely based on primary commodities and agricultural products. In particular, fuel products and the agro-industrial system represented strong comparative advantages. Aside from resource-intensive goods, all other industrial groups registered negative values (comparative disadvantages) in the indicator of contribution to trade balance (ICTB).

In the course of the 1980s, Tunisia changed significantly with its integration into international markets. Facing an increasingly restrictive external constraint, Tunisia adopted an outwardly oriented strategy by generously supporting its exports and gradually liberalizing imports. The correction of the real exchange rates so as to guarantee more competitive values also played an important role in this external adjustment process.

The resulting trade performance was very positive indeed. Tunisia's trade specialization shifted towards industrial goods, especially traditional consumer goods, so that by the early 1990s they covered nearly 75 per cent of total exports. The trade deficit in industrial goods also diminished significantly. This rapid expansion of industrial exports was attributable mainly to the exploitation of lower labor cost advantages in labor-intensive products, mainly textile-apparel and orientation towards privileged access European markets. This positive adjustment, however, has been slowing down over the course of the 1990s. Tunisia's share in world exports has remained roughly the same, and the trade deficit in industrial goods did not improve either in recent years.

Certainly, macroeconomic factors such as the appreciation/stability of the real exchange rate can be used to explain the negative trade performance of Tunisia over the first part of the 1990s. But, the contribution of long-run structural factors has been also important. Like Turkey, the intense industrial restructuring in Tunisia encountered some major obstacles in the more recent years. Tunisia's trade specialization has remained locked into those industrial sectors that comprize low-skill labor-intensive assembly activities, mainly textile-apparel, and unable to diversify into higher value-added and more technologically sophisticated sectors. Besides their sectoral concentration, Tunisia's exports have also been strongly concentrated geographically in European markets, where they have privileged access.

Greece shows very distinctive trade patterns from Turkey and Tunisia (Tables 9.12, 9.13, 9.14 and 9.15). Greece has been characterized by sharp cycles since the early 1970s, with relatively low average growth rates, a few expansionary phases and recurrent slumps mainly due to domestic instability. The external constraint has always been very tight, and Greece has had serious problems to covering its trade deficits because of very weak export performance. All major industrial product groups reflect these unfavorable trends, with the exception of the agricultural products and food industries that had relatively better results, especially in the first part of the 1990s. Over the entire period, Greece had a stagnant market share in world exports. By the mid-1990s, the Greek share was almost the same as in the early 1970s (0.22), equal to half the Turkish share in the same years.

This weak trade performance has been accompanied by a relatively stable trade specialization pattern over time. Greece had an initial phase of structural change up to the first half of the 1970s, based on small-scale industrial restructuring. This favored the upgrading of some dynamic labor-intensive industries, such as textile, clothing and light manufacturing. But, industrial restructuring in general has been quite modest, so that, since the early 1980s, after Greece entered into the European Community's space, a prolonged period of relative industrial decline took place. This is reflected in Greece's trade composition: almost half of overall exports consists of agricultural and other raw materials, while the share of export of industrial products has remained almost the same over the past fifteen years. The import share of industrial goods did not change significantly either, revealing stagnation in industrial transformation process.

The fact that the trade specialization pattern did not display significant changes suggests that Greek comparative advantages *vis-à-vis* the market economies are still based on traditional labor-intensive industries and resource-intensive products. By the mid-1990s, Greek specialization was still dominated by non-industrial products. Food industries made a positive contribution to the trade balance over the period. On the other hand, specialized suppliers (industrial machinery) and science-based goods remained highly negative.

The overall share of scale-intensive, specialized supplier and science-based sectors in Greek exports (a proxy for the technological content of trade pattern) has been extremely low in the past. In the early 1970s, it was around 15 per cent, and remained relatively stagnant over the entire period, up to the first half of the 1990s (almost 15.5 per cent). Even more so, the index of intra-industry trade does not show any significant improvement. This confirms the persistent low technological capability of the Greek economy, both in terms of product and process innovation potential.

4. Trade specialization, technological change and economic performance: A few stylized facts

Given the very different patterns followed by the three groups of economies considered in the previous section, it is not easy to provide an overall evaluation of their evolutions. In what follows, let us try to depict some stylized facts derived from the patterns observed, and relate them to the thematic issues discussed in Section 2 of the paper.

First, we need to sum up first the main features of the performances of the three groups of countries. South-East Asian NICs had a very successful growth and trade performances up to the first half of the 1990s, combined with changing and upgrading their trade composition in the course of the 1980s towards higher value-added and increased technological intensity of goods and sectors. After a short experience of import substitution in the 1950s, all the countries in this group shifted towards trade openness accompanied by various industrial and technological policies. Within this common context, however, there were different patterns for each Asian NIC and the recent crisis also affected each one very differently. As a result, each economy had an individual pattern of export growth, industrialization, technological progress, reliance on FDI and policy interventions.

The second group of countries, the Mediterranean NICs, more specifically Turkey and Tunisia, experienced significant changes in terms of trade specialization and composition in the course of the 1980s in relation with a process of trade openness. Their trade specialization shifted from raw materials and agricultural products towards industrial products, mostly 'traditional' labor-intensive exports. In more recent years however, they registered a much less favorable trade performance and their trade specialization remained locked into less dynamic medium–high technology intensive exports where competitiveness rests primarily on relatively cheap labor costs.

Latin American NICs have performed differently from the other two groups, particularly in relation to structural change and technological upgrading of their production structure. Its trade specialization is, at present, still based on relatively abundant natural resources, such as exports of raw materials and resource-intensive goods. Also, Latin American NICs had very different patterns one to another. Furthermore, in more recent years they had stronger trade performances, especially in the case of Mexico where more trade openness has been accompanied by progress in medium–high technology intensive exports and higher intra-industry trade.

There is no doubt that if we define countries' long-run competitiveness as positive performance in the world market combined with a capacity to sustain economic growth through balance-of-payment equilibrium over a long period of time, wide differences characterize the three groups of countries in their ability to compete in the world economy. These differences can be attributed not only to their different factor endowments, but also to their different accumulated industrial and technological capabilities.

In this regard, one should emphasize that a country's industrial and technological deepening could assume three different forms, such as: (i) a technological upgrading of product and processes within the same industry; (ii) greater local content through an increase of local inputs and linkages; and (iii) entry into progressively more technologically complex new activities (Justman and Teubal 1991; Lall 1995). In other words, countries can exploit their existing strengths in terms of static comparative–competitive advantages and/or can search for new areas of competence in relation to their dynamic advantages. The composite mix of a country's industrialization process is very important since there are systematic differences in productivity and value-added across industrial sectors. Industrial activities also differ between one another by implying distinct 'learning costs' that rise with the degree of technological sophistication, the spread of production linkages and increases in the level of technological capability. The taxonomy adopted here tries to reflect these differences in terms of different technological opportunities, sources and appropriate conditions across industrial sectors (Pavitt 1984; Dosi *et al.* 1990; Guerrieri 1992; Guerrieri and Tylecote 1997).

All this implies that the evolution of industrial structure and the consequent trade specialization do matter to countries' economic growth. The progressive industrial and technological deepening is a crucial part of economic development and is an evolutionary cumulative process that is country specific. Industrial technological modernization therefore is not inevitable. In effect, the tacit, specific and cumulative nature of industrial and technological change can lead – and has historically led to – different divergent accumulation rates, technological capability changes and development paths across countries. The three groups of countries in our sample seem to fully confirm this. Although characterized by common trade openness, countries in our sample have followed very distinct industrialization experiences and trade specialization patterns. Their industrialization paths were characterized by a different mix and sequence of structural changes that in very different ways have upgraded and diversified their production structures.

They also show that trade openness is certainly important, but is not at all a sufficient condition for this progressive industrial and technological deepening. The most successful countries are those that have been able to better exploit trade opportunities over the past two decades. The Asian NICs in particular had very high growth rates combined with strong export growth. But it is an open question as to how the two outcomes were combined and what the direction of causality between the two really is.

In standard neoclassical frameworks, a country's industrial and technological deepening is a market driven result, stemming from trade openness and outward-oriented growth. In these models, the more efficient resource allocation over time is entirely driven by market incentives (relative prices) according to changing factor endowments and evolving country comparative advantages (domestic versus world prices). A specific country's trade specialization is not an issue in this approach, as long as markets are open and efficient, and factor prices change to reflect changing factor endowments. Nor do technological characteristics of different activities matter as technology is freely available and it is freely and instantly absorbed. All that does matter is that returns are equalized across countries. The appeal of opening up to international markets is thus based on the strong promise that international economic integration will promote efficient structural change and improve economic performance. The problem is that there is no sound evidence that openness produces these results given the more articulated linkages between industrialization and economic development.

In a different perspective, such as an 'evolutionary approach', the patterns and impact of trade openness differ greatly across countries, especially according to the different policies these countries can adopt (Nelson 1993; Lall 1995). In this framework, the generation of comparative advantages is a more articulated process in which the accumulation of physical capital interacts with the development of skill and technological capability (Dosi *et al.* 1990; Bell and Pavitt 1995). Within this context, progressive industrial and technological deepening requires a set of conditions, and includes interactive roles and strategies by firms, governments and institutions of individual countries.

One could reconcile, however, the two explanations by assuming, first, that trade openness is able to provide a set of efficient incentives (price structure) for industrial deepening. So, for most developing economies in our sample, trade liberalization reforms were very helpful to restructure their production systems. But, the ability to respond to these incentives crucially depends on the skills and knowledge of the firms concerned, on the measures to overcome the market failures affecting structural change in developing economies, and on the rate of generation diffusion of technology that is not freely accessible.

As shown by the three groups of countries considered, many factors can contribute to explain the different capabilities of individual countries to cope with the needed requirements of positive industrial technological deepening. First of all, macroeconomics has played an important role. There is nothing inherently prone to stability and balance-of-payment equilibrium in an open trade regime, as the payments crisis suffered by many export-oriented countries in our sample fully confirm. Therefore, sound macroeconomic policies should be considered fundamental ingredients in order to avoid instability and foreign exchange crises, and also to maintain factor costs in line with those of other competitors. But, macroeconomic stability, in terms of trade balance and a favorable competitiveness pattern, is not only the result of good macroeconomic policy combined with trade openness as in the standard model. A growing literature, both theoretical and empirical, has emphasized the important microeconomic foundations of macroeconomic stability.

This literature emphasizes the importance of investment and capital accumulation. Many empirical studies have shown that investment is key to economic growth. Cross-country regression analyses have proved that physical investment is one of the strongest determinants of growth (Levine and Renelt 1992). Also in our sample the most successful countries in terms of economic growth were those that in the period considered had very high rates of capital accumulation. Certainly there is no single way of raising the rate of accumulation. Anyway, one should recognize that the financial system, in collecting and allocating resources from savers to firms who can make productive use of them, plays a very important role. A third important factor to strengthen the relationship between trade openness and economic growth is technology and technological change. As already noted, dynamic efficiency does not follow automatically from capital accumulation, but depends heavily on domestic capabilities for generating and managing technical change in production activities. Technological capability therefore is not an automatic by-product of investment and production. Technological change is accumulated through conscious and continuous investment by firms in specialized, change-generating activities (Bell and Pavitt 1995). To create these endogenous sources of technological accumulation, a 'supply-side' upgrading clearly has a vital role to play in countries' industrial development. It depends on firm-specific variable, on the one hand, but also on the effectiveness of specialized support institutions in providing technological knowledge and training incentives.

In this regard, market mechanisms alone are unlikely to be sufficient. Left to itself, the market underprovides technology. Investment in technology is considerably riskier than other types of investment, and there are much larger asymmetries of information that can impede the effective workings of the market. So without industrial and technological policies, there will be too little investment in the production and adoption of new technology. Policy interventions should not be directed to pick up the winners in advance, but to overcome market failures in resource allocation and create favorable conditions for firm restructuring and upgrading.

To this technological 'upgrading', another important contribution could come from closer integration and links of local firms and sectors with major enterprises of advanced countries within the context of global network. In our sample of countries, various channels were used to strengthen these connections. Emerging countries, in particular in Asia and to a certain extent in Latin America, have performed positively in terms of FDI inflows. In contrast, other countries like the

Mediterranean NICs (i.e. Greece and Turkey) have not seen a large influx of FDI, despite the favorable legislation introduced to attract FDI. On the other hand, in many sectors, especially in traditional goods (mostly textile-clothing and leather-footwear), non-equity-based linkages such as subcontracting activities and outward processing (OPT) of firms had significantly contributed to the rapid expansion of the trade, as in the case of Tunisia and Turkey (Hoekman and Djankov 1996).

Both FDI and non-equity linkages can produce advantages for the local economies by developing 'backward linkages' and integrating local firms into networks of large foreign firms, by contributing to improve local levels of managerial, organizational and technical skills, and by favoring the development of new comparative advantages. But in order to benefit from these opportunities, countries must upgrade their domestic skills, firm organization and infrastructures. Again, the potential benefits are neither incorporated in, nor automatically derived from, FDI and the entry of foreign firms.

5. Concluding remarks

The long-term trade performances and specialization of three groups of countries in Latin America, East Asia and Mediterranean region were analyzed in this chapter. The three groups have been all characterized by significant trade openness over the past two decades, although to different extents and in different periods. Each had a different pattern of export performance, trade specialization and economic growth.

Southeast Asian NICs had a very successful growth and trade record up to the first half of the 1990s, combined with changes and upgrades of their trade composition in the course of the 1980s. The recent crisis in East Asia cannot be a refutation of its remarkable results in the past. Nonetheless, each Asian NIC has followed different patterns, and the recent crisis also affected each very differently. The second group of countries, the Mediterranean NICs, and more specifically Turkey and Tunisia, experienced significant changes in terms of their trade composition, but in more recent years they registered a much less favorable trade performance and structural change. Latin American NICs performed differently from the other two groups, particularly with regard to their technological upgrading of production activities. Mediterranean and Latin American NICs had very distinct development patterns and performances.

The effects of trade openness and liberalization on countries' economic performances therefore appear to be, to a large extent, indeterminate in our case studies. In our sample, the countries that experienced positive economic performances have all succeeded with their own specific economic policies. The set of complementary policies adopted by countries at the micro-level were crucial in determining a positive result from trade liberalization. In this regard, essential ingredients are represented by macroeconomic stability, domestic investment and technological changes.

The point here is not to deny the role of trade openness for economic development. It can be a source of many economic benefits. There is also evidence of a positive relationship between trade openness and growth in some cases in our sample. But, one should not overemphasize what openness can accomplish. It is important to outline the various and indirect mechanisms by which trade openness is linked with, and can stimulate, economic growth. In this perspective, trade can be considered a facilitator of growth, but it does not do so automatically. Making trade openness work depends on the country's ability to create strong domestic competitive environments and implement effective economic policies.

All this seems to suggest that to investigate the connections between trade openness and economic development needs a more pragmatic approach. We must rely on the lessons and the guidance that come from a careful consideration of cross-country experiences. This is an area of research that needs to be pursued further in the near future.

Notes

1 Especially in the group of raw materials, the market shares in world exports of Latin American NICs showed a significant increase in the period from the mid-1980s up to the mid-1990s, nearly doubling also Latin American trade surpluses (standardized) (see Tables 9.9 and 9.2).

2 One should add that only in these two industrial categories was Brazil able to significantly increase its share in world industrial exports in the 1980s.

3 By the early 1970s the Asian NICs market shares accounted for a little more than 2.4 percentage points of world exports. By the late 1980s this figure had more than tripled, and throughout the first half of the 1990s has increased so significantly that by the mid-1990s, it was around 10.8 per cent of the world export (see Table 9.8).

4 The increasing role of traditional sectors in the 1980s could be attributed both to privileged access to European markets for textiles and garments, and to a massive increase in subcontracting (OPT), licenses and joint ventures by Western European firms, while production was mainly in the hands of local firms. FDI had a marginal role in manufacturing, aside from the automotive industry. In this regard, Turkey had a low intra-industry trade intensity in comparison with the other NICs.

References

Amendola, G., Guerrieri, P. and Padoan, P. C. (1992) 'International Patterns of Technological Accumulation and Trade', *Journal of International and Comparative Economics* 1(1): 173–97.

Amsden, A. H. (1989) *Asia's Next Giant: South Korea and Late Industrialization*. Oxford: Oxford University Press.

Arthur, B. (1990) 'Positive Feed-backs in the Economy', *Scientific American* 262: 92–9.

Baldwin, R. E. (1992) 'Measurable Dynamic Gains from Trade', *Journal of Political Economy* 100(1): 162–74.

Beckerman, W. H. (1962) 'Projecting Europe's Growth', *Economic Journal* 72(4): 912–25.

Bell, M. and Pavitt, K. (1995) 'The Development of Technological Capability', in I. Haque (ed.), *Trade, Technology and International Competitiveness*. Washington: World Bank.

Bisang, R. and Kosakoff, B. (1995) 'Tres etapas en la búsqueda de una especialización sustentable: exportaciones industriales argentinas, 1974–1993', *CEPAL Documento de Trabajo*, No. 59.

Borrus, M. (1993) 'The Regional Architecture of Global Electronics: Trajectories, Linkages and Access to Technology', in P. Gourevitch and P. Guerrieri (eds), *New Challenges to International Cooperation. Adjustment of Firms, Policies, and Organizations to Global Competition*. San Diego: University of California.

Coe, D. T. and Helpman, E. (1995) 'International R&D Spillovers', *European Economic Review* 39(5): 859–87.

Doherty, E. (ed.) (1995) *Japanese Investment in Asia. International Production Strategies in a Rapidly Changing World*. San Francisco: The Asia Foundation and The Berkeley Roundtable on the International Economy.

Dollar, D. (1992) 'Outward-oriented Developing Economies Really Do Grow More Rapidly:Evidence from 95 LDCs, 1976–1985', *Economic Development and Cultural Change* 40(3): 523–44.

Dosi, G., Freeman, C., Nelson, R., Silverberg, G. and Soete, L. (eds) (1988) *Technical Change and Economic Theory*. London: Frances Pinter.

Dosi, G., Pavitt, K. and Soete, L. (1990) *The Economics of Technical Change and International Trade*. Brighton: Wheatsheaf.

Dowrick, S. (1997) 'Trade and Growth: A Survey, in Technology and International Trade', in J. Fagerberg *et al.*, P. Hanson, L. Lundberg and A. Melchior, (eds), *Technology and International Trade*. Cheltenham, UK and Brookfield, US: Edward Elgar.

Edwards, S. (1993) 'Openness, Trade Liberalization, and Growth in Developing Countries', *Journal of Economic Literature* 31(3): 1358–93.

Edwards, S. (1998) 'Openness, Productivity and Growth: What Do We Really Know?', *Economic Journal* 108(3): 383–98.

Ernst, D. and Guerrieri, P. (1998) 'International Production Networks and Changing Trade Patterns in East Asia: The Case of the Electronic Industry', *Oxford Development Studies* 26(2): 191–212.

Fagerberg, J. (1988) 'International Competitiveness', *Economic Journal* 98: 355–74.

Fagerberg, J. (1996) 'Heading for Divergence? Regional Growth in Europe Considered', *Journal of Common Market Studies* 34(3): 431–49.

Freeman, C. (1982) *The Economics of Industrial Innovation*. London: Frances Pinter.

Fritsch, W. and Franco, G. (1991) 'Competition and Industrial Policies in a Technologically Dependent Economy: The Emerging Issues for Brazil,' *Revista Brasileira de Economia*, 45: 1, 69–90.

Grossman, G. M. and Helpman, E. (1991) *Innovation and Growth in the Global Economy* Cambridge, MA: MIT Press.

Guerrieri, P. (1992) 'Technological and Trade competition: The Changing Position of US, Japan and Germany', in M. C. Harris and G. E. Moore (eds), *Linking Trade and Technology Policies*. Washington, DC: National Academy Press.

Guerrieri, P. (1993) 'Patterns of Technological Capability and International Trade Performance: An Empirical Analysis', in M. Kreinin (ed.), *The Political Economy of International Commercial Policy: Issues for the 1990s*. London: Taylor & Francis.

Guerrieri, P. (1995) *Trade Integration and Changing specialization Patterns in the East Asia Electronics Industry*, Mimeo, Berkeley and University of Rome.

Guerrieri, P. and Tylecote, A. (1997) 'Interindustry Differences in Technical Change and National Patterns of Technological Accumulation', in C. Edquist (ed.), *Systems of Innovation: Technologies, Institutions and Organizations*. London and Washington, DC: Pinter.

Hoekman, B. and Djankov, S. (1996) 'Intra-industry Trade, Foreign Direct Investment and the Reorientation of East Euroepan Exports', *CEPR Discussion Papers*, No. 1377.

Johnson, H. G. (1958) *International Trade and Economic Growth: Studies in Pure Theory*. London: Allan.

Justman, M. and Teubal, M. (1991) 'A Structuralist Perspective on the Role of Technology in Economic Growth and Development', *World Development* 19(9): 212–41.

Kaldor, N. (1970) 'Conflicts in National Economic Objectives', *Economic Journal* 81(321): 1–16.

Kaldor, N. (1981) 'The Role of Increasing Returns, Technical Progress and Cumulative Causation in the Theory and of International Trade and Economic Growth', *Economie Appliquée* 34: 593–617.

Krugman, P. (1992) 'Technology and International Competition: A Historical Perspective', in M. Harris and G. E. Moore (eds), *Linking Trade and Technology Policies*. Washington, DC: National Academy of Engineering.

Lall, S. (1995) 'The Creation of Comparative Advantage: Country Experiences', in I. Haque (ed.), *Trade, Technology and International Competitiveness*. Washington, DC: World Bank.

Landesman, M. and Burgstaller, R. (1997) 'Vertical Product Differentiation in EU Markets: The Relative Position of East European Producers', *WIIW Research Reports* 72.

Levine, R. and Renelt, D. (1992) 'A Sensitivity Analysis of Cross-country Growth Regressions', *American Economic Review* 82(4): 942–63.

Lucas R. E. Jr. (1988) 'On the Mechanics of Economic Development', *Journal of Monetary Economics* 22: 3–42.

Nelson, R. (ed.) (1993) *National Innovation System*. New York: Oxford University Press.

OECD (1992) *Technology and the Economy: The Key Relationship*. Paris: OECD.

Pavitt, K. (1984) 'Sectoral Patterns of Technical Change: Toward a Taxonomy and Theory', *Research Policy* 13: 343–73.

Pavitt, K. (1988) 'International Patterns of Technological Accumulation', in N. Hood and J. E. Vahlne (eds), *Strategies in Global Competition*. London: Croom Helm.

Porter, M. (1990) *The Competitive Advantages of Nations*. London: Macmillan.

Rodriguez, F. and Rodrik, D. (1999) 'Trade Policy and Economic Growth: A Skeptic's Guide to the Cross-National Evidence', *Economic Research Forum Working Paper*, No. 9912.

Romer, P. (1994) 'Endogenous Technological Change', *Journal of Political Economy* 98(2): S71–S102.

Rosenberg, N. (1982) *Inside the Black Box*. Cambridge: Cambridge University Press.

Scherer, F. M. (1982) 'Inter-industry Technology Flows in the United States', *Research Policy* 11: 227–45.

Soete, L. (1987) 'The Impact of Technological Innovation on International Trade Patterns: The Evidence Reconsidered', *Research Policy* 16(4): 101–130.

Thirlwall, A. P. (1979) 'The Balance of Payments Constraint as an Explanation of International Growth Rate Differences', *Banca Nazionale del Lavoro Quarterly Review* 128(791): 45–53.

Urata, S. (1993) 'Japanese Foreign Direct Investment and its Effect on Foreign Trade in Asia', in T. Ito and A. O. Krueger (eds), *Trade and Protectionism*. Chicago: The University of Chicago Press.

Verspagen, B. (1992) 'Endogenous Innovation in Neoclassical Models: A Survey', *Journal of Macroeconomics* 14(4): 631–62.

Von Hippel, E. (1988) *The Source of Innovation*. New York: Oxford University Press.

Wade, R. (1990) *Governing the Market: Economic Theory and the Role of Government in East Asian Industrialization*. Princeton: Princeton University Press.

Young, A. (1991) 'Learning by Doing and the Dynamic Effects of International Trade', *Quarterly Journal of Economics* 106: 369–405.

10 Trade specialization and economic growth[1]

Jaime Ros

1. Introduction

The central question addressed in this chapter is how the pattern of trade specialization can affect long-term economic growth performance. This issue has received little attention in theoretical analysis and empirical studies. Standard trade theory has been interested on the question of how growth – through the changing composition of factor endowment – affects comparative advantages and thus the trade pattern. It has had little to say, however, on the causal links we are interested here, i.e. those running from trade specialization to growth. Neither has modern growth theory paid much attention to this issue. Neoclassical growth theory focuses on the role of factor accumulation, i.e. investment rates in physical and human capital as well as labor force growth. Moreover, its assumption of a constant returns to scale technology leaves little room for economic structure to affect the growth rate. Recent endogenous growth models have brought increasing returns into growth theory but the level of aggregation assumed in these models has led them to focus on factors other than the pattern of specialization. Growth empirics, inspired by these two brands of growth theory, has at most looked (without much success) at how trade openness, rather than trade specialization, may affect differences in growth rates among countries. There is thus a theoretical as well as an empirical gap to fill in this important area.

All this is not to say that there has been complete neglect. In the old literature on trade and in new trade theory, there is a significant list of contributions that are all relevant to our topic – on infant industry protection, the Prebisch–Singer thesis on the terms of trade of primary products, immiserizing growth, and multi-sector growth models with different rates of learning in new trade theory. In looking at how the pattern of specialization can affect growth, a common feature of these contributions is that the pattern of specialization of an economy, as determined by comparative advantages associated with the current factor endowment or locked in by historical accident, may be different from the pattern of specialization that yields the largest long-term economic benefits. This may occur because the economy's static comparative advantage does not coincide with its dynamic comparative advantage in the presence of, for example, technological externalities due to learning by doing, or because the evolution of the terms of trade is such that the

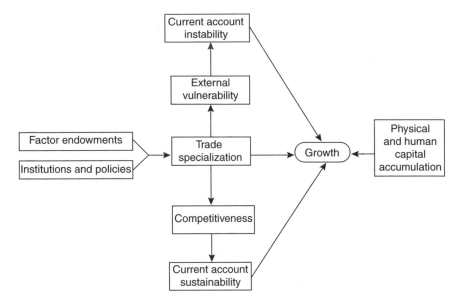

Figure 10.1 Determinants of growth and macro-linkages between trade
        specialization and growth.

economy would benefit from departing from specialization according to comparative advantage. The basic insights from these contributions are well known and we shall largely ignore them except in the empirical part of the chapter.[2]

The main motivation of the chapter comes from another way through which the pattern of specialization can affect the long-term growth rate. This is when a given factor endowment does not determine a unique pattern of specialization and the different patterns of specialization consistent with the same resource endowment have different dynamic implications. This may be due to learning by doing externalities associated to one or the other of the different patterns or to the different linkages with the non-traded sectors associated with these patterns. In any case, there is no conflict here between static and dynamic comparative advantage that can in principle be satisfactorily resolved by a perfect capital market. The source of the problem, when the economy specializes in the less dynamic pattern, is a coordination failure. Recent models following this approach are Rodrik (1994), Rodriguez-Clare (1996), Ciccone and Matsuyama (1996), Skott and Ros (1997) and Ros (1998, chapter 9).

Along with these direct links between trade specialization and growth, there are other, more indirect links that deserve attention.[3] One operates through current account instability to the extent that different patterns of specialization are more or less vulnerable to external shocks. The other operates through current account sustainability, given that different patterns of specialization and growth may be subject to more or less recurrent foreign exchange constraints. These links are presented in Figure 10.1, along with the determinants of growth emphasized by traditional theory and the direct links discussed above.

The chapter is organized as follows. Section 2 discusses the determinants of the pattern of specialization in a standard neoclassical model and in an extended model with increasing returns to scale. This is followed in Section 3 by a discussion of the micro-linkages between trade specialization and growth. The theoretical discussion there is complemented in Section 4 with an empirical analysis of a cross section of developing countries, which includes most of the countries for which case studies were undertaken in the context of the trade and competitiveness project. Section 5, on the macro-linkages between trade specialization and growth, presents an empirical analysis of the links between current account volatility and borrowing constraints, trade specialization and growth performance. A concluding section summarizes the main points and findings of the chapter.

2. International trade theory and the pattern of specialization

In textbook neoclassical theory, the pattern of specialization is uniquely determined by factor endowments in the sense that, independent of initial conditions, the economy converges to a pattern of specialization that can be fully explained by the economy's factor endowments. At the other extreme of the theoretical spectrum, some new trade theory models treat productivity growth as the result of learning by doing and assume away factor endowments as a determinant of comparative advantage (see e.g. Krugman 1987). The pattern of specialization cannot be determined independent of initial conditions and history. Accidents, i.e. real shocks like a temporary resource boom or monetary shocks like a temporary currency overvaluation, are then all important in its influence on the pattern of trade specialization. Industrial policy also becomes crucial in acquiring new comparative advantages independently of factor endowment. This section discusses the assumptions under which these different possibilities can arise. It is useful to begin with a standard neoclassical model.

The pattern of specialization in a small open economy with two tradable goods

Consider an economy that produces two tradable goods (A and B), for which the economy is a price taker in international markets. Technology in these sectors features constant returns to scale and is assumed, for simplicity, to be Cobb–Douglas as in eqns (10.1a,b):

$$A = K_A^a I^{1-a} \tag{10.1a}$$

$$B = K_B^b L_B^{1-b} \tag{10.1b}$$

where A and B are the quantities produced of the two goods, K_A and K_B are the capital input in each sector, L_B is the input of labor in sector B and I is the input of a non-traded good into sector A. The non-traded good (I) is produced with labor (L_I) under constant returns: $I = L_I$.

Competitive conditions are assumed in all three sectors. Given the assumptions about technology and market structure, we can think of sectors A and I as a vertically integrated sector using capital (invested in sector A) and labor (employed in sector I). We shall refer, in this section, to this integrated sector as sector A. As shown in the Appendix, employment in sectors A and B is a log-linear negative function of the product wage and a positive function of the capital stock in sectors A and B, respectively. The profit rates in sectors A and B are log-linear negative functions of the product wage in the respective sectors. Because by assumption A is the capital good, the profit rate in sector B is also a function of the terms of trade (p_B/p_A). The output elasticity of capital is assumed to be higher in sector A than in sector B $(a>b)$. This implies that for the same of the product wage, sector A is always more capital intensive than sector B.

Labor market equilibrium

Equilibrium in the labor market implies a uniform wage and the full employment of the labor force. Consider what happens to the equilibrium wage when, keeping the overall stock of capital constant, capital is reallocated from sector B to sector A. At any given initial wage, the reduction of the capital stock in sector B causes a fall in labor demand in this sector, while the higher capital stock in sector A causes an increase in employment in sector I.

Holding the wage constant and using the labor demand functions for L_I and L_B (see Appendix), the reduction in employment in sector B and the increase in employment in sector I are given by eqns (10.2a,b):

$$-\mathrm{d}L_B = [(1 - b)\, p_B/w]^{1/b}(-\mathrm{d}K_B), \tag{10.2a}$$

$$\mathrm{d}L_I = [(1 - a)\, p_A/w]^{1/a}\, \mathrm{d}K_A, \tag{10.2b}$$

with $-\mathrm{d}K_B = \mathrm{d}K_A$, since by assumption the reallocation leaves the aggregate capital stock intact. Whether the change creates excess supply or demand for labor depends of course on whether the reduction of employment in sector B is more or less than the increase in employment in sector I (i.e. on the size of $-\mathrm{d}L_B$ compared to $\mathrm{d}L_I$). The answer depends on the technological parameters a and b as well as the terms of trade (pB/pA). More precisely, unless high terms of trade for sector A make this sector less capital intensive than sector B, the effect of the technological parameters $(a>b)$ implies that the fall in labor demand in the labor-intensive sector B is larger than the increase in labor demand in sector I. A reallocation of capital from sector B to sector A tends to create excess supply of labor and this requires a fall in the wage in order to clear the labor market. We assume in what follows this to be the case. The reader may check that the analysis of the opposite case (when the reallocation creates excess demand for labor) is symmetrical.

Figure 10.2 illustrates how the market equilibrium wage behaves as capital is reallocated to sector A. Formally, this schedule of labor market equilibrium

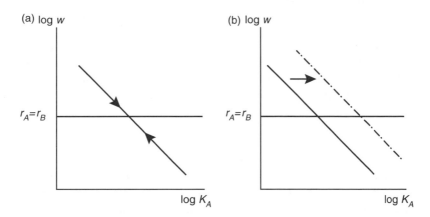

Figure 10.2 The pattern of specialization in a neoclassical trade model.

is obtained by substituting from the labor demand functions into the full employment condition. The schedule slopes downwards in (w, K_A) space since an increase in K_A (and a fall in K_B) creates excess supply of labor, under the conditions assumed, and this requires a fall in the wage to clear the labor market. Along the schedule the overall stock of capital is held constant. A change in the overall capital stock thus shifts the position of the schedule. For example, an increase in the capital stock, holding the overall labor force constant, shifts the locus upwards: intuitively, a higher overall capital–labor ratio raises the market-clearing value of the wage for each given allocation of the capital stock.

Capital market equilibrium

Capital is mobile between sectors A and B. Capital market equilibrium requires the full employment of the aggregate capital stock and a uniform profit rate in the two capital-using sectors. Just as we did for the schedule of labor market equilibrium, we can derive a schedule of capital market equilibrium by substituting from the profit rate functions into the condition for profit rate equalization. In (w, K_A) space, this schedule shows, at each given value of the wage, the value of K_A, and the corresponding allocation of the capital stock, that yields the same profit rate in sectors A and B. Under our present assumptions, there is a unique value of the wage, independent of the capital stock in sector A, that satisfies the condition for profit rate equalization. This value depends on technological parameters and the terms of trade but not on factor endowments. A shift in the terms of trade in favor of the labor-intensive sector (sector B) increases the value of the wage required for profit rate equalization.

What happens when the economy is off the locus of capital market equilibrium? The profit rates in the two sectors clearly cannot be equal. If the wage is higher than its value on the schedule of capital market equilibrium, the profit rate in the capital-intensive sector is higher than in the labor-intensive sector (intuitively, the higher wage reduces the profit rate of the labor-intensive sector to a larger extent than in the capital-intensive one). Capital will thus flow towards the capital-intensive sector (A). Below the schedule, the low wage implies that the profitability of the labor-intensive sector is higher and capital thus flows towards sector B. With labor market equilibrium obtaining at all times, and given the negative slope of this schedule, the allocation at the intersection of the two loci is then stable (Figure 10.2).

The structure of this economy, and the associated pattern of specialization, depend on technology and the terms of trade as well as on factor endowments: the overall capital stock and the total labor force, both of which affect the position of the schedule of labor market equilibrium. Thus, as the capital stock increases, the labor market equilibrium schedule shifts up and more capital and labor are allocated to the capital-intensive sector (see Figure 10.2b). The overall capital–labor ratio increases and as a result the economy allocates more resources to its capital-intensive sector. With no technical progress – so that the capital market equilibrium schedule does not shift – the wage remains constant throughout this process *as long as* the economy remains incompletely specialized.[4] The reason is that with constant returns to scale in sector B, employment in this sector provides an elastic labor supply to sector A. It is only when the economy has fully specialized in sector A that the wage will tend to increase as a result of the excess demand for labor generated by capital accumulation.

The pattern of specialization in an extended model with increasing returns

The model just discussed has a clear-cut answer to the question of what determines the pattern of specialization. Given the technology, the terms of trade and the endowment of factors, there is a unique allocation of resources that satisfies the conditions of equilibrium in the labor and capital markets. This section extends the model in the previous section to show that, under slightly more general assumptions, the analysis of the pattern of specialization suffers from a fundamental indeterminacy that opens the door to the role of other determinants, including institutional factors and policies. This extension can be seen as an amended neoclassical model which allows for the presence of increasing returns in the production of non-traded inputs or, alternatively, as a new trade theory model – such as Krugman's (1987) analysis of the 'competitive consequences of Mrs Thatcher' – which abandons the assumption of a Ricardian technology and allows for the presence of non-traded goods.

The only change with respect to the assumptions made in the previous section refers to sector I. The output of this sector (I) represents now a set of differentiated intermediate goods. Production of these intermediate inputs is subject to internal economies of scale and undertaken by firms operating under conditions of monopolistic competition and facing downward-sloping demand curves. As shown in the Appendix, this change has two consequences. First, employment in sector *I* depends, along with the capital stock and the wage in sector *I* measured in terms of *A*-goods, on the number of producers and the extent to which returns increase, both of which affect the efficiency with which the *I*-goods are produced. Second, the profit rate in sector *A* is now not only an inverse function of the product wage but, given this wage, a positive function of the capital stock invested in this sector. This positive effect of the capital stock is due to the presence of increasing returns in sector *I*. Indeed, a higher capital stock in sector *A* raises the demand and output for *I*-goods; the higher scale of output implies an increase in productivity which, given the wage, reduces the relative price of intermediate goods (in terms of *A*-goods) and thus increases the profit rate in sector *A*.

Labor market equilibrium

As before, equilibrium in the labor market implies a uniform wage and full employment of the labor force. Consider now what happens to the equilibrium wage as capital is reallocated from sector *B* to sector *A*. The fall in labor demand in sector *B* is the same as before. Using the demand function for L_I (see the Appendix), the increase in employment in sector *I* at the initial wage is now given by 10.3:

$$dL_I = \left[\left(\frac{1}{n} \right)^{1-f} G \frac{p_A}{w} \right]^{1/f} \left(\frac{a}{f} \right) K_A \left(\frac{a}{f} \right)^{-1} dK_A. \tag{10.3}$$

Whether the change creates excess supply or demand for labor (the size of $-dL_B$ compared to dL_I) depends now on the level of K_A,[5] i.e. on the initial allocation of the capital stock. When the capital stock invested in sector *A* is small, sector *I* is also small and produces at high costs, given the presence of economies of scale in this sector. The relative price of intermediate inputs (p_I/p_A) being very high, demand for *I*-goods is low and the capital intensity in sector *A* (given by the ratio K_A/I) is very high despite K_A being small in absolute value. With a high capital intensity, an increase in the capital stock in sector *A* has small indirect employment effects in sector *I*. The fall in labor demand in sector *B* is then larger than the increase in labor demand in sector *I*. A reallocation of capital from sector *B* to sector *A* thus tends to create excess supply of labor and this requires a fall in the wage to clear the labor market.

In contrast, when the capital stock invested in sector *A* is large, the indirect employment effects of the expansion of sector *A* can offset the fall in labor demand in sector *B*. The scale of output in sector *I* is now large and this has the effect of making this sector more productive. This higher productivity reduces the relative price of intermediate goods and, as a result, the capital intensity in sector *A* is smaller. With a low K_A/I ratio, the expansion of sector *A* at the expense of sector *B* can then have the effect of generating excess demand for labor and increasing the market clearing wage.

The schedule of labor market equilibrium in ($\log w, \log K_A$) is now U-shaped. The slope of the schedule is negative, tending to zero, at low levels of K_A and becomes positive, tending to '*a*', at high levels of K_A (provided that such high

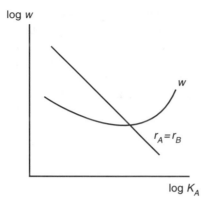

Figure 10.3 Multiple equilibria in a model with increasing returns.

values exist given the size of the overall capital stock). The equilibrium value of the wage first falls as K_A increases, and eventually rises, becoming an increasing function of K_A (Figure 10.3).

Capital market equilibrium

The condition for profit rate equalization yields, as before, the schedule of capital market equilibrium by substitution from the profit rate functions. The new feature is that the value of the wage required for profit rate equalization is no longer independent of the allocation of the capital stock. We now have a locus of (w, K_A) combinations, rather than a unique value of the wage, along which the condition of profit rate equalization is fulfilled. The shape of the schedule depends on how the composition of the capital stock has to change, in order to maintain capital market equilibrium, in the face of an increase in the wage rate. Intuitively, the answer to this question depends on which of the two sectors is more labor intensive, as the higher wage will tend to reduce the profit rate of the labor-intensive sector to a larger extent. The required reallocation would then depend on the effects of K_A on relative profit rates.[6] The problem now is that it is not clear which of the two sectors is more labor intensive directly *and* indirectly. Even though sector A is more capital intensive than sector B (in the sense that $a > b$), the increasing returns parameter (μ) may be large enough to make the 'indirect' labor share of sector A larger than the labor share of sector B. This is due to the presence of increasing returns in sector I, which makes the sum of the capital and labor shares in the integrated A/I sector larger than unity.

We shall carry the analysis on the assumption that the indirect labor share of sector A is less than in sector B.[7] On this assumption, the slope of the schedule of capital market equilibrium is negative (see Figure 10.3): An increase in the wage (given K_A) reduces the profit rate in sector B more than it does in sector A. This requires a fall in K_A (which reduces r_A) to restore the equality of profit rates. The region to the right of the schedule of capital market equilibrium (the $r_A = r_B$ locus) is one in which sector A is more profitable than sector B. This is because it is a region where the capital stock invested in sector A is relatively large and, given the wage, K_A has a positive effect on the relative profitability of sector A through its effect on the productivity of sector I. In this region, capital will be flowing towards sector A and thus K_A/K_B will increase. In contrast, to the left of the schedule the profit rate in sector A is lower than in sector B and capital is flowing towards sector B. It then follows that the capital allocation at the intersection of the two loci is now an *unstable* equilibrium. As shown in Figure 10.3, a capital allocation with more capital in sector A than at the intersection generates a profit rate in sector A higher than in sector B. Capital then moves towards sector A and further depresses the relative profitability of sector B. Analogous mechanisms, in reverse, operate for capital allocations below the intersection.

We can also verify that when the two schedules intersect, this intersection is unique (see the Appendix). It follows then that if an intersection exists, there will be two stable equilibrium allocations in which the whole capital stock is invested in one of the two sectors. In one equilibrium, the economy fully specializes in the production of good B. Since no I sector will exist, not only the capital stock, but the whole labor force is also employed in sector B. We shall refer to this capital and labor allocation as the B-specialization. In the other equilibrium, the economy specializes in the production and export of good A and, since there will be no sector B, the whole labor force is employed in sector I. We call this allocation the A-specialization.

In this economy, a B-specialization always exists whether there are multiple equilibria or not.[8] It follows that the existence of an A-specialization guarantees the existence of an intersection and, therefore, ensures the presence of multiple stable equilibria. As shown in the Appendix, the existence of multiple equilibria depends on the capital–labor endowment and terms of trade. The aggregate capital stock must be sufficiently large so that, when the whole of it is allocated to sector A, the price of intermediate goods, produced under economies of scale, is low enough to make sector A viable. The threshold value of the aggregate capital stock is smaller, the more favorable the terms of trade for sector A, since a higher relative price of A-goods increases the profitability of sector A.[9]

When an A-specialization does not exist because, say, the aggregate capital stock is too small, and thus a unique B-specialization exists, the economy clearly has a comparative advantage in good B and market incentives will lead the economy to specialize in sector B. However, when an A-specialization exists, the existence of multiple patterns of specialization consistent with the same factor endowment makes the notion of comparative advantage equivocal. This indeterminacy opens the door to the role of other factors – related to history, exogenous shocks or institutions and policies – in the determination of the pattern of specialization.

Indeed, initial conditions matter now in a way that was absent in the standard neoclassical model, since depending on the initial allocation of resources the economy will move to one or another of the two patterns of trade specialization and remain locked in that pattern. Temporary shocks brought about by history can also be decisive. Consider, for example, an economy specialized in sector A and suppose that a terms-of-trade shock favorable to sector B makes the A-specialization disappear. The economy specializes in sector B. Then, even if the terms of trade return to their initial level, the economy will remain locked in the B-specialization since this pattern of specialization continues to exist and is a stable equilibrium. The reader will recognize here the concerns with the 'Dutch disease' if we interpret sector B as a resource-intensive sector and sector A as a manufacturing sector. Industrial policy and more generally sector-specific policies can also make a difference even if they are only transitory since by providing sufficient incentives for the reallocation of capital the change in the pattern of specialization will not reverse itself when the policy is dismantled.

3. Direct links between trade specialization and growth

When multiple equilibria exist, does it make a difference to the growth rate of an economy whether it adopts one or the other of the two possible patterns of trade specialization? This is the question addressed in this section. As we shall see, the pattern of specialization, *for the same* factor endowments, can affect growth in two ways: (1) through its effect on the investment share and, thus, the rate of capital accumulation; (2) through the dynamic implications that different allocations of investment may have on the rate of growth. It is worth noting that this second influence is related to the one traditionally addressed by the older literature emphasizing conflicts between static and dynamic comparative advantages and the implications that different resource endowments can have for growth. In this sense, our analysis encompasses and generalizes those more traditional cases.

Two patterns of specialization compared

Suppose that the condition for multiple equilibria is fulfilled and consider two economies, identical in all respects – including capital endowment, size of the labor force, savings rate, rate of depreciation of the capital stock and access to technology – except for their pattern of specialization. For simplicity, assume that there is no growth of the labor force and exogenous technical progress. One economy is specialized in the production and export of good B, the other in the production of goods A and I. Does the fact that the pattern of specialization is different make any difference to their growth rates?

Consider, first, the profit and wage rates in these two economies. As shown in the Appendix, the existence of multiple equilibria ensures that the aggregate capital stock is large enough for the economy with the A-specialization to have an I sector so productive that the rate of profit in this economy is higher than in the economy with the B-specialization. If, in addition, the capital stock is larger than a certain threshold value, the wage rate in the A-specialization is higher than in the B-specialization.

Suppose that this last condition is fulfilled, i.e. the aggregate capital stock is large enough for the wage rate in the A-specialization to be higher than in the B-specialization. As already mentioned, this ensures the existence of multiple equilibria. Since it has a higher wage rate and a higher profit rate (with the same capital endowment), the economy which specializes in the production of A- and I-goods has a higher income per capita than the economy specializing in good B. With identical same savings rates (as well as population growth rates), it would appear according to standard neoclassical growth theory, that the economy with the lower income per capita (the B-specialization) should grow at a faster rate: the parameters determining the steady-state value of income (savings and labor force growth) are the same as in the A-specialization and, since per capita income is lower, the economy would appear to be further away from the steady state than that with the A-specialization. Yet, it is clear that this last economy is the one that grows at the faster rate: with a higher income and the same capital stock and savings rate, its rate of capital accumulation must be higher than in the economy with the B-specialization.

This higher growth rate is the result of the pattern of specialization: it is the associated allocation of the capital stock that raises the rate of capital accumulation for a given investment share (given that for the same capital stock its income level is higher). Moreover, in the presence of international capital mobility this growth advantage is likely to be enhanced since capital will be flowing to the economy with the highest returns to capital and, as we have seen, the existence of multiple equilibria ensures by itself that the profit rate in the A-specialization is higher than in the B-specialization. With a higher profit and capital mobility, the investment share itself is likely to be higher in the A-specialization.

The fact that the higher income per worker does not prevent the second economy from growing faster can be seen from a slightly different perspective. The economy specializing in A- and I-goods is converging to a steady state different from that of the B economy (even leaving aside the fact that the investment share under capital mobility is likely to be higher in the first economy). In this steady state, the capital–output ratio is the same as in the B economy since, by assumption, savings rates and depreciation of the capital stock are the same in both economies. Total output, however, is larger in the economy specializing in sector A. The difference is proportional to the difference in output–capital elasticities in sectors A and B.[10] This steady-state income gap is the result of their different patterns of specialization which appears here thus as an additional determinant of the steady-state level of income.

Further extensions

Our discussion so far has assumed, for simplicity, that the technology available for the production of B-goods does not use intermediate I-goods. How do the properties and conclusions of the model change, when we relax this assumption? Suppose sector B uses intermediate goods (I), although less intensively than sector A. Demand for I-goods will no longer depend exclusively on the capital stock of sector A. The capital invested in sector B will now also affect the demand for I goods and the relative price p_I/p_A of these inputs. The profit rate in sector A will depend not only on K_A and the product wage, but also on K_B and, therefore, on the aggregate capital stock. There will then generally be a sufficiently large capital stock, so that when the whole of it is allocated to sector B, the profit rate in this sector is lower than the profit rate in sector A, evaluated at the market-clearing values of the wage and the relative price of intermediate inputs. At this value of the capital stock, the B-specialization is no longer an equilibrium since sector A is more profitable than sector B, even when K_B is equal to the aggregate capital stock. This implies that, unlike the previous model, it is no longer the case that a B-equilibrium always exists no matter how large the aggregate capital stock.

We have now three configurations. First, over a range of low values of the aggregate capital stock, a unique equilibrium exists. In this equilibrium the economy specializes in trade in the production of good B. A small sector I now coexists with sector B since the technology used requires intermediate inputs. Specialization in this case must be in B, and not in A-goods, because sector B uses intermediate goods less intensively and is thus the only one able to survive under the high costs of production with which the small I sector operates.

Then, over a range of intermediate values of the capital stock, two stable equilibria exist, with specialization in B- and A-goods, respectively. The size of the capital stock is large enough to generate a productive I sector and make sector A viable, but only if capital is invested in sector A. If allocated to sector B, the market for I-goods is insufficient to make it profitable to invest in sector A. In a related model, Rodriguez-Clare (1996) shows that in the A-equilibrium, the profit rate is higher than in the B-equilibrium and the wage rate at least as high. The A-specialization is then unambiguously Pareto superior to the B-specialization, not only for a value of the capital stock above a threshold as in the previous model, but over the whole range values of the capital stock for which multiple equilibria exist.[11] With the same savings rate, the rate of capital accumulation and growth in the A-specialization is also unambiguously higher than in the B-specialization.

Finally, for high values of the capital stock we again have a unique equilibrium. The size of the capital stock is sufficient not only to make sector A viable but to make the B-specialization disappear. The low prices of intermediate goods and high wages make it worthwhile for an individual investor to move away from sector B and start production in sector A. By doing so, intermediate good prices and wages move to reinforce the relative profitability of sector A with eventually all the capital moving away from sector B. This sector is no longer viable at the high wages associated with the large capital–labor ratio in the economy.

Another extension of the model would be to introduce skilled labor and consider differences among sectors in the intensity with which they use skilled labor. This has been done by Rodrik (1994). In Rodrik's model, the sector producing non-tradable inputs under economies of scale is intensive in skilled labor. The level of skills of the work force then plays a role in the existence of multiple equilibria, along with the size of the capital stock. A higher level of skills can partly compensate for the high costs arising from a small market for I-goods and thus reduce the size of the capital stock required for the existence of an A-equilibrium. Similar results follow, if sector A, rather than sector I, is intensive in skilled labor. For example, while the high prices of intermediate goods tend to depress the relative profitability of sector A, when the market for I-goods is small, an abundance of skilled labor tends to raise it, and sector A may be viable depending on the allocation of the capital stock. In any case, multiple equilibria can arise from various combinations of skill levels and capital stocks, rather than simply from an intermediate value of the capital stock.

Policy implications

We are now prepared to address our main concern: the question of whether, and under what conditions, policy-induced changes in the pattern of specialization can effectively increase income per capita and enhance the rate of capital accumulation.

As it is well known, many developing countries have adopted industrial policies in an attempt to accelerate the rate of industrialization and economic growth. The results have been mixed, if we are to judge from the variety of growth performance under similar policies. This explains why the effectiveness of these policies is controversial and why widely different views coexist on whether they made a difference and, if so, whether this was positive or negative. This is the case even though observers and policy makers alike have amply documented the role of industrial policy in fostering a fast rate of industrialization in East Asia (see, on the subject, Amsden 1989; Wade 1989). An important reason for this state of affairs seems to be that consensus is lacking on precisely the key issue of how and under what conditions industrial policy can significantly alter the rate of capital accumulation and growth. The analytical framework developed here helps in clarifying this question.

Industrial policy, the capital stock and the level of skills

It is worth noting, first, that in the more general models discussed above, the economy has a clear comparative advantage in the labor-intensive good B and the capital-intensive good A at low and high levels of the aggregate capital stock, respectively. In both cases a unique equilibrium exists and market incentives lead the economy to specialize in the production of those traded goods in which it has a comparative advantage. This means that when a unique A-equilibrium exists, industrial policy is not needed in order to move the economy towards this pattern of specialization. It also means that when the economy has a unique B-equilibrium, industrial policy can hardly improve on the market outcome. Consider, for instance, a policy attempting to reallocate resources towards sector A in an economy that has a unique B-equilibrium. Suppose that policy succeeds in reallocating the whole of the capital stock towards sector A. Because the A-specialization is not an equilibrium, the wage in this economy would fall compared to that in the B-specialization. The profit rate is also likely to fall, especially if the aggregate capital stock is small and the costs of intermediate goods are high, as a result. With a profit rate in sector A lower than in sector B – evaluated at market wages and prices of intermediate goods – the policy-induced changes in relative prices required to make sector A viable would imply a further reduction of the wage. The A-specialization, in this case, will not feature a growth rate higher than that in the B-specialization. Ultimately, again, this is due to the fact that an A-equilibrium does not exist.

The scope for policy intervention is very different over that range of intermediate levels of the aggregate capital stock that are large enough to make a coordinated development of the A and I industries viable, yet insufficient for any individual firm to be profitable in isolation in sector A. Over this range, the economy is in a transition between different patterns of trade specialization: a transition in which old comparative advantages are being eroded, while the new ones are only slowly emerging. In this transition, as long as the low-level equilibrium exists, market incentives are unlikely to move the economy to the high growth path associated with the superior equilibrium.

The successful policy interventions geared to accelerate this transition are the basis for Rodrik's interpretation of how 'Korea and Taiwan grew rich' (Rodrik 1994). Rodrik argues that, more than their export orientation, the distinguishing feature of these growth experiences was the sharp and sustained increase in their investment rates in the early 1960s. Through an array of government interventions, by subsidizing and coordinating investment decisions, government policy was successful in reallocating resources towards modern capital-intensive industries. With increasing returns in these activities, this reallocation raised the rate of return on capital and pushed the economy into a high growth path. Outward orientation followed, because the higher investment rates increased demand for imported capital goods. The relatively high level of skills of the labor force in both countries was a condition for the success of industrial policy.

The role of the terms of trade

The size of the capital stock and the level of skills are not the only factors affecting the existence of multiple patterns of specialization. As already noted, the existence of multiple equilibria also depends on the terms of trade between A- and B-goods. To illustrate the role of the terms of trade, consider an economy specialized in labor-intensive goods and suppose that, over time, the entry of new low-cost producers in the international market tends to reduce the relative price of B-goods. This has the effect of generating an A-equilibrium without necessarily, at the same time, making the economy move towards this high-level equilibrium. The economy is, in a sense, losing its competitiveness in B-goods, without at the same time acquiring a comparative advantage in A-goods. This may describe the situation of a number of semi-industrialized 'sandwich economies' facing stiff competition from new low-wage producers of labor-intensive goods while still being unable to compete with the more efficient producers of capital-intensive goods in the more industrialized economies. If good B is a primary good, the transition can be interpreted as describing the balance-of-payments problems and, eventually, the beginning of industrialization in resource-abundant countries facing declining terms of trade for their primary exports.

In any of these interpretations, the economy in transition with declining terms of trade is likely to remain largely specialized in the production of the labor-intensive *B*-goods until it eventually achieves the high levels of the capital stock that make sector *A* clearly profitable from the point of view of individual investors (or unless the fall in the price of *B*-goods is large enough to eliminate the *B*-equilibrium). This is so simply because the *B*-specialization is a locally stable equilibrium: no individual investor in isolation will find the investment opportunities in sector *A* more attractive than those existing in sector *B*. In the transition, the economy will suffer a slowdown of its rate of growth, as a result of the decline in the relative price of *B*-goods. As shown by eqns (2) and (11) in the Appendix, the profit rate in this economy is an inverse function of the relative price of *A*-goods. Insofar as the rate of accumulation depends on profitability, the decline in the relative price of *B*-goods will adversely affect capital accumulation and growth. The reduced rate of capital accumulation will in turn prolong the transition towards the capital stock necessary to make *A*-goods spontaneously profitable. Under this 'slow-growth trap', policy intervention can make a substantial difference to the growth rate in the medium term.

4. Trade, investment and growth: An empirical analysis

Trade specialization and growth

The analysis in previous sections suggests two channels through which the pattern of specialization can affect the rate of capital accumulation and growth. First, trade specialization is likely to affect the investment share given that, other things being equal, the rate of return on capital is higher in economies specialized in increasing return industries. Second, at the same level of income per worker, specialization in increasing returns industries is associated with a higher output–capital ratio. The implication is that, for the same investment share, the rate of capital accumulation and growth will be higher when an economy specializes in industries subject to increasing returns. We now turn to an empirical analysis of these relationships.

An important practical question is how to measure the pattern of specialization. As a country's income level increases over time, the trade pattern changes. The economy typically moves from being a net importer of manufactures to being a net exporter of manufactures while manufacturing trade increasingly dominates overall trade. Because the level of income is likely to affect the growth rate in ways independent from the pattern of specialization, we would like to have an indicator of trade specialization, which isolates the effects of resource endowment and policies and adjusts for the influence of income level on the trade pattern.

Such an indicator is available from Chenery and Syrquin (1986). This is their index of trade orientation (TO) which measures the pro-manufacturing bias in the composition of commodity exports after adjusting for the country's income and size.[12] It measures thus the degree to which the economy specializes in manufactures, as influenced by factors other than size and income (i.e. resource endowment and policies). The TO index is available for 1975 and thirty-four countries, most of which were semi-industrialized in the 1970s, and which include most of those considered in the competitiveness project.12 We also consider a smaller sample of twenty-two countries for which the TO index as well as Leamer's ratio of intra-industry trade and other trade characteristics are available. These twenty-two countries were aggregated, according to their TO index, into the following groups:

1   Countries with positive manufacturing export bias: Egypt, Greece, Hong Kong, Israel, Japan, Morocco, Portugal, Singapore, Spain and Yugoslavia, i.e. largely a group of some East Asian and Southern European countries.
2   Countries with a moderate primary export bias: Colombia, Costa Rica, Malaysia, the Philippines, Thailand and Turkey, i.e. some Latin American and East Asian countries.
3   Countries with a strong primary export bias: Argentina, Brazil, Dominican Republic, Ecuador, Ivory Coast and Peru; largely a group of Latin American countries.

Table 10.1 summarizes the information available for the small sample and Table 10.2 presents the cross-country correlations for this group of countries. Table 10.3 presents cross-country correlations for the large sample.

A positive relationship between manufacturing bias in trade and the investment share is apparent in Table 10.1, for the small sample. For the large sample, as shown in Table 10.3, the correlation coefficient between the two variables is 0.35. This is exactly the implication of the models in previous sections, which suggest that specialization in increasing returns industries (a manufacturing bias) should have a positive effect on the investment share.

Table 10.1 Trade orientation, investment and growth (twenty-two countries, average values for country groups)

	Manufacturing bias	*Primary export bias*	
		Moderate	*Strong*
Trade orientation index (1975)	0.45	−1.0	−0.45
Investment share	24.8	19.1	19.5
Growth rate	4.1	2.8	1.5
Trade share	84.8	48.5	39.2
Trade intensity (Leamer 1)	0.08	0.04	−0.5
Intra-industry trade ratio	0.56	0.30	0.17
Number of countries	10	6	6

Notes: Growth rate: growth rate of real GDP per worker 1960–90 (Penn World Table Mark 5.6); Trade share: (exports+imports)/nominal GDP, average of 1970–80 (Penn World Table Mark 5.6); Trade intensity: adjusted trade intensity ratio 1982 (Leamer 1, in Leamer 1988); intra-industry: Intra-industry trade ratio 1982 (Leamer, 1988).

Table 10.2 Cross-country correlations (twenty-two countries)

	TO_{1975}	Intra-industry	Trade intensity	Trade share
TO_{1975}	1.00	0.69	0.42	0.35
Intra-industry		1.00	0.73	0.71
Trade intensity			1.00	0.85
Trade share				1.00

Notes: TO_{1975}: trade orientation index 1975 (Chenery and Syrquin 1986); Intra-industry: intra-industry trade ratio 1982 (Leamer 1988); Trade intensity: adjusted trade intensity ratio 1982 (Leamer 1, in Leamer 1988); Trade share: (exports + imports)/ nominal GDP, average of 1970–80 (Penn World Table Mark 5.6).

Table 10.3 Cross-country correlations (thirty-two countries)

	TO_{1975}	I/Y_{70-80}	Trade share	Growth
TO1975	1.00	0.35	0.33	0.73
I/Y_{70-80}		1.00	0.30	0.54
Trade share			1.00	0.39
Growth				1.00

Notes: TO1975: Trade orientation index 1975 (Chenery and Syrquin 1986); I/Y_{70-80}: real investment share of GDP, Average for the period 1970–80 (Penn World Table Mark 5.6); Trade share: (exports+imports)/nominal GDP, average of 1970–80 (Penn World Table Mark 5.6); Growth: growth rate of real GDP per worker 1960–90 (Penn World Table Mark 5.6).

A second implication of those models refers, as already mentioned, to the effects of the pattern of specialization on the rate of capital accumulation *for a given investment share*. As shown in Table 10.2, the correlation between manufacturing trade orientation and growth is, interestingly, very high (0.73), which is higher than that between the trade orientation index and the investment share. Also worth noting is the highly significant coefficient of trade orientation in a cross-country regression including investment share and the initial level of output per worker, as shown in eqn (10. 4):

$$g = 2.02 + 0.09\,I/Y + 1.47\,\text{TO} - 0.0002\,Y/L_{60}, \quad R^2 = 0.75 \qquad (10.4)$$
$$\quad\;\; (3.73)\;\;(4.02)\qquad (4.39)\qquad (-4.42)$$

where g is growth rate of output per worker in 1960–90, I/Y is real investment share (1970–80), TO is Chenery–Syrquin trade orientation index 1975, Y/L_{60} is real GDP per worker in 1960 and t-statistics are in parentheses.

Equation (10.4) indicates that, holding initial income and the investment share constant, countries specializing in manufacturing exports grew at a faster rate than those exporting primary products. If we think of sector B in the model of Sections 1 and 2 as a resource-intensive sector with few linkages to increasing returns activities, then the equation illustrates the model's basic insight on the growth effects of investment allocation. The initial level of output per worker also has a highly significant (and negative) coefficient in the regression. This suggests that across this group of thirty-four semi-industrial countries there was some degree of convergence: other things being equal, countries with a lower initial level of income tended to grow faster. As implied by the models discussed earlier however, convergence was conditioned by the pattern of specialization: countries specializing in manufactures were converging towards high income levels at a faster rate than those specializing in primary products. They were in fact converging towards higher steady-state income levels as suggested by our previous discussion.

It is worth noting that this last result is consistent with other recent findings on the effects of primary export orientation on growth. In Sachs and Warner (1995, 1997) the ratio of resource-intensive exports to GDP has a negative impact on growth, an influence that the authors largely attribute to Dutch disease effects. In Sala-i-Martin (1997), the fraction of primary products in total exports is one of the few economic variables that systematically appear to be correlated with growth (with a negative sign).

Trade openness, investment and growth

In their 'sensitivity analysis' of cross-country growth regressions, Levine and Renelt (1992) examined the robustness of the empirical relationships between long-run growth rates and a variety of economic, political and institutional indicators. Their assessment reached pessimistic conclusions. While there are many econometric specifications in which a number of indicators are significantly correlated with per capita growth rates, almost all of these are fragile in the sense that 'small alterations in the "other" explanatory variables overturn past results'. Only two relationships pass their test of robustness. One is a positive correlation between growth and the share of investment in GDP. The second is a positive correlation between the ratio of trade to output and the investment share. Table 10.3 shows for our large sample of thirty-four countries results supporting these findings: the positive correlation between growth and investment share (0.54) and that between trade share and investment share (0.30).

The first result is reassuring as it conforms to standard economic theory. The second is very puzzling. First, it is important to emphasize that the robust relationship found by Levine and Renelt is not between investment share and trade barriers but between investment share and trade share. The relationships between the investment share, or alternatively the growth rate, and a number of indicators of trade barriers or trade policy distortions – Dollar's (1992) 'real exchange rate distortion', average black market exchange rate premium, and Syrquin and

Chenery's index of outward orientation – are not robust. Therefore, the robust relationship does not seem to reflect the effects of trade policy. Moreover, when controlling for the investment share, there is no robust relationship between trade share and growth (this is so, incidentally, whether the trade indicator is the export share, the import share or total trade). The fact that the robust correlation is between trade and investment shares suggests that if trade affects growth, it is not through the conventional theoretical channels involving resource allocation, but rather through less conventional effects involving enhanced capital accumulation.

What these less conventional effects may be is unclear in most of the existing literature. Romer (1990a, 1990b) suggested that openness has a positive effect on research and development expenditures and, by increasing the rate of technological change, affects investment share and growth. Other views emphasize the positive effects of openness on technology transfer.[14] Whatever the merits of these views, they can hardly provide a convincing explanation of the Levine–Renelt finding. One reason is that openness in these models does not refer to trade shares and, therefore, in terms of providing an explanation of the statistical relationship between the trade share and investment, they face an old objection recently restated by De Long and Summers (1991). Trade shares pick up differences in national size and proximity to trading partners. If Belgium and Holland merged, it is hard to see how the combined rate of technical progress would fall (or rise) as a result of this new entity being less 'open' than each of the two countries separately.[14]

Even if the objection to viewing trade shares as a measure of openness was not decisive, the puzzle remains: why is it that the robust correlation is only between investment and the trade share and not between investment and other (more appropriate) measures of openness? The analysis in this and previous sections suggests a number of channels that can provide a convincing explanation of the positive relationship between trade and investment shares.[16] Our argument will be that the explanation of the trade–investment nexus may run through the pattern of trade specialization as determined by policy and factor endowment, including the natural resource endowment. Cross-country growth studies have missed these links because, with few recent exceptions, they have neglected the role of these two factors (policy and resource endowment) through their effects on trade orientation.[17]

Our main point is that the positive correlation between trade share and investment share is mediated by trade orientation, i.e. the explanation of the positive relationship between trade and investment is that trade share and investment share are both positively affected by a pro-manufacturing bias in trade orientation. We have already discussed and illustrated the effects of trade orientation on the investment share. Consider now the effects of trade orientation on the trade share. A positive relationship between these two variables is apparent in Table 10.1. Tables 10.2 and 10.3 show positive correlation coefficients of 0.35 and 0.33.

Why should a manufacturing bias in trade orientation positively affect the trade share? One reason involves the positive effect that specialization in increasing returns activities can have on trade creation. Increasing returns favor the expansion of intra-industry trade – two-way flows of trade in similar goods, subject to economies of specialization. Countries with a stronger bias towards manufacturing in the export bundle typically show higher indices of intra-industry trade. The correlation coefficient, as shown in Table 10.2, between the two indices is 0.69.

A second mechanism may be the presence of Dutch disease effects of primary exports. The implication of Dutch disease models is that countries exporting primary goods tend to be less open, other things being equal, since in the long-run equilibrium they have larger sectors producing non-tradable goods (see Ros 1998, chapter 8). In this respect, it is noteworthy that trade orientation shows a positive relationship with Leamer's openness index (Tables 10.1 and 10.2). The Leamer index is an adjusted trade–intensity ratio that represents the difference between the actual level of trade (as opposed to the pattern of trade) and the level predicted by the Heckscher–Ohlin trade model, including factor endowment and distance to markets. The positive relationship with trade orientation indicates that the more the trade pattern is biased towards exports of primary products, the lower the adjusted trade–intensity ratio tends to be, probably as a result of larger non-tradable goods sectors, together with less intra-industry trade.

5. Macro-linkages: Trade specialization and current account volatility

We turn now to explore macroeconomic aspects of trade specialization and their effects on growth. Conventional wisdom asserts that primary exporting countries are more vulnerable to the vagaries of the international market and, thus, face a greater degree of current account instability, which in turn is likely to affect growth adversely. There are two propositions involved here. One links trade orientation to current account volatility to the extent that world prices of primary commodities are more sensitive to the international business cycle. The other involves causal relationships running from current account instability to the rate of economic growth.

Consider the first link. Table 10.4 presents data sorted by the trade orientation index for the twenty-nine countries for which we have information on the TO index, current account volatility and output volatility. The volatility measures were estimated as standard deviations of the first differences of the current account (as percentage of GDP) and of the natural logarithm of GDP (so that in this case the measure reflects the volatility of the GDP growth rate).[18] The real exchange rate refers to the ratio of the US CPI to domestic CPI; real exchange rate volatility was obtained by dividing the real exchange rate series by the mean and then estimating the standard deviation.

No clear relationship emerges from the table: Countries with a strong primary export bias have the highest current account volatility but at the same time countries with a moderate primary bias show less current account volatility than those with a pro-manufacturing bias. Moreover, the scatter diagram in Figure 10.4 suggests that any negative relationship between current account volatility and growth (which is positively correlated with manufacturing bias) is at best tenuous.

Does this mean that trade specialization and growth are related only through the microeconomic links discussed in the previous two sections? It would be too

Table 10.4 Trade orientation, current account volatility and output volatility

Country	TO1975	Current account volatility	Output volatility	Real exchange rate volatility	GDP growth	Time period[a]
Iran	−1.03	6.6	11.5	86.7	−2.3	77–96
Brazil	−0.67	1.6	5.3	25.1	0.6	76–97
Ecuador	−0.6	3.9	3.2	31.0	0.8	76–97
Venezuela	−0.59	9.4	4.5	29.5	−0.2	71–97
Spain	−0.48	1.5	1.8	20.7	1.9	76–97
Argentina	−0.47	2.0	5.6	42.7	0.7	77–97
Chile	−0.4	3.8	5.4	25.6	4.1	76–97
Dominican Republic	−0.35	3.3	4.1	29.0	2.5	68–96
Mexico	−0.35	3.1	3.8	19.0	0.6	80–97
Peru	−0.34	3.5	7.0	48.9	0.1	78–97
Tunisia	−0.23	2.9	14.9	5.1	3.4	77–97
Turkey	−0.19	2.7	4.5	11.3	2.4	88–97
Guatemala	−0.13	2.6	3.1	21.8	0.0	78–97
Philippines	−0.13	2.6	4.1	13.0	0.3	78–97
Colombia	−0.12	2.8	3.0	10.0	5.8	76–97
Thailand	−0.12	2.8	3.0	10.0	5.8	76–97
Uruguay	−0.09	1.8	4.8	28.9	1.9	79–97
Malaysia	−0.03	4.9	2.9	15.2	4.2	75–97
Costa Rica	−0.01	3.3	4.6	17.5	0.6	78–97
Japan	0.07	1.0	1.5	22.8	2.8	78–97
Morocco	0.07	3.7	5.4	20.4	1.5	76–97
Greece	0.18	2.0	2.0	17.4	1.2	77–94
Singapore	0.2	3.6	3.2	16.4	−0.6	77–97
South Africa	0.2	3.6	3.2	16.4	−0.6	77–97
Egypt	0.31	2.8	2.2	34.4	3.0	83–97
Israel	0.77	4.1	10.6	12.3	4.0	69–97
Portugal	0.79	4.5	2.3	21.2	3.0	76–97
Korea	0.97	2.7	3.0	11.4	6.7	77–97
Syria	1.18	3.8	5.8	32.4	1.5	78–97

Source: International Financial Statistics.

Note
a A time period over which GDP growth, capital account and real exchange rate voltatilities calculated.

soon to reach this conclusion. The relationship between current account instability and growth is far more complex than conventional wisdom asserts. To the extent that current account volatility captures the effects of negative external shocks that were transmitted to domestic output, we would indeed expect a negative relationship between current account volatility and growth. In this case, current account volatility is truly an indicator of external vulnerability. Also, to the extent that current account instability generates a large volatility of the real exchange rate, it is likely to affect growth adversely: a large variance of the real exchange rate runs against long-run investment decisions at the firm level.

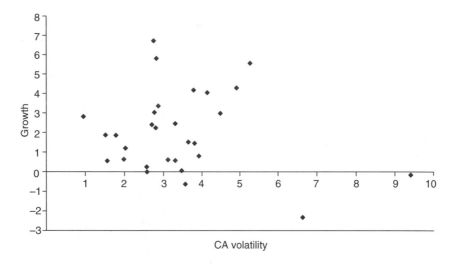

Figure 10.4 Growth and current account volatility.

Yet, under some circumstances, current account volatility may reflect the absence of borrowing constraints, i.e. a country's ability to absorb the effects of external shocks without affecting the growth path of domestic output. In this case, current account volatility does not lead to a high instability of domestic output and reflects the resilience, rather than the vulnerability, of an economy to external shocks. The economy is able to accommodate the external shock through borrowing (or lending) and as a result the increases and reductions in the current account deficit will not be reflected in a large variance of output and the real exchange rate.

This discussion suggests a number of testable hypotheses. First, the relationship between current account volatility and growth should be mediated by output volatility. Table 10.5 aggregates the twenty-nine countries of our sample according to the volatility of their current account and domestic output. This classification yields four groups (low and high are defined in such a way as to have half of the countries in each category):

1   low current account and output volatility: Japan, Spain, Greece, Guatemala, South Korea, Colombia, Egypt and Thailand;
2   high current account and low output volatility: Singapore, Malaysia, Portugal, Ecuador, South Africa and Mexico;
3   high current account and output volatility: Venezuela, Iran, Israel, Syria, Chile, Morocco, Peru, Costa Rica and Dominican Republic; and
4   low current account and high output volatility: Tunisia, Turkey, the Philippines, Argentina, Uruguay and Brazil.

A first remarkable feature of this aggregation is that it shows the absence of a strong correlation between current account and output volatility. Indeed, the

Table 10.5 Growth performance, output volatility and current account
volatility

	Group 1	Group 2	Group 3	Group 4
Current account volatility (%)	2.3	4.2	4.6	2.3
Output volatility (%)	2.3	3.1	6.5	6.5
Growth rate[a] (%)	3.0	2.3	1.3	1.6
Exchange rate volatility (%)	20.4	18.7	33.4	21.0
Trade orientation index	0.085	0.035	−0.016	−0.297

Source: based International Financial Statistics; Chenery and Syrquin (1986).

Note
a GDP per capita for the periods indicated in Table 10.4.

'boxes' that combine high current account and low output volatility and vice versa
are far from empty: over 40 per cent of the total number of countries fall in those
two groups.

What can we expect, based on our previous discussion, about the growth performance of each of these groups? The low output volatility in groups 1 and 2
suggests the absence of borrowing constraints in these countries to the extent that
they were able to accommodate internal and external shocks without affecting the
growth path of domestic output. In the case of group 1, the low current account
volatility may also be reflecting the relative absence of internal and external
shocks during the period. It is interesting to note in this respect that this group
includes the relatively more developed economies in the sample (Japan, Spain
and Greece), two East Asian economies that did not suffer from the debt crisis of
the 1980s, and the Latin American economy (Colombia) that was among the least
affected by the debt crisis given its relatively low debt burden. Other things being
equal (i.e. holding constant other factors that affect growth) we should expect to
find in these two groups the highest growth rates during the period.

The high output volatility in groups 3 and 4 suggests the presence of borrowing
constraints and, as a result, the inability of these countries to prevent the external
(or internal) shocks from affecting the path of output growth. Borrowing constraints, contrary to what may appear at first sight, were probably more severe in
group 4. The low current account volatility should not be interpreted as indicating
the absence of shocks. If this was the case, output volatility should also, as in
group 1, have been low. Rather, the low current account volatility is likely in this
case to indicate the severity of borrowing constraints, i.e. that these countries were
unable to borrow in order to finance an increase in their current account deficit and
thus had to adjust (to a larger extent than groups 2 and 3) through output changes.
Other things being equal, it is in groups 3 and 4, and in particular in group, 4 were
we would expect the worst growth performances.

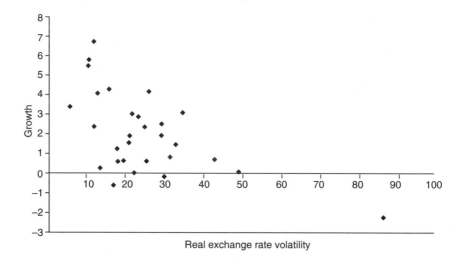

Figure 10.5 Growth and real exchange rate volatility.

Table 10.5 presents the growth performance of each of the four groups, along with other characteristics. The table shows a number of interesting features. First, the growth performance of the first two groups with low output volatility is clearly better than that of groups 3 and 4. Group 1 shows the highest growth rate as one would expect since in this case the low current account volatility indicates the absence, in contrast to group 2, of external or internal shocks. Contrary to our expectations, however, group 4 shows a slightly better performance than group 3. One reason may be the high degree of real exchange volatility in group 3, arising from the large shocks reflected in its current account instability, which created an adverse macroeconomic environment for growth. It is worth noting in this respect, the negative relationship between growth and exchange volatility that is apparent in Figure 10.5.

A second remarkable feature refers to the composition of each group in terms of trade orientation. The fast growing low output volatility groups 1 and 2 are composed by economies with a clear manufacturing bias compared to those in groups 3 and 4. In fact, only two countries in groups 3 and 4 (Israel and Syria) have a clear pro-manufacturing bias and, with the clear exception of Spain and Ecuador, all countries classified as having a *strong* primary export bias are in groups 3 and 4.[19]

All this suggests, after all, a relationship between trade orientation and growth that involves vulnerability to shocks. Vulnerability, however, should not be understood so much as relating to the frequency of shocks as to the inability to absorb these shocks without affecting the path of output growth. That is, trade orientation towards primary exports, to the extent that it is related to external vulnerability, is reflected in a large degree of output volatility rather than in the instability of the current account itself. This is so especially when, due to a lack of export diversification, a primary exporting country finds it particularly difficult to borrow in international capital markets at times of balance-of-payments difficulties. The relationship between primary export bias and output volatility is apparent in Tables 10.4 and 10.5.

Trade orientation also appears to affect the effectiveness with which real exchange rate changes can isolate the domestic economy from external shocks. Consider groups 2 and 3. Both have a high degree of current account instability, which suggests the presence of relatively large external shocks during the period. Output volatility is, however, very different being much larger for group 3 with a primary export bias. There is another key difference: the much large variance of exchange rates in group 3 which suggests that these group of primary exporters found it more difficult to prevent, through real exchange rate changes, external shocks from affecting domestic output.

6. Conclusions

This chapter has investigated the relationships between the pattern of trade specialization and the rate of economic growth. We began by presenting the standard analysis of the determinants of the pattern of specialization and extended it to consider the presence of increasing returns in non-traded goods. This change alone led to a model with multiple equilibria in which the pattern of specialization can be affected by determinants other than the standard ones (the composition of factor endowments, technology, and terms of trade). The model was also useful to compare the dynamic implications of different patterns of specialization. This analysis encompasses the treatment in the traditional literature on the subject (on, e.g. the infant industry argument or two-sector models with different rates of learning) to the extent that the different patterns of specialization compared may or may not be consistent with the same factor endowment. The analysis also helps to elucidate the conditions under which policy intervention geared to change the pattern of specialization can be effective and the role of the terms of trade in generating multiple equilibria.

The analysis highlighted two implications, which were supported by the empirical evidence. First, trade specialization affects the investment share given that, other things being equal (including factor endowments), the rate of return on capital tends to be higher in economies specialized in increasing returns industries. Second, at the same level of income per worker specialization in increasing returns industries is associated with a higher output–capital ratio; the rate of capital accumulation and growth will then be higher, for the same investment share, when an economy specializes in industries subject to increasing returns.

We then moved in Section 5 to an analysis of the macroeconomic aspects of trade specialization and their effects on growth. Our main finding here is that the lack of a clear and direct relationship between primary export bias and current account instability should not be attributed to the fact that primary exporting countries are less vulnerable than manufacturing exporters to external shocks.

Rather, the lack of such a relationship, together with the existence of a clear relationship between primary export bias and output volatility, suggests that primary exporting countries faced particularly severe borrowing constraints during the period analysis (broadly the last two to three decades). These borrowing constraints forced the absorption of the external shocks through changes in the real exchange rate, the level of economic activity or both and resulted in a degree of output and exchange rate volatility in primary exporting economies that were much larger than in economies with a pro-manufacturing bias.

Appendix

The model with constant returns in sector I

The two sectors (A and B) use, as indicated in the text, Cobb–Douglas technologies. Given this technology and the competitive conditions assumed, the first order conditions for profit maximization imply the following employment and profit rate functions in sectors A and B:

$$L_B = [(1 - b)\,p_B/w]^{1/b}\,K_B = L_B\,(w/p_B, K_B), \tag{1}$$

$$r_B = b\,(p_B/p_A)\,[(1 - b)\,p_B/w]^{(1-b)/b} = r_B\,(p_B/p_A, w/p_A). \tag{2}$$

Employment in sector I and the profit rate in sector A are determined as

$$L_I = [(1 - a)\,p_A/w]^{1/a}\,K_A = L_I\,(w/p_A, K_A), \tag{3}$$

$$r_A = a[(1 - a)\,p_A/w]^{(1-a)/a} = r_A\,(w/p_A). \tag{4}$$

The schedule of labor market equilibrium is obtained by substituting from the labor demand functions into the full employment condition: ($L = L_B + L_I$), setting $K_B = K - K_A$. As is readily verified, for $p_B = p_A$ (i.e. considering only the effect of technological parameters on capital intensity) the slope of this locus is negative (see Figure 10.1). An increase in the capital stock, holding the overall labour force constant, shifts the locus upwards. Intuitively, a higher overall capital–labor ratio raises the market-clearing wage for each given allocation of the capital stock. The schedule of capital market equilibrium is derived by substituting from the profit rate functions into the condition for profit rate equalization ($r_A = r_B$). In (w, K_A) space, there is a unique value of the wage, independent of the capital stock in sector A, that satisfies the condition for profit rate equalization. This value depends on technological parameters and the terms of trade but not on factor endowments (see eqns (2) and (4)).

The model with increasing returns in sector I

Non-tradable inputs in sector I are now produced under internal increasing returns and monopolistic competition. More precisely, I represents now the input of a set of intermediate goods,

$$I = ((1/n) I_i^\sigma)^{1/\sigma}, \quad 0 < \sigma < 1,$$

where n is the number of intermediate goods, assumed to be given. Production of these intermediate goods is subject to internal increasing returns:

$$I_i = L_i^{1+\mu}, \quad \mu > 0,$$

where L_i is labor input and μ is the increasing returns parameter in the production of I-goods. Moreover, producers operate under conditions of monopolistic competition and face downward sloping demand curves:

$$I_i^d = D p_i^{-\phi}, \quad \phi > 1,$$

where D is a position parameter and ϕ is the price elasticity of demand facing individual producers. As shown in Skott and Ros (1998), these assumptions imply that, in a symmetric equilibrium in the I sector, employment in sector I and the profit rate in sector A are determined as

$$L_I = [(1/n)^{1-f} G K_A^a p_A / w]^{1/f} = L_I (w/p_A, K_A), \tag{5}$$

$$G = (1 - a)(1 + \mu)(\phi - 1)/\phi, \quad f = a - \mu(1-a),$$

$$r_A = a K_A^{\mu(1-a)/f} [(1/n) G / (w/p_A)]^{(1-f)/f} = r_A (K_A, w/p_A). \tag{6}$$

The slope of the schedule of labor market equilibrium in $(\log w, \log K_A)$ space is now

$$d \log w / d \log K_A = \frac{[a/f - (K_A/K_B)(L_B/L_I)]}{[1/f + (1/b)(L_B/L_I)]},$$

where L_B/L_I, from the labor demand functions, is given by

$$L_B/L_I = (B K_B / A K_A^{a/f}) w^{1/f - 1/b},$$

$$B = [(1 - b) p_B]^{1/b}, \qquad A = [(1/n)^{1-f} G p_A]^{1/f}.$$

The slope of the locus is negative, tending to zero, at low levels of K_A and becomes positive, tending to 'a', at high levels of K_A (provided that such high values exist given the size of the overall capital stock). The equilibrium value of the wage thus first falls as K_A increases, and eventually rises, becoming an increasing function of K_A (see Figure 10.3).

The schedule of capital market equilibrium is derived as before from the condition of profit rate equalization. The slope of the schedule in $(\log w, \log K_A)$ space is now

$$d \log w / d \log K_A = \frac{[\mu(1 - a)/f]}{[(1 - a)(1 + \mu)/f - (1 - b)/b]}.$$

We have two cases depending on technological parameters in sectors A, B and I. The case of $b > f$ implies: $(1-a)(1+\mu) > (1-b)$, which says that the 'indirect' labor share of sector A is larger than the labor share of sector B. In this case, a wage increase (given K_A) reduces the profit rate in sector A more than it does in sector B. An increase in K_A (which affects positively r_A through its positive effect on the productivity of sector I) is required to restore the equality of profit rates, which makes the slope of the schedule positive.

In the second case, we have: $b < f$. This implies: $(1-a)(1+\mu) < (1-b)$, i.e. the 'indirect' labor share of sector A is smaller than the labor share of sector B. An increase in the wage (given K_A) will thus reduce the profit rate in sector B more than it does in sector A. This requires a fall in K_A (which reduces r_A) to restore the equality of profit rates. The slope of the schedule is then negative.

When there is an intersection this intersection is unique: In the first case, this is because the locus of the capital market remains steeper than the locus of the labor market at high levels of K_A. Necessary and sufficient conditions are $a > b$ and $f > 0$. In the second case, the intersection is unique, because the locus of the capital market is steeper, at low levels of K_A, than the locus of the labor market (when the latter is relatively flat).

Existence of multiple equilibria

As stated in the text, the existence of multiple equilibria depends on the existence of an A-equilibrium. An A-equilibrium, in turn, will exist if profitability in sector A, when the whole of the capital stock is allocated to this sector, is higher than that of sector B (evaluated at the market clearing wage corresponding to $L_I = L$). Consider, first, the wage in the A-equilibrium (w_A^*). From eqn (5), setting $L_I = L$ and $K_A = K$ and solving for the wage, we have

$$w_A^* = G(1/n)^{1-f} p_A K^a/L^f. \tag{7}$$

Substituting from (7) into eqn (6), setting $w_A^* = w_A$ and $K_A = K$, we obtain the profit rate in the A-equilibrium (w_A^*):

$$r_A^* = a(L/n)^{1-f}/K^{1-a}. \tag{8}$$

The profit rate in sector B, evaluated at the A-equilibrium wage, is obtained from substitution of (7) into eqn (2):

$$r_A^b = b(p_B/p_A)^{1/b}[(1-b)n^{1-f}L^f/G K^a]^{(1-b)/b}. \tag{9}$$

Note that the profit rate in sector B, evaluated at the A-equilibrium wages, w_A^b, is an increasing function of the number of producers of I-goods (n). A larger number of producers raises the unit cost of each of the I-goods and reduces the demand for labor in sector I. This has a negative effect on w_A^* and therefore tends to increase the profit rates in sector B, which does not use I-goods. This negative effect on the wage is offset in the case of the profit rate in sector A, since a higher number of producers implies higher costs for sector A: r_A^* is a decreasing function of the number of producers (n).

From (8) and (9), the condition for $r_A^* > r_A^b$, and thus for the existence of an A-equilibrium, is:

$$K^{a-b} > K^{*a-b} = (b/a)^b \, (p_B/p_A) \, [(1-b)/G]^{1-b} n^{1-f} L^{f-b}.$$

Comparison of equilibria

Suppose that the condition for multiple equilibria is fulfilled and compare the wage and profit rates in the two stable equilibria. In an A-equilibrium, the wage and profit rate are given by eqns (5) and (6). In a B-equilibrium, we have $K_B = K$ and $L_B = L$. Using eqns (1) and (2), the B-equilibrium wage and profit rate are

$$w_B^* = (1-b) \, p_B \, (K/L)^b, \tag{10}$$

$$r_B^* = b \, (p_B/p_A) \, (L/K)^{1-b}. \tag{11}$$

Comparing (6) and (11) shows that for r_A^* to be higher than r_B^* requires

$$K^{a-b} > K_1^{a-b} = (b/a) \, (p_B/p_A) \, n^{1-f} L^{f-b}. \tag{12}$$

Comparing (8) and (12), we can establish that $K^* > K_1$. The assumption of $a > b$ and the second-order condition for a profit maximum among I_i producers ensure this inequality.[20] It follows that when an A-equilibrium exists $(K > K^*)$, the profit rate in this equilibrium is higher than in the B-equilibrium (since K then is also higher than K_1).

Inspection of (5) and (10) shows that for w_A^* to be greater than w_B^* the aggregate capital stock must be such that

$$K^{a-b} > K_2^{a-b} = (1-b) \, (p_B/p_A) \, n^{1-f} L^{f-b}/G. \tag{13}$$

From (8) and (13), we can establish that $K_2 > K^*$.[21] The existence of an A-equilibrium does not guarantee that the wage in the A-equilibrium is higher than in the B-equilibrium. This requires that the aggregate capital stock is larger than K_2. In this case, with $K > K_2$, and therefore K larger than K^* and K_1, an A-equilibrium will exist and feature both a profit rate and a wage rate higher than in the B-equilibrium.

Notes

1 The author is grateful to Maiju Perala for research assistance.
2 See, on the subject, Ros (1987).

3   These links are emphasized in the research proposal on International Trade, Competitiveness and Finance, CEDES 1996.

4   More precisely, capital accumulation increases the wage at the initial allocation but the increase in the wage itself implies that the initial allocation no longer satisfies the condition of profit rate equalization. The reallocation of capital towards the capital-intensive sector then brings the wage back to its initial value.

5   Note that the labor demand in sector I is an increasing function of K_A ($\mu > 0$ ensures that $a > f$).

6   If there is no effect, i.e. if K_A does not appear in the profit-wage function, there will be no reallocation that is able to restore the equality of profit rates. The schedule would then be a horizontal line at that unique value of the wage that is consistent with the equality of profit rates. As can be readily verified, this is the case if m 5 0, that is when the technology of the integrated A/I sector exhibits constant returns to scale. This is the case examined in the previous section.

7   The appendix examines both cases and the reader may verify that the analysis is symmetrical for the case in which the indirect labor share in A is larger than that in B.

8   As we shall see later, this is due to the assumption that sector B does not use intermediate goods produced under increasing returns. At low levels of K_A, the profit rate in sector A tends to zero while it remains positive in sector B no matter how large the capital stock is. There are thus some capital allocations, at sufficiently low levels of K_A, for which sector B is more profitable than sector A.

9   The threshold value is also smaller, the smaller the number of firms (n) in sector I, which affects positively the profitability of sector A. The effect of the overall labor endowment on the threshold value of aggregate capital stock depends on the sign on the size of the 'indirect' labor share of sector A compared to that of sector B.

10 In the presence of differences in the size of the labor force, the difference in the steady-state level of income would also be proportional to the size in the labor force (due to the existence of increasing returns to scale in sector I).

11 One source of this difference is the adoption by Rodriguez-Clare of a Dixit–Stiglitz–Ethier specification in sector I, with a preference for variety and an ever-expanding number of I goods (and with a zero profit condition in equilibrium).

12 That is, it measures, for a given country, the deviation between the observed manufacturing trade bias and that predicted for a typical country of similar income and size. In Chenery and Syrquin (1986), the trade orientation index measures the primary export bias. We use this index multiplied by -1. This yields the manufacturing export bias.

13 The thirty-four countries are: Algeria, Argentina, Brazil, Chile, Colombia, Costa Rica, Dominican Republic, Ecuador, Egypt, Greece, Guatemala, Hong Kong, Iran, Iraq, Israel, Ivory Coast, Japan, Korea, Malaysia, Mexico, Morocco, Peru, the Philippines, Portugal, Singapore, Spain, Syria, Taiwan, Thailand, Tunisia, Turkey, Uruguay, Venezuela and Yugoslavia.

14 At the same time, it is possible to argue that the effects of openness are dependent on the pattern of specialization that it induces (as in the model of Section 1). In some North–South models, such as Young's (1991), openness can even lead to a lower rate of technological change for the South. Moreover, foreign direct investment is a major vehicle of technology transfers and there is no clear positive relationship between openness to trade and openness to foreign investment.

15 It is worth emphasizing that De Long and Summers' observation is not an objection to models in which openness – in the sense of absence of trade barriers – has a positive effect on investment. Rather, it is an objection to using trade shares as a measure of openness. The implication, however, is that we should not interpret the correlation between investment and trade shares as evidence supporting models in which openness enhances investment.

16 We have already mentioned Rodrik's (1994) argument that a higher investment share may lead to a higher trade share, as result of increased imports of capital goods in industrializing economies. In this argument causality runs from investment to trade and not the other way around. Our main focus in what follows will take a different and complementary direction.

17 Exceptions include, as already noted, Sachs and Warner (1995, 1997) and Sala-i-Martin (1997).

18 See Razin (1996) for a discussion of these measures.

19 Mexico is a marginal country between groups 2 and 3 and thus is not a clear exception. Similarly, Morocco is a marginal case of manufacturing bias (with a TO index of 0.07).

20 For $K^* > K_1$, the following condition must be fulfilled:

$$(1 - b)/b > [(1 - a)/a] (1 + \mu) (1 - 1/\phi),$$

$a > b$ implies that $(1 - b)/b > (1-a)/a$. For the second-order condition for a profit maximum among I_i producers to be fulfilled, it is necessary that $(1+\mu) (1-1/\phi) > 1$. Taken together, these inequalities ensure the fulfillment of the condition above.

21 This requires as in the previous case:

$$(1 - b)/b > [(1 - a)/a] (1 + \mu) (1 - 1/\phi).$$

The fulfillment of this inequality is guaranteed by the same conditions as before ($a > b$, and the second-order condition for a profit maximum among I_i producers).

References

Amsden, A. H. (1989) *Asia's Next Giant: South Korea and Late Industrialization*. Oxford: Oxford University Press.

Chenery, H. B. and Syrquin, M. (1986) 'The Semi-industrial Countries', in H. B. Chenery, S. Robinson and M. Syrquin (eds), *Industrialization and Growth. A Comparative Study*. New York: Published for the World Bank, Oxford University Press.

Ciccone, A. and Matsuyama, K. (1996) 'Start Up Costs and Pecuniary Externalities as Barriers to Economic Development', *Journal of Development Economics* 49: 33–60.

De Long, J. B. and Summers, L. H. (1991) 'Equipment Investment and Economic Growth', *Quarterly Journal of Economics* 106: 445–502.

Dollar, D. (1992) 'Outward-oriented Developing Economies Really Do Grow More Rapidly:Evidence from 95 LDCs, 1976–1985', *Economic Development and Cultural Change* 40(3): 523–44.

Krugman, P. (1987) 'The Narrow Moving Band, the Dutch disease, and the Competitiveness Consequences of Mrs Thatcher: Notes on Trade in the Presence of Dynamic Scale Economies', *Journal of Development Economics* 27(1–2): 41–55.

Leamer, E. (1988) 'Measures of Openness', in Robert Baldwin (ed.), *Trade Policy Issues and Empirical Analysis*. Chicago: University of Chicago Press.

Levine, R. and Renelt, D. (1992) 'A Sensitivity Analysis of Cross-country Growth Regressions', *American Economic Review* 82(4): 942–63.

Razin, A. (1996) 'The Dynamic-Optimizing Approach to the Current Account: Theory and Evidence', in P. Kenen (ed.), *Understanding Interdependence. The Macroeconomics of the Open Economy*, Princeton, NJ: Princeton University Press.

Rodriguez-Clare, A. (1996) 'The Division of Labor and Economic Development', *Journal of Development Economics* 49: 3–32.

Rodrik, D. (1994) 'Getting Interventions Right: How South Korea and Taiwan Grew Rich', *National Bureau of Economic Research Working Paper*, No. 4964.

Romer, P. (1990a) 'Are Nonconvexities Important for Understanding Growth?', *American Economic Review* 80(2): 97–103.

Romer, P. (1990b) 'Endogenous Technological Change', *Journal of Political Economy* 98(5): S71–S102.

Ros, J. (1987) 'Growth and International Trade', in J. Eatwel, M. Milgate and P. Newman (eds), *The New Palgrave: A dictionary of economics*, London: Macmillan.

Ros, J. (1998) *Increasing Returns, Development Traps, and Economic Growth*, Manuscript, forthcoming.

Sachs, J. D. and Warner, A. M. (1995) 'Natural Resource Abundance and Economic Growth', *National Bureau of Economic Research Working Paper*, No. 5398.

Sachs, J. D. and Warner, A. M. (1997) 'Fundamental Sources of Long-Run Growth', *American Economic Review* 87: 184–8.

Sala-i-Martin, X. (1997) 'I Just Ran Two Million Regressions', *American Economic Review* 87: 178–83.

Skott, P. and Ros, J. (1997) 'The "Big Push" in an open economy with Non Tradable Inputs', *Journal of Post Keynesian Economics* 20: 149–62.

Wade, R. (1989) *Governing the Market: Economic Theory and the Role of the Government and East Asian Industrialization*. Princeton: Princeton University Press.

Young, A. (1991) 'Learning by Doing and the Dynamic Effects of International Trade', *Quarterly Journal of Economics* 106(2): 369–405.

11 Two problems in bank lending for development

Rodney Schmidt

1. Introduction: Two problems in bank lending for development

Most investment in developing countries is financed externally, by borrowing from banks. Banks retain this central role because they are the best at monitoring projects and enforcing contracts when public information is limited and the legal and financial infrastructure is immature. They often do this by establishing long-term relationships with firms.

Banks in developing countries, however, tend to lend either too little or too much to firms, with two important effects. First, chronically low lending is associated with low levels of investment and growth, and, moreover, constrained lending restricts growth. Second, periodic surges in lending end in systemic bank and economic crises. For convenience, we refer to the first pattern as 'under-borrowing' by firms, and to the second as 'over-lending' by banks.

The role of financial agency costs in firms and banks helps to understand these related, and seemingly conflicting, lending patterns. Financial agency costs refer to the impact on lending behavior of the stakes that firms and banks have, respectively, in the outcomes of investment projects. These stakes grow out of features of the balance sheets of firms and banks. A simple version of how this works is as follows.

On the one hand, when firms have low net worth, they cannot put up collateral for investment projects. Then banks do not lend to them, since the firms have little to lose from project failure, and are more likely to choose or accept poor projects. This yields under-borrowing. On the other hand, when banks have low net worth, or there is deposit insurance, they also have little to lose from failure, and are more willing to lend to poor projects. This yields over-lending. If deposit insurance is implicit and systemic, then banks may require collateral for individual projects, while ignoring aggregate credit risk associated with inflated asset and collateral values. This simultaneously yields under-borrowing in some sectors where collateral is not available, and over-lending in other sectors where collateral is available.

To assess the explanatory power of this approach, we undertake a selective review and interpretation of evidence on patterns of bank lending, and on how financial agency costs contribute to them. The evidence on lending patterns is mostly from developing countries, while that on agency costs is only available for developed countries. The latter evidence is informative for us, nevertheless, because it identifies both the impact of agency costs on lending behavior, and the types of affected firms and banks. These types are more common in developing countries than elsewhere.

2. Chronic credit shortages constrain investment

The following propositions summarize evidence on the nature of the relationship between bank lending and economic development.

Proposition 1.1. *Over long periods, bank lending to the private sector is strongly positively correlated with macroeconomic investment, productivity and growth in developing countries (Levine 1997, and citations therein).*

That is, if bank lending leads investment and growth, then lending constraints have important macroeconomic effects.

The correlation between bank lending and economic growth has been established largely in cross-country studies, and therefore rests on a relationship of averages across countries. By itself, it does not show that limitations on bank lending constrain investment. Other macroeconomic studies, however, are more definite about this.

Proposition 1.2. *Bank-lending volume predicts subsequent long-term growth, capital accumulation and productivity (King and Levine 1993). Further, industries that rely heavily on external funding, identified outside of the context of financial and economic development, grow faster in countries with deeper financial sectors (Rajan and Zingales 1996).*

Time series evidence from individual countries suggests that causation between financial depth and economic growth changes over time, depending on the institutional context (Arestis and Demetriades 1997). One important feature is agency costs in the market for bank credit. For example, in a theoretical analysis, Sussman and Zeira (1995) show that when low levels of institutional and economic development entail high agency costs, then credit rationing constrains growth. Whereas they build their analysis on monitoring costs, we focus on financial factors underlying effective agency costs, given monitoring technology. This seems practically relevant since, when firms can finance investment projects internally, agency costs are much reduced or eliminated, even if external monitoring costs are high (Gertner *et al.* 1994). Hence, in developing countries the importance of financial agency costs, and macroeconomic lending constraints on growth, varies with financial conditions.

Financial agency costs in firms

Agency costs in external credit markets come from a divergence of incentives between borrower (the firm) and lender (the bank), when the lender cannot fully monitor the borrower's behavior. One important source of these divergences is the state of the firm's balance sheet, and, in particular, its net worth. The value of a firm's net worth indicates its ability to co-finance investment, or put up collateral against external finance.

Posting partial or full collateral reduces the amount of risky lending needed for the project. More importantly, it strengthens the combined interest of the bank and the firm in the outcome of the project, so that they work towards a common purpose. Otherwise the firm, which is closer to the project than the bank, may seek financing for lower quality projects than the bank would choose. The reason is that the opportunity cost of a project is small for a firm which borrows most or all of the funds to finance it, while the gains from a successful outcome may be high. The opposite is true for a bank which lends most of the funds for the same project on a debt contract. (Gertler (1988) reviews this literature. See also Bernanke and Gertler (1990), Bernanke and Gertler (1995) and Holmstrom and Tirole (1997).

When financial agency costs in firms are high, banks may refuse to finance investment projects, even though they would finance the same projects in other circumstances. Then firms cannot obtain working capital or pursue productive and socially beneficial investment activities. This is confirmed by evidence on firm borrowing from banks.

Proposition 1.3. *Following a negative macroeconomic shock, firms' short-term borrowing by commercial paper rises sharply compared to their short-term borrowing from banks (Kashyap et al. 1993).*

Strictly speaking, this finding reflects either of a more restricted supply of bank loans, or an only partially satisfied increase in demand for bank loans, following a shock to firms balance sheets.

Less ambiguous is evidence that some firms, with high financial agency costs, have a harder time borrowing from banks than others.

Proposition 1.4. *During recessions, bank borrowing by large manufacturing firms rises sharply, while that by small manufacturing firms rises modestly, if at all. Further, bank lending to riskier or less transparent firms and to firms without lines of credit falls (Bernanke et al. 1996; Calomiris 1995; Kashyap et al. 1993).*

Large manufacturing firms have easier access to real short-term bank credit than small ones. The former tends to be more mature, established and stable than the latter.

Under-borrowing by firms

Under-borrowing refers to the impact that financial agency costs in firms have on their real economic behavior.

Proposition 1.5. *Investment by firms is excessively sensitive to current cash flow, especially in new and small firms. (For a review of this large body of evidence, see Gertler (1988).)*

Proposition 1.6. *The investment, employment, research and development and inventory behavior of firms with high agency costs and credit constraints, identified independently, is sensitive to cash flow, while that of other firms is not (Fazzari et al. (1988) and citations therein, and Calomiris and Hubbard (1995)).*

This is consistent with the aggregate evidence presented earlier of a strong relationship between bank lending and macroeconomic performance.

Not all firms at a given time and in a given context are equally affected by financial agency costs. More susceptible firms are those with fragile balance sheets and low and variable net worth.

Proposition 1.7. *Firms with high agency costs, identified independently, tend to be small, and to have large debts, low profits relative to sales and high rates of growth of profits. These firms are new, untried and fast growing (Calomiris and Hubbard 1995).*

Developing countries have a preponderance of this type of firm, especially after programs of macroeconomic reform and structural adjustment. Because firm net worth is, on average, structurally lower there than elsewhere, especially relative to the size of investment projects, demand for external finance is higher at both firm or project and aggregate levels.

Proposition 1.8. *In poor countries most investment is financed externally and by borrowing from banks, while in rich countries most is financed from retained savings (Corbett and Jenkinson 1994; Eichengreen 1999; Mayer 1989; Singh 1995; Singh and Hamid 1992).*

Since most investment finance in developing countries must be obtained externally and, equivalently, project co-financing by firms is insubstantial, investment is more expensive there than in developed countries. In the aggregate, the result is underperformance in investment and growth. To the extent that policy can improve on these market outcomes, financial agency costs in firms are a pressing issue for growth and development.

3. Periodic credit surges are not sustainable

In the two decades since developing countries began liberalizing financial sectors, attention has increasingly focused not on under-borrowing, but on the problem of banks lending too much, too quickly. The reason is the rising number and increasing costliness of bank crises (Eichengreen and Rose 1998; Frydl 1999; Goldstein and Turner 1996; Wyplosz n.d.).

A bank crisis is usually set off by a macroeconomic event which, when compared to the succeeding financial upheaval, seems disproportionately minor. Typical events are contagion from crises elsewhere, a devaluation of the currency, an increase in global interest rates, or a decline in the international terms of trade. They often occur at a cyclical economic and stock market peak. Economic output then falls sharply, and the stock and real estate markets collapse. The response of the real estate market is particularly important, as it accounts for a large share of collateral for bank loans. A credit crunch ensues, as banks call in loans to avoid higher credit risk and to meet greater deposit withdrawals. The credit crunch, rising interest rates, deteriorating economy and falling collateral values reduce debt servicing by firms, and bad loans accumulate. A crisis-induced credit crunch is generally more severe, but shorter-lasting, than credit shortages arising from chronically high firm agency costs.

The recent proliferation of bank crises is not due to an increase in macroeconomic volatility, but to events within the banking sector which undermine its ability to withstand shocks.

Proposition 2.1. *Financial liberalization and a rapid rise in bank lending precede most bank crises, and contribute significantly to the probability of a crisis (Gavin and Hausmann 1996; Gonzalez-Hermosillo 1996; Kaminsky and Reinhart 1999; Sachs et al. Velasco 1996).*

Rapid growth in lending leading to bank crises is not expected behavior in developing countries, where information is scarce and firm agency costs are high. Banks ought to ration credit to avoid exposure to poor investment projects. From where, then, do unsustainable bank credit surges come?

Financial agency costs in banks

Banks lend to firms to finance investment projects from their own capital and from funds borrowed from depositors. They may also borrow by issuing securities, but in developing countries where equity markets are immature and illiquid, this is not a viable option on a large scale (Diamond 1997; Singh 1997). In general, ready substitutes for deposits as external borrowing instruments are not available.

If it is hard for depositors and others to monitor bank asset portfolios, then banks with low net worth face high financial agency costs. The mechanism is the same as that for firms, and leads to under-borrowing by banks from depositors just as by firms from banks. Under-borrowing by banks may constrain lending for investment projects even when financial agency costs in firms are low (Bernanke and Blinder 1988, 1992; Bernanke and Gertler 1987, 1995).

Proposition 2.2. *The level and rate of growth of bank lending depend positively on the quantity of bank capital and the capital asset ratio (Holmstrom and Tirole 1997; Sharpe 1995).*

A substitute for high bank net worth, in terms of affecting agency costs in banks, is deposit insurance, since it reduces depositor liability for bank asset portfolios (Stein 1998). For given financial agency costs in firms, insurance releases lending constraints imposed by depositors, leading to an increase in lending to firms.

Proposition 2.3. *An exogenous reduction in insured deposits is accompanied by a shrinking of bank lending (Bernanke and Blinder 1992).*

Information gaps about bank asset portfolios arise in part from individual bank characteristics. Banks with high agency costs are those which have a harder time finding substitutes for insured deposits than others, and they are more vulnerable to shocks.

Proposition 2.4. *Small banks cut loans by more in response to exogenously induced deposit outflows. Among smaller banks, the impact on lending is greater for those with lower ratios of cash and securities to assets (Kashyap and Stein 1995, 1997).*

Following the same reasoning, in developing countries domestic banks face higher agency costs than international banks, since domestic banks have less access to international credit.

Proposition 2.5. *In developing countries, domestic banks experience higher deposit outflows in response to macroeconomic shocks, and take longer to adjust to them, than foreign banks (Ramos 1998).*

This evidence supports an unconventional interpretation of the role of deposit insurance in developing countries. This role is to reduce under-borrowing by firms by overriding financial agency costs in banks. For this purpose, deposit insurance must include an expectation of bank bailouts. Otherwise, banks themselves ration credit to high agency cost firms, even if depositors do not restrict credit to banks.

Over-lending by banks

Deposit insurance, operating through bailout expectations, introduces moral hazard into bank-lending practices, a factor which is distinct from financial agency costs. Moral hazard is present because banks have little to lose from failed investment projects, so they are more willing to lend to poor projects. In the absence of effective prudential regulation and supervision, the quality of bank asset portfolios may be expected to fall.

From experience with bank crises in developing countries, moral hazard operates through rapid growth in bank lending, which is associated with asset price inflation or an economic boom.

Proposition 2.6. *Deposit insurance and credit subsidies contribute to asset price bubbles and bank crises (Calomiris 1995; Carey 1994; Demirguo-Kunt and Detragiache 1998).*

Our concept of over-lending, therefore, goes beyond insufficient project selectivity by banks. It embraces aggressive lending that may simultaneously stem from and reinforce unsustainable stock market or economic activity. In this regard, what appears most important is implicit deposit insurance protecting banks against systemic failure coinciding with, or following, burst collateral and asset value bubbles. In such circumstances, governments cannot usually avoid intervening to support the banking system. Lending in the context of an unsustainable macroeconomic boom accomplishes the same thing; the ensuing bust affects all banks almost equally.

Theory identifies two complementary mechanisms linking deposit insurance, bank lending and asset price inflation. On the one hand, banks underwrite speculative markets, such as real estate, because a potential collapse would affect the entire banking system (Carey 1994). On the other hand, banks take collateral, often real estate, at face value, ignoring the possibility of a price bubble (Kiyotaki and Moore 1997). They lend freely believing themselves to be covered individually by collateral, and collectively by deposit insurance. In either case, asset price inflation may originate either outside the banking system, for example in a consumption boom stimulated by macroeconomic and financial reform (McKinnon and Pill 1997), or within the banking system, fueled by abundant credit itself, which also stimulates the economy (Gavin and Hausmann 1996).

An asset price inflation-based lending surge may or may not be accompanied by a rise in bad loans prior to the collapse of the asset bubble. If there is a large accumulation of bad loans, the banking system may collapse first, followed by equity markets (Gavin and Hausmann 1996). If there is no pre-collapse rise in bad loans, asset prices and collateral values still depend on the expected volume of bank lending. An external shock that reduces expected lending has a much amplified shrinking effect on asset prices, further reducing expected bank lending (Kiyotaki and Moore 1997). Bad loans then appear with or after the financial crash.

4. Under-borrowing versus over-lending

Both under-borrowing and over-lending are financial policy issues in developing countries, as they are patterns of microeconomic lending behavior with important macroeconomic effects. They arise from a common source, namely, insufficient project-contingent liability by borrowers, with respect to under-borrowing, and by lenders, with respect to over-lending.

Under-borrowing can be addressed independently, by improving the transparency of relations between participants in the financial system, and by enhancing loan monitoring technology, skills and institutions. This would reduce financial agency costs in both firms and banks. There are, however, natural limitations to what can be achieved this way, within the context of economic and institutional underdevelopment.

Over-lending can also be addressed independently, by eliminating deposit insurance if possible, or at least by eliminating expectations of bank bailouts. It can also be addressed by enhancing bank regulation, involving high bank capital, or net worth, requirements. However, as already noted, this would likely increase under-borrowing.

Thus arises a serious policy dilemma, or trade-off. In developing countries, it seems that an effective way to address under-borrowing is to tolerate, or to offer, deposit insurance, with the concomitant bailout expectations. Apparently this can only be done by accepting increased over-lending, or financial instability, and vice versa.

One option for responding to the policy trade-off, advanced by Stiglitz (1994), is to return to policies typical of the era of financial repression. These include forcing interest rates below equilibrium levels and directing credit allocation, which would avoid over-lending. This would cause widespread under- and mis-directed borrowing to reappear however, due to the repression itself (which was the reason for liberalizing in the first place (Fry 1997)), and due to high financial agency costs in firms.

A second, widely adopted, option presented by the policy trade-off is to deal with under-borrowing by pursuing financial liberalization. But, as seen earlier, often this has been achieved at the cost of over-lending. McKinnon and Pill (1997) argue that financial and macroeconomic reform stimulate overly opti-mistic or euphoric expectations of success, which seem to be validated by low levels of real interest rates. This is especially so if the reforms encompass capital account liberalization (McKinnon and Pill 1998). The excessive optimism appears as a consumption and macroeconomic boom accompanied by a great demand for bank loans. (McKinnon and Pill (1997) refer to this as an over-borrowing phenomenon.) Depositors and banks are willing to feed the boom with copious lending because they expect to be bailed out in the event it proves unsustainable. Further, the boom creates high rates of profit and sales growth for many firms, so that it is hard for banks, whose market skill levels may be primi-tive, to perceive financial agency costs and other credit risks (Gavin and Hausmann 1996).

In the worst realization of the policy trade-off, deposit insurance in the context of financial liberalization yields simultaneous under-borrowing and over-lending. Here, firms are not able to borrow to finance risky projects, while banks channel lending to self-collateralizing projects, leading to unsustainable asset price inflation.

There are several reasons why banks in developing countries may concentrate lending in real estate and other easily collateralizable sectors, even with deposit insurance. First, deposit insurance may be accompanied by prudential regulation and supervision, including measures to forcibly restructure individually weak banks in a way that is costly to bank capital and management. Then the net worth of individual banks remains at risk, and banks seek to cover themselves, or reduce financial agency costs in firms, by requiring collateral. Regulators may also impose collateral requirements (Stiglitz and Uy 1996). Second, it may be hard for banks to diversify asset portfolios if it requires expertize in many sectors, stretch-ing already low credit skills, or if firm agency costs are high in some sectors. Finally, as seen above, banks may wish to mine high return, high risk sectors, such as real estate.

Can the terms of the under-borrowing–over-lending policy trade-off be improved? The question is relevant if one is not narrowly concerned with elimi-nating financial instability in developing countries. There is evidence that finan-cial and, presumably, economic development already is not fully set back by banking crises (Demirguo-Kunt and Detragiache 1998). Then, under appropriate conditions, additional financial instability in return for easier lending constraints may yield a net gain.

Deposit insurance always introduces moral hazard into the bank-lending problem. The means of addressing this however, embodied in the conventional prescriptions for regulation and supervision, are well known and effective. What one wants to avoid is the positive interaction between lending and asset price inflation.

This can be done, if deposit insurance is coordinated with two complementary policies. The first is to impose portfolio diversification requirements on banks to prevent too much lending to collateralizable sectors and speculative markets. It also restrains rapid growth in bank lending when asset price inflation is exogenous. To achieve diversification, government might also encourage syndicated bank lending, which has the added benefit of pooling information on borrowers.

The second complementary policy is to exert discretionary control over the rate of growth of insured deposits, by adjusting reserve requirements and generally controlling the supply of high-powered money. This also constrains the rate of growth of bank lending, which is especially useful for preempting latent asset price bubbles or unsustainable consumption and macroeconomic booms.

5. Conclusion

Banks in developing countries, the dominant source of finance for investment, have a disturbing tendency to lend too little or too much to firms. The result is unnecessarily low rates of investment and growth, and unnecessarily frequent financial and economic crises.

Evidence indicates that an important part of the explanation for this is inadequate contingent liability for project outcomes on the balance sheets of both firms and banks. For firms, this arises from low net worth, a structural characteristic of developing countries. For banks, it arises from the implicit presence of systemic deposit insurance, also characteristic of developing countries.

From this perspective, deposit insurance is a policy instrument for reducing under-borrowing. To date it has not been effective as such, because reductions in under-borrowing appear limited while increases in over-lending are substantial. Nevertheless, the terms of the trade-off can be improved if deposit insurance is complemented by bank portfolio diversification requirements and discretionary controls on the rate of growth of insured deposits.

These conclusions are tentative. There is still surprisingly little direct evidence on the influence of financial agency costs in bank credit markets in developing countries. The same is true for the nature of the trade-off between under-borrowing and over-lending introduced by deposit insurance of different types, and accompanied by different prudential regulations and policies. Neglecting such evidence carries the risk of too narrow a concern with financial stability and unwitting acceptance of more under-borrowing and less development than necessary.

References

Arestis, P. and Demetriades, P. (1997) 'Financial Development and Economic Growth: Assessing the Evidence', *Economic Journal* 107: 783–99.

Bernanke, B. and Blinder, A. (1992) 'The Federal Funds Rate and the Channels of Monetary Transmission', *American Economic Review* 82: 901–21.

Bernanke, B. and Blinder, A. (1988) 'Credit, Money, and Aggregate Demand', *American Economic Review* 78: 435–9.

Bernanke, B. and Gertler, M. (1987) 'Banking and Macroeconomic Equilibrium', in W. A. Barnett and K. Singleton (eds), *New Approaches to Monetary Economics*. New York: Cambridge University Press.

Bernanke, B. and Gertler, M. (1990) 'Financial Fragility and Economic Performance', *Quarterly Journal of Economics* CV(1): 87–114.

Bernanke, B. and Gertler, M. (1995) 'Inside the Black Box: The Credit Channel of Monetary Policy Transmission', *Journal of Economic Perspectives* 9(4): 27–48.

Bernanke, B., Gertler, M. and Gilchrist, S. (1996) 'The Financial Accelerator and the Flight to Quality', *Review of Economics and Statistics* LXXVIII(1): 1–15.

Calomiris, C. W. (1995) 'Financial Fragility: Issues and Policy Implications', *Journal of Financial Services Research* 9: 241–57.

Calomiris, C. W. and Hubbard, R. G. (1995) 'Internal Finance and Investment: Evidence from the Undistributed Profits Tax of 1936–1937', *Journal of Business* 68(4): 443–82.

Carey, M. S. (1994) 'Feeding the Fad: The Federal Land Banks, Land Market Efficiency, and the Farm Credit Crisis', *Federal Reserve Board of Governors Working Paper*.

Corbett, J. and Jenkinson, T. (1994) 'The Financing of Industry, 1970–89: An International Comparison', *Centre for Economic Policy Research, London Discussion Paper*, No. 948.

Demirguo-Kunt, A. and Detragiache, E. (1998) 'The Determinants of Banking Crises in Developing and Developed Countries', *International Monetary Fund Staff Papers* 45(1): 81–109.

Diamond, D. W. (1997) 'Liquidity, Banks, and Markets', *Journal of Political Economy* 105(5): 928–56.

Eichengreen, B. (1999) *Toward a New International Financial Architecture*. Washington, DC: Institute for International Economics.

Eichengreen, B. and Rose, A. K. (1998) 'Staying Afloat When the Wind Shifts: External Factors and Emerging-Market Banking Crises', *National Bureau of Economic Research Working Paper*, No. 6370.

Fazzari, S. R., Hubbard, G. and Petersen, B. (1998) 'Financing Constraints and Corporate Investment', *Brookings Papers on Economic Activity* 1: 141–95.

Fry, M. J. (1997) 'In Favor of Financial Liberalization', *Economic Journal* 107: 754–70.

Frydl, E. J. (1999) 'The Length and Cost of Banking Crises', *International Monetary Fund Working Paper WP/99/30*.

Gavin, M. and Hausmann, R. (1996) 'The Roots of Banking Crises: The Macroeconomic Context', in R. Hausmann and L. Rojas-Suarez (eds), *Banking Crises in Latin America*. Washington, DC: The Johns Hopkins University Press.

Gertler, M. (1988) 'Financial Structure and Aggregate Economic Activity: An Overview', *Journal of Money, Credit, and Banking* 20(3): 559–88.

Gertner, R. H., Scharfstein, D. S. and Stein, J. C. (1994) 'Internal versus External Capital Markets', *Quarterly Journal of Economics* CIX: 1211–30.

Goldstein, M. and Turner, P. (1996) 'Banking Crises in Emerging Economies: Origins and Policy Options', *Bank for International Settlements Economic Paper*, No. 46.

Gonzalez-Hermosillo, B. (1996) 'Banking Sector Fragility and Systemic Sources of Fragility', *International Monetary Fund Working Paper WP/96/12*.

Holmstrom, B. and Tirole, J. (1997) 'Financial Intermediation, Loanable Funds, and the Real Sector', *Quarterly Journal of Economics* CXII(3): 663–91.

Kaminsky, G. and Reinhart, C. (1999) 'The Twin Crises: The Causes of Banking and Balance-of-Payments Problems', *American Economic Review* 89(3): 473–500.

Kashyap, A. and Stein, J. (1995) 'The Impact of Monetary Policy on Bank Balance Sheets', *Carnegie-Rochester Conference Series on Public Policy* 42: 151–95.

Kashyap, A. and Stein, J. (1997) 'What Do a Million Banks Have to Say About the Transmission of Monetary Policy?', *National Bureau of Economic Research Working Paper*, No. 6056.

Kashyap, A., Stein, J. and Wilcox, D. (1993) 'Monetary Policy and Credit Conditions: Evidence from the Composition of External Finance', *American Economic Review* 83: 78–98.

King, R. G. and Levine, R. (1993) 'Finance and Growth: Schumpeter Might be Right', *Quarterly Journal of Economics* 108(3): 717–37.

Kiyotaki, N. and Moore, J. (1997) 'Credit Cycles', *Journal of Political Economy* 105(2): 211–48.

Levine, R. (1997) 'Financial Development and Economic Growth: Views and Agenda', *Journal of Economic Literature* XXXV: 688–726.

McKinnon, R. I. and Pill, H. (1997) 'Credible Economic Liberalizations and Over-Borrowing', *AEA Papers and Proceedings* 87(2): 189–93.

McKinnon, R. I. and Pill, H. (1998) *International Overborrowing: A Decomposition of Credit and Currency Risks*. Manuscript.

Mayer, C. (1989) 'Myths of the West: Lessons from Developed Countries for Development Finance', *World Bank Working Paper WPS301*.

Rajan, R. G. and Zingales, L. (1996) Financial Dependence and Growth. Manuscript.

Ramos, A. M. (1998) 'Capital Structures and Portfolio Composition During Banking Crisis: Lessons from Argentina 1995', *International Monetary Fund Working Paper WP/98/121*.

Sachs, J. D., Tornell, A. and Velasco, A. (1996) 'Financial Crises in Emerging Markets: The Lessons from 1995', *Brookings Papers on Economic Activity*, No. 1: 147–215.

Sharpe, S. (1995) 'Bank Capitalization, Regulation, and the Credit Crunch: A Critical Review of the Research Findings', *Board of Governors of the Federal Reserve System Discussion Paper*, No. 95-20.

Singh, A. (1995) 'Corporate Financial Patterns in Industrializing Economies: A Comparative International Study', *International Finance Corporation Technical Paper*, No. 2.

Singh, A. (1997) 'Financial Liberalization, Stock Markets and Economic Development', *Economic Journal* 107: 771–82.

Singh, A. and Hamid, J. (1992) 'Corporate Financial Structures in Developing Countries', *International Finance Corporation Technical Paper*, No. 1.

Stein, J. C. (1998) 'An Adverse-Selection Model of Bank Asset and Liability Management with Implications for the Transmission of Monetary Policy', *RAND Journal of Economics* 29(3): 466–86.

Stiglitz, J. E. (1994) 'The Role of the State in Financial Markets', in M. Bruno and B. Pleskovic (eds), *Proceedings of the World Bank Annual Bank Conference on Development Economics 1993*. Washington, DC: World Bank.

Stiglitz, J. E. and Uy, M. (1996) 'Financial Markets, Public Policy, and the east Asian Miracle', *World Bank Research Observer* 11(2): 249–76.

Sussman, O. and Zeira, J. (1995) 'Banking and Development', *Centre for Economic Policy Research, London Discussion Paper 1127*.

Wyplosz, C. (n.d.). 'International Capital Market Failures: Sources, Costs and Solutions', Manuscript.

12 Exchange rates, real–financial and micro–macro linkages

Rohinton Medhora

1. Introduction

It is commonly understood that the determinants of competitiveness are varied and complex, and spring from micro, macro and institutional levels, as also from the monetary and the real side of the economy. A key link between micro and macro, and also between real and financial is the exchange rate. Exchange rates link macroeconomic policies and exogenous events to sector and firm level outcomes; they link financial developments to output and employment; they alter international goods and financial flows and in turn are altered by these flows.

This chapter conceptualizes these linkages into four 'cells', as shown in the table below.

	Short-term exchange rate movements	Long-term movements (i.e. persistent deviations from equilibrium)
Goods flows		
Financial flows		

The bulk of this chapter concentrates on the first row of the table, surveying the issues around the matter of the effect of short-term and long-term exchange rate volatility on international trade. These effects are relatively one way, meaning exchange rates have the potential to alter trade flows, but increasingly it is clear that the classical view of the exchange rate being determined by goods flows is less likely. The relationships in the second row, on the other hand, are likely two way and are examined at the end of the chapter; and equally importantly (though not the subject of this chapter), investment flows in turn determine trade flows.

Section 2 argues that exchange rate variability is a relevant issue in trade modelling, while Section 3 outlines the 'standard' model that is used in most studies. Section 4 addresses some general issues that arise from the model, while Section 5 concentrates on how to define and measure exchange rate variability. Section 6 presents financial flows and Section 7 some concluding remarks.

2. Why variability matters

In making their decisions, economic agents face a range of risk. The international trader – be he an importer or an exporter – must deal with uncertainty of supplies, of the weather, of government policies, and in a world of floating exchange rates, uncertainty in the rates of change of those exchange rates. The traditional literature on portfolio selection stresses that risk in one area – changes in exchange rates – must be seen relative to all the other types of risks that a trader faces, both in trading abroad *and* in trading at home.[1]

While exchange rate risk may be 'just another' risk however, this does not diminish its importance for a number of reasons. While it may be largely avoidable, either by moving away from foreign trade and towards domestic trade, or at the extreme, moving back to a system of fixed exchange rates, neither is a trivial prospect. A move towards autarky, with all its resultant implications on global resource allocation and comparative advantage, while acceptable in portfolio selection terms, is hardly a solution. It essentially means running away from the problem, and turning away from what has been the engine of economic growth and global integration since the industrial revolution – international trade.

The prospect of a world of fixed exchange rates, while eliminating nominal exchange rate risk, does not eliminate real exchange rate risk, and, in any case, has implications on domestic economic policies serious enough to merit further debate. The point being made here is that while exchange rate risk may be avoidable – as proper portfolio selection would dictate – the two results of avoiding it – autarky or fixed exchange rates – are serious enough for this topic to merit closer attention.

Exchange rate changes, of course, can be covered against, by trading on the forward market. But forward markets in foreign exchange offer only partial – and imperfect – cover, for a number of reasons. First, the transaction costs of buying cover increase the cost of foreign trade. Second, forward markets in foreign exchange are incomplete in both length of cover offered, and location – the latter being a problem for traders in small LDCs, the former a problem for all foreign traders. Third, the forward exchange rate is a poor predictor of the future spot rate.[2] Fourth, traders cannot always plan the magnitude or timing of all their foreign exchange transactions.

Whether for reasons stated explicitly or implicitly, all the studies cited in the Appendix assume that in the absence of full information or complete forward markets, exchange rate variability should hurt trade.

It should be noted here that under the Newbery and Stiglitz (1981) mean-variance analysis framework, even this conclusion does not always hold. The argument here is that an increase in exchange rate risk has a substitution and an income effect. The substitution effect leads traders to shift away from foreign trade and towards domestic trade – the usual expected effect, as argued above. The income effect works in the *opposite* direction, however. When exchange rate risk increases, the expected total utility from foreign trade receipts falls. This leads the trader to *increase* his foreign trade activity, to offset the decline in expected utility in this sector.[3]

While this result is counter-intuitive, it should be noted that it follows from a few reasonable assumptions about utility functions and risk averseness. The argument that exchange rate variability hurts trade thus boils down to the assertion that the substitution effect (as described above) outweighs the income effect. This is not an unreasonable line of thought. The idea that a trader, when faced with increased exchange rate risk, decides to *increase* his exposure to the riskier market seems unrealistic, and should be borne out by a conversation with any trader.

Thus, while in theory exchange rate variability need not diminish – indeed, it will enhance! – foreign trade, there are sound practical reasons – imperfect information, and incomplete and costly markets for cover – for it to do just that.

3. The model

The 'standard' model of international trade incorporating exchange rate variability was first rigorously presented by Hooper and Kohlhagen (1978), and this model is still the theoretical basis of the empirical work in this area. Consider, first, the case of a domestic producer who must import some of his inputs, operating in a flexible exchange rate environment. His output (Q) is an increasing function of domestic income (Y) and the price of other goods in the domestic economy (PD), and a decreasing function of the price (P) and non-price rationing (CU) of own output. This can be seen in eqn (12.1):

$$Q = aP + b\text{PD} + CY + d\text{CU}. \tag{12.1}$$

The firm maximizes its utility, over output, as in eqn (12.2):

$$\max_Q U = E\pi - \gamma(V(\pi))^{1/2}. \tag{12.2}$$

That is, utility is an increasing function of expected nominal profits ($E\pi$), and a decreasing function of their standard deviation, $(V(\pi))^{1/2}$. γ is the measure of risk preference, so that $\gamma > 0$ implies risk aversion, $\gamma = 0$ risk neutrality and $\gamma = 0$ risk loving. Equation (12.3) shows the importing firm's profits:

$$\pi = Q \cdot P - C \cdot Q - HP^* iQ, \tag{12.3}$$

where C is the unit cost of production, P^* is the foreign currency price of imports, i is the proportion of imports in output and H is the cost of foreign exchange to the importer. H depends on the proportion of imports denominated in foreign currency (β), and the proportion of these that are hedged in the forward market (α). This is illustrated in eqn (12.4):

$$H = \beta(\alpha F + (1 - \alpha)R_1), \tag{12.4}$$

where F is the forward exchange rate, and R_1 the future spot rate (both defined as the domestic currency price of one unit of foreign currency). This cost, H, would be certain only if all imports were denominated in domestic currency (i.e. $\beta = 0$), or all imports denominated in foreign currency could be hedged on the forward market ($\alpha = 1$).

Since R_1 is assumed to be uncertain, eqn (12.5) is the variance of the importer's profits:

$$V(\pi) = [P^* iQ\beta(1 - \alpha)]^2 \cdot V(R_1). \tag{12.5}$$

Substituting (12.3) for α, and (12.5) for $V(\alpha)$ into (12.2), and solving (12.2) for q (where $q = iQ$, the firm's import demand function) yields eqn (12.6):

$$q = i(a \cdot UC + b \cdot PD + c \cdot Y + d \cdot CU) + ai^2 P^* (EH + \gamma\beta(1 - \alpha)\sigma R_1). \tag{12.6}$$

Since $a < 0$, eqn (12.6) shows that an increase in the cost of foreign exchange (H, or its components, β and α) or an increase in the variability of R_1 (σR_1, the standard deviation) will shift the demand for imports to the left.

The same method is used to derive analogous results for the supply of exports. The exporter sells some of his output at home, and exports the rest, where he faces the import demand function of eqn (12.6), times n, the number of importing firms. Maximizing his utility from profits as before, yields an export supply function which moves to the left when nominal exchange rate variability increases. The import demand and export supply functions are then used to solve for a price equation.

Cushman (1983) extends this framework and assumes that firms maximize expected *real* profits, and that prices and exchange rates are uncertain. This yields the conclusion that it is *real* exchange rate variability that should be measured. This is discussed further in Section 5.

A number of issues – other than how to measure exchange rate variability – arise from this model, and these are discussed next.

4. Issues in the model

First, it should be noted from eqn (12.6), that so long as the trader is risk averse (meaning $\gamma > 0$), trade is adversely affected by an increase in exchange variability (σR_1). As Newbery and Stiglitz (1981: 85–90), Coes (1981: 130–3) and de Grauwe (1988: 64–9) point out, this result follows because of the implicit assumption of constant *absolute* risk aversion of traders. This assumption effectively eliminates the income effect of a change in exchange rate variability.

For the more general case of a concave and separable expected utility function, the two conflicting effects will operate, and the effect of exchange rate variability on trade then becomes an empirical issue.

But whether we assume constant absolute risk aversion – thus eliminating the income effect – or not, measuring the impact of exchange rate variability on trade is a relevant exercise. In the one case it measures the – predicted – adverse effect, and in the other, it measures the net effect of the income and substitution effects discussed above.

The second issue of concern is the degree of aggregation of the dependent variable in question. When total trade – meaning imports or exports aggregated across countries and commodities – is used, this may result in biased coefficients. Theil (1954) showed that unless all the disaggregated coefficients are equal, the aggregated coefficients being weighted averages of the disaggregated ones, will contain a specification bias. Subsequently, Zellner (1969) showed that for a class of regression models with random coefficients and for a certain range of specifying assumptions, there is no aggregation bias. But here, the standard error could be very high.

Brodsky and Sampson (1983) show that exchange rate variations affect different industries in different ways, so that an 'industry-specific' effective exchange rate might be in order. Goldstein and Khan (1985) survey the empirical evidence in trade in this regard and come out in favour of disaggregated studies – by country and by commodity group.

Where the data permit, this approach gives more interesting results. As the Appendix shows, the studies that use disaggregated data – either bilateral or sectoral – invariably reveal differences in the effects of exchange rate variability on trade. As Coes (1981), Maskus (1986) and Belanger *et al.* (1988) report, some sectors have been measurably affected by exchange rate variability, and others have not. Why this is so is not pursued by the authors, but is presumably of further concern to policy makers and those in the affected sectors.

Similarly, the studies using bilateral trade flows reveal differences in the pattern of the impact of exchange rate variability. The most recent and widest ranging study using this approach, Thursby and Thursby (1987), reveals significant bilateral effects. This implies that the *pattern* of world trade, not merely the level, is affected by exchange rate variability. Once again, the implications of differing bilateral effects – are they because bilateral exchange rate variabilities differ, or because of forward exchange rate markets of varying completeness? – are not pursued in any of the studies.

Pooling the data rather than aggregating it will increase the sample size, but may result in heteroscedasticity. In effect, when pooling data of large and small countries, we must first ask – and test for – whether small countries differ in their response to exchange rate variability from large countries. If heteroscedasticity is present, most corrections for it assume knowledge of its correct specification. The MacKinnon and White (1985) procedure has the advantage of not assuming such knowledge. It yields inefficient coefficient estimates, but the t- and F-tests are asymptotically valid.

The third issue we deal with is the capacity utilization variable. Hooper and Kohlhagen (1978) introduce this as a non-price rationing variable that works as the price variable does. As domestic capacity utilization increases, domestically produced inputs are delivered with longer lags, thus decreasing the quantity demanded of imports. On the export side, Coes (1981) suggests that as domestic excess capacity increases, producers are driven to seek markets abroad.

It is not clear why these relative business cycle effects will not manifest themselves via the price and income variables, and indeed, not all studies include a capacity utilization variable. For the industrialized economies, indices of capacity utilization in manufacturing are available. For primarily agricultural economies, it is not clear how capacity utilization should be measured. For Brazil, Coes (1981) uses the residuals from a semi-log time trend of GNP.[4] In Medhora (1990), capacity utilization at home and abroad, thus measured, was found to be insignificant in explaining West African imports, and dropping it did not change the results reported.

Finally, there is some latitude on what the dependent variable should be. Not all the estimations are the result of a rigorously specified model of trade. Thus, whether it is import/export volume, as most of the studies use, or whether it is growth of imports/exports, as Kenen (1979) and de Grauwe (1988) use, or the import/export to GNP ratio, as Coes (1981), Thursby (1981) and Thursby and Thursby (1985) use, depends on the authors' notion of what is being affected by exchange rate variability. Similarly, it is not always explicitly stated why only imports or exports are used as the dependent variable. In a general equilibrium framework of the Hooper–Kohlhagen–Cushman type, both imports and exports are affected by exchange rate variability. Yet they do not estimate separately demand for imports and supply of exports equations – their export equations incorporate the effect of exchange rate variability on imported inputs.

While most studies that have estimated separate import and export equations have found no asymmetric effects, Akhtar and Hilton (1984) and Belanger *et al.* (1988) have. Moreover, Kenen and Rodrick (1986) found an adverse effect on imports of exchange rate variability for many of the industrialized countries whose exports had been found to have been unaffected by exchange rate variability – see, for example, Bailey *et al.* (1986, 1987) and Côté (1986). Even allowing for slight differences in sample size, time period and the measure of exchange rate variability, these results seem anomalous, and an estimation of both, imports and exports, seems appropriate. For LDCs, changes in government policies – especially producer prices – and the weather, along with movements in relative prices and world income, may well dwarf the effects of exchange rate variability on the supply of exports. But, properly modelled to incorporate these factors, a study of LDC exports may yield interesting results.

5. Defining and measuring exchange rate variability

Two issues will be addressed here. First, are we concerned with real or nominal exchange rate variability? Having made this decision, second, what statistical measure of variability should be used?

At the outset it should be noted that measured variability is only a proxy for what is really at issue – uncertainty. It is possible for a low level of variability to be associated with a high degree of uncertainty, and vice versa. Some measures are better than others at overcoming this dilemma, as will be seen below. But to the extent that forward exchange markets do not exist everywhere and for long time horizons, measured variability captures the uncertainty well. But different variability measures have different characteristics.

The use of real exchange rate (meaning nominal exchange rates corrected for differing relative price changes across countries) variability is advocated primarily because it takes into account the possible offsetting nature of price movements to nominal exchange rate changes. Optimal resource allocation decisions should, of course, be made on the basis of nominal exchange rate *and* price – that is, based on *real* exchange rate – changes. But nominal variability should not be ruled out entirely, for a number of reasons.

First, because the real exchange rate is composed of two (possibly) offsetting components, it does not follow that real variability is always less than nominal variability. Indeed, as Helleiner (1981), Lanyi and Suss (1982) and Akhtar and Hilton (1984) show, through most of the 1970s and early 1980s, real variability has often exceeded nominal variability in many countries. Whatever variability is chosen should depend on stronger reasons than which type has been larger.

Exchange rates both influence, and are influenced by prices. The individual trader faces two separate risks – a nominal exchange rate risk, and a price risk. By fusing the two, a measure of real exchange rate variability obscures this distinction. For example, even if, on day thirty, a price inflation is perfectly offset by a nominal exchange rate depreciation, leaving the real exchange rate unchanged, on day one the trader faced *two* uncertainties – the price movement and the exchange rate movement. His decisions of day one – how much to import/export, and from/to who? – must thus be based on these actual uncertainties, not the happy *ex post* coincidence of day thirty, which shows zero variability – and also zero uncertainty.

If we assume traders have a short time horizon in a world where nominal exchange rates move more often (or, at least more visibly) than prices, then a measure of nominal variability should be used. But if we assume that traders are more sophisticated, keeping in mind not just nominal exchange rate changes but also the impact of monetary and fiscal policies at home and abroad, then a measure of real variability should be used.

Having determined which type of variability should be of concern, it remains to be decided on how it should be measured. The range of measures available include the standard deviation, deviations from trend, difference between previous forward and current spot rates, Gini mean difference coefficient (GMD), coefficient of variation and the scale measure of variability.

The use of deviations from trend assumes that the trend itself is predictable and costless, thus leaving only the misfits as 'true' measures of the cost of uncertainty. In economies where forward exchange markets are thin and/or expensive, even the *trend*, known and predictable as it may be, will have welfare implications because allowing for it consumes resources. If it is determined that deviations from trend best approximate exchange rate uncertainty, there is still the question of how to 'de-trend' the data.

IMF (1986) uses two measures that do this: (1) a weighted average of the standard deviation of changes in the natural log of the exchange rate, and (2) the standard deviation of changes in the natural log of a weighted average of bilateral rates (i.e. of effective exchange rates). Lanyi and Suss (1982) show that so long as the covariance between two exchange rates is non-zero, (1) and (2) will diverge, so that both measures should be used in estimation.[5]

The standard deviation measure, while it does not take the trend and deviations from it into account, does not render the trader completely uninsightful. Rather, it assumes that deviations from an intra-period mean of observations best reflect uncertainty. Since the mean of a group of observations is easier to compute than their trend, the standard deviation measure is less informationally demanding of the trader than the deviations from trend measure.

The use of the difference between the previous forward and current spot rates to measure variability assumes that hedging is a viable alternative to cover foreign transactions. As noted earlier, this measure reflects uncertainty only insofar as hedging is costless (which it is not), or can cover *all* foreign transactions (which it cannot).

The relative merits of the GMD and scale measure of variability as against the standard deviation has been the subject of a debate between Rana (1981, 1984) and Brodsky (1984). Rana argues that if the variability measure is a non-normal stable Paretian distribution (as he finds for his sample of effective exchange rates), then the second moment does not exist, making the sample standard deviation unstable, and therefore, statistically inappropriate in use. As alternatives, he suggests the GMD and scale measure. The GMD is the average of the difference in all possible pairs of values regardless of the sign, while the scale measure uses only the middle 44 per cent of the range of observations.

Whereas Rana speaks of leptokurtosis and interfractile ranges, Brodsky's arguments are based on economics, or as he puts it 'a somewhat more practical point of view than that employed by Rana' (1984: 295). Essentially, a non-normal distribution has too many observations in the tails, thus giving them more weight than they would have in a normal distribution. Brodsky asserts that if we assume risk aversion, then in fact greater weight *should* be given to extreme observations. On the other hand, the scale measure *drops* 28 per cent of the observations at each end, making it economically meaningless.

The GMD is similar to the standard deviation in that all observations are given equal weight, but while the former uses absolute differences, the latter uses second-order (i.e. squared) differences, making it more relevant under the assumptions of risk aversion. It may well be argued that the GMD could be modified to use squared differences as well, but then it still pairs all observations with one another, rather than with an intra-period mean – as the standard deviation does – which at least implies some intelligence for the trader. After all, the point of the variability measure is to closely approximate uncertainty. By averaging all possible pair differences, the GMD makes any and all exchange rate changes 'uncertain'. The standard deviation, on the other hand, grounds all changes to a base – the intra-period mean.

Finally, it should be noted that the issue of periodicity has been largely ignored in the discussion on measuring exchange rate variability. In the context of export earnings instability, Gelb (1977, 1979) posed this question – for a given degree of fluctuation around a mean, does it matter whether the frequency of fluctuations is high or low? He found that low frequency variability, meaning a deviation from trend that persists for over two years, is more costly than high frequency variability because the financial system is unable or unwilling to give medium- or long-term credit to exporters facing such an earnings risk.

In the absence of complete forward exchange markets, it is unclear whether low frequency exchange rate variability is more or less harmful to trade than high frequency variability. Indeed, none of the measures outlined above allow for the impact of persistently misaligned exchange rates on trade, which has also become a feature of the post-Bretton Woods system.

The decision, then, on variability – real or nominal? how measured? – depends on the researcher's a priori belief of the system at hand. Is it fairly well covered by forward exchange markets? How well informed are traders?

Studies that use multiple measures of variability in effect avoid this problem by trying to take into account all, or most, possibilities. If all the measures used show consistent results – one way or the other – then all is well. But it must be remembered that such an approach has no basis in theory. The author is saying, 'I can't say much about the system and its traders, so let's try everything.'

6. Financial flows

The literature and methodology to assess the impact of exchange rate volatility on financial flows is less extensive than that for trade flows. The Newbery–Stiglitz framework can be used here too, and is the standard wherein savings and investment decisions are analysed. Typically, this is done with respect to an uncertain rate of return, which captures exchange rate movements in addition to other concerns such as the interest rate or country risk. Aizenman (1992) distinguishes between real and nominal shocks to show that in an intertemporal model with monopolistic competition and *risk neutrality*, a fixed exchange rate regime is more conducive to FDI relative to a flexible exchange rate. Empirical evidence presented in Goldberg and Kolstad (1994) confirms a negative correlation between real exchange rate volatility and FDI in US bilateral FDI flows with Canada, Japan and the United Kingdom. A more extensive survey of the empirical evidence on the matter is contained in Bailey and Tavlas (1991). They conclude that the ambiguity predicted in the theoretical findings is reflected in the empirical literature (which, to be sure, is focused on developed countries).

The theoretical and procedural issues involved in analysing the link between exchange rate volatility and investment are much the same as those discussed earlier in this chapter. Questions of the basic underpinnings of the theoretical model, of how to measure volatility and what to make of the results remain. It is this last issue that is the focus of the concluding section of this chapter.

7. Conclusion

Historically, and using admittedly crude methods of measurement, Yeager (1976) argues that throughout the nineteenth century and during the interwar years, there was no correlation between exchange rate variability and world trade. Several authors, among them Bailey and Tavlas (1991), Bini-Smaghi (1991), Dellas and Zilberfarb (1993) and Willett (1986) attempt to assess the reasons behind the admittedly mixed bag of results that we possess. Interestingly, while most are common to trade and investment flows, the policy implications of each set of results differ. Put more precisely, the policy implications for each of the four cells in the figure at the start of this chapter are different.

Interestingly, there is convincing evidence to suggest that most exchange rate changes during the past three decades have been unexpected. This is borne out by the failure of most models to consistently and accurately predict exchange rate movements, survey data on the topic, and indicators of expected exchange rate movements such as interest rate differentials and forward discount premia (Frenkel and Goldstein 1989). Exchange rates have also become more not less variable over time. Why then, do exchange rates that have become *more volatile and more unpredictable* still yield ambiguous results in their impact on trade and investment?

The results of the early studies reported in the Appendix, while mostly showing no adverse effect, must be reconsidered in a critical light. First, many straddle the period of transition from fixed to floating exchange rates. This regime shift is strong enough to cast doubts on any trade model that ignores this fundamental structural shift – the standard Lucas critique.

But even for the studies that use as their time period the early part of the post-Bretton Woods era, there are two counter-acting reasons why their results should be considered tentative.

First, contracts, trade and investment relationships are made over a number of years, and will not be broken or changed right after a new exchange rate regime begins. This 'inertia' effect, then, may result in understatement of the true costs of exchange rate variability on trade.

Second, in the early phase of the new regime, there may well be greater uncertainty among traders, as they adjust to the new rules of the game. Forward markets need time to develop, and the early jumps in exchange rates may only be the inevitable result of a system finding its equilibrium. This 'growing pains' effect would overstate exchange rate variability costs on trade.

The evidence for the more recent period – the mid-1970s and after – is mixed, although it is fair to say that there are more studies that find no effect than there are that do. This, however, is not the last word on the issue.

For one, the evidence is quite convincing that exchange rate variability, both real and nominal, has, indeed, *increased* over time.[6] Studies of the mid- and late 1980s may well show more convincingly an adverse effect of exchange rate variability on trade.

It is possible, of course, for the 'no effect' results to have economic meaning. As Willett (1986) argues, if exchange rate variability merely *reflects* other (meaning policy) variability, or if relative to domestic variability, exchange rate variability has not increased, then empirical studies will, in fact, find no adverse effects.[7] The call here is for trade and investment models to be set in a more general framework in which exchange rate variability is not the only type of variability that traders and investors must face. Indeed, Bailey and Tavlas (1991) report that during the 1970s and 1980s, exchange rate volatility has been *less* than volatility of commodity prices and interest rates, a trend that holds for the 1990s. One also needs a measure of changes in country risk over time before exchange rate volatility on trade and investment decisions can be situated in a more general (and germane) context.

Indeed, the studies reported in this chapter do not address the other effects of exchange rate variability on trade and investment. As mentioned earlier, persistent misalignments of exchange rates have resource allocation implications that are not addressed here.[8]

If, in fact, a persistently over-valued exchange rate in a country squeezes the traded-goods sector and thus provokes calls for increased protection which is then not removed when the exchange rate falls back into line, then trade will be further affected.[9]

Another possible reason to answer the question posed at the start of this section is given in Gonzaga and Terra (1997). In comparing their results on the impact of exchange rate volatility on exports in Brazil with those of Gagnon (1993) for industrial countries, they postulate that Brazil's much higher exchange rate volatility might explain their more significant and robust results. That decision making is not a linear or even predictable function of risk or volatility is a very intuitively appealing concept, which merits further examination.

Finally, it should be noted that the bulk of the literature uses developed country data. In LDCs, where forward markets are less developed and the cost to adjust to changes in the economic environment is higher, exchange rate variability – coupled with developed country protectionism – may have a measurable impact on trade and income. Yet, to the extent that financial markets are less developed (and therefore carry higher transactions costs) in developing countries, it is there that the policy implications of volatile exchange rates need to be best understood.

Clearly, there is no substitute for complete financial markets. There is an extensive theoretical and empirical literature that links the level of financial sector development with favourable growth outcomes. More germane to this chapter, Rajan and Zingales (1998) show that in a sample of forty-one developed and developing countries during the 1980s, industrial sectors that need relatively more external finance developed disproportionately faster in countries with well-developed financial sectors. The principal policy conclusion, then, even (or perhaps especially) bearing in mind the large recent outpouring of thought in relation to the East Asian crisis, is that there is no substitute for a deep and efficient financial sector to minimize risk (i.e. allow economic agents to minimize risk) and permit an optimal allocation of resources.

But as a guide to policy, this statement may be more helpful in principle than in practice. For a given state of the financial sector, the causes of short-term exchange rate movements differ from those of long-term (i.e. persistent) exchange rate movements. The current preoccupation with Tobinesque taxes, indeed capital account regimes more generally (summarized in chapters one and six of Helleiner 1998), is most suited to addressing issues related to short-term volatility. Even here, diminution of said volatility is likely to have a greater impact on goods flows and short-term investments, which have a relatively short time horizon, than investment flows, rather than medium- and long-term investments with a longer pay-off period. So 'sand in the wheels' types of policies are likely to be a useful addition to the arsenal of macroeconomy managers so long as: (1) they do not impede financial sector development (relative to the alternative), and (2) their limits in effectiveness even if ideally applied are understood.

Persistent misalignments of exchange rates pose a different set of issues. The most obvious case that can be assessed relates to 'Dutch disease', where it is the attraction of a country's natural resource endowments (or size of overseas remittances) rather than a capital market imperfection *per se* that is the root cause of the disequilibrium. Sterilization policies assuming the domestic financial sector permits this, are not long-term solutions, and often lead to significant side effects even in the short term.

A second and no less important dimension of this problem is the potential for international capital flows themselves to lead to persistent misalignment problems. The jury is still out on whether domestic policies alone (as is alleged for many East Asian countries and some European ones) could have created the environment within which persistent capital movements lead to persistent exchange rate misalignment.

The important things to understand here are that (1) exchange rates alter and are altered by trade and financial flows, especially the latter; (2) but that they are but one factor in the decision-making process of economic agents. Also, (3) while there is no obvious substitute for complete markets, the policy implications for dealing with various sets of outcomes vary, not only depending on the nature of the volatility (short or long term) but also the context within which policies are framed and implemented.

Appendix – Summary of salient studies

Study	Data, period, countries	Measure of variability	Dependent variable	Results
Clark and Haulk (1972)	Quarterly, 1952–72, Canada, US	Standard deviation of forward exchange rate of (moving average) previous four quarters	Aggregate real imports and exports	No effect
Makin (1976)	Quarterly, 1960–73, Canada, Federal Republic of Germany, Japan, US	Standard deviation of spot exchange rate	Aggregate real imports	No effect
Hooper and Kohlhagen (1978)	Quarterly, 1965–75, France, Federal Republic of Germany, Japan, UK, US	Average absolute difference between forward and spot rates in each quarter	Bilateral export volume and price	No volume effect except US and UK. Adverse price effect.
Abrams (1980a)	Annual, 1973–6, 19 developed countries (pooled)	Variance of previous year's spot rates, monthly	Bilateral export volume	Adverse effect

Study	Data	Measure of variability	Dependent variable	Effect
Abrams (1980b)	Annual, 1973–6, 19 developed countries (pooled)	Variance of previous year's real exchange rates (monthly)	Bilateral export volume	Adverse effect
Gupta (1980)	India, Israel, Mexico, Korea, Taiwan	Standard deviation of exchange rate changes around trend	Aggregate export volume	No effect
Kenen (1980)	Annual, 1974–6, 33 countries (cross-section)	Monthly standard deviation of nominal and real spot rates	Growth of aggregate real exports	No effect
Thursby (1980)	Quarterly, 1953–77, Canada	Per cent difference between a hypothetical 'fixed' rate and actual rate, in each quarter	Aggregate real exports	No effect
Coes (1981)	Annual, 1957–74, Brazil	Integral difference cumulative distribution of real exchange rate and the 'certain' exchange rate	Export–production ratio, by sector for two industries	Adverse, except for two countries
Thursby (1981)	Quarterly, 1972–9, 15 developed countries + Brazil, Spain, Ireland, Turkey	Variance of nominal and real effective exchange rates	Aggregate export–GNP ratio	No effect

Appendix Continued

Study	Data, period, countries	Measure of variability	Dependent variable	Results
Cushman (1983)	Quarterly, 1965–77, France, Federal Republic of Germany, Japan, UK, US	Standard deviation of changes in spot real exchange rate, four quarters	Bilateral export volume and prices	Adverse volume and price effects in some cases
Justice (1983)	Quarterly, 1973–81, UK	Average changes and average standard deviations of nominal and real exchange rates	Bilateral export volume and price	Adverse effect in some cases
Akhtar and Hilton (1984)	Quarterly, 1974–81, Federal Republic of Germany, US	Standard deviation of effective exchange rate	Aggregate export and import volume, price of exports and imports	Adverse effect except US imports
Bank of England (1984)	Quarterly, 1976–83, UK	Average absolute changes in daily rates; standard deviation within each quarter	Aggregate import and export volume, price of imports and exports	No effect on trade. Adverse price effect

IMF (1984)	Quarterly, 1965–81, Canada, France, Federal Republic of Germany, Italy, Japan, UK, US	Standard deviation of changes in spot real exchange rate, past five quarters	Bilateral export volume	No effect
Gotur (1985)	Quarterly, 1975–83, France, Federal Republic of Germany, Japan, UK, US	Standard deviation of effective exchange rate	Aggregate import and export volume	No effect
Thursby and Thursby (1985)	Annual, 1973–77, 20 countries (pooled)	Trade-weighted algebraic mean of the per cent change in bilateral exchange rates; trade-weighted mean of absolute values of per cent changes in bilateral rates; trade-weighted standard deviation of per cent changes in above series	Bilateral real exports; change in export–GNP ratio	No aggregate effect; adverse bilateral effects

Appendix Continued

Study	Data, period, countries	Measure of variability	Dependent variable	Results
Bailey et al. (1986)	Quarterly, 1973–84, Canada, France, Federal Republic of Germany, Italy, Japan, UK, US	Absolute value of per cent change in nominal effective exchange rate	Aggregate real exports	No effect
Côté (1986)	Quarterly, 1972–83, Canada	Standard deviation of changes in spot real exchange rate, four quarters; standard deviation of effective exchange rate	Aggregate import and export volume, price of imports and exports	No effect
Kenen and Rodrik (1986)	Quarterly, 1975–82, 11 developed countries	Standard deviations of real exchange rate; standard deviations of the trend in real exchange rate; standard deviation of the real exchange	Volume of aggregate manufactured imports	Adverse effect in many cases

Study	Data	Exchange rate variability measure	Trade measure	Result
		rate from an AR1 equation		
Maskus (1986)	Quarterly, 1974–84, US	Three-month spread between spot and forward rate, adjusted for expected inflation	Bilateral real exports, by sector	Adverse aggregate effect, no effect in some sectors/countries
Bailey et al. (1987)	Quarterly, 1973–84, Canada, France, Federal Republic of Germany, Italy, Japan, UK, US	Absolute value of per cent change in nominal and real effective exchange rate, standard deviation of nominal and real spot rates	Aggregate real exports	No effect
Thursby and Thursby (1987)	Annual, 1974–82, 17 countries (pooled)	Variance of spot rate around its trend	Bilateral real exports and export price	Adverse effect
Belanger et al. (1988)	Quarterly, 1974–87, Canada, US	Variance in per cent difference between spot and forward rate	Bilateral real imports and exports, sectoral	Adverse effect in some sectors
de Grauwe (1988)	Annual, 1960–9 and 1973–84, 10 industrial countries (pooled)	Standard deviation of exchange rate changes around mean, real and nominal	Change in nominal exports	Adverse effect

Appendix Continued

Study	Data, period, countries	Measure of variability	Dependent variable	Results
Medhora (1990)	Annual, 1976–82, Benin, Burkina, Faso, Côté d'Ivoire, Niger, Senegal, Togo (pooled)	Standard deviation of weekly, monthly and quarterly rates	Aggregate real imports from non-franc zone	No effect
Gonzaga and Terra (1997)	Daily, weekly, monthly, 1980–95, Brazil	Standard deviation, REER	Export volume, X/GDP	No to slight adverse effect

Notes

1 See, for example, Markowitz (1952), Debreu (1959), Sharpe (1964), Lintner (1965), Mossin (1966) and Arrow (1971).
2 The empirical evidence here is quite strong. See, for example, Hodrick and Srivastava (1987), Cumby and Obstfeld (1981, 1984), Hsieh (1984), Dooley and Shafer (1983), Hansen and Hodrick (1980, 1983), Bilson (1981) and Frankel (1980).
3 For a more rigorous discussion of the Newbery–Stiglitz framework in this context, see de Grauwe (1988) and Coes (1981).
4 For more on measuring capacity utilization, see Lim (1976), Artus (1977) and Christiano (1981).
5 Cuddy and Della Valle (1978) proposed a measure to de-trend time series data, which was subsequently refined by Duggan (1970). On this matter, see also Della Valle (1979) and Brown (1979). The method essentially involves 'correcting' the conventional coefficient of variation by a factor reflecting the goodness of fit of past observations to a time trend. Tsui (1987) shows that Duggan's measure of variability will always be less than the conventional coefficient of variation.
6 See, for example, Kenen (1979), Gupta (1980), Brodsky *et al.* (1981), Helleiner (1981) and Kenen and Rodrick (1984, 1986).
7 Some studies like IMF (1984) and Gotur (1985) have found a 'perverse' sign on the exchange rate variability measure, meaning it is positive and significant. In the Newbery–Stiglitz framework, of course, this is not perverse, but rather evidence of their income effect overriding their substitution effect – difficult to conceive as this may be.
8 Cushman (1986) has found significant 'third country' effects on US exports to its six largest partners. That is, an increase in, say, the variability of the dollar–DM rate will shift exports away from Germany and towards, say, the UK. This is consistent with Thursby and Thursby (1987), who find that exchange rate variability affects not just the *volume* but also the *pattern* of world trade.
9 This is what de Grauwe (1988: 69) calls the 'political economy of exchange rate variability'.

References

Abrams, R. K. (1980a) 'International Trade Flows under Flexible Exchange Rates, Federal Reserve Bank of Kansas City', *Economic Review* 65(3): 3–10.
Abrams, R. K. (1980b) 'Exchange Rate Volatility and Bilateral Trade Flows', Draft, Federal Reserve Bank of Kansas City.
Aizenman, J. (1992) 'Exchange Rate Flexibility, Volatility, and the Patterns of Domestic and Foreign Direct Investment', *International Monetary Fund Working Paper*, No. WP/92/20.
Akhtar, M. A. and Spence Hilton, R. (1984) 'Exchange Rate Uncertainty and International Trade: Some Conceptual Issues and New Estimates for Germany and the United States', *Federal Reserve Bank of New York Research Paper*, No. 8403.
Amsden, A. H. (1989) *Asia's Next Giant: South Korea and Late Industrialization*. Oxford: Oxford University Press.
Arrow, K. J. (1971) 'The Role of Securities in the Optimal Allocation of Risk-Bearing', in K. J. Arrow (ed.), *Essays in the Theory of Risk-Bearing*. Chicago: Markham Press.
Artus, J. R. (1977) 'Measures of Potential Output in Manufacturing for Eight Industrial Countries, 1955–78', *International Monetary Fund Staff Papers* 24(1): 1–35.
Bailey, M. J. and Tavlas, G. S. (1991) 'Exchange Rate Variability and Direct Investment', *Annals* 516: 106–29.

Bailey, M. J., Tavlas, G. S. and Ulan, M. (1986) 'Exchange-Rate Variability and Trade Performance: Evidence for the Big Seven Industrial Countries', *Weltwirtschaftliches Archiv* 122(3): 466–77.

Bailey, M. J., Tavlas, G. S. and Ulan, M. (1987) 'The Impact of Exchange-Rate Volatility on Export Growth: Some Theoretical Considerations and Empirical Results', *Journal of Policy Modelling* 9(1): 225–44.

Bartov, E., Bodnar, G. M. and Kaul, A. (1995) 'Exchange Rate Variability and the Riskiness of US Multinational Firms: Evidence From the Breakdown of the Bretton Woods System', *National Bureau of Economic Research Working Paper*, No. 5323.

Belanger, D., Gutierrez, S. and Raynauld, J. (1988) 'Exchange Rate Variability and Trade Flows: Preliminary Sectoral Estimates for the US – Canada Case', *Ecole des Hautes Etudes Commerciales: Cahiers de Recherche*, No. 89(01).

Bilson, J. F. O. (1981) 'The Speculative Efficiency Hypothesis', *Journal of Business* 54(2): 435–52.

Bini-Smaghi, L. (1991) 'Exchange Rate Variability and Trade: Why Is It So Difficult to Find Any Empirical Relationship?', *Applied Economics* 23: 927–35.

Brodsky, D. A. (1980) 'Decomposable Measures of Economic Instability', *Oxford Bulletin of Economics and Statistics* 42(4): 361–74.

Brodsky, D. A. (1983) 'Exchange Rate Changes and the Measurement of Export Instability', *Oxford Bulletin of Economics and Statistics* 45(3): 289–96.

Brodsky, D. A. (1984) 'Fixed versus Flexible Exchange Rates and the Measurement of Exchange Rate Instability', *Journal of International Economics* 16(3/4): 295–306.

Brodsky, D. A. and Sampson, G. P. (1983) 'Exchange Rate Variations Facing Individual Industries in Developing Countries', *Journal of Development Studies* 19(3): 349–68.

Brodsky, D. A., Helleiner, G. K. and Sampson, G. P. (1981) 'The Impact of the Current Exchange Rate System on Developing Countries', *Trade and Development* 3: 31–52.

Brown, A. (1979) 'On Measuring the Instability of Time Series Data: A Comment', *Oxford Bulletin of Economics and Statistics* 41(5): 249–50.

Christiano, L. J. (1981) 'A Survey of Measures of Capacity Utilization', *International Monetary Fund Staff Papers* 28(1): 144–98.

Clark, P. B. and Haulk, C. J. (1972) 'Flexible Exchange Rates and the Level of Trade: Preliminary Results of the Canadian Experience', Federal Reserve Board, unpublished.

Coes, D. (1981) 'The Crawling Peg and Exchange Rate Uncertainty', in J. Williamson (ed.), *Exchange Rate Rules: The Theory, Performance, and Prospect of the Crawling Peg*. New York: St Martins Press.

Côté, A. (1986) 'Effets de la Variabilite des Taux de Change Sur le Commerce International – Une Analyse Pour le Canada', *L'Actualite Economique* 62(4): 501–20.

Côté, A. (1994) 'Exchange Rate Volatility and Trade, a Survey', *Bank of Canada Working Paper*, No. 94–5.

Cuddy, J. D. A. and Della Valle, P. A. (1978) 'Measuring the Instability of Time Series Data', *Oxford Bulletin of Economics and Statistics* 40(1): 79–85.

Cumby, R. E. and Obstfeld, M. (1981) 'A Note on Exchange-Rate Expectations and Nominal Interest Differentials: a Test of the Fisher Hypothesis', *Journal of Finance* 36(3): 697–704.

Cumby, R. E. and Obstfeld, M. (1984) 'International Interest-Rate and Price-Level Linkages Under Flexible Exchange Rates: A Review of Recent Evidence', in J. F. O. Bilson and R. C. Marston (eds), *Exchange Rate Theory and Practice*. Cambridge, MA: National Bureau of Economic Research.

Cushman, D. O. (1983) 'The Effects of Real Exchange Rate Risk on International Trade', *Journal of International Economics* 15(1/2): 45–64.

Cushman, D. O. (1986) 'Has Exchange Risk Depressed International Trade? The Impact of Third-Country Exchange Risk', *Journal of International Money and Finance* 5(3): 361–80.

Debreu, G. (1959) *Theory of Value*. New York: John Wiley.

Della Valle, P. A. (1979) 'On the Instability Index of Time Series Data: A Generalization', *Oxford Bulletin of Economics and Statistics* 41(1): 247–9.

Dellas, H. and Zilberfarb, B.-Z. (1993) 'Real Exchange Rate Volatility and International Trade: A Reexamination of the Theory', *Southern Economic Journal* 59(4): 641–7.

Deppler, M. C. (1974) 'Some Evidence on the Effects of Exchange Rate Changes on Trade', *International Monetary Fund Staff Papers* 21(3): 605–36.

Dooley, M. and Shafer, J. (1983) 'Analysis of Short-Run Exchange Rate Behaviour: March 1973 to November 1981', in D. Bigman and T. Taya (eds), *Exchange Rate and Trade Instability*. Cambridge, MA: Ballinger.

Duggan, J. E. (1979) 'On Measuring the Instability of the Time Series Data', *Oxford Bulletin of Economics and Statistics* 41(3): 239–46.

Elbadawi, I. A. (1997) 'Real Exchange Rate Policy and Export Competitiveness in sub-Saharan Africa', Mimeo, Nairobi: African Economic Research Consortium.

Frankel, J. A. (1980) 'Tests of Rational Expectations in the Forward Exchange Market', *Southern Economic Journal* 46(4): 1083–101.

Frenkel, J. A. and Goldstein, M. (1989) 'Exchange Rate Volatility and Misalignment: Evaluating Some Proposals For Reform', *National Bureau of Economic Research Working Paper*, No. 2894.

Gagnon, J. (1993) 'Exchange Rate Variability and the Level of International Trade', *Journal of International Economics* 34: 269–340.

Gelb, A. H. (1977) 'Optimal Control and Stabilization Policy: An Application to the Coffee Economy', *Review of Economic Studies* 44(136): 95–110.

Gelb, A. H. (1979) 'On the Definition and Measurement of Instability and the Costs of Buffering Export Fluctuations', *Review of Economic Studies* 46(142): 149–62.

Goldberg, L. S. and Kolstad, C. D. (1994) 'Foreign Direct Investment, Exchange Rate Variability and Demand Uncertainty', *National Bureau of Economic Research Working Paper*, No. 4815.

Goldstein, M. and Khan, M. S. (1985) 'Income and Price Effects in Foreign Trade', in P. B. Kenen and R. W. Jones (eds), *Handbook of International Economics*, Vol. II. Amsterdam: North Holland.

Gonzaga, G. M. and Terra, M. C. T. (1997) 'Equilibrium Real Exchange Rate, Volatility, and Stabilization', *Journal of Development Economics* 54: 77–100.

Gotur, P. (1985) 'Effects of Exchange Rate Volatility on Trade: Some Further Evidence', International *Monetary Fund Staff Papers* 32(3): 475–512.

de Grauwe, P. (1988) 'Exchange Rate Variability and the Slowdown in Growth of International Trade', *International Monetary Fund Staff Papers* 35(1): 63–84.

Gupta, S. (1980) 'Exchange Risk in International Trade Under Alternative Exchange Systems: The Developing Countries' Experience', Ph.D. dissertation, Michigan State University.

Hansen, L. P. and Hodrick, R. J. (1980) 'Forward Exchange Rates as Optimal Predictors of Future Spot Rates: An Econometric Analysis', *Journal of Political Economy* 88(5): 829–53.

Hansen, L. P. and Hodrick, R. J. (1983) 'Risk Averse Speculation in the Forward Foreign Exchange Market: An Econometric Analysis of Linear Models', in J. A. Frenkel (ed.), *Exchange Rates and International Macroeconomics*. Cambridge, MA: National Bureau of Economic Research.

Harwood, A. and Smith, B. L. R. (eds) (1997) *Sequencing? Financial Strategies for Developing Countries*. Washington, DC: Brookings Institution Press.

Helleiner, G. K. (1981) 'The Impact of the Exchange Rate System on the Developing Countries', in S. Dell (ed.) (1987) 'The International Monetary System and its Reform: Papers Prepared for the Group of Twenty-Four', *Contribution to Economic Analysis Series*, No. 162.

Helleiner, G. K. (1998) *Capital Account Regimes and the Developing Countries*. London: Macmillan.

Hodrick, R. J. and Srivastava, S. (1987) 'Foreign Currency Futures', *Journal of International Economics* 22(1/2): 1–24.

Honohan, P. (1983) 'Measures of Exchange Rate Variability for One Hundred Countries', *Applied Economics* 15(5): 583–602.

Hooper, P. and Kohlhagen, S. W. (1978) 'The Effect of Exchange Rate Uncertainty on the Prices and Volume of International Trade', *Journal of International Economics* 8(4): 483–512.

Hsieh, D. A. (1984) 'Tests of Rational Expectations and No Risk Premium in Forward Exchange Markets', *Journal of International Economics* 17(1/2): 173–84.

International Monetary Fund (IMF) (1983) 'The European Monetary System: The Experience, 1979–82', *International Monetary Fund Occasional Paper*, No. 19.

IMF (1984) 'Exchange Rate Volatility and World Trade', *International Monetary Fund Occasional Paper*, No. 28.

IMF (1986) 'The European Monetary System: Recent Developments', *International Monetary Fund Occasional Paper*, No. 48.

Ito, T., Isard, P. Symansky, S. and Bayoumi, T. (1996) 'Exchange Rate Movements and their Impact on Trade and Investment in the APEC Region', *International Monetary Fund Occasional Paper*, No. 145.

Kenen, P. B. (1979) 'Exchange Rate Variability: Measurement and Implications', Princeton University (mimeo.).

Kenen, P. B. and Rodrik, D. (1984) 'Measuring and Analyzing the Effects of Short-Term Volatility in Real Exchange Rates', *Princeton University Working Papers in International Economics*, G-84-01.

Kenen, P. B. and Rodrik, D. (1986) 'Measuring and Analyzing the Effects of Short-Term Volatility in Real Exchange Rates', *Review of Economics and Statistics* 68(2): 311–5.

Klein, M. and Rosengren, E. (1992) 'The Real Exchange Rate and Foreign Direct Investment in the United States: Relative Wealth vs Relative Wage Effects', *National Bureau of Economic Research Working Paper*, No. 4192.

Krugman, P. (1997) 'What Should Trade Negotiators Negotiate About?', *Journal of Economic Literature* 35(1): 113–20.

Kulatilaka, N. (1996) 'Direct Investment, Hysteresis, and Real Exchange Rate Volatility', *Journal of the Japanese and International Economies* 10(1): 1–36.

Lanyi, A. and Suss, E. C. (1982) 'Exchange Rate Variability: Alternative Measures and Interpretation', *International Monetary Fund Staff Papers* 29(4): 527–60.

Lim, D. (1976) 'On the Measurement of Capital Utilization in Less Developed Countries', *Oxford Economic Papers* 28(1): 149–59.

Lintner, J. (1965) 'The Valuation of Risk Assets and the Selection of Risky Investments in Stock Portfolios and Capital Budgets', *Review of Economics and Statistics* 47(1): 13–37.

MacKinnon, J. G. and White, H. (1985) 'Some Heteroskedasticity-Consistent Covariance Matrix Estimators with Improved Finite Sample Properties', *Journal of Econometrics* 29: 305–25.

McKinnon, R. I. (1986) 'Comments on Willett', *Journal of International Money and Finance* 5, Supplement: S113–5.

Makin, J. H. (1976) 'Eurocurrencies and the Evolution of the International Monetary System', in C. H. Stern, J. H. Makin and D. E. Logue (eds), *Eurocurrencies and the International Monetary System*. Washington, DC: American Enterprise Institute.

Markowitz, H. M. (1952) 'Portfolio Selection', *Journal of Finance* 7(1): 77–91.

Maskus, K. E. (1986) 'Exchange Rate Risk and U.S. Trade: A Sectoral Analysis', *Economic Review*, Federal Reserve Bank of Kansas City 71(3): 16–28.

Medhora, R. (1989) 'Effect of Exchange Rate Variability on Trade: A Survey', *Economic and Political Weekly*: 579–86.

Medhora, R. (1990) 'The Effect of Exchange Rate Variability on Trade: The Case of the West African Monetary Union's Imports', *World Development* 18(2): 313–24.

Melvin, M. and Yin, X. (1996) 'Public Information Arrival, Exchange Rate Volatility and Quote Frequency', Mimeo, Arizona State University.

Mossin, J. (1966) 'Equilibrium in a Capital Asset Market', *Econometrica* 34(4): 768–83.

Newbery, D. M. and Stiglitz, J. E. (1981) *The Theory of Commodity Price Stabilization, A Study in the Economics of Risk*. Oxford: Clarendon Press.

Rajan, R. G. and Zingales, L. (1998) 'Financial Dependence and Growth', *American Economic Review* 88(3): 559–86.

Rana, P. B. (1981) 'Exchange Rate Risk Under Generalized Floating: Eight Asian Countries', *Journal of International Economics* 11(4): 459–66.

Rana, P. B. (1984) 'Fixed versus Flexible Exchange Rates and Measurement of Exchange Rate Instability: Comment', *Journal of International Economics* 16(3/4): 307–10.

Sharpe, W. F. (1964) 'Capital Asset Prices: A Theory of Market Equilibrium Under Conditions of Risk', *Journal of Finance* 19(3): 425–42.

Theil, H. (1954) *Linear Aggregation of Economic Relations*. Amsterdam: North Holland.

Thursby, M. C. (1980) 'The Resource Reallocation Costs of Fixed and Flexible Exchange Rates: A Counterexample', *Journal of International Economics* 10(1): 79–90.

Thursby, M. C. (1981) 'The Resource Reallocation Costs of Fixed and Flexible Exchange Rates', *Journal of International Economics* 11(4): 487–94.

Thursby, M. C. and Thursby, J. G. (1985) 'The Uncertainty Effects of Floating Exchange Rates: Empirical Evidence on International Trade Flows', in S. A. Arndt, R. J. Sweeney and T. D. Willett (eds), *Exchange Rates, Trade, and the US Economy*. Cambridge, MA: Ballinger.

Thursby, M. C. and Thursby, J. G. (1987) 'Bilateral Trade Flows, the Linder Hypothesis, and Exchange Risk', *Review of Economics and Statistics* 69(3): 488–95.

Tsui, K. Y. (1986) 'The Measurement of Export Instability: A Methodological Note', Draft, University of Toronto.

Tsui, K. Y. (1987) 'A Social Cost-Benefit Analysis of Exports Processing Zones in Some Asian Countries', Ph.D. dissertation, University of Toronto.

Willett, T. D. (1986) 'Exchange-Rate Variability, International Trade and Resource Allocation: A Perspective on Recent Research', *Journal of International Money and Finance* 5, Supplement: S101–12.

Yeager, L. B. (1976) *International Monetary Relations: Theory, History and Policy*. New York: Harper and Row.

Zellner, A. (1969) 'On the Aggregation Problem: A New Approach to a Troublesome Problem', in K. A. Fox (ed.), *Economic Models, Estimation, and Risk Programming*. Berlin: Springer-Verlag.

Index